SECOND EDITION

Intercultural Communication

A Peacebuilding Perspective

Martin S. Remland
West Chester University of Pennsylvania

Tricia S. Jones
Temple University

Anita Foeman
West Chester University of Pennsylvania

Bessie L. Lawton
West Chester University of Pennsylvania

WAVELAND

PRESS, INC.

Long Grove, Illinois

For information about this book, contact:
Waveland Press, Inc.
4180 IL Route 83, Suite 101
Long Grove, IL 60047-9580
(847) 634-0081
info@waveland.com
www.waveland.com

10-digit ISBN 1-4786-4937-2
13-digit ISBN 978-1-4786-4937-3

Printed in the United States of America

7   6   5   4   3   2   1

Contents

1
Intercultural Communication and Peacebuilding   1

2

Elements of Intercultural Communication   61

3
Contexts of Intercultural Communication   211

10 Intercultural Communication in the Classroom. 265

11 Intercultural Communication in the Workplace 265

Preface

This introduction to intercultural communication addresses the perils and opportunities emerging in a shrinking world, where the realities of war, migration, international markets, natural calamities, and more, demand global attention and cooperation. Working and living with people of other cultures is no longer a choice with little consequence; it is a necessity for survival in the 21st century.

We developed our approach to intercultural communication for readers interested in developing intercultural competence, not just for the sake of becoming more skilled communicators, but also for the greater good of building peaceful communities. This peacebuilding perspective accomplishes the following:

1. It places the goal of building peaceful communities in the foreground, using it as both a moral compass and guiding framework for the book. At the core of our approach is the unwavering conviction that today's students see the need for peaceful coexistence with other cultural groups and the need for constructive dialogue as a vital step toward peace.

2. It highlights and elaborates the connections between intercultural communication and the ideology and practice of building peace. For instance, intercultural communication shapes and is shaped by the *beliefs* we hold about the nature of, and the prospects for, peace. Also, the *skills* of effective and ethical intercultural communication contribute substantially to peaceful outcomes across a variety of intercultural contexts, where divisive conflict and numbing indifference often prevail.

3. It focuses on how students can make a difference in the world by forging healthy and productive relationships with people of other cultures—in their personal lives, in the workplace, in the classroom, through the media, and during their travels at home and abroad. We believe this approach cultivates an untapped spirit of volunteerism and encourages students to become activists for peace in ways that go beyond customary approaches to the subject.

4. It endorses a broad conception of culture, favoring a view that privileges shared identities over geographic borders. This conception of culture not only reflects a growing movement away from restrictive definitions of culture, but also draws attention to the intercultural challenges and opportunities most likely to arise in a particular context (e.g., the classroom, the workplace, etc.), and mirrors a world in which intergroup tensions are not confined to differences in religion, race, ethnicity, or social class.

Conceptual Framework and Organization

We introduce the peacebuilding perspective in the first part of the book, "Intercultural Communication and Peacebuilding." Chapter 1 includes a discussion of culture, communication, and intercultural communication as they relate to the notion of building peaceful communities. In chapter 2 we establish the basic connection between developing intercultural communication competence and building peaceful communities. This includes an extended discussion of how everyday interactions and the tools of dialogue enhance the prospects of peace. We also introduce and develop a *peacebuilding model* of intercultural communication that serves to preview the chapters that follow. The model begins with cultural identity (chapter 3), which affects each of the key elements present in all intercultural interactions: cultural frames (chapter 4), emotions (chapter 5), nonverbal communication (chapter 6), and verbal communication (chapter 7). These chapters (3–7) constitute the second part of the text, "Elements of Intercultural Communication." In each of these chapters, we highlight important cultural differences, consider various obstacles to peacebuilding, and conclude with a focus on developing intercultural communication competence.

Our peacebuilding model of intercultural communication emphasizes the fundamental idea that our interactions occur in a particular intercultural context, and that each context presents a unique set of challenges and opportunities. These chapters (8–13) highlight the influence of culture on each context and consider the potential of intercultural contact and dialogue as instruments of peace, building a sense of community that invariably affects the core of one's cultural identity. This third part of the book, "Contexts of Intercultural Communication," includes chapters on friendship (chapter 8), families (chapter 9), the classroom (chapter 10), the workplace (chapter 11), the media (chapter 12), and the sojourn experience (chapter 13). In each of these chapters, we offer myriad opportunities for readers to become actively engaged in the task of building peaceful communities.

Special Features

Each of the chapters in the book contains several features to engage readers and facilitate learning. In addition to opening page *summary outlines* of the chapter's contents, along with an accompanying list of *key terms* discussed in the chapter, we provide an end-of-chapter list of *questions* to stimulate further reflection and discussion. Each chapter also contains the following *boxed inserts*:

- *A Closer Look:* Readings and resources from a variety of outside sources (news stories, abstracts of studies, provocative essays, websites).
- *Put It Into Practice:* Exercises that enhance student learning (assessments, reflections, observations, quizzes, discussion questions, etc.).
- *Culture Shock:* Personal first- and second-hand accounts of people who experienced "culture shock" while visiting another culture.

Acknowledgments

We couldn't be more pleased that Waveland Press has given us this opportunity to present our peacebuilding view of intercultural communication. First and foremost, we want to thank Neil Rowe for inviting us to work with Waveland, for his unequivocal and generous support of the project, and for his reassurance that we would get to print sooner rather than later. We are also indebted to our highly talented editor at Waveland, Dakota West, for his meticulous and insightful work on our manuscript and his desire to make each chapter the best it could be. We have never worked with a better publisher and editor and we are grateful for having had such a positive experience. On a personal note, each of us would like to acknowledge the special people in our lives that have helped make this book a reality.

Marty

This book has been a work in progress for many years and none of it would-have been possible without the hard work, passion, and expertise of my coauthors—Trish, Anita, and Bessie—each of whom brought something special(and indispensable) to this project, along with their shared commitment to the peacebuilding model that frames our book. Thanks also to our colleague, Bessie Lawton, for her hard work on the Instructor's Manual. I am grateful for having the support and encouragement of a family dedicated to scholarly growth and always striving for a healthy balance between work and play! I want to thank Trish for bringing her "A" game to all of the work she did on this book; our son, Alex, the most gifted author in our family, for continuing to inspire us with his own work; and Annie, for waking us up and getting us out of the house.

Trish

My sincere gratitude to all of my coauthors on the first and second editions—Marty, Anita, Bessie, and Dolores—for their work and wisdom in making this book a reality. A very special thanks to Marty—the champion behind this project. Marty had the original vision for this book, developed the proposal, and supportively guided us all through the ups and downs of both editions. Sincere thanks to all of the students who have used the first edition and provided feedback that informed this second edition. To all the peace-builders out there helping to create constructive communities among diverse individuals and groups—may your work yield outcomes equal to your passion for peace!

Anita

I would like to thank my husband Nate; my Mom, Dad, and brother Jerry; my kids Nikki, Chelsea, and Darqui; my wonderful research partners Phil Thompsen and Bessie Lawton; my coauthors Marty, Trish, and Dolores; and my students, all of whom have demonstrated patience and support in all of my endeavors!

Bessie

I am very grateful to Trish, Marty, and Anita for inviting me to be part of the second edition of this book. I have really enjoyed the conversations about what it means to live in a multicultural society and how we can encourage our students to open their minds to the world. I am also thankful to my family—Grant, Ralph, and Gaea—for all the support they continuously give me. They are the best part of my world.

Intercultural Communication and Peacebuilding

1

Intercultural Communication in the Global Community

CHAPTER OUTLINE

KEY TERMS

co-culture
communication
cultural diversity
culture
ethnicity
ethnocentrism

intercultural communication
negative peace
nonverbal communication
peacebuilding
peacekeeping

peacemaking
positive peace
symbol
verbal communication
xenophobia

R eflecting worldwide trends, the United States population continues to become a more culturally diverse nation. The 2020 United States census showed a decline in the nation's White population between 2010 and 2019 (Frey, 2021). This trend makes the 2010–2020 decade the only one since the first census was taken in 1790 when the white population did not grow. This decline is largely due the older age of the white population when compared to other racial and ethnic groups, leading to fewer births and more deaths in relation to its population size. In 2019, for instance, the median age for White Americans was 43.7, compared to 29.8 for Latino or Hispanic Americans, 34.6 for Black Americans, 37.5 for Asian Americans, and 20.9 for persons identifying as two or more races.

The portion of the population identifying with two or more races is projected to be the fastest-growing racial/ethnic group between 2010 and 2020, with a 36 percent increase. The Asian American population is projected to increase by 32 percent, followed by the Latino population (23 percent). The non-Hispanic white population is projected to increase by just 1 percent, with a net gain of 1.3 million people (Mather & Lee, 2020).

Recent Census Bureau population estimates also revealed that more than half of the nation's total population are now members of the millennial generation or younger. And while these younger generations—born in 1981 or later—are not growing as rapidly as older age groups, they are far more racially diverse. While some 75% of the older age groups (i.e., baby boomers and older) identify as non-Hispanic White, no more than half of the younger age groups do so (Frey, 2021).

In many ways, from the 1980s through the early 2000s, immigrants and their children have contributed to both the growth and diversity of the nation's younger population—however, more recently, natural increase rather than immigration is the primary source of Latino or Hispanic population growth.

But while statistical projections confirm that cultural diversity is a fact of life in the new century, they do not attest to the growing recognition that cultural diversity is a universal good. On this point, the United Nations Educational, Scientific, and Cultural Organization (UNESCO) declared in 2001 that cultural diversity represented "the common heritage of humanity . . . as necessary for humankind as biodiversity is for nature" (see A Closer Look 1.1).

As you will see throughout this book, cultural diversity creates both obstacles and opportunities for peaceful coexistence. This book introduces an approach to the study and practice of intercultural communication—the *peace-building perspective*—that highlights the unique and indispensable role of communication in building and sustaining peaceful communities. In this chapter, we begin our discussion of this approach with an introduction to the concept of intercultural communication. Although it may seem obvious what intercultural communication is and why it is important, you may be surprised to learn that definitions of *culture* and *communication* raise questions that have confounded scholars for a long time. In addition, while intercultural communication has always been important, it has never been more vital for the well-being of our rapidly "shrinking" planet than it is today.

A CLOSER LOOK   **1.1**

UNESCO Universal Declaration on Cultural Diversity

Adopted unanimously a short time after the September 11, 2001, terrorist attacks on the United States, UNESCO's formal acknowledgement of the need for and benefits of cultural diversity is clear and compelling. Of the 12 Articles contained in the Declaration, Articles 1–4 express, perhaps most directly, the case for cultural diversity.

Article 1: Cultural diversity: The common heritage of humankind

Culture takes diverse forms throughout time and space. This diversity is embodied in the uniqueness and plurality of the identities and the groups and societies making up humankind. As a source of exchange, innovation, and creativity, cultural diversity is as necessary for humankind as biodiversity is for nature. In this sense, it is the common heritage of humanity and should be recognized and affirmed for the benefit of present and future generations.

Article 2: From cultural diversity to cultural pluralism

In our increasingly diverse societies, it is essential to ensure harmonious interaction among people and groups with plural, varied, and dynamic cultural identities as well as their willingness to live together. Policies for the inclusion and participation of all citizens are guarantees of social cohesion, the vitality of civil society and peace. Thus defined, cultural pluralism gives policy expression to the reality of cultural diversity. Indissociable from a democratic framework, cultural pluralism is conducive to cultural exchange and to the flourishing of creative capacities that sustain public life.

Article 3: Cultural diversity as a factor in development

Cultural diversity widens the range of options open to everyone; it is one of the roots of development, understood not simply in terms of economic growth, but also as a means to achieve a more satisfactory intellectual, emotional, moral, and spiritual existence.

Article 4: Human rights as guarantees of cultural diversity

The defense of cultural diversity is an ethical imperative, inseparable for respect for human dignity. It implies a commitment to human rights and fundamental freedoms, in particular the rights of persons belonging to minorities and those of indigenous people. No one may invoke cultural diversity to infringe upon human rights guaranteed by international law, nor to limit their scope.

(UNESCO, 2001)

What Is Culture?

Most modern definitions of the term *culture* refer to the shared beliefs, values, customs, and symbols of a large group of people (see Table 1.1 for some typical definitions). A key element of culture, *sharing* produces a sense of community and belonging, the cornerstone of a culture. Most importantly, culture is a product of *learning*. Each generation passes lessons on to the next about what to value, what to believe, and how to behave. Because of the ambiguities contained in most definitions of culture, we may not always agree on whether a particular group represents a culture. To illustrate, using any of the definitions offered in Table 1.1, which of the groups listed in the exercise below (Put It Into Practice 1.1) would you identify as a culture?

As you can see from the list of definitions above, culture is a broad concept, not limited to nations, races, religions, or ethnic groups, thus allowing for the presence of many different cultures, or *co-cultures*, within and alongside other cultures. For example, *ethnicity*, or one's affiliation with an ethnic group, ordinarily refers

Table 1.1 Definitions of Culture

"A learned system of meanings that fosters a particular sense of shared identity and community among its group members."	—Ting-Toomey (2005)
"A set of fundamental ideas, practices, and experiences of a group of people that are symbolically transmitted generation to generation through a learned process."	—Chen & Starosta (1998)
"A population of people who have similar attitudes, values, beliefs, and share a system of knowledge through unstated assumptions."	—Triandis (1995)
"The total way of life of a people, composed of their learned and shared behavior patterns, values, norms, and material objects."	—Rogers & Steinfatt (1999)
"A learned set of shared interpretations about beliefs, values, norms, and social practices, which affect the behaviors of a relatively large group of people."	—Lustig & Koester (2006)
"The set of distinctive spiritual, material, intellectual, and emotional features of society or a social group . . . it encompasses, in addition to art and literature, lifestyles, ways of living together, value systems, traditions, and beliefs."	—UNESCO (2001)

PUT IT INTO PRACTICE   **1.1**

Counting Cultures

We defined a "culture" as a large group of people who share beliefs, values, customs, and symbols. Based on this definition or the ones found in Table 1.1, how many of the following groups would you classify as a cultural group?

Group	Culture	
Bodybuilders	Yes	No
Asians	Yes	No
Gays	Yes	No
Italian Americans	Yes	No
Bikers	Yes	No
Westerners	Yes	No
Arabs	Yes	No
Native Americans	Yes	No
Amish	Yes	No
Gamers	Yes	No
Evangelicals	Yes	No

---

to a culture rooted in a shared language, historical origin, religion, or nationality. Within the American culture, ethnic co-cultures include Hispanics, Arab Americans, Muslims, and Italian Americans. Interestingly, however, the US Census, which classifies Americans by race and ethnicity, has chosen to limit ethnic classifications to Hispanic or non-Hispanic, while using racial classifications of Black, White, American Indian or Alaskan Native, and Asian or Pacific Islander. But the multitude of co-cultures that truly reside in a given society, representing the *cultural diversity* of that society, belies simple classifications.

Sometimes regarding a group of people as a culture can change the way we think about the group. In 2002, a deaf lesbian couple in Maryland made headlines for purposefully conceiving a deaf child through artificial insemination using the sperm of a donor who had a family history of deafness. Accused of being selfish and uncaring, one critic claimed: "This couple has effectively decided that their desire to have a deaf child is of more concern to them than is the burden they are placing on their son." The same critic continued: "To intentionally give a child a disability, in addition to all the disadvantages that come as a result of being raised in a homosexual household, is incredibly selfish" (Pyeatt, 2002). Would the same charge apply to an Asian couple who wants to raise an Asian child, or an African American couple who wants to raise an African American child? If we think of

A culture refers to the shared beliefs, values, customs, and symbols of a large group of people. Do each of the groups pictured above represent a distinct culture?

sexual orientation and deafness as cultural constructs, what remains of the charges against the Maryland couple? What is your reaction to the arguments raised in A Closer Look 1.2?

Metaphors of culture (especially diverse cultures) conjure up many images. A long-standing metaphor is that of a melting pot, which initially referred to the melding together of the many immigrant European cultures residing in the United States. In recent times many people have found the term offensive because it implies that co-cultures have to "melt away" and one generic "Eurocentric" culture has to emerge. Today, the metaphor of the salad bowl or quilt resonates because it allows people to maintain their unique cultural identity and learn about people of other cultural groups. In fact, we can picture every culture as many different pies, puzzles, or quilts, because each culture includes an array of characteristics on which its members are judged. For example, think of five or six demographic characteristics that define you, such as your race, age, gender, region, religion, sexual identification, or any number of other qualities. Each piece gives you a different view of reality and shapes who you are and how you fit into the culture at large, as well as how you view other cultures. Looking at these pieces, for example, you may see that your social class and educational background place you on one rung

A CLOSER LOOK   **1.2**

Debating Deafness: Disability, Culture, or Both?

Indeed, it is more convenient to be hearing than deaf, but such convenience does not de-facto lead to an increased value of one's life. Presumptions about the horrors of deafness are usually made by those not living Deaf lives. Deaf lives reveal that disability affects people in different ways, and that hearing loss has catalyzed deaf persons to convene a culture with members who experience a depth of affiliation comparable to any other ethnic group and linguistic minority. Clearly, my colleagues and friends are more culturally Deaf than I am culturally Irish or German. . . .

In reworking the language of disability, we must also ask our questions differently. *Where* is disability? If it is not only (or not at all) on the body but also in the social, physical, and political environment, where does it take place? Most Deaf people would grant that there is little disability in an all-signing environment. It is only once there is no access to communication that the conditions of disability become evident. Thus, it is only within the contact zone between hearing and deaf worlds, between auditory and visual modalities, that the conditions of disability make themselves present. Such contact zones may be described as "social spaces where disparate cultures meet, clash, and grapple with each other, often in highly asymmetrical relations of domination and subordination."* It is only in the hearing/deaf contact zone where the site of disability emerges. It is here that there are no text telephones, no captions, and no (or inadequate) interpreters. It is here that hearing people enjoy systems of advantage and deaf persons systems of disadvantage. . . .

What do Deaf people make with their four senses? They have made their own epistemological path in the world; together, they have convened a visual culture with its own traditions, literature, and heritage, and, yes, with its flashing lights and text phones. To begin to grasp the worth of living a Deaf life is to begin the reworking of the language of disability and our entire moral perspective. Such a reworking may lead toward a more dynamic intersection between disability and culture.

* Pratt, M. (1992). *Imperial eyes: Travel writing and transculturation*. New York: Routledge.

(Bauman, 2005)

of society. Your age, gender, or ethnicity may place you on another. Some scholars use an iceberg metaphor to visualize culture, where the tip of the iceberg represents the most "noticeable" features of a culture, such as members' physical appearance, rituals, and symbols, while beneath the surface lies the core of a culture: its values, norms, and beliefs (Oetzel, 2009).

As we compare one culture to another, we see similarities as well as differences. For example, religion may be very important in two cultures, yet the ways members express their religious commitment can be quite distinct. Monica

McGoldrick (2005) studied intermarriages between Irish and Italian Americans based on their common Catholic and immigrant heritages. She found that conflict sometimes occurred in marriages when the role of the church, as well as their distinct cuisines, did not always match. Add to this that culture changes and evolves over time and culture is a difficult concept to fully comprehend. For example, in the United States the role and definitions of race have shifted dramatically. In many states in the late 1800s, a person with one drop of African ancestry was considered Black and stripped of many human rights. Anti-miscegenation laws were enforced to keep the White race pure and privileged; only in 1964 did the right to marry a person of another race become protected under federal law. Further, DNA testing is demonstrating that many people who identify themselves as a "White American" indeed have significant African ancestry—a discovery that makes little to no difference in their rights as American citizens.

What Is Communication?

In one sense, communication is the lifeblood of a culture, for only through communication can all the distinguishing features of a culture survive from one generation to the next. Communication also builds a sense of community, strengthening the ties that exist among members of a culture. Throughout history, when societies wanted to severely punish someone for a social transgression, the harshest punishment was *excommunication*—banishment from the community. In Catholicism this means to cast out someone from the church. In ancient Rome the process was called *ostracism*, a ritual in which citizens used clay shards (ostraca) to vote for someone to be sent away from the community for 10 years. In modern Amish communities the practice is called *shunning*. The shunned person is allowed to physically remain in the community but is prohibited from any social interaction with others. The shunned individual is not allowed to eat at the same table, worship in the same space, or even have others face them unless it is a matter of life and death. One of the authors of this text recalls how the idea of shunning affected her, even as a small girl in grade school:

> When I was a young girl in third grade, I read a story that I have always remembered. It was one of those stories in our history books that is meant to impress on us the importance of our nation. But its message was more powerful for me. The story was called "Man Without a Country." Supposedly, it was a true story about a young American naval officer in the War of 1812. In the midst of battle, he had acted without bravery and was summarily brought up on charges. At the military trial he was found guilty and awaited sentencing. Upon pronouncement of his guilt, the officer exclaimed, "I care not for this nation and wish never to lay eyes on the United States of America again." The judge, looking somber, decreed that the officer had issued his own sentence. From that day forward, the officer would be sent to sea, always transported from ship to ship but never allowed to land. Always provided the means for physical survival but never allowed to be spoken to by any member of the crews of the vessels he would inhabit for the remainder of his life. The sentence was carried out. The officer lived as sentenced until his death. The other crew

members found among his personal effects a handmade American flag that he had created from cloth scraps through the years. He lived and died completely alone. I cannot remember his crime. But I have never forgotten his punishment. (Jones, Remland, & Sanford, 2007, p. 4)

The profound cumulative impact of social interaction on culture and community represents a "big picture" view of communication's consequences. But even a single interaction, one of the countless and ongoing exchanges that reinforce and reflect a society, offers a clear view of what happens when communication takes place. Consider the following scenario:

On her way home from work, Maria stops at the local pharmacy to pick up the prescription medicine her doctor phoned in earlier that day. Waiting at the counter, she catches the attention of Dennis, the pharmacy technician working the evening shift, and tells him she's there to pick up her prescription. Dennis replies that he'll be with her in just a few minutes.

This brief interaction is an example of the kind of routine, taken-for-granted communication we experience every day. These instances of **communication** occur whenever two individuals exchange meaningful messages. When the two individuals represent different cultural groups, their exchange becomes an instance of **intercultural communication**. While there appears to be nothing remarkable about Maria's interaction with Dennis, in any interpersonal interaction there is always much more going on than we may know. Moreover, since Maria happens to be from Venezuela and Dennis happens to be from Japan, we can examine their interaction as a case of intercultural communication. Their brief exchange also illustrates the basic process underlying any communication between two or more individuals. In this section we present a model of communication as a social transactional process in which two persons use various channels of communication to exchange meaningful messages in a particular context (see Figure 1.1).

Communication Is Social

You are probably familiar with the conundrum, "If a tree falls in the forest, and no one is there, does it make a sound?" The implication of the question is that sound requires a hearer. In order for there to be communication, we must have more than one person exchanging a message. Thus, communication is an *interpersonal* or social activity. While some people speak about *intrapersonal* communication, or communication with the self, we maintain that this is a form of thought or perception rather than communication. As Figure 1.1 shows, communication is a *connection* between two persons. In the brief interaction between Maria and Dennis described above, the communication that transpired between them depended on one of them sending a message and the other getting a message. So when Maria said she was there to pick up her prescription, and Dennis received and interpreted her message, communication occurred. Of course, this minimal condition for communication does not address the more troublesome question of whether two persons fully understand each other; that is, whether there is *shared meaning*. If, for instance, Maria had given her last name as "Chavez" and Dennis thought she had said "Sanchez" he would have looked for the wrong prescription. More significantly, if Maria inferred that

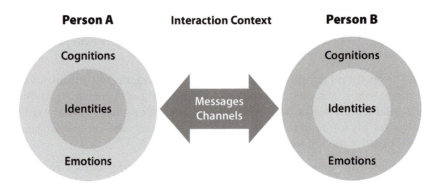

Figure 1.1   Model of Communication

Dennis was being impolite when he said he would be with her in just a few minutes (without making eye contact) even though he didn't "mean" to be impolite, Maria might have decided to take her business elsewhere. But a miscommunication, regardless of the consequences, is not necessarily the absence of communication.

Communication Is a Process

To begin with, what does it mean to say that communication is a process? A process is something that is constantly changing and has no definite beginning or end. It is a flow of actions with consequences. Communication is a process in every sense. Although we may trick ourselves into thinking that we can freeze a communication moment, in reality we cannot—no more than we can freeze a beat of our heart. We may learn to separate communication into episodes and segments in order to make sense of it, but doing so always risks oversimplification. As you can see in Figure 1.1, Person A and Person B are communicating because they are exchanging messages. But when does the communication begin or end? In our example of Maria and Dennis, does their communication begin when Maria first speaks to Dennis or when Dennis first hears what she said? On the other hand, if speech is not the only way to exchange messages, maybe their communication began when Maria first saw Dennis, or perhaps when Dennis first saw Maria approaching the counter.

Communication Is Transactional

Notice that Figure 1.1 shows various *channels* of communication carrying messages in two directions at the same time (two-sided arrow): from Person A to Person B and from Person B to Person A. This represents the *transactional* nature of communication. Earlier so-called *linear* models of communication focused on what people said to each other, depicting message exchanges as a sequential "turn-taking" activity: Person A (the sender) speaks to Person B (the receiver); when the speaking-listening roles switch, Person B becomes the sender and Person A becomes the receiver. But because messages are not limited to a single channel of communication (i.e., spoken words), these linear models did not represent the true nature of communication as a *multichanneled* exchange. For example, while Maria tells Dennis she wants to pick up her prescription, she may be receiving *feedback* from Dennis in the form of (1) a head nod that says "I'm listening," (2) a hand gesture that says "Just a second, I'll be right with you," (3) a facial grimace that says "I don't understand," or (4) an eyebrow raise that says "Can I help you?"

Communication Is Symbolic

Human communication is unique because it relies on symbolic codes. A *symbol* is anything that stands for or represents something else. All languages are symbolic codes in which symbols refer to objects, events, experiences, and/or thoughts. When we use words, spoken or written, we are using **verbal communication** or language (see Chapter 7). But we communicate in many other ways, using facial expressions, clothes, tattoos, gestures, vocalizations, and more to exchange messages about ourselves and the outside world (see Chapter 6). These types of **nonverbal communication** often involve the use of symbols, such as when we roll our eyes in ridicule, shake someone's hand in greeting, or get a tattoo as a sign of group affiliation. The arbitrary connection between a symbol and what it means increases the likelihood that a nonverbal signal in one culture may have no meaning or a very different meaning in another culture. For example, the well-known "ring" gesture (thumb and forefinger creating the shape of a circle) is a sign of approval in many cultures but an obscenity in others. One sign of assimilation into a culture is the ability to exchange the symbolic messages of the new culture, as in the example above of Maria and Dennis speaking a common language (i.e., English) and sharing a head nod, a hand gesture, or an eyebrow raise.

Although most forms of human communication rely on arbitrary, symbolic codes, some rely on natural, nonsymbolic forms of expression that we share with other living creatures. Physical features that convey information about our gender, age, fitness, and race; and spontaneous facial and vocal expressions of emotions such as anger, fear, and joy suggest a universal form of communication we inherit rather than learn.

Communication Is Personal

A well-known maxim about communication is that meanings are in people, not in the messages they exchange. Notice that Figure 1.1 shows two persons, each with a unique set of identities, cognitions, and emotions, shaping the messages they send as well as receive. In every interaction we have with another person, what we say and do depends on our thoughts and feelings, which in turn depend on our cultural background, gender, age, personality, social role, occupation, and more. While each of these identities is important, our concern is with the impact of one's cultural identity (see Chapter 3). One way that cultural identity affects our communication is through stereotyping. For example, while Maria and Dennis may not know each other personally, they may have judged each other according to some stereotype related to intelligence, work ethic, religion, attitude, or family values associated with South American and East Asian cultures. Cultural identity also affects our communication through public displays of emotion, which tend to vary from one culture to another (see Chapter 6). With his strict Asian upbringing,

A gesture that sends a clear message is a type of nonverbal communication that relies on the use of symbols.

for example, Dennis may be less likely to express his feelings in public settings than Maria would be to express hers.

Communication Is Contextual

There are two overarching contexts in which communication takes place: relational and cultural. The *relational* context provides information about the level of intimacy, the balance of power, and the socially constructed roles that exist between people. This information helps us understand how we should interpret the behavior of others. For example, say you see the following: a young man walks up to an older woman, throws his arms around her, and picks her up. Now, consider how the meaning of that behavior changes if you know that the young man is (a) the woman's son, (b) the woman's student, or (c) a stranger on the street. If he is her son we see the behavior as affectionate; if he is her student we would see the same behavior as inappropriate, even sexual; and if he is a stranger the behavior would probably seem threatening. The relational context for Maria's brief interaction with Dennis is that of a customer service transaction, a pharmacy technician assisting a customer. While the "script" for such routine encounters is quite predictable, how might their interaction differ if they saw each other as a casual friend or as a romantic prospect?

The *cultural* context adds another layer of information that determines the meaning and consequences of our communication. Culture creates the communication rules we use in different contexts. We can think of family culture, regional culture, religious culture, racial/ethnic culture, professional culture, national culture, and so on. In fact, we can even think of two people creating a cultural context. Each cultural context presents a complex set of rules about how to behave. For example, according to traditional Korean belief, death does not mean the end of a life, so it is not something to grieve. Communication rules for Korean funerals are to behave casually and cheerfully—rules that may strike Westerners as bizarre and even uncaring. Cultures also create their own rituals. Muslims, like other religions, hold rituals to welcome a new birth. Many Muslims have a welcoming ceremony for babies that is called *aqiqa* (pronounced similar to akika), a party at the new parents' home to welcome the baby into the family and community. But the welcoming often starts before that. Moments after birth a call to prayer may be spoken in the baby's ear. The baby's hair is often shaved and may be weighed as a means of having parents donate the weight in silver to a mosque.

When the cultural context of an interaction differs from the cultural identity we bring to the interaction, we face the challenge of adapting to another culture. For example, as relatively new immigrants to America—Maria came from Venezuela and Dennis from Japan—Maria and Dennis are still learning the customs of their new culture. Even in the context of a customer service transaction, cultural norms dictate what we should do and say as an employee (e.g., smile when greeting a customer) and as a customer (e.g., wait your turn). The same kind of adaptation applies to co-cultures. How much of a challenge would it be, for instance, if Maria and Dennis went to an Arab wedding ceremony and they didn't know what to expect?

Why Study Intercultural Communication?

If you were to surf the hundreds of channels offered by your cable/streaming service, scan the endless internet blogs and social media platforms, or stroll down the magazine aisle of your favorite bookstore, two things will become immediately clear. First, there is an astonishing diversity of people, perspectives, and ideas available to us in the world community. Second, this mind-boggling number of options can allow, even lead, us to retreat into a smaller world of people who share our opinions and make the same generalizations we make. The stress that comes from attempting to incorporate so many perspectives can feel overwhelming. Yet, because of technology, economics, and limited resources, we must learn to live peacefully and productively with our neighbors. To do this, we must develop a healthy curiosity, basic understanding, and human empathy in the diverse world we inhabit.

Intercultural interactions are an everyday part of life in a multicultural society, presenting us with both challenges and opportunities.

Look around your college campus. The students you come in contact with will most likely be from different cultural backgrounds than your own and hold very different worldviews than you. In the workforce, you will be more likely to have colleagues and supervisors with different cultural backgrounds. To be effective in your career you will need to learn to collaborate with and work in virtual global teams. This increased global interdependence creates the possibility of being drawn into the political, economic, and humanitarian issues of other nations. The potential for conflict and misunderstanding grows as we come into contact with nations and peoples who do not share our personal worldview.

Shifting Demographics

The most recent census data shows that the United States is becoming a country with historically low population growth, rapid aging, and greater racial and ethnic diversity, especially among the nation's youth (Frey, 2021). The US grew by a total of 22.7 million people between 2010 and 2020. Latinos or Hispanics contributed 11.6 million people to that total—over half of the nation's growth. Asian Americans and Black Americans contributed 5.1 million, 2.2 million, respectively, while persons identifying as two or more races rose to 7.5 million. These groups constituted the main engines of the nation's growth and are likely to do the same going forward.

Dramatic changes in the demographic makeup of the US population notwithstanding, all of us are likely to encounter growing numbers of people from different cultural groups throughout our everyday lives. We need the skills to make the most of these interactions. *This is the work of intercultural communication.*

A Global Community

From the invention of the bicycle in the fifteenth century to the democratization of the airline industry following World War II, access to transportation has made it even more possible for us to traverse the planet. Still, most people tend to live in a relatively small geographic zone, and according to statistics reported in *The Economist*, only one-third of Americans own a valid passport (Frankovic, 2021). But today, global 24-hour cable news operations, the internet, social media, and smartphones allow for ubiquitous and constant interaction without borders for anyone with access to modern technology. Many activists and tech companies are working hard to extend that access to every land and every person, especially young people. Even global positioning systems mean that we are never lost and never out of touch. Our neighbors near and far are constantly in contact and always up to date.

Of course, it is not surprising to anyone that the COVID-19 pandemic has had a devastating impact on the global economy. Well before that, the burst of the housing bubble in the United States in 2008 triggered an economic crisis in this country and triggered an economic calamity around the globe. In addition, wildly fluctuating fuel costs in oil-producing countries keep international economies reeling. Further, the rapidly expanding economies of China and India influence wages around the planet. The ratification of the North American Free Trade Agreement (NAFTA) in 1993, the establishment of the euro in 1999, the withdrawal of the United Kingdom from the European Union (i.e., Brexit) in 2020, and other economic and political events are likely to affect global economies well into the future.

You need look no farther than the tags on your clothing as evidence of a global manufacturing economy. It is likely that your clothing is made in China, India, and places with which you are completely unfamiliar. Pick up the phone to request computer help and the call may be answered anywhere around the globe. Some even predict that the fast-food order you place though a voice kiosk will eventually be answered in a developing country far away.

While the demands of the world to participate in the information age and the global economy increase, natural resources do not. Shifting rain patterns and decreasing oil reserves place us at odds with our world neighbors. Shrinking resources coupled with modern weaponry can be a volatile mix that demands attention. And of course, global warming and other weather anomalies cross borders and harm the innocent and polluters alike. Attempts to solve one crisis can trigger another. For example, the use of corn crops for ethanol fuel has caused an increase in grocery prices so that families already struggling to pay for food suffer even more. The idea that no one is an island has new meaning on every front. All of these changes, and more that you can probably identify, call on us to participate in understanding and finding solutions. *This is the work of intercultural communication.*

Peaceful Coexistence

As the foregoing discussion suggests, our global community demands that we forge productive relations with people everywhere. To be sure, this means taking advantage of the opportunities we have to interact with individuals of other cultures. These myriad opportunities exist in our homes and neighborhoods, in our schools and workplaces, in our virtual communities, and in our travels abroad. We know that successful intercultural exchanges in these contexts not only enrich our personal and professional lives and help us solve global problems in an interdependent world, but most importantly, they lay the groundwork for a more peaceful future as well. What does it mean to achieve peace and what are the challenges we face?

Sociologist Johan Galtung (1990), one of the pioneers in the field of peace and conflict studies, suggested that peaceful coexistence means much more than the absence of war and bloodshed, which constitutes a type of violence he called *direct violence* (i.e., violent conflict). Eradicating this type of violence gives us **negative peace**. In this respect, the job of **peacemaking** is to stop the violence taking place between conflicting parties as quickly as possible, while the job of **peacekeeping** is to prevent the recurrence of such violence. According to Galtung, however, genuine peace requires the absence of two other no less significant (though *indirect*) types of violence: structural and cultural. *Structural violence* emanates from political, economic, and social institutions that produce or permit various forms of human suffering (e.g., death, illness, starvation, poverty). Government policies and business practices that widen the gap between the rich and the poor (e.g., disproportionate spending, tax breaks for the wealthy, corporate greed) and exploit the helpless (e.g., human trafficking, cheap labor) are examples of structural violence. *Cultural violence* is a more indirect and insidious form of violence, resulting from the prejudiced beliefs we hold about the relative value of other cultural groups.

Often, this type of violence manifests itself in feelings of indifference toward the plight of others, as though the victims were in some way undeserving of aid. But cultural violence also includes the discriminatory practices that deprive individuals of basic human rights afforded to all citizens. According to Galtung, efforts to eradicate structural and cultural violence, the ***peacebuilding*** enterprise, create the conditions needed for the attainment of ***positive peace***. In the final analysis, *this is the work of intercultural communication.*

The peacebuilding approach to intercultural communication stresses the urgency and possibility of curtailing the various forms of intercultural violence all too prevalent in the world today. Driven by extreme ignorance and prejudice, stoked by adversity, hate crimes represent one of the more heinous examples of such violence. To assist in the collection of data regarding hate crimes in the United States, Congress formally defined a hate crime as a "criminal offense against a person or property motivated in whole or in part by an offender's bias against a race, religion, disability, ethnic origin, or sexual orientation" (Federal Bureau of Investigation, n.d.). After the passage of the Hate Crimes Statistics Act in 1990, the FBI has been collecting and publishing hate crime statistics, beginning in 1992. During the period from 1995 to 2019, the total number of reported hate crimes have been remarkably consistent, usually in the range of 7,400 and 8,100 cases (11 of 13 years). One striking exception was for the year 2001 during which the 9/11 terrorist attack occurred. Following the attack, a spike in the incidence of anti-Islamic and other religion-based hate crimes brought the total number of reported cases to well over 9,000 (Federal Bureau of Investigation, 2001). Recently, the FBI reported that in 2020 there was a 32% increase in hate crimes over the previous year, including a 77% increase in anti-Asian incidents (US Department of Justice, 2021a).

Of course, statistics alone do not reveal the human tragedy of these crimes (see A Closer Look 1.3); and some hate crimes are particularly shocking in their scope and brutality, arising from an irrational state of mind known as ***xenophobia***—an abnormal fear or hatred of foreigners. One example is the horrific case of Pennsylvania death row inmate Richard Baumhammers. The son of Latvian immigrants, Baumhammers was an immigration attorney who hated immigrants. He believed that immigration was destroying America and he wanted to champion the rights of European Americans. To that end, he tried to organize an extremist group called the "Free Market Party." Living at home with his parents in an upscale community a few miles south of Pittsburgh, he awoke the morning of April 28, 2000, with a plan to rid the world of as many "foreigners" as he could. First, he stopped by the home of his Jewish neighbor, Anita Gordon. After shooting her six times he set her house on fire. Then he drove about a mile to the India Grocers and shot two of their employees, Anil Thakur and Sandip Patel. Next, he fired on two synagogues, stopping to paint swastikas on both. Then, he drove to the Ya Fei Chinese restaurant, killing the owner, Ji-ye Sun, and a Vietnamese delivery man, Theo Pham. The final stop on his killing spree was the C. S. Kim School of Karate, where he killed an African American student, Garry Lee. Though most cases of xenophobia do not end in this kind of senseless barbarism, there is never any justification for hatred directed toward others simply because they belong to a racial or ethnic group different from our own.

A CLOSER LOOK   **1.3**

Some Recent Cases of Hate Crimes Across America (FBI Hate Crime Statistics)

Utah man charged with hate crimes for attacking three men

> A federal jury in Salt Lake City, Utah, found defendant Alan Covington guilty on three hate crime charges. The Utah man is charged with attacking three men with a metal pole because he believed the men were Mexican.
>
> After a five-day trial, a federal jury in Salt Lake City, Utah, found defendant Alan Covington guilty on three hate crime charges stemming [from] an incident in which the defendant attacked three men with a metal pole because he believed the men were Mexican. . . .
>
> Evidence presented at trial established that on November 27, 2018, Covington entered a tire store, shouted at employees that he wanted to "kill Mexicans," and then struck an employee in the head with a metal pole. The father of the victim rushed to help his son, who had been knocked to the ground with a serious head injury. While the father cradled his son's head, Covington used the metal pole to strike the father in the back. When a third man tried to intervene to chase off the defendant, Covington swung the metal pole in an attempt to injure him. . . . A sentencing date has not been set. (US Department of Justice, 2020a)

Federal jury convicts Illinois man for bombing the Dar-Al Farooq Islamic Center

> A federal jury returned guilty verdicts against [the offender] for his role in bombing the Dar al-Farooq ("DAF") Islamic Center in Bloomington, Minnesota, on August 5, 2017. Previously, two other defendants pleaded guilty to their roles in the bombing. As proven at trial, during the summer of 2017, [the offender] established a terrorist militia group called "The White Rabbits" in Clarence, Illinois. [He] recruited co-defendants . . . to join the militia, which he outfitted with paramilitary equipment and assault rifles. On August 4 and 5, 2017, [they] drove in a rented pickup truck from Illinois to Bloomington, Minnesota.

The group bombed the DAF Islamic Center at about 5 a.m., when worshipers were present for morning prayers. In 2021, the offender was sentenced to 53 years in prison (US Department of Justice, 2020b; Ibrahim & Forliti, 2021).

Indiana man pleads guilty to hate crime for racially motivated threats toward black neighbor

The offender made threats to intimidate his Black neighbor, and interfered with their right to fair housing, because of the neighbor's race. The offender learned about his neighbor's plans to remove a tree from the neighbor's property:

> [He] placed and burned a cross above the fence line facing his neighbor's property; created and displayed a swastika on the outer side of his fence, facing his neighbor's property; created and displayed a large sign containing a variety of anti-Black racial slurs next to the swastika; visibly displayed a machete near the sign with the racial slurs; loudly played the song "Dixie" on repeat; and threw eggs at his neighbor's house.

In early 2021, the offender was sentenced to 46 months in federal prison, along with three years of supervised release. (US Department of Justice, 2021b; Harris, 2021)

(continued)

Hate crime charges in connection with the shooting deaths of two transgender individuals during an alleged carjacking

> [A] federal grand jury in the District of Puerto Rico returned an indictment against two defendants charged with the murder of two transgender women. . . . The four-count indictment includes charges for using a firearm in relation to crimes of violence, carjacking resulting in death, and destruction of property using explosive materials. . . . The crimes of violence underlying the firearms offense charged in Counts One and Two, were a carjacking and a hate crime based on gender, sexual orientation or gender identity. . . . If convicted, the defendants face up to life in prison or the death penalty. (US Department of Justice, 2020c)

Colorado man pleads guilty to federal hate crime for plotting to blow up synagogue

The offender pled guilty to a federal hate crime for plotting to blow up the Temple Emanuel Synagogue in Pueblo, Colorado. According to the affidavit, he self-identifies as a Neo-Nazi and a white supremacist:

> [The offender] visited Temple Emanuel to observe Jewish congregants. After one such visit, Holzer told undercover FBI agents that he wanted to do something that would tell Jewish people in the community that they are not welcome in Pueblo, and they should leave or they will die. . . . [He] repeatedly expressed his hatred of Jewish people and suggested using explosive devices to destroy the Synagogue. [He] told the undercover agents that he wanted to "get that place off the map."

On November 1, 2019, the offender took custody of "inert explosive devices" with the plan to detonate them the next morning. In early 2021, he was sentenced to over 19 years in prison (US Department of Justice, 2020d; US Department of Justice, 2021c).

The Ethics of Intercultural Communication

Although we believe that intercultural communication can build more productive and peaceful communities, we do not subscribe to the notion that any communication between people of different cultures is better than no communication between people of different cultures. We begin with a brief discussion of the ethical principles guiding our commitment to and understanding of intercultural communication. These principles are derived from the general guidelines offered by the National Communication Association (see A Closer Look 1.4).

Understandably, most of us feel some measure of pride in our cultural heritage due to the emotional attachment and sense of belonging we have with our culture. This *cultural identity* develops over time, takes many forms, and varies from one person to another (see Chapter 3). A strong attachment to one's cultural group can inspire patriotism and a willingness to sacrifice for the welfare and survival of the group; but it can also create animosity and insensitivity toward persons of other cultural groups.

William Graham Sumner, a nineteenth-century sociologist, coined the term *ethnocentrism* for the belief that one's culture is the "center of everything" and therefore superior to other cultures. Ethnocentrism encourages people to apply the norms and standards of their own culture when judging other cultures: "This is the way we

---

A CLOSER LOOK   1.4

National Communication Association Credo for Ethical Communication

Questions of right and wrong arise whenever people communicate. Ethical communication is fundamental to responsible thinking, decision-making, and the development of relationships and communities within and across contexts, cultures, channels, and media. Moreover, ethical communication enhances human worth and dignity by fostering truthfulness, fairness, responsibility, personal integrity, and respect for self and others. We believe that unethical communication threatens the quality of all communication and consequently the well-being of individuals and the society in which we live. Therefore, we, the members of the National Communication Association, endorse and are committed to practicing the following principles of ethical communication.

We advocate truthfulness, accuracy, honesty, and reason as essential to the integrity of communication.

We endorse freedom of expression, diversity of perspective, and tolerance of dissent to achieve the informed and responsible decision making fundamental to a civil society.

We strive to understand and respect other communicators before evaluating and responding to their messages.

We promote access to communication resources and opportunities as necessary to fulfill human potential and contribute to the well-being of families, communities, and society.

We promote communication climates of caring and mutual understanding that respect the unique needs and characteristics of individual communicators.

We condemn communication that degrades individuals and humanity through distortion, intimidation, coercion, and violence and through the expression of intolerance and hatred.

We are committed to the courageous expression of personal convictions in pursuit of fairness and justice.

We advocate sharing information, opinions, and feelings when facing significant choices while also respecting privacy and confidentiality.

We accept responsibility for the short- and long-term consequences for our own communication and expect the same of others.

---

do it, so this is the way everyone should do it" (see Put It Into Practice 1.2 for a self-assessment). Rather than cultivating an attitude of respect, much less an appreciation for differences, ethnocentrism breeds feelings of contempt that can lead to apathy, discrimination, and intergroup hostilities. Research shows, for example, that ethno-centric persons are more likely to lack knowledge of and respect for another culture than are persons with less ethnocentric beliefs (Wiseman, Hammer, & Nishida, 1989).

Alarmingly, recent studies suggest that ethnocentrism plays a role in the dehumanization of outsiders—members of other cultural groups (outgroups). For instance, in one series of experiments, researchers found that individuals were less sensitive to the number of outgroup lives at stake in a disaster than they were to the number of ingroup lives at stake in the same disaster (Pratto & Glasford, 2008). Eth-nocentrism also fosters the belief that outsiders—people of other racial and ethnic

---

PUT IT INTO PRACTICE   **1.2**

Ethnocentrism Scale

In the space provided please indicate the degree to which each statement applies to you by marking whether you (5) strongly agree, (4) agree, (3) are undecided, (2) disagree, or (1) strongly disagree with the statement. There are no right or wrong answers and some of the statements are similar to others. Remember, everyone experiences some degree of ethnocentrism.

1. _____ Most other cultures are backward compared to my culture.

2. _____ My culture should be the role model for other cultures.

3. _____ People from other cultures act strange when they come to my culture.

4. _____ Lifestyles in other cultures are just as valid as those in my culture.

5._____ Other cultures should try to be more like my culture.

6. _____ I'm not interested in the values and customs of other cultures.

7. _____ People in my culture could learn a lot from people in other cultures.

8. _____ Most people from other cultures just don't know what's good for them.

9. _____ I respect the values and customs of other cultures.

10. _____ Other cultures are smart to look up to our culture.

11. _____ Most people would be happier if they lived like people in my culture.

12. _____ I have many friends from different cultures.

13. _____ People in my culture have just about the best lifestyles anywhere.

14. _____ Lifestyles in other cultures are not as valid as those in my culture.

15. _____ I am very interested in the values and customs of other cultures.

16. _____ I apply my values when judging people who are different.

17. _____ I see people who are similar to me as virtuous.

18. _____ I do not cooperate with people who are different.

19. _____ Most people in my culture just don't know what is good for them.

20. _____ I do not trust people who are different.

21. _____ I dislike interacting with people from different cultures.

22. _____ I have little respect for the values and customs of other cultures.

To calculate your ethnocentrism score complete the following four steps:

Step one: Add your responses to items 4, 7, and 9.

Step two: Add your responses to items 1, 2, 5, 8, 10, 11, 13, 14, 18, 20, 21, and 22.

Step three: Subtract the sum from step 1 from 18.

Step four: Add results from step two and step three. This is your ethnocentrism score. Higher scores indicate greater ethnocentrism. Scores above 55 are considered high in ethnocentrism.

(Neuliep & McCroskey, 1997)

groups—are less likely to experience "uniquely human" emotions. Unlike "universal emotions," such as anger and fear, uniquely human emotions (also called "secondary emotions") are those not found in the animal kingdom, and thus "uniquely" human. In one provocative study of helping behavior in the aftermath of Hurricane Katrina, researchers asked White and Black participants to infer the emotional states of an individualized White or Black hurricane victim. Participants were also asked about their willingness to help such victims. Not only were the participants less likely to believe that an outgroup individual felt uniquely human emotions (e.g., anguish, mourning, remorse), but these beliefs predicted who would volunteer for hurricane relief efforts. Those less likely to attribute uniquely human emotions to the victims were also the least likely to offer help (Cuddy, Rock, & Norton, 2007).

While recognizing the inherent value of one's cultural affiliations, we endorse ethical guidelines for intercultural communication that lessen the destructive impact of ethnocentrism. Research shows that we can reduce ethnocentrism through efforts aimed at promoting intercultural sensitivity and multiculturalism (Dong, Day, & Collaco, 2008), so what are some useful ethical guidelines? Communication scholar David Kale (1994) offers the following:

1. Ethical communicators address people of other cultures with the same respect that they would like to receive themselves.

2. Ethical communicators seek to describe the world as they perceive it, as accurately as possible.

3. Ethical communicators encourage people of other cultures to express themselves in their uniqueness.

4. Ethical communicators strive for identification with people of other cultures while still retaining the uniqueness of their cultural identities; they strive for unity of spirit . . . the human spirit.

The following recommendations for ethical intercultural communication are consistent with these guidelines.

Seek to Understand Rather than Predict

Any statement about culture and cultural style is a generalization. As you learn about cultural patterns, remember that what is true at the macro level is not always true at the micro level. In other words, what we discover about patterns of cross-cultural communication (e.g., comparing Japanese communication styles with American communication styles) does not necessarily reflect what we observe when an individual from Japan interacts with an individual from America. As communication scholars Timothy Levine, Hee Sun Park, and Rachel Kim (2007) explain:

> The findings from cross-cultural communication research do not necessarily transfer automatically to predictions about intercultural communication. Just because members of one cultural group have high frequencies of apologizing to their fellow members, it does not mean that they will also show high frequencies of apologizing to a member of another cultural group. Although it is certainly informative to know cultural characteristics of members of one cultural group when predicting what might happen when the group members encounter/interact with members of another cultural group, there is no guarantee that cross-cultural communication differences will be fully exhibited in intercultural communication. (p. 209)

Be Respectful

The world is full of different ways of meeting human challenges. Any culture in existence today is here because it has successfully met its challenges in the past. Be careful of ethnocentrism that leads you to assume that your ways of doing things are the best or only ways. This is not to say that you have to abandon what you feel is best for you. Still, before you make such decisions, try to keep an open mind about why a person might think differently than you do. Understand before you judge. It may take years of living in another culture before you can truly understand how the culture works, so suspend judgment as long as you possibly can. Lead with your curiosity, not your judgment, and you may be surprised what you can learn. Anthropologist Wade Davis, for example, studied zombies in Haiti in the 1980s. Although most people assumed that zombies were mythological figures used to frighten children into good behavior, Davis made one important assumption in his research: he would believe what the Haitians believed, without question. As a result, he was able to discover that zombies did exist and that the state of the zombie was produced by the use of poisoned powder that could be delivered through the skin. His discovery added to what modern science knows about anesthesia. Would this discovery have been possible had he not been willing to suspend his disbelief? Can we suspend ours?

Find People Who Will Engage and Challenge You

One of the challenges of intercultural communication is that we tend to learn about cultural styles, values, and so on in a vacuum. As much as we read, none of this is a substitute for lived experience. Even when faced with the opportunity for cross-cultural contact, our clumsy curiosity can lead us to be imposing as we approach people different than ourselves to learn more. We have to work hard to make real and meaningful contact across cultures. Challenge yourself to live outside of your comfort zone. Go to places you don't usually go, talk with people you might typically ignore, and visit different places, even in your own town. The facility to interact with a variety of people is a gift that will serve you throughout life. If you live in this way, you will be better able to ask the hard questions about a culture and more likely to get honest answers. For example, approaching a person in a wheelchair and asking, "What's it like to need a wheelchair?" is a lot different than walking alongside a friend in a wheelchair when she encounters an access problem at a building entrance. Develop the capacity to accept your own discomfort. If your friend in a wheelchair expresses anger or frustration, just listen. Don't argue or try to minimize by simply agreeing or disagreeing. Empathize with them and learn from their feelings.

Never Stop Learning

Never believe that you know it all, even about your own culture. Ask questions of your grandparents, parents, siblings, and neighbors, as well as unfamiliar others to allow yourself to deepen your understanding. Keep up with current events and think about your place in making the world you desire. When visiting another culture keep an open mind and allow yourself to be surprised, even though some surprises can arouse feelings of anxiety, confusion, and disapproval—a disorienting condition known as *culture shock* (see the following Culture Shock box on parenting styles for an example).

Studying intercultural communication from a peacebuilding perspective means adopting the view that we need to interact with people of other cultures so we can move closer to a world that resolves its greatest differences through personal contact and dialogue rather than apathy or aggression. It means that people do not try to understand each other in order to take advantage of an insider's knowledge of another culture, but instead use their knowledge to make sense of another's experience and worldview. It means embracing the idea that building peace is everybody's business, not just the politicians or those with the power to make decisions. Finally, it means embracing the idea that each new intercultural relationship represents a new link in the chain of relationships fortifying communal life. In the next chapter, we introduce this approach to the study and practice of intercultural communication.

Summary

While the global community recognizes the inherent value of cultural diversity, the clash of cultures in a multicultural society poses a major challenge to the prospects of peaceful coexistence. The peacebuilding approach to the study and

CULTURE SHOCK

What's a Parent to Do?

During a panel discussion in which several students from Korea and Japan spoke with a class of American students about their different backgrounds, the discussion turned to parenting styles. First, one classroom student asked our Asian visitors, "Aren't you just sick when you see American parents in the market whacking their kid on the bottom?" The panel of students responded, "No, we are shocked at how young children shame their parents in public." Another classroom student then said, "It's good that you don't spoil your children and help them to be respectful and independent. Some American parents spoil their kids and turn them into real brats. Some even have their children in the bed with them!" There was some confusion at this point. When the panel of visitors finally realized that many American parents put a newborn baby in a crib to sleep alone, they were shocked. One explained, "In Japan a parent will keep a child very close and sleep with them for a long time." "How long?" asked one student. As we went down the row of visitors the first responded, "I slept with my parents until I was 5." The next said, "Until I was eight." The next said, "I am looking forward to going home over break and sleeping with my parents." No one said a thing for several seconds. Later an American student said almost under her breath, "That's way inappropriate" as one of the Japanese students said to another panelist, "What a mean thing to do to a child."

practice of intercultural communication highlights the unique and indispensable role of communication in building peaceful communities. Most definitions of culture refer to shared beliefs, values, customs, and symbols of a large group of people that are passed down from one generation to the next. Because many co-cultures often reside within a larger culture, differentiating cultural groups is no easy task. Yet, regarding a group of people as a culture can change the way we treat and think about the group.

Intercultural communication involves the exchange of meaningful messages between individuals of different cultural groups. Most models of communication view it as a social and transactional process in which two persons use various channels of communication to exchange meaningful messages in a particular context. The social nature of communication requires some kind of connection between individuals, although a misunderstanding does not imply a lack of communication. Communication is a process because it is constantly changing with no clear beginning or end. The transactional nature of communication suggests a multichanneled exchange in which the participants are both senders and receivers of messages at the same time. It consists largely of verbal and nonverbal symbols— arbitrary signs that may differ from one culture to another—even though many messages involve the use of nonsymbolic, universal forms of expression (e.g., an angry facial expression). Communication is highly personal in that meaning resides not in the message itself, but in the identities, emotions, and thoughts of the individuals involved. It is also affected by the context in which it occurs. The relational context provides information about the level of intimacy, the balance of power, and the socially constructed roles that exist between communicators; the cultural context creates the rules and rituals we take for granted in our everyday interactions. Shifting demographics, globalization, and the importance of peaceful coexistence in an increasingly complex and interconnected world underline the urgency of ethical and successful intercultural communication.

QUESTIONS

1. As noted in the opening of this chapter, the global community recognizes the value of cultural diversity. Based on your reading of the UNESCO Declaration on Diversity (A Closer Look 1.1), which of the benefits of diversity (as stated in Articles 1–4) do you believe represents the most convincing case for cultural diversity?

2. Based on the definition of the term culture presented in this chapter, what are your cultural affiliations? How would you rank-order these cultural groups in terms of their importance to your own sense of identity? What factors determined your rankings?

3. Think of an instance in which you experienced a "breakdown" in communication; that is, you or someone you were interacting with got the wrong message. Why do you think this breakdown occurred? Could it have been prevented? What were the consequences of the breakdown? How does the breakdown illustrate one or more of the characteristics of communication (social, process, transactional, symbolic, personal, and/or contextual)?

4. How does ethnocentrism interfere with the goals of peacebuilding through intercultural communication? What do you think are the main causes of ethnocentrism? To what extent do you believe that ethnocentrism is a personal trait that cannot be changed? What do you believe are the best ways to lessen the negative effects of ethnocentrism?

A Peacebuilding View of Intercultural Communication

CHAPTER OUTLINE

I. Intercultural Communication Competence
   A. Elements of Intercultural Communication Competence
   B. Models of Intercultural Communication Competence

II. Intercultural Communication Competence and the Peacebuilding Process
   A. Initiating Contacts that Build Community
   B. Creating Dialogues that Build Community

III. A Peacebuilding Model of Intercultural Communication
   A. Cultural Identity Shapes Communication in Context
   B. Intercultural Contexts Offer Opportunities to Build Community

KEY TERMS

automatic stereotyping
common ingroup identity model
conflict transformation
contact hypothesis
dialogue
extended contact effect
ingroup favoritism
intercultural communication competence
intercultural dialogue

outgroup homogeneity bias
prejudice
self-segregation
sense of community
social capital
social identity theory
social justice
stereotype
ultimate attribution error

The symbolism at play was mind-boggling. For decades Mandela had stood for everything White South Africans most feared; the Springbok jersey had been the symbol, for even longer, of everything Black South Africans most hated. Now suddenly, before the eyes of the whole of South Africa, and much of the world, the two negative symbols had merged to create a new one that was positive, constructive, and good. Mandela had wrought the transformation, becoming the embodiment not of hate and fear, but of generosity and love. (Carlin, 2008, p. 223)

In the book *Invictus*, which recounts former South African President Nelson Mandela's unimagined journey from prisoner to peacebuilder, author John Carlin tells the story of how Mandela's vigorous and steadfast support of South Africa's nearly all-White rugby team, the Springboks, helped unify the country around a new collective identity—one that transcended the brutal legacy of apartheid and the ongoing rivalries between Blacks and Whites. Working together under the banner of "one team, one country," Mandela and his backers, both Black and White, turned their improbable 1994 Rugby World Cup championship into much more than a sports team victory; they turned it into a triumph of the peacebuilding enterprise and a model of how an entire nation can move, at least for a time, away from the forces that weaken and toward those that strengthen the ties of a community. In many ways, as we will see in this chapter, the South Africa story is a story about the paramount role of intercultural communication competence in building peaceful communities.

We begin this chapter by discussing the meaning and fundamental elements of intercultural communication competence. We will then consider how competent communication contributes to peaceful communities and present a

Separate entrances for races, like at this train station, were commonplace in the apartheid era in South Africa.

peacebuilding model of intercultural communication that provides the foundation for the remainder of the book.

Intercultural Communication Competence

Although ethical principles provide the moral grounding for competent intercultural communication (see Chapter 1), they do not contain the fundamental criteria for judging our level of competence or for determining the relative success of our intercultural interactions in specific situations. This chapter introduces the concept of *intercultural communication competence*, which presupposes that some people are more "able" communicators than other people, and that most people can learn to improve these skills if they choose to do so.

Elements of Intercultural Communication Competence

The idea to promote both the scientific study and practice of competent intercultural communication gained considerable momentum during the 1970s, fueled in part by the need to train volunteers for the Peace Corps program, and alongside the growing recognition that social, economic, and political survival will depend increasingly on interactions with members of other cultural groups (Spitzberg & Changnon, 2009). In their seminal work on this subject, communication scholars Brian Spitzberg and William Cupach (1984) suggested that competent communication should include at least two outcomes: (1) it should be appropriate and (2) it should be effective. Appropriate behaviors follow prescribed rules; effective behaviors produce desired results. While there may be some overlap between these two factors, they are reasonably distinct. For example, suppose Tina makes a phone call to get product information from a department store employee. If she gets the information she needs, her communication was effective; but if she insults the employee in the process, her communication was inappropriate. Of course, judgments of whether a person's communication is competent may depend on the cultural background of the judge. To briefly illustrate, picture this scene:

> A 19-year-old college student arrives for a meeting with a history professor. The student wants to find out if he can get course credit for an independent study project he would like to do under the professor's guidance and supervision. During the meeting the student speaks very little, giving very short answers to the professor's questions. When the student speaks he smiles a bit nervously, hesitates slightly, speaks softly, and looks down, averting the professor's steady gaze. The meeting lasts about 10 minutes. The professor is undecided about taking on the project and asks the student to check back in a couple of days. The student thanks the professor and leaves.

How would you interpret and evaluate the communication that took place in this meeting? Specifically, what is your opinion of the student's demeanor? Was his communication with the professor appropriate and effective?

Some of you might regard the student's communication as timid and lacking in confidence. Perhaps the professor shared this assessment. But others might see the same behavior as polite and respectful. In fact, this difference in judgment reflects a cultural divide over what constitutes proper conduct between a lower-status and a higher-status person—a fundamental difference about the *appropriateness* of one's communication. The prevailing norms in many cultures prescribe that lower-status persons be highly respectful (i.e., submissive, deferential) toward persons of higher status, in contrast to the norms of other cultures that recommend strong, assertive communication styles (see Chapters 6 and 7). The *effectiveness* of the student's communication, which represents the other primary dimension of communication competence, depends on whether the student achieved his goal. But even this judgment is not free of cultural bias. For example, one viewpoint would say the student's main goal was to get independent study credit from the professor, while a different point of view would say the student's main goal was to begin building a positive relationship with the professor. In fact, as we will see in Chapter 4, these two viewpoints represent different cultural orientations. Therefore, in judging the communication competence of someone in a particular situation, our cultural *frame of reference* influences how we interpret and how much we value the appropriateness as well as the effectiveness of someone's communication behavior (Kim, 2005). Despite these cultural variations, however, we recognize the need to distinguish between appropriateness and effectiveness as the essential and overarching features of competent communication (Lustig & Koester, 2006; Spitzberg & Changnon, 2009).

As noted earlier, the notion of intercultural communication competence implies that some of us are more competent than others. But it also assumes that we can increase our level of competence, which raises the question: what are the prerequisites for competent communication? According to Spitzberg and Cupach (1984), competence requires *knowledge* about the communication practices of a particular culture and the *motivation* and *skills* to apply that knowledge in a particular *context*. Accordingly, our knowledge, motivation, and skills combine to determine our level of competence in a particular situation.

The "knowledge" element includes what we know about a culture that informs and guides our choices of what to think, say, and do in a particular situation. Ignorance of a culture's norms, rules, rituals, symbols, and expressions can lead to missteps and misunderstandings. Sometimes these gaffes produce only awkward or embarrassing moments, as would happen, for instance, if when greeting a person from a foreign country, you freeze, not knowing whether to kiss the person, bow, place the palms of your hands together, or shake hands with the other person. But other times the consequences can be serious and far-reaching, endangering a fragile peace and creating an international incident. In a highly publicized case at the time, Gillian Gibbons, a British woman teaching school children in the Sudan in 2007, came up with a nice idea for a class project. She asked one of her students, a 7-year-old girl, to bring a teddy bear to class. The students voted to name the teddy bear "Muhammad" after considering several other names. Each of the 23 students in the class took turns taking the teddy bear home and writing in a diary what the teddy bear did during the visit. Gibbons collected the students' entries and compiled them in a book called *My Name Is Muhammad*, putting a picture of the teddy bear on the cover. Upon finding out, outraged parents and school officials complained that using the name of the prophet Muhammad for a teddy bear was an extreme insult to Islam. Gibbons was arrested and jailed and hardline Muslim clerics and angry protesters called for her execution. After lengthy negotiations, the Sudanese president pardoned Gibbons and within days she left the country. Her punishment could have included up to 40 lashes and 6 months in prison. In a written statement, Gibbons declared, "I have a great respect for the Islamic religion and would not knowingly offend anyone" (Associated Press, 2007).

Though vital, knowledge alone is not sufficient for intercultural communication competence. We also need the *motivation* to interact with people of other cultural groups. Many factors conspire to keep us apart: anxiety, disinterest, ignorance, prejudice, ethnocentrism, and so on. Research sometimes shows that increased diversity in schools and neighborhoods encourages people to "hunker down" along racial and ethnic lines (Moody, 2001; Putnam, 2007; Anicich et al., 2021). Even on college campuses, where diverse student populations offer plentiful opportunities for intercultural interactions, we still see a reluctance to reach out to persons of other cultural groups. This tendency toward *self-segregation* rarely escapes notice, leading to some skepticism over whether efforts to increase campus diversity actually achieve their desired effects. For example, in a widely cited survey of undergraduate students at the University of California at Los Angeles, more than 90% of the respondents believed that students cluster largely by race and ethnicity, and a majority (52%) felt that students rarely socialize across racial lines (Antonio, 2001).

Research shows that campus diversity encourages intercultural interactions. However, it may take more than mere contact with someone of another culture to reduce prejudice.

But how accurate is the perception that college students avoid interactions with peers from other cultural groups? In the UCLA survey noted above, only 17% of the UCLA students reported having friendship circles that did *not* include at least one student from a different racial or ethnic group. Indeed, there is ample evidence of a gap between the perception and the reality of self-segregation on college campuses. In a study of intercultural socializing at 390 campuses across the country, students reported frequent contacts outside their own cultural groups. As one example, 78% of Mexican American, 69% of Asian American, 55% of African American, and 21% of White students frequently dined with someone of a different racial or ethnic group (Hurtado, Dey, & Trevieo, 1994).

Research confirms that campus diversity encourages intercultural interactions, contrary to any claims of widespread and growing trends toward self-segregation. Using data from the National Longitudinal Survey of Freshmen, which questioned 4,000 White, Black, Hispanic, and Asian students on 28 college and university campuses during the fall and spring terms of their freshman year, Mary Fischer (2008) found a clear relationship between campus diversity and friendship diversity. Students on highly diverse campuses were more likely to report having intercultural friendships than were students on less diverse campuses—a finding that was especially true for the White students in the survey. Systematic observations of casual interactions reveal a similar pattern. Studying more than 2,000 student interactions inside and outside various buildings of six California State University campuses, Gloria Cowan (2005) found no overall differences between the percentages of interethnic and intraethnic groups. She also found that interethnic interactions constituted a greater percentage of the total number of observed interactions on those campuses, with the most diverse student populations compared to those with the least.

Even though cultural diversity generally brings greater opportunities for intercultural interactions, there is less evidence that contact with someone of another culture heightens the chances of *friendship* with that person or automatically reduces the level of prejudice we may have toward that person's cultural group. Although increased immigration has created more diverse populations in many countries, there are some studies that do not report reduced prejudice as a consequence of greater diversity and opportunities for more intercultural contact. For instance, one series of studies in Germany found that contacts with members of another cultural group, under some circumstances, can actually increase rather than decrease prejudice against members of the other cultural group (Kotzur & Wagner, 2021).

Our attitudes toward the members of other cultures are often a consequence of the stereotypes we hold about them. In this regard, stereotyping can increase or decrease prejudice toward that culture. Researchers tend to offer two competing theories about the impact of cultural diversity on stereotyping and prejudice. One theory suggests that we will judge members of a culture in ways that reinforce what we already believe about them (i.e., confirmation bias). The other theory suggests that increased exposure and contact with members of other cultures will encourage us to abandon the stereotypes we hold about them (we discuss this "intergroup contact theory" later in the chapter). A recent series of studies offers convincing evidence that, in general, increased cultural diversity decreases our reliance on stereotypical thinking about cultural groups (Xuechunzi, Ramos, & Fiske, 2020). In the first study, data collected in 46 countries around the world showed that people living in countries with greater ethnic diversity were more likely to feel a sense of community with the members of other ethnic groups than were people living in countries with less diverse populations. In their second study, the researchers surveyed 1,500 Americans living in all 50 states and found that the more diverse a state was, the more likely it was for the participants in the study to feel a sense of commonality with the members of other ethnic groups. So, it would appear that the more we're exposed to diverse groups, the more we're going to find that they're not actually much different than ourselves.

What's more, surveys show that most people around the world generally welcome greater diversity in their populations despite the challenges they also acknowledge. According to a 2019 Pew Research Center survey, in 27 countries, home to more than half of the world's international migrants, roughly 23% of those surveyed in each country were opposed to greater diversity and viewed it as more of a bad thing than a good thing for their country. In contrast, a much higher percentage (45%) had a favorable opinion. The research also found a gen-erational gap—younger people tend to welcome diversity more than their older counterparts. Education also made a difference in attitudes; the more education survey respondents had, the more likely they were to favor ethnic and racial diver-sity (Poushter & Fetteroff, 2019). Focusing on just American citizens, another 2019 Pew Research Center survey of a representative sample of more than 6,000 people found that 57% of Americans believed that racial and ethnic diversity was a very good thing for the country, while another 20% believed it was somewhat good (Horowitz, 2019).

As we will see later in this chapter, positive outcomes from contact with persons of other cultural groups often depends on a variety of factors, such as whether one person holds power over another. In addition, we do not share the same desire to pursue these opportunities. Two of the most influential factors are: (1) how much discomfort we expect to feel in such interactions and (2) how ethno-centric we happen to be. In one study, for example, researchers asked college stu-dents how likely it was that they would participate in a campus program giving them the opportunity to meet and talk to international students once a week. As expected, students' levels of anxiety and ethnocentrism predicted their desire to participate in the program (Lin & Rancer, 2003).

Knowing a lot about a particular culture and being highly motivated to apply what we know can make it easier for us to communicate effectively and appropriately with members of that culture. But knowledge and motivation are not enough. Even the most informed and well-intentioned person needs certain *skills* to achieve high levels of intercultural communication competence. We dis-cuss these specific skills in Chapters 3 through 7, including the abilities to (1) manage the anxiety associated with meeting and talking to individuals of different cultural groups; (2) recognize and resist ethnocentric impulses in our thoughts and actions; (3) understand and take the perspectives of individuals from different cul-tural groups; (4) respect and appreciate cultural differences in taken-for-granted modes of communication; (5) reject stereotyped and preconceived judgments of individuals from different cultural groups; (6) recognize and manage emotions tied to cultural conditioning and socialization; (7) empathize with the experiences of persons from other cultural groups; and (8) send and interpret verbal and non-verbal messages according to the demands of the cultural context.

The final element of intercultural communication competence is the *context* in which an interaction takes place. Although contexts can vary in countless ways, the most important factors are: (1) our *relationship* with another person (friend, stranger, sibling, parent, employer, etc.); (2) the *purpose* of the interaction (get acquainted, persuade, exchange information, give advice, entertain, comfort, etc.); (3) the *cultural rules and norms* embedded in the interaction (ethnicity, race, religion, sexual-orientation, etc.); (4) the *occasion* for the interaction (business meeting, dinner date, interview, wedding reception, party, informal visit, college course lecture, etc.); and (5) the *setting* of the interaction (restaurant, dorm room, doctor's office, friend's home, shopping mall, cyberspace, movie theatre, etc.). No sensible discussion of communication competence is possible without considering these contextual factors; as you will see throughout this book, behavior that may be effective or appropriate in one context may be highly ineffective or inappropriate in another.

Models of Intercultural Communication Competence

Graphic representations, or *models*, of intercultural communication competence tend to vary according to their main purpose. For instance, some models show only the relations among the core elements contributing to competence; others focus on showing competence as a developmental process, something we attain over time; while still other models highlight the role of cultural adaptation as a prerequisite for competence. One of the most useful and comprehensive models of relations among the core elements contributing to competence is Darla Deardorff's (2009) pyramid model, shown in Figure 2.1. To construct the model, Deardorff asked 23 recognized experts on intercultural competence to suggest, independently, what they believed were the key elements. Her model reflects those beliefs about which there was the greatest consensus among the experts. As represented in the model, each level contributes directly to the level above, leading ultimately to desired outcomes. Lower levels include the core elements of motivation (i.e., attitudes), knowledge, and skills, while the top two levels of the pyramid include various outcomes associated with appropriate and effective communication.

Developmental and adaptation models offer another view of intercultural communication competence, focusing on the acquisition of attitudes, knowledge, and skills over time. Illustrative of this approach is Milton Bennett's (1986) stage model of intercultural sensitivity shown in Figure 2.2. The model begins with a series of ethnocentric stages marking a person's movement away from a monocultural worldview and proceeds in turn through a series of "ethnorelative" stages marking a person's transition to a deeper and more dynamic multicultural worldview. The stages reflect a person's growth or maturation as he or she gains

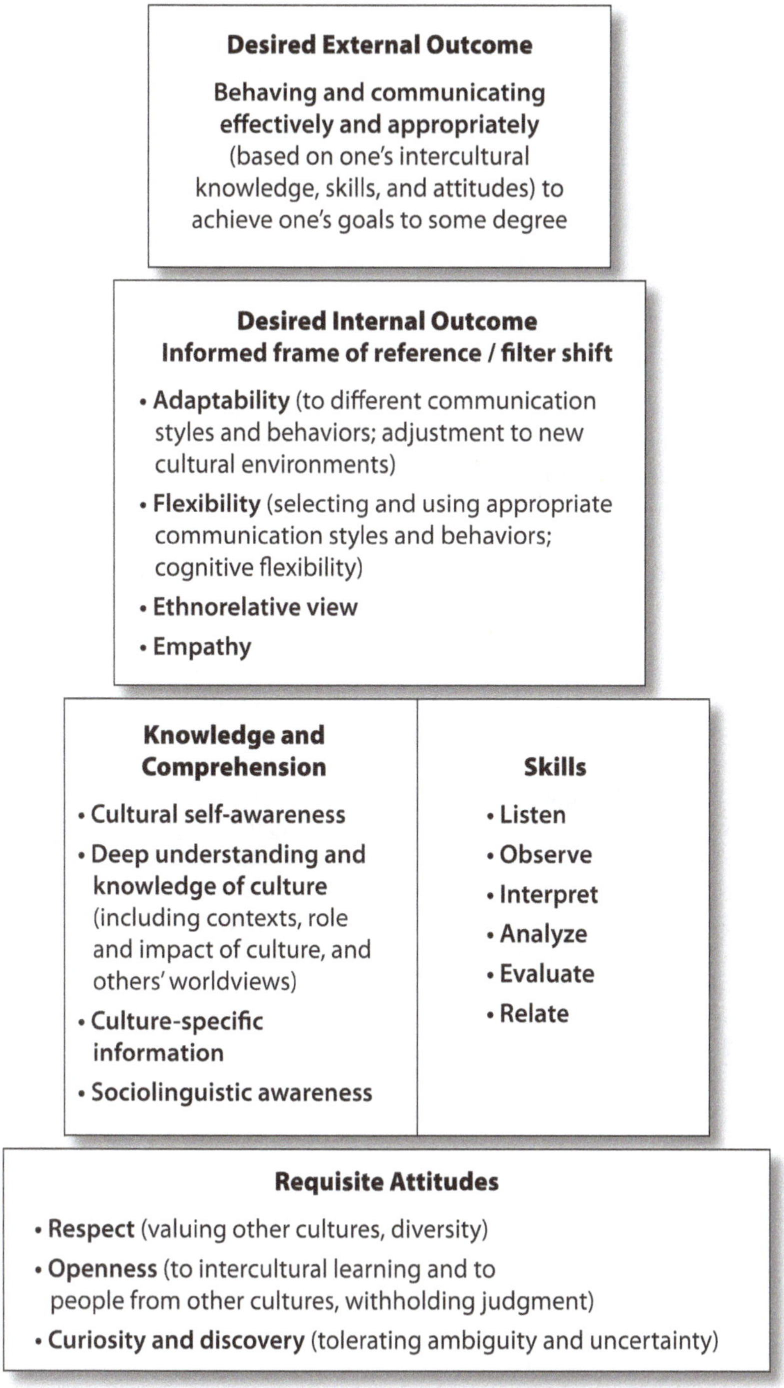

Desired External Outcome

**Behaving and communicating
effectively and appropriately**
(based on one's intercultural
knowledge, skills, and attitudes) to
achieve one's goals to some degree

**Desired Internal Outcome
Informed frame of reference / filter shift**

- **Adaptability** (to different communication
  styles and behaviors; adjustment to new
  cultural environments)
- **Flexibility** (selecting and using appropriate
  communication styles and behaviors;
  cognitive flexibility)
- **Ethnorelative view**
- **Empathy**

**Knowledge and
Comprehension**

- **Cultural self-awareness**
- **Deep understanding and
  knowledge of culture**
  (including contexts, role
  and impact of culture, and
  others' worldviews)
- **Culture-specific
  information**
- **Sociolinguistic awareness**

Skills

- **Listen**
- **Observe**
- **Interpret**
- **Analyze**
- **Evaluate**
- **Relate**

Requisite Attitudes

- **Respect** (valuing other cultures, diversity)
- **Openness** (to intercultural learning and to
  people from other cultures, withholding judgment)
- **Curiosity and discovery** (tolerating ambiguity and uncertainty)

Figure 2.1   Deardorff's Model of Intercultural Competence (Deardorff, 2009)

Figure 2.2 Bennett's Developmental Model of Intercultural Competence (Adapted from Bennett, 1986. In Spitzberg & Changnon, 2009)

experiences with a wide range of cultural differences. In the *denial stage* we fail to acknowledge the existence of legitimate cultural differences and cling to the belief that other cultures are not as worthy as our own; in the *defense stage* we acknowledge cultural differences but largely in terms of a threatening "us" vs. "them" orientation; in the *minimizations stage* we tend to trivialize cultural differences as having little significance compared to assumed similarities; in the *acceptance stage* we begin to both understand and respect cultural differences; in the *adaptation stage* we begin to develop intercultural communication skills, such as taking the perspective of others; and finally, in the *integration stage* we acquire a multicultural worldview, expanding the boundaries of our own cultural identity process.

In their review of the literature on models of intercultural communication competence, Spitzberg and Changnon (2009) express a number of concerns. First, the models generally ignore the relatively nonconscious emotional processes that can help or hinder the acquisition of competence, focusing instead on highly conscious, rational decision-making processes (e.g., choosing to accept or reject the customs of a culture). Second, most of the models tend to reflect a "Western" bias in their assessments of competence. That is, they favor a view of competence that equates successful communication with the task of achieving personal goals (e.g., being assertive)—a perspective that differs from the more relationship-oriented paradigms of many non-Western cultures (e.g., being respectful or saving face). Third, the models fail to account fully for the consequences of adaptation. For instance, it is not clear in a two-person interaction whether one or both persons should adapt to the other. As Spitzberg and Changnon point out:

> If both are adapting, it seems possible that both interactants become chameleons without a clear target pattern to which to adapt. If adaptation results in excessive compromise of personal identity, such a trade-off may exact costs on other aspects of competent performance. (p. 35)

The idea of intercultural communication competence focuses on the traits and abilities that help people achieve a clearly defined goal in a socially acceptable manner. It also encourages us to focus on the *individuals* involved in a particular interaction and their respective levels of competence. The peacebuilding perspective takes us in a different direction, asking us to consider intercultural communication competence first and foremost as a means of attaining the larger goal of building peaceful communities. It suggests further that in even the most seemingly inconsequential intercultural exchanges, the stakes may be higher than we realize; and instead of judging the competence of each individual in an interaction, the peacebuilding view, insofar as it regards each intercultural interaction as a *partnership* striving for a greater sense of community, shifts our attention to the shared burdens and responsibilities of all the participants in the interaction.

Peacebuilding initiatives are multilayered and wide in scope, encompassing work at all levels of society, from international partnerships to personal friendships (Maiese, 2003). Most relevant to the study and practice of intercultural communication is the social or relational dimension of peacebuilding, the task of building a human infrastructure of people committed to "bridge-building" systems of communication. In the sections that follow we discuss these various communication systems and then introduce a model of the peacebuilding approach that guides the remainder of the book.

Intercultural Communication Competence and the Peacebuilding Process

As we noted in Chapter 1, the task of peacebuilding involves more than the cessation and prevention of violent conflict (negative peace). In one sense, while peacemaking and peacekeeping are reactive strategies designed to keep conflicting parties apart, peacebuilding is a proactive means of bringing them together—a relationship-changing, reframing, and healing process known as *conflict transformation* (Lederach, 2003). But peacebuilding goes beyond repairing and transforming relations between disputants and works incrementally over time toward the attainment of positive peace, curtailing indirect forms of violence—the deeply rooted structural and cultural systems in a society that condone hatred, prejudice, discrimination, and indifference. In this sense, peacebuilding works in pursuit of *social justice*, the belief in fair treatment and equal access to valued resources for all citizens in a multicultural society. Finally, by encouraging intercultural ties and expanding social networks (i.e., friendship circles), peacebuilding aims to reinforce the sense of community we need to sustain the health and vitality of democratic institutions adapting to the demands of new demographic trends. In this sense, peacebuilding strengthens the *social capital* of a society (i.e., the value of social networks) by raising levels of voter participation, civic engagement, volunteerism, trust in government, altruism, and the like (Putnam, 2007).

The peacebuilding approach to intercultural communication is an interdisciplinary perspective that draws on the work of scholars in many fields, including sociology, social psychology, education, political science, anthropology, and communication, to name a few. The central question is: *How does intercultural communication competence contribute to the peacebuilding enterprise?* Our interactions with persons of other cultures invariably present *obstacles* on the road to more peaceful communities. More than mere "speed bumps," these obstacles, originating from cultural differences in identity, worldview, emotional experience, and nonverbal as well as verbal communication, are like unexpected "forks in the road," that can steer us away from our destination. Intercultural communication competence helps us navigate this cultural terrain. Our interactions with persons of other cultures also offer *opportunities* along the road to more peaceful communities. Whether in our homes, schools, neighborhoods, places of work, or virtual communities we have more chances than ever before to create new pathways to peace. Intercultural communication competence gives us the tools we need to build bridges over the cultural divides that lie ahead. The peacebuilding approach offered in this chapter draws on two substantial bodies of theory and research clarifying the connection between intercultural communication competence and peacebuilding. The first addresses the social capital implications of personal contact between members of different cultural groups as a means of reducing prejudice, and the second explores the nature and consequences of intercultural dialogue as a tool for conflict transformation and social justice.

Initiating Contacts That Build Community

Shortly after World War II, in the hopes of shedding some much-needed light on one of the major impediments to peace, social scientists began a systematic study of the nature, causes, and consequences of **prejudice**, generally defined as a negative attitude toward a group or members of a group (Stangor, 2009). As early as 1946, a study of desegregation in the United States Merchant Marines found that the more voyages White seamen took with Black seamen, the more positive their attitudes were toward Blacks in general (Brophy, 1946); and in 1949, researchers studying racial prejudice in the military found that, when asked how they would feel about having Black soldiers serving in the same platoon with them, White soldiers reporting the least amount of contact with Black soldiers were most likely to oppose the idea. As expected, integrated units were much less prejudiced than were the segregated units (Stouffer, 1949). In addition to these early studies of interracial contact in the military, several large-scale sociological studies of public housing projects confirmed the positive effects of intergroup contact. Researchers in one study, for example, found that White women assigned to desegregated housing projects were more likely to have contact with and hold positive views of Blacks and to support interracial housing than were White women assigned to comparable but segregated housing projects (Deutsch & Collins, 1951). More than six decades of social science research now informs our understanding of how "making contact" with persons of other cultural groups builds peaceful communities. In this section we review the findings of this research and then consider the implications for understanding and developing intercultural communication competence.

Drawing on the field research and sociological theory available at the time, one of the pioneering psychologists of the twentieth century, Gordon Allport (1954), wrote extensively about the positive effects of frequent contact between racial groups. His **contact hypothesis**, referred to more broadly as *intergroup contact theory*, originally held that interracial contact does not automatically or always reduce prejudice, but will under four conditions: (1) equal status among group members, (2) group members working toward a common goal, (3) cooperative interaction among group members, and (4) clear institutional forms of support for intergroup contact (see A Closer Look 2.1). The impact of this work has been

---

A CLOSER LOOK   **2.1**

The Contact Hypothesis

In his classic and highly influential 1954 book, *The Nature of Prejudice*, Gordon Allport introduced the contact hypothesis in the statement that follows:

> It would seem fair to conclude that contact, as a situational variable, cannot always overcome the personal variable in prejudice. This is true whenever the inner strain within the person is too tense, too insistent, to permit him to profit from the structure of the outer situation.
>
> At the same time, given a population of ordinary people, with a normal degree of prejudice, we are safe in making the following general prediction. . . . Prejudice, unless deeply rooted in the character structure of the individual, may be reduced by equal status contact between majority and minority individuals in the pursuit of common goals. The effect is greatly enhanced if this contact is sanctioned by institutional support (i.e., by law, custom or local atmosphere), and provided it is of a sort that leads to the appropriation of common interests and common humanity between members of the two groups. (p. 267)

(Allport, 1954)

---

far-reaching, beginning most notably with its use as part of the scientific rationale underlying the Supreme Court's landmark 1954 decision in *Brown v. Board of Education*, paving the way for desegregation in public schools. Today, research in the tradition of the contact hypothesis continues to elucidate the myriad effects of cultural diversity in all walks of life.

Although Allport's work concentrated initially on race relations, intergroup contact theory has widened over the years to include prejudice based on ethnicity, religion, age, disability, sexuality, and even professional associations. After reviewing more than 500 different studies on the contact hypothesis published during the period beginning in 1940 and through the year 2000, Thomas Pettigrew and Linda Tropp (2006) concluded that intergroup contact, as Allport predicted, typically reduces prejudice. They concluded further that the four conditions Allport identified as necessary are instead only more likely to enhance the positive effects of contact on prejudice. Thus, their conclusion supports a *mere exposure effect*—that all things being equal, contact and familiarity between members of different cultural groups breeds enough liking to reduce the levels of prejudice that members of one group may feel toward the members of another group.

Yet despite the apparent simplicity and optimism of the claims reported above, it would be a mistake to conclude that getting rid of prejudice requires little more than a few brief intercultural encounters. Even the most encouraging interpretation of the research acknowledges Allport's own contention that mere contact alone is unlikely to change the attitudes of individuals with "prejudiced personality traits," such as authoritarianism and social dominance orientation (i.e., predispositions that embrace various forms of social inequality). In addition, studies suggest that *implicit forms of prejudice*—the mental associations and knee-jerk reactions we have in response to other cultural groups (see section below on social categorization)—may be more resistant to change than are *explicit forms of prejudice* (e.g., reports of negative attitudes; hostile behavior) from regular contact with persons of other cultures (Henry & Hardin, 2006). Finally, since contact does not always reduce prejudice (even under the most favorable conditions), and when it does the effects can range from trivial to transforming, questions remain about how to maximize and extend the positive impact of intergroup contact from one context to another, which requires a clear understanding of how intergroup contact reduces prejudice.

Social Categorization and Prejudice

Our starting point in discussing how intergroup contact reduces prejudice is to consider briefly how the process of *social categorization*—categorizing people according to their group affiliations—creates and nurtures intergroup prejudice. Put simply, group categories produce stereotypes that we apply to the members of a group. **Stereotypes** are knowledge structures that serve as mental images of a group, including the traits we view as characteristic of the group or of its individual members (Stangor, 2009). Acquired early in life from parents, peers, the media, and other sources of influence, these relatively static images shape, simplify, and distort our judgments of cultural groups, particularly when we have little first-hand knowledge of these groups (see A Closer Look 2.2 for an example).

Perhaps the most troublesome quality of stereotypes, aside from their basic unfairness and resistance to change, is how quickly and uncontrollably they come to mind when we think about a group. Indeed, at a time when few people condone or openly and actively endorse negative attitudes toward other cultural groups, most of the negative stereotyping that persists in the world today escapes our notice through a nonconscious process called *automatic stereotyping* (Devine, 1989). In contrast to the willful stereotyping that reflects our conscious thoughts and beliefs, automatic stereotyping includes some or all of the following characteristics (Bargh, 1994):

- *Spontaneity*—we apply the stereotypes without any deliberate intent to do so.
- *Efficiency*—we do not need to pay much attention to the stereotyping.
- *Uncontrollability*—we cannot immediately stop the stereotyping once it begins.
- *Unconsciousness*—we are not aware of how the stereotyping takes place.

To a large degree, all of us are inclined to harbor prejudicial feelings toward other cultural groups because of a natural impulse to favor *ingroups* (groups to which we belong) over *outgroups* (groups to which we do not belong). In addition to the material rewards of group membership (e.g., the benefits of national citizenship), ingroups are a source of valuable information, and they comfort us with a sense of belonging and security. Moreover, according to *social identity theory*, our group affiliations satisfy a fundamental need for positive self-esteem and instill in us as much pride as we derive from our own individual achievements (Tajfel & Turner, 1979; see Chapter 3). Picture, for example, football fans congratulating

A CLOSER LOOK

Cultural Images: Myths and Messages

In the passage below, modern Arabic literature and culture scholar Miriam Cooke describes how stereotyped images of American and Muslim women foster prejudice toward both groups.

> I argue that the major block to respect of and communication with the unknown is preconception built on the weak and resilient foundations of myth and image.
>
> Images are flat impressions that provide pieces of information. They are like photographs that frame and freeze a fragment of the real and then project it as the whole. What was dynamic and changing becomes static. Just as a snapshot provides a true, if partial, picture, so these cultural images contain some truth. That is why they are so hard to change. Just as the image of the amoral, free-living American woman epitomizes for many pious Muslims all that is wrong with Western culture, so the image of the veiled woman encapsulates for the Western observer all the coercion imagined to mark Islamic culture. Women are easily turned by outsiders into emblems of their culture, for within culture itself women are often made into custodians of their culture's values. No matter how many nonpromiscuous, modest Western women the Muslim may meet, no matter how many assertive, independent, unveiled Muslim women the Westerner may meet, there is a possibility that the basic image will not change as these individuals come to be seen as exceptions to a rule that they thereby serve to reinforce. These images are the context of a first encounter between two people who know little if anything about each other.
>
> Images we have of each other are always part of the baggage that we bring to dialogue. Sometimes we are at the mercy of the image our addressee has of us or chooses to invoke. Sometimes we hide behind the image. Sometimes we act *as though* neither of us had an image of the other. Sometimes, those ideal times, the image disappears and the contact is unmediated by the myth. Then we can act as individuals between whom messages pass easily regardless of the contact, code, or context.

Cooke, M. (1997). Listen to the image speak. *Cultural Values*, 1, 101–102.

each other after watching their home team score a touchdown. Perhaps most surprising is the fact that group members tend to share these feelings of self-worth even when the group to which they belong is trivial, as when researchers in laboratory experiments randomly assign individuals to groups on the basis of meaningless categories (Billig & Tajfel, 1973). An important element of prejudice, in fact, has more to do with the positive feelings we have toward ingroups than with any negative feelings we have toward outgroups.

This expression of *ingroup favoritism* takes many forms, some less apparent to us than others. For instance, we are more likely to show empathic concern for the plight of ingroup members than for the same plight experienced by out-group members; and numerous field studies show that in all sorts of situations in which someone needs help, we are more likely to help the person if he or she is a member of an ingroup than if he or she is a member of an outgroup. Studies also reveal that our basic judgments of people depend on whether they are ingroup or outgroup members. One line of such research confirms the existence of an *outgroup homogeneity bias*, a common tendency to exaggerate similarities and overlook individual differences among outgroup members compared to ingroup members—a bias that facilitates the use of stereotypes in judging the members of outgroups, while weakening the use of stereotypical thinking for ingroup members. Another line of research reveals that our explanations for the actions of ingroup members tend to be more generous and supportive than they are for outgroup members, a type of *attribution bias* favoring ingroups known formally as the **ultimate attribution error** (Pettigrew, 1979). Studies show that we are more likely to attribute the bad behaviors of ingroup members to things beyond their control (i.e., the situation) than we are for out-group members; and further, we are more likely to attribute the good behaviors of ingroup members to their inner qualities (i.e., personality, intelligence, character) than we are for outgroup members (Duncan, 1976; Pettigrew, 1979; Wittenbrink, Gist, & Hilton, 1997). For example, if we learn that an ingroup member showed up late for work we are more likely to attribute the behavior to some situational factor like a family emergency or a transportation problem than we would if he or she was the member of an outgroup ("he/she is irresponsible"). On the other hand, if we hear that an ingroup member found and returned a lost puppy we are more likely to attribute the behavior to that person's good character than we would if he or she was the member of an out-group ("he/she just happened to be in the right place at the right time").

Thus, the process of social categorization leads to stereotypical thinking and biased judgments in favor of ingroups over outgroups. That much of this prejudice takes place outside our conscious awareness and control makes it highly resistant to change. Viewed in this light, making contact with persons of other cultural groups is a powerful way to loosen the grip of social categorization in ways that reduce all forms of intergroup prejudice.

How Does Contact Reduce Prejudice?

Consider your own experience. When was the last time you had contact with someone of a different cultural group? How often do you interact with individuals of other cultural groups? Do your contacts with these persons influence your judgments and feelings about them and their cultural ties, or even about your own cultural identity? Answers to these questions give us some clues about how intergroup contacts may reduce prejudice. Extensive research suggests that when intergroup contact is the catalyst for reductions in prejudice, it tends to happen as a result of greater knowledge, increased empathy and perspective taking, and decreased levels of stress and anxiety (Hodson, Hewstone, & Swart, 2013; Pettigrew & Tropp, 2008).

One way that contact reduces prejudice is by *increasing knowledge about other cultural groups*. The more we interact with persons of other cultures the more we learn about them as individuals and as representatives of various cultural groups. This knowledge includes ways in which other cultures are similar to and different from our own culture, making it possible for us to find common ground while also appreciating cultural differences. Information that personalizes our contacts (i.e., self-disclosures) often shows us that the members of other cultures rarely fit the simple stereotypes we have of them. Greater knowledge may also change our attitudes when it makes us more aware of past injustices endured by other groups (Dovidio, Gaertner, & Kawakami, 2003).

Another way that contact reduces prejudice is by *facilitating empathy and perspective taking*. Intergroup contact, especially when it fosters close personal relationships, makes it easier for us to take and understand the perspective of outgroup members, share their emotional experiences, and empathize with their concerns, thereby improving intergroup attitudes (Pettigrew & Tropp, 2008). In fact, some research suggests that intergroup contact may involve processes of "identity expansion" and "identity inclusion" in which we extend our sense of self to include outgroup members (Aron & McLaughlin-Volpe, 2001). This is what happens when we think of ourselves and the members of other cultural groups as sharing a common identity (e.g., we're all Americans, college students, women, baby boomers, etc.).

Contact also reduces prejudice by *lessening the stress and anxiety associated with intercultural encounters*. Feelings of stress and anxiety have multiple adverse consequences: forestalling contact with outgroup members (fewer interactions), hindering efforts to build rapport when we do make contact (signs of discomfort),

Contact with persons of another culture is likely to reduce prejudice when it increases our knowledge of the culture, facilitates empathy and perspective taking, and lessens the stress and anxiety we may feel in these interactions.

and coloring our perceptions following contact (negative judgments and attributions). But intergroup contact over time can allow us to feel less uncertainty, less
threat and more competent in our interactions with outgroup members, which
in turn lowers levels of stress and anxiety (Hodson, Hewstone, & Swart, 2013;
Blascovich et al., 2001).

Our contact with people from other cultures equips us with greater knowledge, empathy, and perspective taking, and makes us feel less threatened and anxious about our intercultural interactions. These contacts are likely to improve our
attitudes toward other cultural groups. In recent years, scholars have been high-
lighting two factors in particular that seem most likely to enhance and extend these
positive effects: establishing a common identity and building strong friendships.

The Importance of a Common Identity

As noted above, intergroup contact reduces prejudice in part because our
interactions with the members of other cultures reveal their personal, rather than
stereotypical, qualities. The "interpersonal" nature of these contacts over time
allows us to regard the members of other cultures as unique individuals with a
complex set of interrelated identities that we cannot easily ascribe to a particular
group. This process of decategorization works against the tendency to pigeon-
hole people as members of ingroups and outgroups and may reduce prejudice
as a result (Brewer & Miller, 1984). However, a different perspective claims that
decategorization, while leading us to abandon the stereotypes that fuel intergroup
prejudice, does not encourage us to think and act more positively toward other
cultural groups. In addition, seeing people as individuals rather than as members of a distinct cultural group can be threatening and sometimes degrading to
persons for whom culture and identity are closely aligned and inseparable. So,
another viewpoint recommends interpersonal interactions (decategorization), but
with some awareness of the intercultural context in which they occur (Hewstone
& Brown, 1986). According to this position, the positive effects of contact will
most likely generalize to other outgroup members and contexts when the contact
includes representative or typical members of the outgroup.

Building on these two perspectives, Samuel Gaertner and John Dovidio (2000)
proposed a *common ingroup identity model*. Instead of focusing on decategorization (seeing people as individuals) or categorization (seeing people as members of
a particular culture), the model focuses on *recategorization*, whereby we see people
as members of one inclusive, overarching, or superordinate group with a shared
identity. Unlike other approaches to intergroup contact, this model suggests that
a common ingroup identity makes it possible for outgroup members to benefit
from the effects of *ingroup favoritism*. This is what happens, for example, when
the members of a soccer or basketball team see each other first and foremost as
team members rather than as member of diverse cultural groups. According to the
model, ingroup and outgroup categories (e.g., Blacks and Whites, Muslims and
Jews, Anglos and Latinos, etc.) begin to function primarily as subgroups within
the more inclusive and salient cultural group, so that individuals maintain dual
identities (e.g., primary/superordinate identity as a team member and second-
ary/subordinate identity as a Muslim). Over a decade of empirical research in a

Regarding persons of other cultural groups as fellow members of a common ingroup, such as the fans of a sports team, is one way of reducing prejudice and building community.

wide range of contexts with diverse populations within and outside the United States generally supports the efficacy of this model (Gaertner & Dovidio, 2009). We review much of this research in Chapters 8–13.

The Importance of Intercultural Friendships

The concept of friendship occupies a special place in the literature on intergroup contact because, by its very nature, it usually encompasses all of the conditions for reductions in prejudice identified in Allport's (1954) seminal work (e.g., equal status, common goals); but also because it exerts a powerful influence on the task of peacebuilding beyond the reduction of prejudice (i.e., encouraging extended intergroup interactions and strengthening the *social capital* of a community). In addition, efforts to build and sustain intercultural friendships present greater communication challenges than those that we face in other types of relationships (see Chapter 8).

A growing body of research clearly documents the beneficial effects of intercultural friendships. Studies show that these friendships help create positive intergroup attitudes, not only toward the members of outgroups with whom we have contact but also toward the outgroup in general and even toward other outgroups (Hodson, Hewstone, & Swart, 2013). In one large scale survey of respondents in four Western European countries, Thomas Pettigrew (1997) found that having more friends of another nationality, race, religion, culture, or social class is associated with less prejudice toward minority group members, even after taking into account the respondent's political ideology, education, age, national pride, and other relevant variables. In a study of friendship groups at the University of California at Los Angeles (UCLA), Anthony Antonio (2001) found that students with more diverse friendship circles were more likely to engage in interracial interactions outside their friendship groups, express a stronger commitment to racial understanding, and exhibit more intercultural awareness. In the largest such study to date, Sidanius et al. (2008) conducted a longitudinal survey of more than 2,000 UCLA students during the period 1997–2001. In part, they found that students who had a greater proportion of friends from different ethnic groups (Asian, Latino, African American, and Anglo) in their sophomore and junior years in college, reported less bias in favor of their ethnic group and less anxiety interacting with members of different ethnic groups at the end of their senior year of college. In contrast, they found that having more ingroup friends led to greater ingroup bias and intergroup anxiety.

Research on intercultural friendships also supports what researchers call an *extended contact effect*—learning that members of your in-group have friends from other cultural groups is sufficient in itself to cause a reduction in prejudice toward those other cultural groups (Hodson, Hewstone, & Swart, 2013). In a review and summary of 20 years of research on the extended contact effect, Zhou, Page-Gould, and Hewstone (2019) found strong support for this hypothesis. Put simply, even if you personally do not have any friends or direct contacts with members of another racial or ethnic group, just knowing that others of your own racial or ethnic groups do, will tend to reduce the prejudice you may have toward those other racial or ethnic group. In fact, what's interesting is the researchers' discovery that the perception of extended contact (i.e., believing that someone in your racial or ethnic group has friends in other racial ethnic groups) is more important than whether they actually do or don't.

Contact and Intercultural Communication Competence

We began this chapter by asking how intercultural communication competence contributes to the peacebuilding enterprise, and now close this section on intergroup contact by considering the role and importance of intercultural communication competence in reducing prejudice through intergroup contact. As we reviewed the theory and research on both topics, you may have been struck by the convergence of findings around the basic theme that intergroup contacts are much less likely to build peaceful communities without some degree of intercultural communication competence. In their exhaustive review of more than 500 studies on the contact hypothesis, Pettigrew and Tropp (2008) concluded that reductions in prejudice depended on three factors: knowledge of other cultures, anxiety reduction, and the skills of empathy and perspective taking. You may recall from our earlier discussion of intercultural communication competence that these findings mirror precisely the three core elements identified in most models of intercultural communication competence: knowledge (cognitive element), motivation (emotional element), and skills (behavioral element). You may also have noticed some parallels between developmental models of intercultural communication competence that show a desired progression from "ethnocentric" to "ethnorelative"

PUT IT INTO PRACTICE   **2.1**

A Case Study of Contact and Prejudice

Using the principles and concepts presented in this chapter, analyze how inter-group contact may have reduced prejudice in the following case. On a sheet of paper, answer the questions listed after reading the case.

Linda gets together twice a month with her physical therapist, Nour, a 36-year-old devout Muslim, born and raised in Syria. Nour earned her college degree in the United States and has been living in Pennsylvania for more than 15 years. Linda is a middle-aged, Anglo-American sales representative for a software manufacturer and grew up in the suburbs of Indianapolis, Indiana. She describes herself as a "conservative" Christian. Before meeting each other for the first time, both Linda and Nour had fairly strong negative feelings about the other person's cultural affiliations. But after several months of meeting on a regular basis, they started enjoying each other's company and began looking forward to their sessions together. Eventually they became friends, no longer meeting just for therapy appointments, and doing things together on the weekends, often with mutual friends. Today, Linda and Nour have more positive feelings about each other's cultural ties and show few signs of the kind of prejudice they once had.

1. Linda and Nour began their relationship holding certain stereotypes about the other person's cultural groups. What might have been some of those stereotypes?

2. Is it likely that the contact between Linda and Nour satisfied the four conditions Allport identified as necessary for contact to reduce prejudice? Explain.

3. How would you explain the change in their initial attitudes toward the other person's cultural groups from negative to positive? What three factors probably account for this change in attitude?

4. How would the common ingroup identity model explain their change in attitude?

5. What role did their friendship play in changing their attitudes?

stages, and models of intergroup contact that show a desired progression from categorization to recategorization. In both cases, we would expect reductions in prejudice as persons move from exclusive "us-them" orientations to inclusive "we" orientations. Finally, research suggests that making contact with persons of other cultural groups depends on one's level of intercultural communication competence. For example, one study of Asian and American college students living in China and in the United States found that scores on a measure of self-perceived intercultural communication competence predicted Asian students' willingness to interact with American students and American students' willingness to interact with Asian students (Lu & Hsu, 2008).

Creating Dialogues That Build Community

Communication scholars W. Barnett Pearce and Stephen Littlejohn (1997) characterize parties enjoined in moral and intractable conflict as "compelled by its highest and best motives to act in ways that are repugnant to the other" (p. 13) and conclude that peace requires processes that can encourage those same people to risk being changed. In this section we describe the nature of intercultural dialogue and its theoretical foundations and present some examples of intercultural dialogue processes in the United States and abroad. In the next section we relate intercultural competence—necessary skills to interact competently across cultures—with the skill development necessary for but also developed through participation in intercultural dialogue. We briefly review some of the research on the effectiveness of intercultural dialogue on developing intercultural communication competence.

The Nature of Dialogue

From his experience as founder and consultant with the *Transcendent Communication Project*, Stephen Littlejohn (2021) explains that **dialogue** differs from conventional interaction in terms of change potential. Conventional discussion and debate concentrates on "first order change" or changing a participant's point of view about the content being discussed. "Second order change" concerns transformation of the relationship between the parties or transformation of the social system of which they are a part. The goal of dialogue is a deeper understanding of self and other in order to redefine relationships. For example, imagine a dialogue that is held about racial tensions in a community. Conventional discussion about that issue may concentrate on the facts of racial tension in terms of personal and economic costs. But a dialogue, focusing on second order change, encourages participants to consider how they can become more engaged in building community networks that will decrease those racial tensions and encourage participants to reflect on how their current attitudes and behaviors may be contributing to racial tension.

Stewart, Zediker, and Black (2004) reviewed major theories of dialogue and reported that all major theories of dialogue emphasize its power to use communication to bring together the "different." One of the most influential theorists of dialogue, Martin Buber (1958) wrote about dialogue as a special kind of communication marked by speaking and listening in which the speakers are communicating their uniqueness and their sameness at the same time and for the purpose of transcending difference and aloneness. Dialogue, in Buber's sense, involves an exceptional openness to otherness, but it is not an unreflective or gullible acceptance or tolerance (Cissna & Anderson, 2002).

Paulo Friere, a great social activist who devoted his work to understanding the power of education and interaction for social justice, felt that dialogue is a way that people humanize and transform an unjust world into a just one. Since cultures are formed in and through communication, a communication perspective on dialogue underscores the consequence of dialogue for changing social relations and creating new social meaning (Pearce & Pearce, 2004). For these same reasons, the Russian philosopher of dialogue and dialectics, Mikhail Bakhtin, saw dialogue as

A CLOSER LOOK   **2.3**

The Importance of Intercultural Dialogue for World Peace

In 2010, the United Nations Security Council laid out the importance of intercultural dialogue for achieving global peace. Then-Secretary-General Ban Ki-moon warned that just because the world is becoming more connected through social, political, and economic forces (e.g., technology, trade, and migration), it is simultaneously experiencing change in different, more negative, ways that can drive it further apart:

> At a time when prejudice and hatred are all too common, when extremists seek new recruits through incitement and identity-based appeals, when politicians use divisiveness as a strategy to win elections, dialogue can be an antidote. . . . Dialogue can defuse tensions, and keep situations from escalating. It can promote reconciliation in the aftermath of conflict. It can introduce moderate voices into polarized debates. (United Nations, 2010)

Ban highlighted the recent creation of the United Nations Alliance of Civilizations (UNAOC) as a valuable initiative for overcoming prejudice among nations, cultures, and religions.

especially critical in *intercultural* situations. Bakhtin's theory of dialogue emphasizes the necessity of interaction and understanding between inherently different persons or perspectives (Strine, 2004).

Overview of Dialogue Processes

Dialogue practitioners distinguish between dialogue and "nondialogic" forms of communication like debate and diatribe. Dialogue has certain properties that help create a social condition that is connective, creative, and restorative. As you review the contrast between debate and dialogue from in Table 2.1, think about how these differences in process help to reinforce a sense of openness and possibility (for dialogue) versus threat and certainty (for debate).

David Bohm (1996) uses the term "dialogue" to mean a particular process that occurs between a group of people who, seated in a circle talking together, communicate to understand each other and to develop mutual respect on which community can be built, sustained, or repaired. Using a similar general process, in their Public Dialogue Consortium work, Pearce and Pearce (2004) see dialogue as a way of helping people tell their stories:

> We teach facilitators to treat any statement as an anecdote rather than a complete story, and to ask questions inviting the speaker to describe the fuller story . . . to probe for unheard and untold stories, to explore the differences between their stories lived and stories told, and to bring in other voices to tell the story more systematically. (p. 47)

Table 2.1   Distinguishing Debate from Dialogue

Debate	Dialogue
Pre-meeting communication between sponsors and participants is minimal and largely irrelevant to what follows.	Pre-meeting contacts and preparation of participants are essential elements of the full process.
Participants tend to be leaders known for propounding a carefully crafted position. The personas displayed in the debate are usually already familiar to the public. The behavior of the participants tends to conform to stereotypes.	Those chosen to participate are not necessarily outspoken "leaders." Whoever they are, they speak as individuals whose own unique experiences differ in some respect from others on their "side." Their behavior is likely to vary in some degree and along some dimensions from stereotypic images others may hold of them.
The atmosphere is threatening; attacks and interruptions are expected by participants and are usually permitted by moderators.	The atmosphere is one of safety; facilitators propose, get agreement on, and enforce clear ground rules to enhance safety and promote respectful exchange.
Participants speak as representatives of groups.	Participants speak as individuals, from their own unique experience.
Participants speak to their own constituents and, perhaps, to the undecided middle.	Participants speak to each other.
Differences within "sides" are denied or minimized.	Differences among participants on the same "side" are revealed, as individual and personal foundations of beliefs and values are explored.
Participants express unswerving commitment to a point of view, approach, or idea.	Participants express uncertainties as well as deeply held beliefs.
Participants listen in order to refute the other side's data and to expose faulty logic in their arguments. Questions are asked from a position of certainty. These questions are often rhetorical challenges or disguised statements.	Participants listen to understand and gain insight into the beliefs and concerns of the others. Questions are asked from a position of curiosity.
Statements are predictable and offer little new information.	New information surfaces.
Success requires simple impassioned statements.	Success requires exploration of the complexities of the issue being discussed.
Debates operate within the constraints of the dominant public discourse. (The discourse defines the problem and the options for resolution. It assumes that fundamental needs and values are already clearly understood.)	Participants are encouraged to question the dominant public discourse, that is, to express fundamental needs that may or may not be reflected in the discourse and to explore various options for problem definition and resolution. Participants may discover inadequacies in the usual language and concepts used in the public debate.

(Herzig & Chasin, 2006). With permission.

A detailed description of how practitioners in the field define dialogue can be found on the National Coalition for Dialogue and Deliberation website (www.ncdd.org). Also, Dessel, Rogge, and Garlington (2006) offer a summary of community and academic intergroup dialogue centers that implement intergroup dialogues and offer dialogue training.

Examples of Intercultural Dialogue Projects

The use and endorsement of dialogue processes in intercultural conflict is increasing, as former United Nations Secretary General Ban Ki-moon's comments in A Closer Look 2.3 suggest. Here we present only a handful of examples to help you appreciate the flexibility and power of intercultural dialogues in domestic and international peacebuilding.

Many individuals and organizations have engaged in dialogue processes in the Middle East to address perhaps the most intractable conflict in human history. For example, Halabi (2000) described the goals of the School for Peace model of Arab-Jewish intergroup dialogue. He stated that rather than attempting rational conflict resolution, the school's dialogues aim to promote a genuine exchange about the inequities that exist for Arabs in Israel. Mary Jane Collier (2009) studied the reactions of Palestinian, Israeli, and Palestinian/Israeli young women in a US peacebuilding program called Building Bridges for Peace. Earlier work with Arab-Jewish coexistence models including dialogue were studied by Abu-Nimer

While formal debates are an essential means of resolving disputes between conflicting parties, intercultural dialogue offers a more promising way of finding common ground, reducing prejudice, and building a sense of community.

(1999). It is important to note that these scholars caution that while these dialogue processes can have very positive consequences, they also can co-opt—dampen the challenge of nondominant groups to dominant power structures.

One model of intercultural dialogue used in high conflict situations is the sustained dialogue model developed by former Secretary of State Harold Saunders. Saunders (2005) reflected on dialogue processes in Tajikistan that he has been involved with since 1993. He emphasized that the focus is on transforming relationships:

> In this process of sustained dialogue there is always a dual focus: Participants, of course, focus on concrete grievances and issues, but always the moderators and participants are searching for the dynamics of the relationships that cause the problems and must be changed before the problems can be resolved. (p. 130)

Large-scale intercultural dialogue processes have been used successfully in the United States. Richard Corcoran (2010), in his book *Trustbuilding: An Honest Conversation on Race, Reconciliation, and Responsibility*, discusses the process that thousands of citizens of Richmond, Virginia, used to address racial tensions in their city. The process, which he called the "Hope in the Cities" model, involved a series of interventions, heavily dependent on dialogue processes, to create trust in a community that had been torn with racial and ethnic conflicts. He reminds us that dialogue at times of division can be scary and difficult:

> Someone once said that the four most frightening words in the English language are, "We've got to talk." It's one thing if you are the person who is saying this, observes Harlon Dalton, "but if you are on the other side, if you are the person who thought things were fine the way they were, or at least you understand that things can be worse, these are scary words indeed. What our partner is saying is that attention must be paid, that respect must be given, and that perhaps power must be shared; that in some significant way the relationship must be altered. (p. 204)

As an example of the use of intercultural dialogue for peacebuilding and policy-making purposes, in July 1998, the Michigan Department of Civil Rights (MDCR) was approached by Community Uniting for Peace (CUP) to conduct a major research and assessment project in Muskegon County on racial/ethnic relations and equity issues. This project designed and implemented a series of large-scale dialogues throughout the state that contributed to community building and improved understanding in race relations policy and practice in Michigan. As Orbe (2006) describes, "the Michigan project is an exemplar for public dialogues as advanced by Cissna and Anderson (2002)" (p. 195).

Dialogue and Intercultural Communication Competence

In the beginning of this chapter we discussed a variety of skills that are critical for intercultural communication competence. Among the most important skills were managing anxiety, resisting ethnocentric impulses, engaging in perspective-taking, empathizing, and using culturally sensitive and appropriate verbal and nonverbal communication behaviors. As we have described, the process of intercultural dialogue incorporates the very competencies we hope to develop and use as peacebuilders.

But, what does the research tell us about the ability of dialogue processes to create or improve these competencies in participants? The evidence from dialogue programs used in large-scale interethnic conflicts is strongly supportive. Abu-Nimer (1999) conducted a program evaluation over a six-year period with 156 facilitators, administrators, participants, and community leaders involved with 15 coexistence programs between Arabs and Jews in Israel. Results of this extensive evaluation indicated that, in part, individuals experienced changes in perceptions of each other and the conflict, an increased sense of knowing each other culturally and personally, increased awareness of Arab-Jewish relations in Israel, and more positive assessments of their intercultural interactions. In Central America, Diez-Pinto (2004) evaluated dialogues conducted in Guatemala that aimed to promote trust and establish a foundation for a long-term national peace agenda. She found that dialogues influenced both personal and national processes through the breakdown of stereotypes, facilitation of personal relationships that would not have otherwise formed, and establishment of trust that led to the start of consensus building.

Promising social science research findings from the United States reveal the power of intercultural dialogue to reduce prejudice and ease ingroup/outgroup tensions. Nagda and Zuniga (2003) found that the more participants valued dialogue, the more positive they were on a variety of outcomes: more reflection about their racial identities, better perspective taking abilities, more comfort in communicating across differences, and more motivation to bridge differences. Other studies have reported that involvement in dialogue fosters comfort in interracial/interethnic situations, learning from diverse peers, and reduction in unconscious prejudice immediately after sustained intergroup encounters (Werkmeister-Rozas, 2003; Yeakley, 1998). In terms of reducing prejudicial attitudes, two studies compared people in dialogue and people in control groups, where no special activity for peacebuilding occurred (Gurin et al., 1999; Gurin, Nagda, & Lopez, 2004). The studies found that dialogue improved perspective taking and a sense of commonality for both dominant and marginalized groups.

Nagda's (2006) study confirmed that dialogue strengthens relationships and builds alliances. Five cohorts of students in a Bachelor of Arts in Social Welfare (BASW) program were enrolled in a "Cultural Diversity and Justice" course that incorporated intergroup dialogue. Nagda hypothesized that communication would be more important than psychological factors, and found strong support for four communication factors that significantly reduced prejudice:

1. Alliance building—relating to and thinking about collaborating with others in taking actions toward social justice. Looking at biases and assumptions and working through disagreements and conflicts are integral to alliance building.

2. Engaging self—being involved as a participant in interactions with others through personal sharing, inquiry, and reconsideration of perspectives as part of the intergroup interaction.

3. Critical self-reflection—examining one's ideas, experiences, and perspectives as located in the context of inequality, privilege, and oppression.

4. Appreciating difference—learning about others, hearing personal stories, and hearing about different points of view in face-to-face encounters; being open to learning about realities different from one's own.

A Peacebuilding Model of Intercultural Communication

We opened this chapter with the story of South Africa's transformation from a nation divided in bitter conflict to a nation in pursuit of peace. We highlighted their 1994 Rugby World Cup championship as a moment in history symbolizing much more than international rugby supremacy. In this special case, it represented a triumph of the peacebuilding enterprise. Even a quick reading of the events leading up to and surrounding that special moment reveals a process that exemplifies the peacebuilding model of intercultural communication we present below (see Figure 2.3). In this section we consider the two core principles represented in the model.

Figure 2.3   Peacebuilding Model of Intercultural Communication

Cultural Identity Shapes Communication in Context

The cyclical process shown in the peacebuilding model begins with (and returns to) our cultural identity—our sense of membership in a particular group or collective—because of its tremendous influence on our everyday lives, shaping our beliefs, attitudes, and actions. South Africa's story begins with a legacy of racism and violence based on the most extreme forms of ingroup privilege and outgroup subjugation. As John Carlin (2008) writes in his book *Invictus*, "Nowhere, since the fall of Nazism had this dehumanizing habit been institutionalized more thoroughly than in South Africa. Mandela himself had described apartheid as a 'moral genocide'—not death camps, but the insidious extermination of a people's self-respect" (p. 2).

Chapter 3 addresses the nature and development of cultural identity, with a particular emphasis on the social construction of identities that constitute obstacles to community, encouraging the powerful to oppress the powerless (i.e., majority and minority identities). It also considers the role of intercultural communication competence insofar as it helps us overcome perceived threats to our identity, initiate contacts with persons of other cultural groups, and create new more inclusive identities. As shown in the model, cultural identity directly influences our intercultural interactions, which includes the emotional and cognitive predispositions we bring with us to all of our interactions (see Chapters 4 and 5), as well as the communicative behaviors we use (see Chapters 6 and 7). The model also shows that cultural differences in these predispositions and behaviors create obstacles to peace, but that we can work to overcome these obstacles with the knowledge, motivation, and skills of competent intercultural communicators.

Despite the compelling drama of the rugby match that captured the attention of the world, the real story of South Africa's transformation, as told in Carlin's book, unfolds in the casual face-to-face conversations of the Black and White leaders and citizens of post-apartheid South Africa. Mandela, of course, was chiefly responsible for charting the course of forgiveness, redemption, and unity that led the way to a new collective identity. His leadership reveals countless instances of intercultural communication competence: empathizing with the emotional concerns of the White population (fear of retribution; pride in the rugby team), recognizing and lessening the anxiety of outgroup members (making White Afrikaners feel comfortable instead of threatened), appreciating and using the symbols that instilled pride among Whites (like wearing the green jersey of the rugby team—a symbol of oppression to most Black South Africans), facilitating personal contacts between the rugby team and the Black population, convincing the rugby team to sing the Black (unofficial) national anthem before the World Cup final match (a song that symbolized White suppression of Blacks), actively persuading Black groups to forgive and embrace the predominately White rugby team, and so forth.

Intercultural Contexts Offer Opportunities to Build Community

In his seminal book on the nature of community, Seymour Sarason (1974) defines our *sense of community* as the perception of similarity to others, an acknowledged interdependence with others, a willingness to maintain this interdependence by giving to or doing for others what one expects from them, and the feeling that one is part of a larger dependable and stable structure. (p. 157)

The peacebuilding model highlights intercultural contexts as places where we make contact and interact with persons of other cultural groups in ways that build friendships (Chapter 8) and the shared identities that lead ultimately to a greater sense of community. These contexts include our home and family (Chapter 9) our schools (Chapter 10), our places of work (Chapter 11), in the media (Chapter 12), and during our travels at home and abroad (Chapter 13).

Nelson Mandela used every opportunity he could imagine to promote his vision of a united South Africa. That tensions between Blacks and Whites lessened and friendly interactions grew with each victory of the Springboks, made the vision seem more real. In the end, following the World Cup victory, signs of a new, more peaceful community were evident. As Carlin (2008) writes:

Reports washed in from the affluent suburbs of Cape Town, Durban, Port Elizabeth, and Johannesburg that White matrons were shedding generations of prejudice and restraint and hugging their Black housekeepers, dancing with them on the leafy streets of prim neighborhoods like Houghton. For the first time, the parallel apartheid worlds had merged, the two halves had been made whole. (p. 245)

Summary

The peacebuilding view of intercultural communication explains how the basic elements of communication competence contribute to the peacebuilding enterprise. Competent communication includes at least two outcomes. First, it should be appropriate, which means it does not violate the rules of proper conduct in a particular situation. Second, it should be effective, which means it produces the desired result. In judging a person's communication competence, our cultural frame of reference will influence how we interpret and how much we value the appropriateness and effectiveness of that person's communication. Competent communication requires knowledge of another culture, as well as the motivation and skills to apply that knowledge in a particular context. Models of intercultural communication competence differ according to the main purpose of the model; but regardless of the model's purpose, they all contain certain strengths and limitations.

While peacebuilding includes the process of repairing and reframing relationships known as conflict transformation, it also includes efforts in pursuit of social justice and practices that strengthen the social capital of a society. One way that intercultural communication competence contributes to peacebuilding is by facilitating the favorable impact of intercultural contact on the reduction of prejudice. Another way is by encouraging the regular and effective use of dialogue as a means of building a sense of community across diverse cultures. The peacebuilding model of intercultural communication begins with the premise that our cultural identity influences our emotions and worldviews, which in turn shape the verbal and nonverbal communication we use in various contexts. The model also includes intercultural contexts as places where we make contact and interact with persons of other cultural groups in ways that build friendships, shared identities, and peaceful communities.

QUESTIONS

1. Consider Brian Spitzberg and William Cupach's central idea that competent communication should be both effective and appropriate. Can you recall any instance of ineffective or inappropriate communication that you have had with someone of another cultural group? What happened? To what extent was the outcome due to a lack of knowledge, motivation, and/or skill? How could the communication have been more effective or appropriate?

2. As noted in this chapter, college campuses are becoming increasingly diverse. What impact do you think these changing demographics have had on intercultural communication competence? What is your view regarding the claim that increased racial and ethnic diversity only produces a tendency toward self-segregation?

3. Intergroup contact theory (i.e., the contact hypothesis) suggests that contact with persons of other cultural groups will reduce prejudice against members of those groups if four conditions exist. What are those four conditions? How would you rank-order them (from most important to least important)? Do you have any personal experiences that support or fail to support the basic ideas of intergroup contact theory?

4. Are the goals and methods of dialogue realistic (or perhaps overly optimistic) when trying to build community between conflicting parties that harbor deeply ingrained feelings of hostility toward each other? Why or why not? Are there situations in which debate is more likely to build peace than dialogue is?

5. What are the four main elements in the peacebuilding model of intercultural communication? Why does the model begin and end with cultural identity? How does the movie *Avatar* illustrate the peacebuilding model?

2

Elements of Intercultural Communication

3

Cultural Identity

CHAPTER OUTLINE

KEY TERMS

critical theory
cultural contracts theory
cultural identity
intergroup threat theory
intractable conflicts
majority identity development
mindfulness

minority identity development
overlapping identity
social construction of identity
social identity theory
standpoint theory
third culture

Persian or Iranian? Negro, colored, Black, or African American? Girl or woman? Gay or Queer? What we are called is an important indicator of our identity. Ethnicity, race, gender, and social class, among other sources of culture, shape our identity. This chapter explores the genesis of cultural identity, definitions of cultural identity, the social construction of cultural identity, minority and majority identity development, obstacles and challenges to peacebuilding, and identity and intercultural communication competence to sharpen our understanding of this complex phenomenon, particularly as it relates to the peacebuilding view of intercultural communication.

The Genesis of Cultural Identity

Some 60,000 years ago about 10,000 people living in sub-Saharan Africa were the totality of humankind (Wells, 2007). From that small band of people, all of modern humanity evolved. The map below shows the human migration beginning in sub-Saharan Africa and extending across the globe.

As members of that initial group traversed the globe, they underwent physical and cultural changes that helped them survive and adapt to the world around them. These changes influenced their social identities; they became mountaineers, hunters, storytellers, healers, and so forth. Even today, family names reflect roles in the community (e.g., Smith, Tailor, Weaver, Baker).

Does your name reflect your cultural identity or your parent's identity? A young man in a training seminar conducted by one of the authors said he was named "N" because his parents (described as "hardcore hippies") allowed his 2-year-old older brother to name him. His brother selected the "letter of the day" on *Sesame Street*. Afrocentric parents have named their children Olubola, Efani, and Karanja as a link to their cultural identity. A first-generation Korean student in an intercultural class named her son Kevin because it sounded like a "real American name." Many transgender people fight for the right to establish a new name

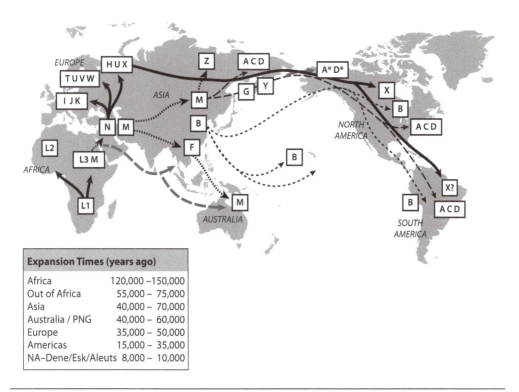

Figure 3.1   Map of human migration (Courtesy of Family Tree DNA)

that is in line with their true identity. In fact, their name assigned at birth is often referred to as their "dead" name.

Naming and identity are so intertwined that some names are illegal. In Germany, for example, names must be approved by a central clearinghouse and are required to reflect the sex of the child and not endanger them (see A Closer Look 3.1). Only in 2008 was the obligation to make a name gender-specific dropped. There was also an uproar in New Jersey when Neo-Nazis tried to have their 3-year-old son's name written on his birthday cake. The child's name is Adolf Hitler Campbell (McShane, 2010).

Defining Cultural Identity

The concept of identity is one of the most researched in the social sciences (Hogg & Vaughan, 2002). Hogg and Abrams (1988) describe identity as a person's awareness that he or she belongs to a particular group or society, and psychologist Erik Erikson (1959) sees identity as both individual and group related.

A CLOSER LOOK 3.1

Approval of Baby Names in Germany

So you've endlessly searched for baby boy names and finally found the fit for your upcoming arrival. Since you love Mark Twain novels, you've decided to name your baby boy "HuckleBerry." You're done, right? Well, not if you live in Germany. All German baby names must be approved by the German Standesamt, also known as the "Office of Vital Statistics." And your name HuckleBerry is going to be rejected!

German law mandates a baby name must reflect the sex of the child, and not endanger the well-being of the child. Once a baby name is chosen, the expectant parents must register the name with the Standesamt. The Standesamt relies on a guide book which translates to "the international manual of the first names."

The Standesamt's website lists recent baby-names decisions which went through the appeal process. The name "Matti" was recently rejected as a baby boy name because the name did not clearly identify the gender. The name "Calotta" was recently rejected because it was similar to the French word "Calotte" which means cap. But the Standesamt ruled the names "Legolas" and "Nemo" were acceptable baby-boy names.

And now back to the name "HuckleBerry." The Standesamt's website states they "were surprised by the HuckleBerry application." The name was considered "a strange thing," and besides, HuckleBerry was considered an outsider in Mark Twain's novels. It is for these reasons the Standesamt rejected this name!

(YeahBaby, 2010)

Cultural identity is our sense of membership in a particular group or collective. We are proud of their accomplishments and feel humiliated by their defeats. We feel that our destiny is tied to theirs (Kriesberg, 2003). Researchers explore many kinds of group associations that make up cultural identity. Race, language, history, gender, age, ability, even hobbies are all mentioned as possible bases for cultural identity (Held & McGrew, 2007). Most theorists agree that multiple factors are at work simultaneously in the development of cultural identity (Tajfel & Turner, 1986); one likening identity to a "yellow dandelion" with each leaf representing an element (Jensen, 2001, p. 13). Some scholars talk in terms of a set of widening circles of membership or "nested" identities (Kriesberg, 2003), for example, a feminist, Christian, American. We all have some version of nested identities; our "layers" of identity are interacting, expanding, retracting, and shifting in intensity throughout our lives.

Developing a Cultural Identity

A common assumption among scholars is that identity is established in concert with others—we cannot solely define ourselves. Identities are what anthropologist Jonathan Friedman (1994) refers to as "socially constructed realities" (p. 238).

Social Construction of Identity

Berger and Luckmann (1966) proposed the concept of *social construction*—that social systems create identities through interaction. Numerous cultural identities have been explored from this perspective. What it means to be beautiful, kind, humorous, appropriate, intelligent, or honest grows out of social agreement between and among people and may therefore differ from one culture to another. For example, Mokros (2003) explores the construction of age and gender. Lee (1996) and Reyes (2007) discuss the construction of Asian American identities, and Carbaugh (2005) examines the construction of a variety of ethnic identities.

In her book *Inter/Cultural Communication: Representation and Construction of Culture*, Anastacia Kurylo (2013) offers the concept of social construction as a useful way to understand intercultural communication and resolve cross-cultural dissonance. Kurylo (2013) and Mokros (2003) agree that culture is produced in interaction. Rather than something that *is*, it is something that we *do*. The opportunity to construct workable realities together exists between people with different, even initially incompatible identities if they are motivated.

Supporting a person's cultural identity in one setting may undermine it in another; cultural identity is contextual and situational. For example, new college students are often motivated to ask who they are and what they value. They interact with people who grew up differently, who encourage them to question their assumptions. This new dissonance can create conflict with their school peers, family, and friends from home. One young man came from a community where men and women have very separated and defined roles. He was initially flabbergasted by the egalitarian gender roles valued by his new college friends. Back at home, he suggested to his male friends that they listen to their wives/girlfriends and negotiate roles and responsibilities. His friends told him he was losing his manhood and becoming a wimpy college boy. He felt internal and external conflict about his masculine identity. Seeing how manhood was constructed in different communities ultimately helped him learn to select what he saw as the best of both worlds and negotiate relationships with a wider range of people.

When identities come into conflict, we can feel attacked; and the stronger one's sense of cultural identity, the more anxiety may be provoked. Thus, we may feel we're at risk of losing something that sustains us and anchors us to a set of "real values." Yet, this does not have to be the case. Later in this chapter we will explore how a strong identity actually supports cross-cultural communication and personal development. Scholars including Kurylo (2010), Mokros (2003), and Carbaugh (2005) have helped to develop a rich interactive view of identity that is steeped in the communication process and useful when we focus on bridging differences.

Majority/Minority Identity Development

There may be different processes in the construction of identity for minority verses majority people. Identity development is different for people who grow up with the protection of the preferred group and for others who develop identity in a context of social marginalization and stigma. Foundational work on minority/majority identity development is from scholarship in Black identity development (Parham, 1989), and White identity development (Ponterotto, 1988). Some theorists developed models to integrate majority and minority experiences (Poston, 1990).

Here, we highlight three key experiences associated with developing identity awareness of majority or minority group members. In this discussion, the terms *majority* and *minority* refer to those in and out of power rather than to the numerical majority and minority. Remember that we are all members of the majority and the minority in different ways. As you read this discussion, think about your own experiences as a member of a minority or majority group, be it in terms of body type, social class, country of origin, age, race, or some other defining quality. Then, see if these stages ring true for you.

Majority Identity Development

The literature on majority/minority identity grew out of ethnic studies and evolved into "whiteness" studies (Nakayama & Krizek, 1995). Nell Irvin Painter (2010), in her book *The History of White People*, explores how whiteness came into existence. Others question the evolution of a White identity in a rapidly diversifying American culture. In the popular book *Cheerful Money: Me, My Family, and the Last Days of Wasp Splendor*, author Tad Friend posits that the WASP (White Anglo-Saxon Protestant), once the very definition of White privilege and the "gold card" standard of mainstream society (Jackson, 1999, p. 48), is being absorbed or shrunk down to a small eccentric group. This provocative assertion is certainly one in the ongoing dialogue of a society in transition.

Whiteness studies are one version of looking at the majority culture and identifying the assumptions and privileges of that culture. But whiteness is not the only form of majority. Anytime that one characteristic (e.g., age, race, gender,

PUT IT INTO PRACTICE   **3.1**

Majority and Minority Identities

1. Write five ways in which you are a minority.

2. Write five ways in which you are a member of the majority group.

   - Compare your list to the lists of others.

   - Are there categories you never even thought of?

   - Are these more likely to be areas in which you are in the majority or minority?

   - Suppose, also, that you are in the minority but that minority holds all of the power. How does that shape identity development?

3. In general, do you think of yourself as a minority person or a majority person?

religion) is treated as superior, you have a majority culture. A question for this chapter is how that majority culture influences identity development.

There are three key experiences that characterize majority identity development: (1) acceptance of the status quo, (2) a growing awareness of the disparity in how people are treated, and (3) the integration of a majority identity in a larger social context.

Acceptance of the status quo.   The first experience of the majority person is paradoxically no experience at all—what some scholars call a lack of social consciousness (Hardiman, 1982). At this stage majority members are "unaware of the complex codes of appropriate behavior" in a differentiated world (Pedersen, Ponterotto, & Utsey, 2006, p. 88). As a result, the majority person acts and thinks of themselves as an individual rather than as part of a group. At this stage the majority members may learn not to make social gaffes (like referring to a person with spina bifida as "crippled") but fundamentally have "not been led, or forced, to examine their own roles" in society (Pedersen, Ponterotto, & Utsey, 2006, p. 89). The person simply sees themselves as "regular" or "normal" and cultureless. At this stage the person sees other people as having cultural, ethnic, or exotic traditions.

Examples of unexamined majority acceptance are easy to find. In a class project in intercultural communication, students designed research to explore how other students used facial features to categorize people by race. As part of their research, they wanted to identify the features associated with different racial groups. To the students' surprise, they could find little research on features associated with Whites. The students did notice that whenever an "ethnic" feature was described (for example, the full lips of African Americans, the "blue black" hair of Mexicans, or the epicanthic fold of Asians) the assumption was that the reference group was White. Think, for example, of the shade that comes to mind when a

We are all members of both minority and majority groups.

color is described as "flesh tone." How often do we assume that people are of the majority or privileged group (in terms of race, ability, sexual identity, body type, social class, etc.) unless otherwise informed?

In this early stage of majority identity development, it is quite common for the majority person to boast that he or she is unaware of difference and/or treats everyone the same. This individual denies any suggestion of his own invisible advantage; often rejecting the idea that people have an unconscious mental profile of "best" that corresponds with a majority image. They are generally unaware or unconcerned about their preference for their own group but are uncomfortable that minority groups cluster together or openly support each other based on the minority characteristic (Tatum, 2003). The preference for the majority might lead the person to *compliment* a person in a wheelchair saying, "'He never seemed disabled to me" (Shapiro, 1994). A Jewish colleague once said that people often say to her, "You don't act Jewish," to which she feels she is supposed to reply, "Gee, thanks." Even when the majority person sees value in the minority identity, it is often an objectification (e.g., "I love your spirituality" or "rhythm" or "math and science skills").

At this initial stage, when the majority person does notice discrimination, the solution is the responsibility of the minority person. Sometimes the minority person is advised to act like the majority (e.g., talk, act, and dress as the majority does); to restrict their behaviors to make the majority feel comfortable (e.g., don't talk, act, dress like that); or to play the fool or rube rather than expressing one's full character. As early film portrayals of African Americans and gays suggested, making fun of one's self may be part of the acceptable minority role.

None of this analysis is meant to demonize the majority person. But it does highlight the fact that when we are in the majority we have to work hard to understand how easy it is to thoughtlessly accept the privileges that come with that status. It behooves us all to be mindful of our majority status when communicating across cultural lines.

Growing awareness of disparity.   A majority individual can frequently avoid meaningful contact with minority people, so it's possible for the majority person to remain unaware of their privilege (Martin & Nakayama, 2000). As the majority individual matures and moves into the larger environment, she becomes aware that the treatment of minority people is often the result of their inability to control their experience rather than an innate deficiency.

In terms of race, Helms and Carter (1990) explain that the majority person comes to a view of Self as a racial being and begins to understand the "relative nature" of experience. This new awareness challenges the person's identity, one that was taken for granted and accepted as superior. For the first time, the majority person may see what it means to be "one-up" by virtue of being born middle class, sighted, tall, or smart, etc. They must face their role in the treatment of minorities if they accept unearned privilege. People have different reactions to this realization. They may justify it ("I worked hard for everything I have"), accept it ("Life isn't fair"), or feel shamed by it. They may respond to shame by idealizing minority people and disparaging their own group, or may feel guilty about disliking or disagreeing with a minority person. They may also feel uncomfortable around minority people. Over time, however, they will learn, hopefully, to live with the ambiguity in human relationships, and educate themselves about their own group and others.

Integration of a majority identity in social context.   In reaching what theorists identify as a mature identity, the majority person learns to value positive qualities in both majority and minority culture, to question damaging qualities in both, and to explore issues in dialogue. Majority individuals can create valuable coalitions with people who have learned to survive under challenging minority circumstances (e.g., older people who have lived through good and bad economic times; poor people who know how to live on less).

Majority people can also share their insights with other majority people who cannot hear the voices of outsiders. Thus, an element of the last stage can be seeking social justice. Through research and exposure to worldwide organizations, majority members can find opportunities in organizations like Teach for America, The Peace Corps, Jesuit Volunteer Corps, City Year, and Habitat for Humanity. They can explore social movements like Black Lives Matter and #MeToo. These are but a few of the social, religious, secular, private, and governmental groups and agencies dedicated to supporting and honoring people in a diverse world.

Minority Identity Development

The stages of minority development run parallel to the stages of majority development. The challenge of the minority person is to develop a healthy identity in the face of assaults on their value as a member of society.

CULTURE SHOCK

My Working-Class Neighborhood

A young man newly arrived to college recounts: I came to college and learned to be ashamed of what my father does for a living. In my working-class neighborhood, being a trash man is considered a great job. It pays well and provides benefits and my father had lots of time at home with us kids. When I told people at college that my father is a trash collector, they laughed. Now I just say that my dad works for the city.

A minority person realizes their relative status translates into being "less than." One student in an intercultural class said, "I knew that it was bad to be a *fag* and then I realized that I was one." So while there is significant payoff for a person in the majority culture to linger in the early stages of avoidance, indifference, or denial, minority persons are less likely to have these options because the constructions of society chafe against them. The minority person seeking well-being may move more determinedly through stages of acceptance of majority domination and awareness of difference, to learning to value self and other.

Acceptance of majority dominance.   Acceptance of majority dominance occurs because of the sheer overpowering and ubiquitous presence of the majority culture and its behaviors, images of beauty, standards, and habits. To the extent that the minority person is surrounded by this culture, the minority person, like the majority person, initially assumes that the dominant culture is superior (Atkinson, Morten, & Sue, 1989). Morten and Atkinson (1983) find the minority person will "express an unequivocal preference for cultural values and behaviors associated with the dominant group over those associated with their own minority group" (p. 157). Phinney (1993) speaks in terms of the unexamined ethnic identity and discusses the "lack of exploration of ethnicity" (p. 66). In this context, the person who is "different" accepts the burden of always having to bend to the majority and may even dislike their own group. This person may try to differentiate themselves from others of the group, even referring to their own as "they."

There is often self-disparagement in this phase. It may be expressed subtly by taking pride in features of the majority group (e.g., praising and desiring straight hair and light skin). Or, it may be expressed through self-disparaging jokes (fat, trans, racial, short, blind, etc.). The minority person may act silly and/or incompetent; and, as you would expect, shame is associated with this phase.

At this stage of identity development, the minority person is not able to see the contradiction in wanting to be judged as an individual while judging their own group as harshly as majority members. The minority person is faced with the paradox of disassociating from a group that defines them; sometimes even "passing" as a majority member to break from the group completely. For example, during the apartheid era in South Africa, people regularly applied to change their racial status, almost always to a group that received more rights than the category they were assigned at birth (Carlin, 2003).

It is important not to view the profile of a minority person in the first stage of identity development as an indictment of any person in the minority. This person is working very hard to manage in a situation that is demanding and perhaps treacherous. It is not surprising that exhaustion alone can thrust the minority person toward the next two phases.

Awareness of difference.   Awareness of difference occurs as the minority person questions and resists unfair treatment by the majority. Phinney (1993) sees this ethnic realization as an integral part of the "ethnic identity search" and a kind of "turning point" for a minority person (p. 69).

The minority person may take on the role of educating people in the majority or may reject them. They may view their group as victimized and majority members as victimizers, and may "completely endorse minority values and behaviors to the complete exclusion of those values and behaviors associated with the dominant group" (Morten & Atkinson, 1983, p. 157). Majority members may experience this behavior as mean spirited and divisive, but the minority individual may be seeking to find a mental space of their own, one not defined by the majority.

Many support groups and mentors provide some reinforcement for minority people and encourage recognition of the unique identity and contribution of people in minority groups. In this phase, the minority person may learn to take pride in behaviors that were once shaming. A student once ashamed of a mother

Sources of identity are varied and can shift over time.

who is "just a cleaning lady" can express pride at what this parent sacrificed so that her child could receive a good education.

Learning to value self and other.   At this stage, the minority person is able to "ascribe selectively to values and behaviors from both the minority and dominant cultures" (Morten & Atkinson, 1983, p. 157). This person is able to see positive and negative qualities of each group and learns to manage the ambiguity of cross-group relations. At this phase, an identity develops that brings the person comfort in many settings and may lead the individual to work for equality, equity, insight, and justice. Much of the work for social justice today is focused on making invisible social structures noticeable. One rendering of the new perspective (Figure 3.2) illustrates the difference between inequity, equality, equity, and true justice that requires reorienting the entire systems.

Sources of Cultural Identity

Dialogue across cultural groups happens often, even among groups that initially appear homogeneous. This is because the sources of identity are so varied. One way to begin to build cross-group communication competence is to manage the identity conflicts that appear in relationships we already have.

A challenge with discussing sources of cultural identity is the risk of excluding cultures that are important. Still, there are common sources of cultural identity

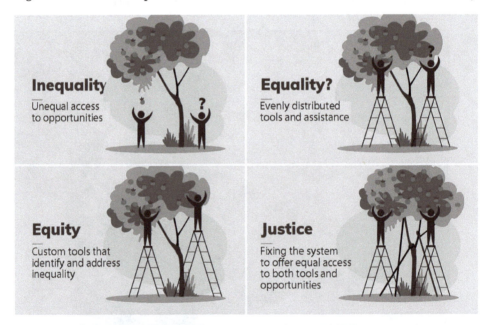

Figure 3.2   The differences between inequity, equality, equity, and true justice. Recreated from Tony Ruth's depiction of Shel Silverstein's *The Giving Tree.* (Courtesy of the Busara Center for Behavioral Economics)

that many of us value and are influenced by. We briefly touch on some of these sources while encouraging you (like in Put It Into Practice 3.2) to see your own cultural influences.

Social Class and Structural Inequity

In *Limbo: Blue-Collar Roots, White-Collar Dreams*, social class "straddler" and Italian American Alfred Lubrano (2005) discusses growing up as a working-class child. He tells his story of working his way to the upper middle class but experiencing difficulty reconciling different communication systems, values, perspectives,

---

PUT IT INTO PRACTICE   **3.2**

Culture Map Exercise

1. List all of the various cultures that you belong to (or that you would say have influenced the way you communicate). There are no right or wrong answers. You can identify any and all cultures (as we have defined that term) that make sense to you.

   Example: American, Woman, White, Christian, Feminist, on the spectrum.

2. Graphically "map" all of the cultures by their importance in your life now and their relation to each other in contributing to your identity. You can use any format you wish to map things. You may use different geometric shapes and sizes for various cultures, and so on. Whatever mapping captures your sense of your cultures is fine.

   Example::

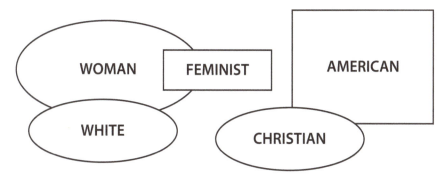

3. Draw points of tension between your cultures. Which cultures tend to have norms for behavior that differ? That conflict? Which cultures are most in tension in this way? Draw arrows or other indicators to show that.

4. Which of these cultural tensions are most likely to cause you internal conflict? Which of these cultural tensions are most likely to cause conflict with others?

behaviors, and identities. He describes his lifelong journey as a person straddling two different worlds that never fully come to terms. Barbara Ehrenreich's (2008) memoir, *Nickel and Dimed: On (Not) Getting by in America*, describes the journalist's challenge to survive working minimum-wage jobs. Both authors bring into focus how social class shapes identity.

Academic scholars have explored the intransigent nature of poverty and the structural realties that favor some and disadvantage others. The intersection of race, social class, gender, and other factors is addressed by many (Collins, 2000; McCall, 2005; Meyer, 2002). Conflation of race and class make unpacking the influence of each difficult (Almanac of Policy Issues, 2004).

Many people who refer to themselves as American have ancestors who came from other lands, often having come to America to escape poverty or oppression in the "old country." Today, the influx of Americans from south of the border and other places creates a new profile of class and race. Ongoing examination of social inequity is part of exploring one's identity. Critical theory and feminist theory are schemas that consider social inequity based on various factors of power that shape identity.

Critical theory argues that we exist in systems of power and injustice. French sociologist and philosopher Michel Foucault (1980), one of the key thinkers associated with this perspective, saw power as a social construction that confines our behaviors. Thus, power can dictate what it means to be mentally well, socially appropriate, and acceptably gendered. The work on power explores the idea that normality is socially constructed and that much of identity is a struggle for control over definition. He comments that "if you are not like everybody else, then you are abnormal, if you are abnormal, then you are sick" (Foucault, 2004, p. 95). Thus, people in power confer power from one generation to the next, sustaining the status quo and perpetual ingroups and outgroups that continue the power dynamic. Critical *race* theory explores how systems have made racism a normal part of the functioning of society.

Many of the theorists who consider gender identity look at the power dynamic between men and women. Authors make the argument that, until recently, academic theories were White- and male-oriented and women (and people of color) were marginalized. As a result, the identities of women formed out of a context of the outsider. Cheris Kramarae's (1981) muted group theory looks at the experience of women as a group whose voice has been subdued and muted. *Standpoint theory* (or feminist standpoint theory) is used to explore gender inequity (MacKinnon, 1999; Wood, 2005).

Sexual Identity

People who consider themselves sexual minorities due to sexual orientation have been in an ongoing struggle to control their identity and receive equal rights. Key elements of the American movement have included codifying what some call "Queer History" as part of queer studies and theory (Safe Schools Coalition, 2007). The term "queer" is selected consciously as a political term that acknowledges both the history and diversity within the movement and claims a word that has been used against people who do not fit traditionally "approved" sexual categories. Key milestones in the gay rights movement include the following:

- In 1924 the Society for Human Rights in Chicago was established as the country's earliest known gay rights organization.
- In 1948 the Kinsey Report revealed to the public that homosexuality is far more widespread than was commonly believed.
- In 1969 the patrons of the Stonewall Inn, a gay bar in New York's Greenwich Village, fought back during a police raid. This event was commemorated by the Obama Administration in 2009 (Barrios, 2009).
- In 1973 the American Psychiatric Association removed homosexuality from its official list of mental disorders.
- In 2000 Vermont became the first state in the country to legally recognize civil unions between gay or lesbian couples.
- In 2010 the US Congress passed a law that repealed "Don't Ask Don't Tell," the policy that maintained secrecy for gays in the military (Herszenhorn, 2010).
- In 2015, the US Supreme Court struck down all state bans on same sex marriage and required states to honor out-of-state same sex marriage licenses.

The history tracks a movement from identification as "perverts" and "deviants" toward full and equal citizenship that includes legal marriage, rights for transgender people, and goals still to be achieved.

Internationally, attitudes toward sexual minorities vary widely. Gays are allowed to serve in the military in many countries, including the Netherlands, Israel, the United Kingdom, and the United States. On the other hand, homosexuality is illegal in countries like Algeria, Pakistan, and Iran. In 2003, Gene Robinson, the first openly gay, noncelibate priest, was ordained as a bishop in the American Episcopal Church (AEC). Some of the individual churches in the AEC wanted to pull away. Many of these churches are in Africa (Heneghan, 2010), where attitudes can be particularly unaccepting of same sex (especially male) partnerships (Ottosson, 2006). In 2023, Uganda legalized the death penalty for "aggravated homosexuality" and long prison sentences for those "promoting" homosexuality. (Reuters, 2023). Yet, even in these most restrictive environments, civil rights organizations continue to work to secure rights and protect this vulnerable population (Baume, 2010).

Scholar and activist James Sears (1997) uses the Sexual Diversity Wheel to attempt to educate people on how human sexuality varies beginning with human biology through worldwide social and cultural roles to personal behavior and identity. His work helps us appreciate the range of sexual orientation and sexual identity throughout the world. Our understanding of sexual identity continues to evolve with research in a wide range of identities that are non-binary.

Nationality

National identity lies at the root of many instances of human conflict, and people express national pride and identity in different ways. Both German and Japanese students in intercultural classes have expressed surprise about Americans' tendency to wave the flag to demonstrate patriotism. In their countries, they explain, such displays call up nationalistic identities linked to past wars and shame. In the United States the identity of the Northern and Southern states remains distinct. Even to this day, the war that threatened to pull this nation apart is often referred to as "The Civil War" in the North and the "War Between the States" in the South.

National identity is shown in how we present ourselves in public and even in what we eat for lunch. An American reporter living in France recounted the lunch menu for her child's school explaining that "no single meal is repeated over the 32 school days in the period, and every meal includes an hors d'oeuvre, salad, main course, cheese plate and dessert" (Walt, 2010). The identity of the French is clearly shaped by their relationship with food and fashion. An American colleague living in France was encouraged to improve her public attire. Her French friend advised, "Eat for yourself, dress for others."

Religion

Like nationality, religion shapes identity and has been a source of serious conflicts throughout history. Nationality and religion often intersect. India and Pakistan became separate nations in 1947 based primarily on incompatible religious traditions and identity of majority Hindu India and the newly formed Islamic Republic of Pakistan.

Church and state can come into conflict in secular nations. In 2004, the French government outlawed wearing the traditional Muslim head covering in public schools. The law states, in part, that:

> Behaviors and signs expressing a religious or political affiliation are prohibited in schools and colleges. Any appropriate sanction is to be taken after the pupil is invited to conform to his obligations. The prohibited behaviors and religious signs are open signs, such as large crosses, veils, or kippas. Discrete signs are not included, for example medals, small crosses, stars of David, hands of Fatimah, or a small Koran. (Huda, 2010, p. 1)

Advocates of this law argue that such "conspicuous religious symbols" inhibit a secular school environment and are inconsistent with French identity. More recently, a French law has been proposed to ban the hijab in competitive sports (Woodyatt, Bashir, & Mawad, 2022). The Muslim population is 5–10% of the French population, the largest Muslim population in any European country. In the United States, as in France, religion and government are intentionally (although not completely) separated. In many countries, however, the state is an arm of the predominant religion.

Age

Both our chronological age and the era in which we live shape our identity and those with whom we identify. Advocates for a new view of aging are exploring both of these factors.

In August of 1970, lifelong social activist Maggie Kuhn and a group of like-minded friends founded the Gray Panthers, a group committed to examining new life options for older adults. Maggie Kuhn worked to change the perceptions of older people, famously correcting President Gerald Ford, who referred to the

The Hagia Sophia is a museum in Istanbul, Turkey, that was once an Eastern Orthodox church and later an imperial mosque. Religion is an important source of identity to billions of people throughout the world.

senior citizen as "young lady," by telling him that she was, in fact, an "old woman" (Kuhn, 1991). Her work helped to usher in a new era of aging as the average life expectancy has increased from 49 for a person born in 1900 to 78.7 for a person born in 2018 (Kochanek, Anderson, & Arias, 2020).

As we all age, we have Maggie Kuhn and people like her to thank for a better quality of life in an age we all hope to reach. Of course, some people age more successfully than others. Research conducted by Fisher and Specht (1999) identified six features of successful aging, most of them related to a positive identity and meaning-centered life: a sense of purpose, personal growth, self-acceptance, autonomy, interactions with others, and health. Beyond chronological age, our generation (e.g., Depression Era, Baby Boomer, Generation X, Y, and so on) influences identity that is distinct from others born at other points in time. It is not uncommon today to find up to four generations working and living side by side, making the ability to find commonality of identity and purpose paramount.

Ability

In the widely read book *No Pity: People with Disabilities Forging a New Civil Rights Movement*, Joseph Shapiro (1994) documents the progress toward the passage of the Americans with Disabilities Act in 1990. Shapiro recounts an experience at the funeral of a disabled person saying that "the highest praise these nondisabled friends could think to give a disabled attorney" was that they did not think

---

PUT IT INTO PRACTICE   **3.3**

Age and Cultural Identity

Make a list of the following items that define your generation: film, song, fashion, sociopolitical event, and technology. Now, find two people at least 20 years away from your age in either direction so that together you each represent three different generations. Have each respond to the same questions. What do your answers to these questions say about the identity of your generation and the times in which you live?

---

of him as disabled (p. 3). As with other minority groups, a goal of the disability movement is to remove the stigma from their group and reframe their experience. For example, Shapiro refers to "nondisabled" as "temporarily abled" to clarify that we all join the ranks of the "disabled" if we just live long enough. Since the most common cause of disability is aging (Shapiro, 1994), we all have a vested interest in supporting the dignity of this group.

Many of the adaptations we make for people with disabilities benefit us all. Curb cuts, for example, benefit parents pushing baby carriages, travelers with rolling luggage, and bicyclers. Closed captioning was developed by the National Captioning Institute to serve 28 million people who are deaf or hard of hearing in the United States, but the organization also notes that millions of other people benefit as well. They explain that the broader audience includes, "people learning English as a second language, young children learning to read, remedial readers, illiterate adults, and people watching television in noisy environments such as restaurants, bars, and airports" (National Captioning Institute, n.d.). Similarly, parents of hearing children teach them sign language to improve their early language learning skills (Daniels, 2000). A local zoo created a large print version of their zoo pamphlet for visually impaired guests only to find that many more people preferred the easy-to-see format. You may be able to think of examples in your own experience when adjustments for the disabled benefited all.

Social Identity

It would be hard to overstate the emerging importance of social media in identity formation, especially for younger generations. Almost paradoxically it connects people in activism and empathy to a global community that crosses national and racial barriers (Renner, 2019). It also spreads "fake news." It separates people into familiar collectives through social media like Black Twitter and Facebook's Subtle Asian Traits community. This can narrow our focus but can also help people who feel isolated to preserve a known association. Social media can create pressure to maintain a public image and undermines us with feelings like FOMO (fear of missing out) or it can and help in difficult times and times of transition. The ability to strategically reach across lines and bolster positive self-identity may be a key to helping people of different backgrounds relate to one another and work toward a peaceful world.

Obstacles and Challenges to Peacebuilding

Managing relations across identities is not easy. Threats to our identity cut to our core. In this section we consider why threats to our identity are so likely to trigger dysfunctional and sometimes explosive conflicts.

Social Identity Theory

Henri Tajfel's *social identity theory* (Tajfel & Turner, 1979) addresses the relationship between group affiliation and identity. In early research, boys were divided randomly into groups and then given money to distribute as they wished (Tajfel et al., 1971). As you might expect, the boys showed preference for those in their own groups, even though there was no direct benefit to them. The researchers concluded that we build and support the groups tied to our identity and we try to put that group at a relative advantage to other groups. People experience their group's survival and accomplishment as linked to their own.

Seen from this perspective, establishing group membership is crucial. The idea of outing a person as gay, for example, is an attempt to claim or control a person's identity. Creating broader definitions of concepts from "disability" to "senior citizen" can be attempts to forward a political agenda in relation to those with characteristics that are "identity controlled."

People who identify themselves as mixed heritage may find that they define ingroups and outgroups differently than others assume they would. Tiger Woods may define himself as "Cablinasian" (Moore, 2009) because he claims ethnicity that is Caucasian, Black, Native American, and Asian. Yet, African Americans may claim him as "African American." One popular Black sports journalist excoriates Woods for claiming this identity, asking provocatively, "Where are your Cablinasian backers?" and declaring "Wake up, Tiger. This is America and that means you're Black" (Moore, 2009).

For some, their identity can shift from setting to setting and under different conditions. In her exploration of biracial and bicultural individuals, Harris (2004) writes that some biracial and bicultural people may have static or constant cultural identity while others have fluid ones that can bend to suit their current circumstances. In Mexico, "Indians" can become "Mestizos" by wearing Western clothing and speaking Spanish (Kriesberg, 2003). Several older celebrities like Raquel Welch (Navarro, 2002) and Carol Channing (Channing, 2007), who were once assumed to be White, have recently claimed Latino and African American ancestry, respectively.

People in multicultural marriages may find that, during times of conflict, people who had lived in harmony (and with positive multiple identities) must revisit identity in times of hostilities. In Iraq, one couple in a mixed Sunni and Shi'ite marriage find that recent conflict between their two sects of Arab Muslims caused the couple to have to, in their own words, "be strong to show our children that those committing sectarian violence are doing wrong" (IRIN, 2006). These people now have a politicized identity and are facing concerns about where they will live and who will have them.

Stereotypes and Social Stigma

If you have ever been reluctant to reveal your background to others (some invisible disability, the circumstances of your birth, a relative that a mutual friend might know) you know what it is to be stigmatized. Sociologist Erving Goffman (1986) says that a person can be stigmatized because of "tribal" identities like race, nationality, or ethnicity; visible conditions of the body like physical disabilities; or perceived problems of individual character such as substance abuse. How these stigmas are managed depends on whether the stigmatized quality can be concealed, if the stigma has existed for a long time, how much the stigma interferes with social interaction, how unattractive or dangerous the stigma is in society, or the extent to which the behavior is seen as a choice.

Zambian economist Dambisa Moyo expresses frustration with stars like Bono who raise millions of dollars for Africa but may reinforce a stigmatized image of Africans as pathetic and perpetually helpless (Solomon, 2009). Similarly, people in the disabilities movement have pushed organizations like Easter Seals, United Cerebral Palsy, and Jerry Lewis MDA Telethons to move beyond stigmatizing images of people with disabilities (Johnson, 1992).

Intergroup Threat Theory

Thus far we have talked about the sources of cultural identity and the tendency people have to see others who are different from them as somehow inferior or needing to be kept at arm's length. But these tendencies alone do not explain why categorizing people into cultural groups is so challenging to peace and community-building efforts.

Intergroup threat theory (Stephan, Ybarra, & Morrison, 2009) provides further explanation, suggesting that relations between groups are more likely to be antagonistic than friendly because, "[p]erceived threats when none exist may be a less costly error than not perceiving threats when in fact they do exist" (p. 47). This "best defense is a good offense" approach to intergroup relations is hardly compatible with the goal of building peaceful communities. According to the theory, threats from outgroups come in two forms: *realistic threats* include threats to a group's power, resources, and general welfare; and *symbolic threats* are threats to a group's religion, values, belief system, ideology, philosophy, morality, or worldview. On an individual level, realistic threats concern actual physical or material harm, whereas symbolic threats concern a loss of face, honor, or self-esteem.

Research shows that perceptions of threat depend on a large number of factors, such as prior relations between groups, power differences between groups, cultural values of group members, the amount of intergroup contact, and the situations in which groups interact. For example, some research suggests that while low-power groups (e.g., African Americans) are more likely to experience threat than higher power groups (European Americans), higher-power groups, because they may have more to lose, will tend to react more strongly than lower-power groups when they feel threatened (Morrison & Ybarra, 2008; Stephan, Ybarra, & Morrison, 2009).

According to intergroup threat theory, there is a strong link between the perceived degree of threat and the tendency for conflicts to escalate, even to the point of intractability—a topic we will explore in more detail in Chapter 5 when we explore the emotional underpinnings of these processes.

Burgess and Burgess (2003) studied conflicts between groups and distinguished between tractable conflicts and **intractable conflicts** that defy resolution. Among the tractable conflicts are "most labor-management conflicts, some family conflicts, many workplace conflicts and even many international conflicts that can be successfully resolved through negotiation or mediation." The most challenging are intractable conflicts—"conflicts that involve irreducible, high-stakes, win-lose issues that have no 'zone of possible agreement'" and with potential to do substantial harm. Middle East conflicts are often seen in this category. The authors spell out three types of conflict, *all tied to group identity*. These include issues of moral differences (such as those related to religion), ideas of how we distribute resources, and "pecking order" (conflicts driven by status categories related to who is most worthy or good).

Understanding the challenge of threats to our identity can help us work to solve identity-based discord. It is easier to mistreat, mistrust, and objectify someone with whom we do not identify. This is one of the reasons that in conflict one of the key communication strategies is naming the "Other" in disparaging and stereotyped ways—indeed, it is one of the first levels of the escalation toward intractability (Burgess & Burgess, 2003).

In a controversial classroom activity called the Name Game, students identify all of the names people use to label groups based on nationality, race, ethnicity, gender, ability, age, religion, and so on. Students find immediately that many (if not most) of the names are negative. Invariably, they are struck by the sheer number of negative names we have for outgroups. Sometimes the words are attached to people whom we find exotic or unfamiliar, but often we reserve the most offensive names for those with whom we have intimate contact (women, for example). Our tendency to demean the identities of others can be hard to overcome and the ability to cast others as outside of our experience and protection can challenge understanding.

Identity and Intercultural Communication Competence

Given the strong drive to advantage those with whom we identify and to disparage the *Other*, one might become discouraged about communicating across cultures. And yet, more than ever people have the opportunity to interact beyond our familiar world. People are traveling more for enrichment, marrying more freely for love, crossing borders physically and electronically for goods and services, and otherwise coming in contact with others who are culturally different.

As we discuss here, there are strategies to help us interact effectively across the barriers of identity. Some important competencies include learning more about your own cultural identity, working to find an identity that you might share with someone who may initially seem very different, building a transcendent culture with a culturally different person that draws on parts of both cultures, and learning to manage your discomfort with strangers. All of this assumes an attitude of abundance, the belief that everyone can get what they need.

Exploring Your Own Identity

Intercultural researcher Young Kim (2009) suggests a strong identity allows one to be open-minded and reach out. Low self-esteem, conversely, may increase one's feeling of anxiety. Kim explores the process of moving from a focus on in-group identity that may lead to a rigid sense of self and cultural blinders to a perspective that includes both individualization and universalization. A man who feels secure about his identity can accept and value women. A woman of one ethnicity can value another's culture if she feels secure in her own. Kim states, "With this capacity, one is better able to transcend conventional in-group and out-group categories and to see ourselves and others on the basis of unique individual qualities" (2009, p. 56). Identity inclusivity (individualization and universalization) and identity security (feeling secure with one's identity) allows a person to empathize with others "without losing the ability to maintain one's integrity and to be creative and effective in responding to impending problems" (2009, p. 57).

Negotiating Cultural Identities

Cultural contracts theory (Jackson, 2002; Hecht, Jackson, & Pitts, 2005) posits that individuals negotiate and establish identity through social contracts with others. Individuals initially have their own values and priorities that in turn are brought into their new relationships. Cultural contracts theory extends Ting-Toomey's (2005) concept of identity negotiation, which explains how individuals choose which of their multiple identities they will bring to the forefront in any particular communication context. *Cultural identity negotiation* is a "conscious and mindful process of shifting one's worldview and/or cultural behaviors" (Jackson, 2002, p. 362). Our identities are multifaceted and related to background, such as race, and role, like mother or friend. Successful relationships are products of dynamic and ongoing negotiation of individual-level values with others. Cultural contracts theory identifies three types of relational contracts that can result from identity negotiation. First, *ready-to-sign cultural contracts* are usually held by dominant groups in society that impose their worldview on others. The groups are not interested in learning about other cultures or adjusting their beliefs and behaviors. *Quasi-completed cultural contracts* are mostly used by nondominant groups. These groups want to keep their worldview but are open to adjusting them temporarily. Finally, *co-created cultural contracts* are engaged in by those who are open to fully negotiating cultural differences with others and can be seen as a give and take between equals. According to the theory, contracts are multidimensional and fluid, much like relationships often are. The theory gives hope to the idea that people from different backgrounds can find some common ground if, based on a variety of factors, they can find areas of accord between them and negotiate a workable contract. Too often, the power differential between cultures disproportionately tips the scale toward the culture of power.

Finding an Overlapping or Transcendent Identity

As we noted in Chapter 2, a good deal of research documents the community-building effects that result from the formation of a *common ingroup identity*.

Research on interracial and intercultural couples also shows that a common or *overlapping identity* as "parent" often helps them work cooperatively, despite different cultural perspectives, when making decisions on behalf of their children (Lawton, Foeman, & Braz, 2013).

In the Middle East crisis with such strong identity conflicts, many people are searching for common ground and historical ties to bring these divergent groups together. Some religious thinkers have made attempts to reconcile nationality and religion by identifying a common identity among Jews, Christians, and Muslims based on a common Abrahamic tradition (Feiler, 2004). While some of the religious narratives explain the conflicts among these groups (for example, the two conflicted offspring of Abraham are said to be the genesis of Judaism and Islam), the core beliefs in the three religious traditions call for believers to make peace among one another despite the difficulties. And, lest we be too cynical about the possibilities, we should remind ourselves of other successes in peacebuilding. For example, who would have thought that after centuries of struggle in Ireland the parties could negotiate a holding agreement that would give some relief to Protestant and Catholic adversaries? We should also remember the achievements of Mandela in South Africa (see Chapter 2) and the role of the Truth and Reconciliation Commission that allowed victims to tell their stories and perpetrators to acknowledge their part in apartheid-era atrocities (Truth and Reconciliation Commission, 2009). There are also tiny steps toward reconciliation after genocide in Rwanda (Mojon, 2009). In each case, before the pragmatic work of repair begins, a common destiny and respected identities had to be conceived.

On a local level, efforts to honor identity are important as well. In an intercultural communication class several years ago, two students engaged in daily battle. One young man described himself as a conservative, born-again Christian and his counterpart was a young woman who described herself as a lesbian and a feminist. The two, predictably, clashed over every topic from marriage and adoption laws to workplace rights. When the topic of abortion was mentioned, they launched into another predictable fight and, as always, their conflict was as much about how they saw one another as it was any particular topic at hand. They just weren't supposed to agree on anything. At the moment they began to launch into the abortion battle, one student called out, "Can't you two agree on anything?" There was a moment of silence. Then, for the next several minutes the class brainstormed the issues related to abortion that these two combatants might find agreement on. The class came up with a list of over 20 items. Top among them were commonalities related to their identities. Both talked about feeling out of the mainstream and both talked about a sense of alienation. Each had felt peer pressure to have sex before they were ready and each felt that his or her identity had been disrespected. They both cared about social justice. Moreover, they agreed that if we focus on the areas in which they agree (that young people should not be pressured into sex before they are ready, and women should not feel pressured into abortions by negative judgments) they could end a large number of abortions. We did not solve every problem that day but the two softened their stance in the classroom. Even in future sessions in which they had disagreement, their dialogue was more fruitful and their treatment of one another was more respectful. Finding the intersection of their identities provided a basis on which to build. Larger, more intractable problems in our communities and in the Middle East, Rwanda, North and South Korea, Darfur, Tibet, and other parts of the world might benefit if we can establish more commonality and community.

In addition to learning about ourselves and finding commonalities with others, we can use the constructed nature of culture to learn to build a unique culture together. For some time, theorists have referred to these hybrid cultures as "third" cultures (Earley & Ang, 2003). The *third culture* is a blend of the contributing cultures. Casmir (1999) and Foeman and Nance (2002) observe that successful mixed-culture marriages develop a shared meaning system and a larger, transcendent identity that involves the creation of something new that is informed and influenced by each spouse's individual cultural identity—ideally the best of both. This transcendent culture allows them to live in both worlds and interpret meaning across groups.

So, establishing a skill set that is based on a strong sense of self (individualization), other (mindfulness), and context (universalization) are central in building intercultural communication competence. The exploration of whiteness mentioned earlier is an example of White Americans working to gain personal insight and individualization. Establishing the Martin Luther King national holiday is an example of a step toward weaving the identity of African Americans into the lives of all United States citizens, thus creating a common culture and an expansion of cultural context that is universalization. The increase in the number of diversity courses is evidence of the attempt to learn to respectfully engage one another that is *mindfulness*. Even together these examples seem small, but they are part of a major and centuries-old struggle for equality in the United States. Every step is a step that facilitates a more peaceable world.

Summary

Modern humanity evolved from a common ancestry. As our ancestors migrated to different parts of the globe, they underwent physical and cultural changes that helped them adapt and survive. These changes led to the construction of diverse social and cultural identities. Our cultural identity is our sense of membership in a particular group or collective. In large part, these identities are socially constructed; that is, they are created through processes of social interaction. The process of majority group identity development differs from that of minority group identity development. *Majority identity development* consists of three key experiences: acceptance of the status quo, growing awareness of disparity, and integration of a majority identity in social context. The stages of *minority identity development* include: acceptance of majority dominance, awareness of difference, and learning to value self and other. There are many sources of cultural identity, including social class and structural inequity, sexual identity, nationality, religion, age, and ability. These identities may intersect, creating even more possibilities for unique identities.

Managing relations across diverse cultural groups is the paramount goal of the peacebuilding enterprise. A number of theories and concepts clarify the nature of the challenge. According to social identity theory, group membership plays a central role in defining an individual's sense of self and self-esteem. Strong cultural identities can contribute to the formation of stereotypes and the creation of social stigmas that impede efforts to build peaceful communities. Intergroup threat theory offers additional insight by specifying the conditions under which relations between cultural groups are most likely to be antagonistic. Intercultural communication competence provides the basis for meeting the challenges associated with identity-based sources of conflict, the most trying conflicts being those that are intractable. Competence in this regard includes exploring your own cultural identity, negotiating differences in cultural identities, finding an *overlapping identity* (or transcendent identity), and maintaining a sense of abundance and possibility.

QUESTIONS

1. Interview members of your family to learn about your heritage. Ask about names and titles that are consistent with that heritage. How would you describe your family identity? How is that identity defined by what your family is and also what it is not? Who is identified as the Other?

2. Think of ways in which you identify as a minority person. Try to remember when you became consciously aware of that status. What practical impact did that status have on your life? Do the same with a majority identification.

3. Indicate two or three groups with which you identify. How do the different groups either reinforce a particular identify or challenge it? When your different reference groups differ, how do you make choices about how you will identify?

4. Identify a conflict situation you have been involved in. Was there an element of identity that fueled the disagreement? How might attention to the identities of the persons involved been able to create a positive outcome?

5. Identify a group with which you have had little contact. What are the images that you have of that group? How many of them are based on stereotype rather than any real and meaningful information about the group? How might you reach out to people who are from other groups to overcome meaningless generalizations? What such stereotypes might others have of your group?

6. Think of a person with whom you have little in common. Challenge yourself to list 20 ways in which you are alike. Does this provide you any opportunity to find common ground and identification with that individual?

Cultural Frames of Reference

KEY TERMS

analytic thinking	holistic thinking	person perception
Confucian dynamism	individualism/collectivism	perspective-taking
Confucianism	ingroup/outgroup	power distance
cultural frames	long-term/short-term	reframing
face	orientation	uncertainty avoidance
face negotiation theory	masculinity/femininity	worldview
facework	monochronic/polychronic	
high context/low context		

Think of someone you have trouble seeing eye to eye with. You say up, they say down. You say yes, they say no. Your conflict may be based as much on your stylistic and value differences as on the issue at hand. For example, you may be more comfortable with open conflict while the other person prefers a more subtle interchange or avoids conflict altogether. You may think of yourself as an individual, speaking only on your own behalf while the other person sees themselves as speaking for a particular interest group. These types of interpersonal styles are not random. They often grow out of a cultural context that we are largely unaware of. Ethnocentrism may lead us to assume that everyone thinks as we do. Hegemony may allow some to impose their perspectives on others. But the ability to stand back and realize that people view reality differently based on their personal and cultural history is vital in building the insight needed to successfully coexist with people who are different than us.

What Are Cultural Frames?

Our *cultural frames* are those structures we impose on reality based on our background and experience. Some scholars write in terms of *worldview* or worldview frames (LeBaron, 2003). Cultural anthropologist Clifford Geertz (1973) described worldview as the collection of notions about how reality is. Biologist Mary Clark (2002) refers to the "set of ground rules for shared cultural meaning" (p. 5). These views can be carried forward in stories, myths, rituals, metaphors, and other communication passed from one generation to the next, from elder to child or from older kids to younger ones. Just as you can think of values that your family passed down in the same story told every year at Thanksgiving, you can probably also think of some insight shared through social media about what makes life worth living. Both help to create the frames that you use to process new information, and both are affected by the larger culture in which we live.

Why Are Cultural Frames Important?

Cultural frames impose meaning on life experience. As you can imagine, when we use certain basic assumptions about how the world works (e.g., "It's us against them" versus "We're all in this together") we set the trajectory for the communication and relationships that extend from that core cultural belief. If different interpretations of reality cast groups in opposition, resolving misunderstanding and conflict and building peaceful communities is hindered. Learning about the assumptions that operate for different cultural groups is vital in developing cross-cultural communication competence.

Several prominent scholars have attempted to organize cultural frames along different lines. These schemas take into account a range of factors such as: focusing on the individual versus the group, the relationship of people to nature, emphasis on materialism, public displays of emotion, what constitutes proof within a culture, immediate verses ultimate values, and even the role of enjoyment in shaping behavior choices. Each schema has benefits and limitations. Factors like economics, politics, environmental conditions, and religious affiliation both shape and are shaped by cultural styles; so describing an entire culture as definitively one way or another will always be inaccurate. Therefore, before presenting some of the major frameworks for examining culture, we want to note a few precautions.

Cultures Change

First, keep in mind that perspectives change over time. None of these styles is set in stone. Think of your personal journey. How have your education and life experiences caused you to shift your perspective? Dealing with a serious illness or other traumatic experience may change your view about the stability of the world and may move you from a future-based orientation to a day-to-day survival mode. Or discussing gender stereotypes in a college class may change what you see as appropriate roles for men and women.

On a national scale, when a country like Ireland experiences a rapid expansion and then contraction of its economy, it may reinforce a fatalistic view of the world. When the economies of China and India continue to expand and several countries in Africa begin to rapidly ramp up, everything in these historical and complex cultures, from the roles of individuals in their communities to attitudes toward authority, begin to shift (Trading Economics, 2022). On the other hand, the relative youth and wealth of the political entity of the United States may cause Americans to feel that progress, change, and self-determination are inherently positive and the answer to every woe. Yet, as we mature and meet challenges as a nation, we may become more reflective and drawn to honor our defining past. Other ancient cultures in the Middle East also have layers of old and new traditions in intricate interplay that pull them in several directions and complicate their outlook. The 2006 election of Ellen Johnson Sirleaf as Liberia's (and Africa's!) first female president began to change an entire continent's view of the roles of women in society Yet, the progress of women has stagnated and there is much exploration of the potential for more gender parity in Africa to continue the considerable potential across the continent (Moodley et al., 2019). A worldwide pandemic changes all the assumptions about how we work and live. Thus, we should avoid developing rigid cultural frames that are maintained even in the face of new information. Unyielding assumptions about cultural styles can be offensive and misleading and can encumber understanding, which is, after all, the ultimate goal of intercultural communication competence.

Individuals and Groups Vary

Second, keep in mind that individuals and groups within cultures vary. Any broad statement cannot describe every individual or collective within that society. Generalizations, by their very nature, oversimplify experience. This fact alone should keep us from making sweeping claims. Yet, in her discussion of gender differences, linguist Deborah Tannen (1990) argues that we *must* address broad, systematic differences between groups. She posits that ignoring such differences leaves us without a helpful perspective in understanding how group distinctions disparately shape our worldviews. Studying these categorical differences helps us find common ground. But we must approach generalizations with care.

In your own life, you are aware of the complexities of personal reality versus broad group patterns. Think of the ways you fit neatly into your reference groups (i.e., family, ethnic, social clubs, gender) and how you simultaneously defy categorization. In one of the authors' intercultural communication classes, for example, several American women engaged in an animated debate on whether women are by nature different than men and whether we should strive to erase gender distinctions or celebrate each gender's uniqueness. There was no consensus. At the same time, a Japanese student shared that she had lived all her life in Japan and had always felt out of step with what she saw as traditional roles of women there. When she arrived in the United States, she immediately noted the relative flexibility of gender roles in this country, which she saw reflected in the very debate among the women in her class. Further, despite the fact that this international student had never set foot in this country before, she said she finally felt at home when she arrived here. So while this Japanese student saw a pattern in the gender roles of American women students, the American students experienced their styles, attitudes, and perspectives as quite diverse. And while the Japanese student grew up in a society often described as homogeneous, she herself reflected an expanded gender role. In each case the individuals within cultures reinforced, challenged, and redefined the nature of gender.

Different Does Not Mean Wrong

Lastly, keep in mind that reasonable people can see the world differently. The challenge of people who hope to build a world of understanding is to build tolerance for different perspectives. This is more important than memorizing some static list of cultural characteristics and behaviors attached to any particular culture. For example, knowing that some people believe that we find truth in words while others seek understanding in silence is as valuable as pinning down which cultures value words and which value silence in conversation. In fact, while most of the research we review here grew out of studies based on ethnic and geographic groupings, our discussion extends these frames to consider gender, ability, and other categories of culture. Knowing the range of possibilities gives us all more options in attempting to achieve insight. Granted, we may reach a point where some cultural values and beliefs are irreconcilable, but we must give ourselves an opportunity to understand that with which we are unfamiliar before we judge.

So, our daunting task as we explore cultural frames as a way of moving toward intercultural competence is to acknowledge the difficulties and take advantage of the opportunities this broad examination provides. Our task presents the challenge of looking at the world from another person's point of view (perspective-taking) and seeing how we can reconcile our cultural frames (reframing) to build peaceful communities. In achieving these goals, we have to build trust and relationships with a variety of people so that when we make mistakes while interacting with people of other cultures (and we will inevitably make mistakes) we have the honesty to admit our blunders; the credibility to be trusted in our motives; and the hopefulness to forgive, make appropriate changes, and move forward together.

Important Cultural Frames

In the last chapter, we discussed identity and talked about a range of identities based on various group memberships; here we examine broader cultural frames. While we obviously cannot cover the full range of possible frameworks, we will address the most significant work that has helped shape the study of intercultural communication. These paradigms have risen to the top because they are based on extensive research or they ring true in explaining human cross-cultural contacts. We will look at the work of Geert Hofstede (Hofstede, 1980, 1986, 1991; Hofstede & Bond, 1988; de Mooij & Hofstede, 2010; Hofstede, 2009) on cultural dimensions, the impact of *Confucianism* (Smith, 1991) in framing culture, Richard Nisbett's work on cognitive frames, Edward Hall's work on the communication dimensions of culture (Hall, 1959; 1966; 1976; 1983; 1990), and Kluckhohn and Strodtbeck's Value Orientations (Kluckhohn & Strodtbeck, 1961). We will also mention a few other well-known frames.

Geert Hofstede's Cultural Dimensions

Geert Hofstede was a Dutch scholar whose work on cultural dimensions is among the most widely cited for understanding cultural variation. His research program ran from 1967 to 1973 and explored the behaviors of over 100,000 people in work settings. Despite the large number of participants, the narrow focus on the workplace has led to questions about generalizing the research to other populations and places. Still, this work represents one of the most comprehensive attempts to compare aspects of culture. Hofstede identified five cultural dimensions. While initially there were only four, he later added a fifth to address Eastern and Western differences. The dimensions include Individualism/Collectivism, Power Distance, Masculinity/Femininity, Uncertainty Avoidance, and Confucian Dynamism (Long-term/Short-term Orientation) (see Table 4.1). Even later he added indulgence versus restraint related to freedom for self-gratification. Since there is less data on this relatively new dimension, we will not be covering it here.

Individualism/Collectivism

Of Hofstede's five dimensions, his most cited by far is his measure of the extent to which people in a culture are expected to "do their own thing" (*individualism*), or act as part of a group (*collectivism*). For example, suppose you fell deeply in love with a person that your family found completely inappropriate for you. Do you feel that you should and would follow your heart and pursue the relationship or would you feel obligated to do what your family prefers? In general, to what extent do you distinguish between what you think as an individual and the voice of the groups with which you identify, be it a political party, ethnic group, or family unit? The dimension of individualism and collectivism explains the powerful hold on how members of a culture see themselves in relation to others, how they develop self-esteem, and how they choose to interact with members of their society.

It is informative that the top four individualistic cultures on Hofstede's scale are the United States, the United Kingdom, Australia, and Canada. These four societies share a great deal of history, a common language, and important world perspectives. We should keep this in mind when approaching other people from other cultures (even various co-cultures within the United States) because the tendency to believe that people should be accountable only to themselves and make their own way may be at odds with the values and perceptions of many people with whom we interact. On the other end of the scale are highly collectivist cultures including Ecuador and Guatemala. As our neighbors to the south, it is important to note that we may be geographically close to others and still see the world through different lenses.

Power Distance

Power distance is the extent to which all groups in a society assume that power is distributed unequally. It is important to note that the system is based on the perspective of those in the "one down" position (Hofstede, 2009). This implies that systems of power work only when the "haves" and the "have-nots" both somehow endorse the inequality. Some societies tend more toward the egalitarian. Israel, for example, is identified as a very low power distance culture. It is a country characterized by lots of active political debate and many varied political parties. Elections are not winner-take-all; rather, proportional representation allows

CULTURE SHOCK

Family Connections

I'm of Irish-American descent and married to a man from Ecuador. I remember traveling to meet my Ecuadorian relatives for the first time and feeling completely overwhelmed that during every minute of our two-week visit we were inundated with relatives up until an uncle actually boarded the plane and saw my husband and I to our seats. Upon returning to the United States, I was once again jolted when not one of my relatives came to the airport to meet us!

—Dolores

smaller constituencies to share power. Of course, the challenge within the Israeli system, often identified as the only democracy in the Middle East, is to find a way of extending the sense of inclusion, respect, and participation to Palestinians living in that part of the world.

In thinking about your own personal experience of power distance, consider the degree to which people in your family or group defer to those in authority by virtue of age, education, or gender. One of the authors has students who refer to parents (and teachers) by first names and argue with their elders as they would peers. Others *never* contradict their parents or teachers and just assume these authority figures (even older siblings) know what is best. Some students live in families where their fathers and brothers eat dinner first, served by their mother and sisters who later eat the leftovers.

Power, of course, can be distributed along many lines. Age, education, gender, and financial wealth are only a few determinants. Body type, skin color, and other factors can be elements of power in various social groups. In January of 2010, Senator Harry Reid caused controversy when past comments of his about Barack Obama (then a presidential candidate) were reported in a new book. Reid was quoted as having said that Obama had a real chance of winning the election because he had light skin and did not have a Negro dialect (Preston, 2010). He saw this as more acceptable to White Americans than a darker-skinned African American with "ethnic" speech. In many societies skin color is a currency that can place one in a power dynamic with others of that same group. Skin- and hair-lightening products are common in the world market, symbolizing power imbalances within a culture.

Masculinity/Femininity

Hofstede's *masculinity/femininity* dimension refers to the distribution and distinction of roles between the genders. In high-masculinity societies, gender roles are clearly distinguished and qualities like competitiveness and assertiveness are valued. In what are identified as feminine cultures male and female roles converge and qualities like caring and cooperation are prized. Japan is regarded as a highly masculine culture (although Japan is certainly a culture in transition) and integration of women into the workplace, for example, has been a challenge in some instances. In the United States, while gender equality is high on our cultural agenda, the strong competitive nature of our culture—for example, we rank everything from sports teams to flower displays (ListVerse.com, 2010)—pushes us toward the masculine end of the scale (see Table 4.1). On the feminine side are many Scandinavian countries. Sweden, for example, offers 480 days of paid parental leave (240 for each parent, or the full 480 for single parents), with 390 of those days based on a percentage of the parents' income, and the remaining 90 days based on the minimum level of pay (Info Norden, n.d.). The far more masculine United States offers 12 weeks with no guaranteed pay.

In your own life, consider how you think about gender roles. Are there "boy" chores and "girl" chores in your family? Are certain behaviors acceptable for males and not females or vice versa? Does your family tend to compare siblings on certain qualities and encourage siblings to overtly or tacitly compete? One of the authors once taught a student whose family held a huge reunion every year that included dozens of cousins. Every year they gave out prizes at the gathering. When the student began to mention some of the prizes, it was interesting that not one was based on competitive standings. Instead, the prizes went to the oldest, youngest, attendee with new teeth coming in, and so on. Also, every single cousin in her generation received some type of award. Awards, in this instance, were intended to demonstrate love and support rather than position, which would place this experience on the feminine end of the continuum. This student said that the most important thing was that everyone felt valued and included. Family members would never want to pit one relative against another or demean a cousin in any way. On the other hand, another student said that her family spends all of their time competing and comparing siblings to one another on every characteristic, from who is the smartest to who is the most attractive. Encouraged by their parents, they were constantly trying to outperform one another to determine who was "the most worthy" among them. This family would fall on the other end of Hofstede's feminine/masculine scale.

As you might imagine, there is some criticism that the feminine/masculine dimension presents stereotypical images of male and female behaviors and supports gender stereotyping. And yet, the idea of masculinity and femininity is so ingrained in many societies that the very language reflects gender designation. Americans struggle to eliminate what is identified as sexist language, so today what was once a mailman is now a mail carrier and a waiter or waitress is now a server. But assumptions about gender roles continue to be reflected in our speech. We may refer to someone as a "male" nurse or use the generic "he" when referring to a physician only to shift to the generic "she" when referring to a kindergarten teacher.

Uncertainty Avoidance

The dimension of *uncertainty avoidance* refers to the degree of comfort with ambiguity. Countries high on uncertainty avoidance tend to focus on identifying one best way and establishing clearly defined rules. In low-uncertainly settings a wider range of behaviors are acceptable and tolerance for variation is more common.

Think about debates in our own society about gay marriage or public religious displays. The United Sates tends to be a country that is willing to accept a level of ambiguity and debate on important issues reflecting our belief in expressing a variety of attitudes and opinions. The college setting in particular is tasked with the challenge of presenting and exploring a range of ideas. For this reason, one of the first things that repressive governments do is jail college professors, burn books, and today, attempt to cut off internet access. For example, after the questionable results of the 2009 presidential election in Iran (a country high on the uncertainty-avoidance scale), citizens spontaneously took to the streets in protest and the government attempted to jam Twitter contact and swear in incumbent Mahmoud Ahmadinejad as head of state, maintaining control over the political climate (Grossman, 2009). Some reporters comment that Iran is a government not set up to make deals and suggest that the ambiguity of negotiating a compromise with dissenters is not built into the system. Yet, in a country where the median age is 30.3 (World Population Review, 2022), and with a history that has included wild swings from major Western influence to ultraconservative leadership, one can see the rumblings of change again, and ambiguity is only likely to increase.

Long-term/Short-term Orientation

Hofstede added **Confucian dynamism** (also referred to as **long-term/short-term orientation**) as a fifth and final dimension because one critique of his work was that it did not adequately reflect Eastern Asian values and perspectives. A long-term, Eastern orientation places emphasis on perseverance, thrift, and humility. This is in contrast to a focus on the immediate gratification and relative excesses of short-term cultures. The impact of Confucianism (discussed in more detail below) shapes this orientation and is credited by some for driving the economic emergence of certain Asian cultures including China, Japan, and South Korea. While the thrifty, delayed gratification attitude of Eastern culture is touted, over time cultures change, converge, and diverge. In Japan, for example, the rate of savings used to be much higher than in the West, at one point reaching 15% of income in 1991 (compared to an American low of less than 0%). But today, after decades of recession in Japan, followed by a worldwide recession in recent years, the savings rates in the United States have trended above that of Japan. The coronavirus pandemic has caused Japan's savings rates to increase once again (OECD, 2021).

While both East and West African societies rank as short-term on Hofstede's dimensions, some have made the case that the Chinese have developed a different relationship in investing in Africa than both British and Americans because they have brought a more long-term perspective and similarity in history in their relationship on the continent (Voice of America, 2009). The challenge for China (and the rest of the world) in dealings with Africa is to forge long-term relationships among equals rather than those based on exploitation, hierarchy, and hegemony to achieve peace and prosperity in all parts of the shrinking globe (Behar, 2008). As the continent of Africa struggles, but continues to rise, there is literature that explores the relationship between African countries and China. The coronavirus pandemic changed world dynamics. While the continent initially did well in curbing COVID-19 cases, attesting to a level of planning that might have surprised some, receiving the COVID-19 vaccine was a challenge. In terms of updated relations with China, China seeks to diversify its imports and Africa may benefit in their relations. According to *The Economist*, China is currently "Africa's largest trading partner, bilateral creditor and a crucial source of infrastructure invest-ment." (*The Economist*, 2022) The future remains complicated, and the United States has yet to fully engage most African countries. The evolution of our post pandemic long-term/short-term orientation may be a factor in all our futures.

In your own life you can consider how you think about planning and struc-ture. Do you tend to spend every dime you earn without a clue where your funds went, or are you the person who saves every penny to buy your first car with cash? Do you like to live for today or think about tomorrow? The fact that you are in col-lege suggests some level of long-term planning. The book *The Millionaire Next Door* (Danko & Stanley, 1996) suggests that the many "average" Americans who are mil-lionaires today got there because they avoid "living large" in favor of a step-by-step plan for spending frugally. They tend to buy secondhand cars, eat at home, shop for bargains, and purchase homes that are less than their means. They also tend to invest in the education of their children and are more likely than most to send them to private schools. In the best "Eastern" tradition, they plan for the future.

Keeping in mind the risks of overgeneralizing that we noted earlier, Hofst-ede's five dimensions assist us in comparing and contrasting a large number of countries in a way that clarifies the impact of cultural frames on our beliefs, values, emotions, and patterns of communications. Table 4.1 includes a list of nations rated highest and lowest on these five dimensions. In the next section we examine the impact of Confucianism in shaping some Eastern societies.

Themes of Confucianism

As stated above, Hofstede referred to Confucian philosophy in laying out the dimension that distinguishes short-term and long-term perspectives. Born in China around 551 BCE, Confucius came along at a time of political and social turmoil when individualism threatened their culture. As an antidote to a corrupt every-man-for-himself system, social harmony and appropriate relationship roles were key elements in Confucian philosophy, with a focus on self-discipline being central (Smith, 1991). The influence of Confucianism spread from China through-out East Asia.

Of course, Asia is quite varied and the unique history of each country inter-plays with the influence of Confucianism. For example, China is a huge landmass with over a billion people under the influence of communism for decades, while Japan is a tiny capitalist nation. Still, the influence of Confucianism on both coun-tries is profound.

Confucian doctrine can be characterized by key themes described in the *Ana-lects*, a collection of sayings written by his disciples. The following are six key themes of Confucianism:

1. *Jen*. Focuses on the idea of relationship between people and represents the golden rule of reciprocity. It is a concept that highlights both respectful treatment of others and oneself.

2. *Chun-tzu*. Emphasizes a state of maturity and grace.

3. *Cheng-ming*. Refers to playing one's part well, whether that of a king, farmer, parent, or child.

Table 4.1   Nations Rated Highest or Lowest on Hofstede's Five Dimensions (in descending order)

Individualism

Highest		Lowest	
United States	Netherlands	Peru	Columbia
Australia	New Zealand	Costa Rica	Venezuela
Great Britain	Italy	Trinidad	Panama
Canada	Belgium	Indonesia	Ecuador
Hungary	Denmark	Pakistan	Guatemala

Power Distance

Highest		Lowest	
Malaysia	Venezuela	Great Britain	Ireland
Guatemala	Arab countries	Switzerland	New Zealand
Finland	Denmark	Panama	Ecuador
Philippines	Indonesia	Norway	Israel
Mexico	India	Sweden	Austria

Masculinity

Highest		Lowest	
Slovakia	Italy	Portugal	Yugoslavia
Japan	Switzerland	Estonia	Denmark
Hungary	Mexico	Chile	Netherlands
Austria	Ireland	Finland	Norway
Venezuela	Jamaica	Costa Rica	Sweden

Uncertainty Avoidance

Highest		Lowest	
Greece	El Salvador	Philippines	Hong Kong
Portugal	Japan	India	Sweden
Guatemala	Yugoslavia	Malaysia	Denmark
Uruguay	Peru	Great Britain	Jamaica
Belgium	France	Ireland	Singapore

Long-term / Short-term Orientation

Highest		Lowest	
China	South Korea	Australia	Canada
Hong Kong	Brazil	New Zealand	Philippines
Taiwan	India	United States	Nigeria
Japan	Thailand	Great Britain	Czech Republic
Vietnam	Singapore	Zimbabwe	Pakistan

4. *Te.* Calls on those with power to use it for good and with integrity and to inspire obedience in others.

5. *Li.* The ideal that people should act as role models striving to capture the essence of their parts and display them with propriety for all to see and emulate.

6. *Wen.* Emphasizes the importance of the arts such as music, painting, and poetry that reflect its highest character.

Together these ways of being define one's existence, behavior, and perspective on every level. When these ideals are implemented broadly, sincerely, and fully, society operates in a harmonious, almost theatrical performance. A Closer Look 4.1 captures the feeling in Japanese culture as families thrive and rear children in a culture that often frames reality quite differently than in the West. Author and therapist Linda Bell describes it as a "song without words."

A CLOSER LOOK 4.1

Excerpts from Linda Bell's "Song Without Words"

We Americans know how to talk; the Japanese, with their emphasis on empathy and intuition, know how to listen. To the Japanese, Westerners' talkativeness makes us seem arrogant and hyperactive. They sometimes wonder if we are afraid of silence. In Japan, the most important communication takes place nonverbally. Restrained and disciplined in public, the Japanese nonetheless have rich inner lives, and perhaps more inner emotional freedom than many in our overtly less inhibited society. . . .

Nowhere are the differences more apparent than in attitudes toward childrearing. When I first saw my own newborn child, I thought about how helpless and dependent he was; I wanted to help him grow strong and self-sufficient. A Japanese mother by contrast wants to strengthen her child's connectedness within a loving family. Mother-child symbiosis lasts longer and is valued more highly in Japan than in America. Until the child's sixth birthday, the parents focus almost exclusively on nurturing that child, accommodating themselves to childish whims. Even during the later years of childhood and adolescence, the child/student is the center of the family and almost no sacrifice is considered excessive if it will contribute to his or her educational advancement.

Although the Japanese are trying to integrate modern values of individualism and autonomy with traditional patterns of family and social harmony, their cultural priorities are still the reverse of ours. Americans cherish individual expression. Japanese cherish harmony in the group. Japanese parents put family harmony first when raising children; American parents are more likely to emphasize individual self-actualization. I want my children to be independent, to take a stand against the group and fight for their rights, if necessary. I distrust "groups," which might

(continued)

negatively influence my children's lives or potentially lead them into trouble. In Japan, however, the word for "different" is the same as the word for "wrong." For them, the group is more likely to offer a comfortable, familial experience, in which people feel nurtured and protected.

Whereas Americans "launch" their adult children—send them "out into the world"—Japanese children never "break away." The family maintains a strong sense of connectedness throughout the life cycle. While American mothers threaten to punish children by making them stay at home, Japanese mothers threaten to punish children by putting them out of the house. My four-year-old learned quickly that ghosts come out after dark in Japan; for safety, he had to come inside the house. In Japan, the mother and baby are one unit. Many American mothers carry babies on their backs in specifically designed sling packs, but only in Japan have I seen coats that cover both mother and baby together. . . .

American children learn to express their ideas orally; Japanese children learn to pay attention to the face, to read nonverbal cues, and to listen well. In a healthy American family, family members share their feelings by talking; in a healthy Japanese family, such verbal sharing is not considered necessary or even desirable. For a Japanese man to say that he can take his wife for granted is a compliment—she is like the air, and he can count on her.

When having our son tested for a private school in the United States, his Japanese teacher was asked to fill out an American form with a question about whether the child could "control his feelings." On the corresponding Japanese questionnaire, which the teacher showed us, was a question about whether the child "manages to express his feelings." Several times, Japanese colleagues in sharing their feelings with me said, "I can't say that in Japanese," suggesting that the very structure of the language forbade the verbal expression of emotions. The Japanese distrust words and verbal skills: "words are just words." Greater weight is placed on intuition and experience—sensing, touching, doing. . . .

Japanese culture is organized around principles of wholeness and complementarily, a respect for all elements of being, and a refusal to divide experience into mutually contradictory categories. . . . The awareness of the indivisibility of creation extends to the Japanese acceptance of death as part of the fullness of life. A Japanese painting of a flower bouquet is likely to include all stages of life, from fresh new buds, to wilted and decaying blossoms. The Japanese never see evil in a child; children are gods—or gifts of gods. Basic human nature is thought to be good. They do not share our dualistic tendency to regard human motivation as either good or evil. Japanese are more likely to accept the whole of human nature, defects and grace alike, and thus may have less need for protecting themselves from guilt or for blaming others. In our litigious society, with about 15 times as many lawyers per capita as Japan, we put enormous energy into protecting ourselves from blame, assigning blame to others, going to court to discover who is to blame. In Japan, even the criminal is partly right, the victim partly wrong. The

(continued)

Japanese are more likely to accept blame and apologize. Apology, they believe, is the gateway to forgiveness, rehabilitation, and social acceptance.

Americans tend to polarize experience, isolating individual elements into good or bad, right or wrong, truth or falsehood. The Japanese, on the other hand, are more likely to see opposites flowing from or even fulfilling each other. In success is the seed of failure, in sadness the germ of future happiness. Matriarchy and patriarchy are Yin and Yang, each intrinsic to an indivisible whole.

These two principles—wholeness and complementarily—underlie the social relativism for which the Japanese are famous. Americans are uncomfortable with relativism; they prefer seeing themselves and their families as unified, stable, single entities. When asked to make a symbolic picture of their family, Americans will usually make one picture, whereas the Japanese families will make more than one—"this is us when father is home," "this is the family at dinner time," "this shows the family's emotional relations," "this shows the different interests and personalities in the family." A Japanese colleague teased me about my "one true self," because like other Westerners, I believe that if my behavior is inconsistent in different situations I am being somehow false, untrue to myself. If I think one thing and say another, I feel dishonest. The Japanese understand that different roles and contexts allow or even demand different aspects of the self to emerge. External behavior and inner feelings are separate, though coexisting, worlds, and society's requirements do not bind the life of the mind.

What seems like contradictions to us work quite harmoniously in the Japanese temperament. For example, they believe that commitment and effort can achieve anything; they are highly ambitious, and prepared to endure much suffering to achieve their goals. At the same time, they relish the experience of being passively nurtured; the experience of dependency is central to the Japanese personality. Pre-school children are cherished and indulged. By our standards they are given little discipline. But, by the time they are elementary school students, they are far more self-disciplined than their American counterparts. The Japanese believe in accommodation to the group, self-sacrifice on behalf of society and family, apology, and humility as a means to peaceful reconciliation. Yet, they also admire the strong, determined individual, the independent spirit of the samurai.

Undoubtedly, there are many ways to understand the truth. Westerners seek to understand their world through intellect—logic and reason; Japanese, through intuition. Japanese culture is distrustful of language and reveres the nonverbal. Nevertheless, as a Westerner, I have had to analyze the essence of the Japanese experience and set it down in the medium of words. I am aware that while I have jotted down some of the notes, the music of Japanese culture will always escape description.

Source: L. G. Bell. (1992). Song without words. In R. Simon, C. Barrilleaus, M. S. Wylie, & L. M. Markowitz (Eds.), *The evolving therapist* (pp. 81–86). New York: Guilford. Used with permission.

Richard Nisbett's Cognitive Frames

Our cultural background influences the way we think about other people, a process known as *person perception*. Perhaps the most important way is the degree to which we see other people as "part of" rather than "apart from" the overall situation they are in. In his book *The Geography of Thought*, the distinguished experimental psychologist Richard Nisbett (2003) shows how this focus (or lack of focus) on *context* is a fundamental difference between East Asian and Western societies. Much of this difference has its origins in the longstanding collectivistic orientation of the East, which encourages *holistic thinking*, and the individualistic orientation of the West, which encourages more *analytic thinking*. Nisbett explains that

> to the Asian, the world is a complex place, composed of continuous substances, understandable in terms of the whole rather than in terms of the parts, and subject more to collective than to personal control. To the Westerner, the world is a relatively simple place, composed of discrete objects that can be understood without undue attention to context, and highly subject to personal control. (p. 100)

This difference in thought and perception shows up in how individuals describe what they see. In the first of three experiments, Nisbett and his student, Takahiko Masuda, showed students from Japan and the United States an animated underwater scene in which one "focal" fish (larger, brighter, faster moving) swam among several less noticeable fish and other aquatic scenery like plants and rocks. When they were asked to describe what they saw, Japanese students usually began by describing the environment ("it looked like a pond"); but the American students were three times more likely to begin by referring directly to the focal fish. Overall, the Japanese descriptions contained over 60% more references to background elements, including water, rocks, bubbles, plants, and so on, than did the descriptions of the Americans. In a second experiment, the researchers showed the students pictures of many different objects, half of which they had seen before. The students had to say whether or not they had seen the objects before. Some of the objects seen before were shown in their original environment and some were shown in a new environment. Compared to the Americans, the Japanese had much more difficulty remembering an object if it was shown in a new environment. This finding supports the idea that for the Japanese, the perception and subsequent recall of an object is more context-bound than it is for the Americans. In their third experiment, Masuda and Nisbett asked students to pick out the differences they saw between two images, such as the ones presented in Figure 4.1. Take a few seconds and compare these two images yourself. What differences between the two versions do you notice the most? The researchers found that the Japanese were much more likely than the Americans to see differences in the background and in the relationships between objects (e.g., distances between background planes, different control towers, etc.). The Americans were more likely to spot differences between "focal" objects in the foreground than the Japanese were, once again illustrating how Japanese perceptions are more attuned to context than American perceptions (Masuda & Nisbett, 2001; Masuda & Nisbett, 2006).

Frame from Airport Site Movie: Version 1   Frame from Airport Site Movie: Version 2

Figure 4.1   Contrasted images from the Masuda and Nisbett experiment. (With permission from Masuda & Nisbett, 2001)

How do these differences affect perceptions of people? One implication is that *attributions*—judgments about why people do what they do—are likely to differ. When explaining a person's behavior, East Asians may tend to focus more on the situation and less on the person than Westerners do. Person-focused explanations are known as *internal attributions* and situation-focused explanations are called *external attributions*. In fact, researchers have found that Chinese are more likely than Americans to rely on external rather than internal attributions. For instance, when they explained why a person committed a murder, in two studies Chinese newspaper reporters were less inclined than American reporters to rely on internal attributions and more likely to rely on external attributions (Morris & Peng, 1994). In one of these experiments, participants read about the killing spree and suicide of an American postal worker in Michigan named Thomas McIlvane. Distraught over losing his job and unable to find employment, McIlvane returned to the post office where he previously worked and opened fire on his supervisor, the person who handled his appeal to the union, several workers and bystanders, and then killed himself. When the researchers analyzed newspaper accounts of the incident, they found striking differences between American and Chinese reporters. Americans generally attributed the killings to McIlvane's personal qualities, such as "he had a short fuse," "he was mentally unstable," etc.; Chinese reporters emphasized situational factors, such as "he had recently been fired," "the post office supervisor was his enemy," and "he was influenced by a recent mass slaying in Texas."

Edward Hall's Communication Dimensions

Edward T. Hall was an American anthropologist who used fieldwork and direct experience to examine many "hidden" elements of communication and is well known for his observations on how culture influences our use of personal space (Hall, 1963). But Hall also developed the concepts of high-context and low-context cultures, ingroup and outgroup membership, and monochronic and polychronic time orientations that relate to intercultural communication. (See Table 4.2 for examples of various high-low context and monochronic-polychronic cultures.)

High Context/Low Context

High context and *low context* refers to the degree to which we depend on words versus situational factors to convey meaning. In a low-context culture, such as the broader American culture, words are the focus. We are supposed to say what we mean and mean what we say. We are taught to speak up for ourselves and be precise in our use of language; so if I say, "Close the door," the acknowledged meaning is carried in the words of the directive.

On the other end of the continuum is a high-context culture in which the words carry a smaller part of the entire message and the "field" or context carries key information regarding the communicators' relationship and the full meaning of the verbal message. In the example above, one might be expected to know that the door should be closed as well as who should close it, even without any statement being made. A Korean-born student in a class of one of the authors shared an expression that captures the essence of a high-context culture: "We hear one word and we understand 100." The same student said that she was shocked that in America young couples are constantly telling each other, "I love you," but miss interpersonal cues that give partners the opportunity to demonstrate caring, such as putting a sweater around a loved one's shoulders when the room has a chill.

Ingroups/Outgroups

Edward Hall's work on *ingroup* and *outgroup* dynamics reveals that people who share similar cultural backgrounds can communicate more easily with one another and are more able to create a distinct ingroup experience that distinguishes

Table 4.2 Some Cultures Classified as High Context or Low Context and as Monochronic or Polychronic

Lower-Context Cultures	Higher-Context Cultures		
German	French	Italian	Native Americans
Scandinavian	Spanish	Mexican	African Americans
Switzerland	Japanese	Korean	Chinese
United States	Greek	Arab	
Monochronic Cultures	**Polychronic Cultures**		
United States	Middle Eastern		
Canada	Sub-Saharan Africa		
Northern Europe	Native American		

them from outgroups with different cultural backgrounds. Not surprisingly, members of an ingroup often have different standards for the treatment of people within their ranks versus outsiders to whom the same protections, and even common courtesies, may not be extended. In fact, it is common to see outgroups as less worthy, even less human than insiders. Indeed, one of the first strategies in conflict and war is to label the Other with disparaging terms, extending negative frames to everything about outsiders that distinguish them from insiders.

Outgroups and stigmatized groups develop strategies in response to the labeling and treatment they receive. For example, over the years one of the authors has observed extensive discussions among her students about the use of the N-word. Of course, the history of the word includes its use by Whites, often as a precursor to lynching, especially in the American South. More fundamentally, framing someone as "just a nigger" gave justification to inhumane systems that enslaved an entire people for centuries. Paradoxically, today some African Americans use the term with relative freedom, and the feeling that they have co-opted its meaning and power. Now the term can be dangerous to use for those who are not African American. Judith Butler in her book *Excitable Speech* (Butler, 1997) analyzes racist, sexist, and homophobic speech and explores how incendiary language is framed differently at different times, for different purposes, by different groups, and under different circumstances, much of this relating to the group status of the user. Butler concludes with the possibility that "the conventional relation between word and wound might become tenuous and even broken over time" (p. 101). In exploring the many uses of the N-word, we can see how the ways that we frame language and experience can be contested and cause ambiguity and conflict in social interactions.

The experience of African Americans as insider and outsider is surely a situation in flux. In today's multiracial society, the dynamics of ingroups and outgroups are increasingly multifaceted and often strained. In a school in Philadelphia, a group of Asian students boycotted classes because they felt that African American students and the African American school power structure were nonresponsive to their concerns (Miller III, 2009). Now that America has had its first African American president and multiracial vice president, the face of power is becoming more diverse. Will the cultural styles of a wider range of Americans begin to merge to create more understanding, or will different groups simply become the winners and losers? Or will the reaction to cultural change challenge us further learn to live as a racial society?

Monochronic and Polychronic Time

Finally, in addition to verbal patterns and group membership, Hall (1966) talked about the use of time as a factor distinguishing cultures. Some cultures are more *monochronic* and others more *polychronic*. Monochronic cultures like the United States, with its history steeped in progress, the industrial revolution, and the assembly line, are focused on linear clock time, efficiency, and schedules. In its most stripped-down form, Americans believe that time is money. On the other hand, cultures like Mexico and Saudi Arabia are polychronic and comfortable with many things going on at once. Relationships rather than schedules are at the focus of human interaction.

This polychronic orientation was articulated best for one of the authors by a visitor to class whose ethnic background was Italian, although he grew up in South America (both polychronic cultures). At the end of his presentation on his background and culture, the speaker turned to the class and asked, "What are you working for?" His perception was that North Americans are hardworking, driven, and always chasing the clock, but that we live shallow lives devoid of real joy and connection. As the saying goes, "We live to work rather than working to live."

Kluckhohn and Strodtbeck's Values Orientations

Florence Kluckhohn worked first with her husband Clyde on cultural research and later with Fred Strodtbeck interviewing individuals from Texas, Mormon, Mexican, and Native American cultures in the Southwest, developing their values orientation theory (Kluckhohn & Strodtbeck, 1961). The influence of the culture of the Southwest is seen in their value dimensions but the work has been extended to cultures all over the world and is one of the most referenced theories in this area. They proposed that cultures could respond to universal problems and the ways in which they respond characterize the cultures.

Though not meant to be an exhaustive list, they offer five value orientations that distinguish cultures from one another:

1. We can examine if a culture views *human nature* as basically good, mixed or evil, mutable, or immutable. Is a baby born as a reflection of God and perfection, as suggested in the reading on the rearing of Japanese children by Linda Bell; as the blank slate to be written upon reflected in the training in British educational systems; or touched by original sin as in some Christian traditions?

2. We can explore how *humans and nature are seen in relationship*. Does the culture believe that humans are subordinate to nature and its forces or should people dominate nature and control everything from procreation to how many hours of sunlight shine each day? Or should people live in harmony with nature and its forces?

3. We can consider how cultures vary in *time orientations* from a past orientation that honors history, precedent, and tradition, to a present orientation in which one lives for the moment, to a future orientation that assumes the best is yet to come and that progress is inherently good.

4. A perspective toward *activity* can honor the very act of being or existence, or being-in-becoming, which is more focused on ongoing internal growth and development, or doing which focuses on accomplishing things, external evaluation, and visible activity.

5. A relational orientation can view *human social relationships* as hierarchical and based on power differences, equal where power and decision making is shared, or individualistic where people have the right to live for their own goals and purposes.

We have highlighted some of the most influential theories for the field of intercultural communication. In our discussion, we have not considered other cultural frames including Rokeach's instrumental (short-term) versus terminal (ultimate) values (1973; 1979) and Schwartz's 10 value types (Schwartz, 1992; 1994) (power, achievement, hedonism, stimulation, self-direction, universalism, benevolence, tradition, conformity, security). We also have not considered the impact of religious and political frames. Further, we have only touched on the interplay of cultural frames and the dynamics of power and hegemony when cultures come into contact (see Chapter 3). The ability to force the less powerful group into submission, based on the worldview and rules of the more powerful group, has led to the devastation of cultures within America and around the globe. For example, over the last 100 years, around 400 languages (about one every three months) have been lost, with experts estimating that 50–90% of the world's remaining 7,000 languages will be gone by the start of the next century (Nuwer, 2014; Strochlic, 2018). Learning that "might does not make right" and the importance of showing respect for people and their worldviews is a small step in the process of building peaceful communities.

Obstacles and Challenges to Peacebuilding

When people frame the world differently, the potential for intractable conflict increases greatly. Even well-intentioned people often find that circumstances deteriorate when they fail to grasp the complexity of perspectives that weigh on a situation. Take, for example, the highly publicized conflict between Harvard Professor Henry Louis Gates and Cambridge Police Sergeant James Crowley (Goodnough, 2009). In July of 2009, Dr. Gates was returning to his home after attending an overseas conference and was having difficulty entering his house. A neighbor saw someone attempting to force his way into the home and called the police. Police officers approached Dr. Gates, now inside his home, and Officer Crowley asked Dr. Gates to step outside. Accounts differ on whether Dr. Gates immediately produced identification but according to Sergeant Crowley, "While I was led to believe that Gates was lawfully in the residence, I was quite surprised and confused with the behavior he exhibited toward me." According to the police report, Dr. Gates said to the police officers, "This is what happens to Black men in America!" and, when asked by Sgt. Crowley to speak with him outside the residence, Dr. Gates replied, "I'll speak with your mama outside." One thing led to another and eventually the 58-year-old Gates, who walks with a cane, was taken to the police station and charged with disorderly conduct.

In his classic book, *Black and White Styles in Conflict*, communication scholar Thomas Kochman (1983) offers insights regarding the frames of Black and White Americans who live parallel lives and see the world through different sets of experiences. For a Black man like Dr. Gates, his experience as an African American of his particular generation may have led him to be both suspicious of police officers and wary that people might underestimate his intelligence and minimize his value as a human being. His question, "Do you know who I am?" may have reflected his attempt to recontextualize himself in the eyes of a person he saw as an adversary. Sergeant Crowley, on the other hand, may have seen himself as a figure of authority who must demand compliance and respect in order to do his job. Officer Crowley

Can awareness of the cultural frames help us manage disagreement in a more civil manner?

construed the words and actions of Professor Gates as inappropriately aggressive and challenging. Further, the police officer, who himself had taught racial sensitivity classes, felt that he was a fair-minded and racially sensitive person. Some have also suggested that beyond race, the fact that these two individuals felt they had to *save face* as men may have caused the situation to spin further out of control. Whatever the contributing factors, might awareness of the cultural frames specified above have allowed one or both of these men to manage their disagreement in a more civil manner? Are such misunderstandings inevitable in a country with our racial past? Will future generations share more common frames of reference? Will the multiracial Black Lives Matter movement and others like it create new sensitivity and awareness?

As we discussed in Chapter 3, a fundamental issue at the heart of many intractable conflicts is the need to protect one's identity. In this regard, ***face negotiation theory*** offers some useful insights into how differences in cultural frames can impede conflict management initiatives (Ting-Toomey, 2005). According to the theory, threats to one's ***face***, defined as the projected image of one's self, are more likely to trigger conflict in self-focused individualistic cultures than in group-focused collectivistic cultures. In contrast, threats to the face of one's group (or other group members) are more likely to trigger conflict in collectivistic cultures. Face negotiation theory also suggests that individualistic cultures are more likely to encourage direct, confrontational, and aggressive tactics, as well as third-party interventions, than collectivistic cultures. The reason for this stems from the idea that persons in collectivistic cultures are less concerned with "winning" a dispute and more concerned with harmonious relations (i.e., avoiding another person's loss of face) than are persons in individualistic cultures.

Cultural Frames and Intercultural Communication Competence

Our discussion of cultural frames assumes that the ability to first imagine that groups use different frames to organize the world is the foundational step to understanding people who are different than us. After this acknowledgement, we have to work on our ability to think within the perspective of another. This is referred to as *perspective-taking*. We can then begin to consciously work on our ability to see commonality in different frames, which is referred to as *reframing*. We can thereby find our common interests to overcome obstacles. We will talk about perspective-taking and reframing in turn.

Perspective-Taking

A primary goal of perspective-taking is to increase empathy and insight regarding co-communicator's points-of-view. The idea of seeing the world through others' eyes is captured in expressions like "walking a mile in another man's shoes" and Peggy McIntosh's (1990) seminal essay in which she makes an extensive list of why her life is easier as a member of the majority culture (see A Closer Look 4.2). Popular films like *Freaky Friday* capture the challenge of feeling empathy across generations. Indeed, there is evidence that perspective-taking can work and is used in a variety of settings.

An experiment in a Polish-Czech borderland community high school demonstrated that Polish students who were made to imagine that they became members of another dissimilar youth group were more willing to help out-group members

---

A CLOSER LOOK   **4.2**

When Life Is Easier

Peggy McIntosh (1990) outlines dozens of ways in which she received privilege because of her status as a member of the majority culture in American society. Among the privileges she lists:

- I can go shopping alone most of the time, pretty well assured that I will not be followed or harassed.

- I am never asked to speak for all the people of my racial group.

- I can remain oblivious of the language and customs of persons of color who constitute the world's majority without feeling in my culture any penalty for such oblivion.

- I can be sure that if I need legal or medical help my race will not work against me.

- If my day, week, or year is going badly, I need not ask of each negative episode or situation whether it has racial overtones.

(Bilewicz, 2009). In the United States, Foeman and Nance's (2002) research interviewing interracial couples confirms that partners find that they see the world differently because their partnership allows them to see reality from the perspective of their spouse. In yet another instance, a local nursing facility builds empathy by having new hires participate in an orientation training activity that requires them to navigate in wheelchairs for several days and attempt other tasks like tying their shoes while wearing mittens over gloves or reading training material through Vaseline-smeared glasses. The first step in using our knowledge of frames is to seek to truly understand the other person. Try Put It Into Practice 4.1 as a start.

Reframing

The act of extending an olive branch is an apt metaphor as a symbol for peacemaking because olive trees grow slowly. Learning to see things from the perspective of another is a slow and arduous process. Using that insight to then find common ground is another difficult step. Frame analysis involves consciously examining the frames of communicators in order to consider how frames compare, often with the goal of finding commonality and overcoming an impasse.

In conducting frame analysis, we must first attempt to mine the understandings and perspectives of people involved in an interaction (Goffman, 1974). This can include extensive and deep listening. In fact, one listening project (The Listening Project, n.d.) operates to allow people of different backgrounds and views to tell their stories for as long as they need so that they may feel fully heard and understood. In your own life, can you think of a person who cares enough about you to listen to you without judgment? Several of the best parents we know have a code word or phrase that their kids can use when they need to share something that they think is going to upset the parent. When the child says something like, "Mom, I just need for you to listen and not say anything," the parent shifts into a mode in which they listen without comment or interruption until the child has said all they need to say. The parent generally then acknowledges that they have heard and offers to talk more about the issue when the child is ready. Any subsequent conversations are then colored by the understanding and sensitivity established in the first listening interaction. Try it yourself using the guidelines in Put It Into Practice 4.2.

PUT IT INTO PRACTICE   **4.1**

Taking Another Person's Perspective

Think of a person with whom you disagree most of the time. How would you describe this person? Now think, how would they describe you? Why? Can you think of this individual as doing the best they can? What factors are driving their behavior? How might you behave similarly given their same circumstances? These are the first steps in trying to take the perspective of another. Now extend this personal example to larger cultural and social situations.

PUT IT INTO PRACTICE   **4.2**

Listening for a New Insight

Use this class as an opportunity to approach someone that you have trouble seeing eye to eye with. Think particularly of someone who may view you as unfair or a bully. Tell that person that you are required to simply listen on a topic about which you disagree. Listen sincerely and intently to the person for a set amount of time. Articulate to that person exactly what you think they are saying. Ask for verification on your interpretation. Monitor your emotions to note if you feel impatient or if you want to interrupt. At the end of the session ask if your listening was meaningful and seemed genuine. Offer to engage in dialogue at a later date if the other person wants to. End the session by thanking the person for their perspective. Afterwards, analyze what this activity means for you and how this skill might benefit you in a variety of relationships.

Generally, in reframing, once all shareholders in a situation have had a chance to share their perspective, reframing works to place the conflict in a larger context in which all people in conflict can see the mutual benefit in finding common ground. In the best-case scenarios, perspective-taking and reframing can solve seemingly intractable problems and create amazing opportunities.

Consider the rise of microloans pioneered by Dr. Muhammad Yunus, a professor of economics who founded the Grameen Bank in 1983. This bank grew out of Dr. Yunus' ongoing work that began in the 1970s of making loans to poor female basket weavers in Bangladesh. This bank is not a nonprofit agency and provides small loans to entrepreneurs (the majority of them women) with no collateral. The loans fund projects such as buying a goat or work supplies. Borrowers can get money at very competitive rates and the repayment rate is extremely high. While the programs have faced their share of problems, the concept has been successful enough to be replicated around the world. It is an example of a person reaching across social class, gender, and other cultural barriers to see a common goal.

In this case, Dr. Yunus did not view these poor women dismissively, worthy only of a handout. Rather, he framed them as entrepreneurs like himself. He saw them as part of the solution rather than part of a problem. His reframing opened a door for real partnership and communication. The United Nations declared 2005 the International Year of Microcredit. In 2006, Dr. Yunus received the Nobel Peace Prize, and in 2009 President Barack Obama presented Yunus with the Presidential Medal of Freedom.

What unchallenged beliefs do you cling to about how different you are from others? How often do you step out of your comfort zone to include "outsiders" as part of your community of friends and peers? That is how you begin to recognize your own frames and those of others. The opportunity to do perspective-taking and reframing can provide a breakthrough in understanding and appreciating other cultures and in building stronger more peaceful communities.

PUT IT INTO PRACTICE   **4.3**

Taking a Cultural Group Inventory

Identify a group to which you belong. Select a group you feel truly reflects your attitudes and values and is important to you. Then review the various cultural frames discussed above (Hofstede's Cultural Dimensions, Hall's High and Low Context, etc.). Identify where you feel your group falls in each area. What does this say about the group? How does the group's awareness of these factors shape their identity? How neatly do you fit into your group? What does this say about you? How do the qualities put this group in sync or in conflict with other groups? How can tensions be managed for the best outcomes?

Summary

Our cultural frame of reference refers to the taken-for-granted structures we impose on reality, based on our background and experience. Cultural frames produce worldviews that filter our perceptions of reality and shape the way we interact with others. But cultural frames are dynamic and change over time; they also vary across individuals and groups. The peacebuilding perspective reminds us to respect differences in worldviews and to resist the ethnocentric impulses that impede progress toward peaceful communities.

There are a number of well-known theories and programs of research about cultural differences in frames of reference. We reviewed Hofstede's theory of five dimensions of culture, perhaps the most referenced in intercultural communication. We discussed the six basic themes of Confucianism and its profound influence in shaping Asian culture. In Nisbett's research on cognitive frames we explored Eastern holistic thinking and Western analytic thinking. Hall's work on high- and low-context cultures, ingroup and outgroup communication, and monochronic and polychronic styles offers another way to explore the orientations of various cultures. Finally, Kluckhohn and Strodtbeck's work on human nature, the relationship between humans and nature, time orientation, activity, and social relationships offers insight into various value orientations. When people frame the world differently, the potential for intractable conflict greatly increases, as individuals of different cultures experience difficulty understanding, appreciating, and relating to each other. Face negotiation theory offers one explanation of how cultural frames affect the management of intercultural conflict. Intercultural communication competence involves the development of skills in perspective-taking and reframing.

QUESTIONS

1. Identify an event that touched your life and profoundly changed the way you view the world. At that point, what elements of your worldview changed and how did your new perspective change your attitudes and behaviors going forward?

2. Using Hofstede's Cultural Dimensions, deconstruct a cross-cultural conflict trending in the media currently to see how worldviews of the co-communicators may differ.

3. Identify a group that you have difficulty understanding. How do you think that group's worldview may differ from yours? Is it possible for you to imagine what worldview might explain behaviors that now appear random to you?

4. What elements of someone else's worldview test your limits for tolerance? What view of the world is very hard for you to accept or comprehend?

5. Exploring the concept of high- and low-context culture, recall a time when you have experienced silence within your family or peer group. How did you interpret that silence? What is the value of silence for you?

6. Identify an issue on your campus or in the news with intercultural implications. Use one of the frames presented in Chapter 3 (e.g., ingroups and outgroups) to explore the nature of cross-cultural confusions. Explore what steps can help in improving communication.

Culture and Emotion

Chapter Outline

Key Terms

action tendencies
cognitive element of emotion
cultural sensitivity
ego-focused and other-focused emotions
emotion scripts
emotional awareness
emotional competence
emotional perspective taking
emotional regulation
goal-congruent and -incongruent emotions
honor culture
infrahumanization
intergroup emotion theory
physiological element of emotion
primary and secondary appraisals
self-conscious emotions
shame reparation
strategic expression
transferred shame

The exchange between the Canadian government and the Residential School Survivors of Canada (see A Closer Look 5.1) document the importance of appreciating emotional experiences that lie "at the heart of" any attempt at reconciliation and repair in every peacebuilding process. These letters are painful and poignant reminders of the difficulty of peacebuilding in the aftermath of interpersonal and social violence.

In this chapter, we explore the fascinating topic of emotion and culture. We begin by discussing the nature of emotion and the cognitive, physiological, and expressive components of emotion. While emotion is central to all human experience, cultures exert influence on emotional experience and responses to emotional situations—a topic for the second section of the chapter. In the third section we explore how cultural differences in emotion and assumptions about the emotions of others contribute to conflict and escalation of dysfunctional conflicts. In the final section we address the challenging yet hopeful processes of peacebuilding through development of *emotional competence* and reconciliation.

The Nature of Emotion

Emotion has several different elements: a cognitive, physiological, and behavioral or expressive component (Kitayama & Markus, 1994). In this chapter we concentrate on the cognitive part of emotion because it relates so strongly to identity, which is the focus in our later discussion of cultural influences on emotional experience. However, as discussed in Chapters 6 and 7 on verbal and nonverbal communication in intercultural communication, the expressive and communicative function is also critical to consider, especially in intercultural conflict.

A CLOSER LOOK   5.1

The following is an exchange between the Canadian government and the Residential School Survivors Association in June 2008. The words provide one example of the emotional reality in intense intercultural conflict and the difficulty in repairing harm from that conflict. Both letters have been abbreviated for presentation.

Open Letter to the Prime Minister

Dear Prime Minister Harper:

On behalf of the Residential School Survivors of Canada, we welcome your announcement of an apology.

. . . It is with deep respect, we boldly put forward what survivors expect in the apology.

1. Survivors expect Canada to recognize what was done was wrong and Canada accepts TOTAL responsibility for what they did to survivors and their families and their communities. . . .

                              *   *   *

4. Canada must confess publically, what they did to each survivor. Survivors were "kidnapped" from their families, they were "imprisoned" . . . . Children were beaten, humiliated, starved, introduced to contagious diseases like tuberculosis, sexually abused, some were "murdered," in an environment whose goal was to " . . . take the Indian out of the child" . . .

5. Canada must make restitution. Canada must put back what was taken away by committing to rebuilding individuals, families and communities. . . .

                              *   *   *

7. Canada needs to commit that it will never, never, never let this happen again. Anything less than the above is not in our view a sincere apology. . . . Anything less will not be an expression of reconciliation.

Once again, we welcome the announcement of the apology and applaud your decision to acknowledge a part of Canadian history that many deny was as intense as it was or even happened.

—Ted Quewezance, Executive Director, Residential School Survivors of Canada

---

(*Windspeaker*, 2008)

(continued)

The Government of Canada Apologizes

I stand before you today to offer an apology to former students of Indian residential schools. The treatment of children in Indian residential schools is a sad chapter in our history. . . . Two primary objectives of the residential schools system were to remove and isolate children from the influence of their homes, families, traditions and cultures, and to assimilate them into the dominant culture. . . . Indeed, some sought, as it was infamously said, "to kill the Indian in the child."

Today, we recognize that this policy of assimilation was wrong, has caused great harm, and has no place in our country. . . . First Nations, Inuit and Métis languages and cultural practices were prohibited in these schools. Tragically, some of these children died while attending residential schools and others never returned home. . . .

The government now recognizes that the absence of an apology has been an impediment to healing and reconciliation. Therefore, on behalf of the government of Canada and all Canadians, I stand before you, in this chamber so vital, so central to our life as a country, to apologize to Aboriginal peoples for Canada's role in the Indian residential schools system. . . . We now recognize that it was wrong to separate children from rich and vibrant cultures and traditions . . . and we apologize for having done this. . . . We now recognize that, far too often, these institutions gave rise to abuse or neglect and were inadequately controlled, and we apologize for failing to protect you. . . .

There is no place in Canada for the attitudes that inspired the Indian residential schools system to ever again prevail. . . . The government of Canada sincerely apologizes and asks the forgiveness of the Aboriginal peoples of this country for failing them so profoundly. We are sorry.

—Prime Minister Stephen Harper, delivered to the Canadian parliament

(Legacy of Hope Foundation, n.d.)

Cognitive Element of Emotion

You may be wondering, "What does cognition have to do with emotion—isn't emotion the opposite of thinking?" You may think of emotion and rationality as polar opposites. On the contrary, cognition is a very important component of emotion. When we have feelings they are feelings about something; they are based on judgments or appraisals we make about an event, a person, or a situation. *Appraisal theories of emotion* (Lazarus, 1991; Ortony, Clore, & Collins, 1988) explain how judgments about actors, behaviors, and events lead to emotional experiences. The key point of these theories is that the judgment comes first, and then the emotional experience is realized.

Lazarus (1991) argued that we have an emotion because of two judgments labeled **primary appraisals** and **secondary appraisals**. Our emotional experience is a function of both appraisal processes acting in tandem. You can think of primary appraisals as pointing to a generally positive or a generally negative emotional experience. The secondary appraisals lead to a specific kind of positive or negative emotion. Using a simple map metaphor, the primary appraisal lets us know we're in Pennsylvania, but the secondary appraisal lets us know whether we're in Pittsburgh or Philadelphia.

Slightly expanding Lazarus' theory of language to acknowledge both individualist and collectivistic orientations to identity, let's explore how primary and secondary appraisals shape emotion. Primary appraisals focus on the question, "Is the event or situation personally/communally relevant?" ("Does this matter to me/us?"). There are three elements to be considered in making the primary appraisal: Does it impact on my/our personal goals (goal relevance)? Does it make it easier or harder for me/us to achieve my/our goals (goal congruence)? Is it related to my/our identity in some important way (ego-involvement)?

According to Lazarus, all negative emotions arise from appraisals that the situation impacts on personal/communal goals (is goal-relevant) in a way that makes it harder for a person/community to achieve those goals (is goal-incongruent). All positive emotions come from appraisals that the event, person, or situation is relevant to our personal/communal goals and makes it easier for us to achieve them. As we will see in the next section, the "self" orientation of the person, in terms of individual versus collective goals, shapes emotional reactions.

Secondary appraisals focus on additional issues that help determine the specific emotion felt. According to Lazarus, there are three additional issues to consider: What or who is to blame for the event/situation (judgments of accountability)? How well can I/we solve this problem and manage my/our feelings (coping potential)? How likely it is that things will get better or worse (future expectancy)?

Gudykunst, Ting-Toomey, Sudweeks, and Stewart (1995) distinguished between *goal-congruent emotions* (or positive emotions) and *goal-incongruent emotions* (or negative emotions) using Lazarus' theory as a foundation (see Table 5.1). In a Western model, they conclude there are six goal-congruent emotions: compassion, happiness, hope, love, pride, and relief. And, there are at least nine goal-incongruent emotions: anger, anxiety, disgust, envy, fright, guilt, jealousy, sadness, and shame.

Various appraisal explanations can be offered to distinguish key emotions—especially emotions that are consistently linked with intercultural conflict or relational difficulties. For example, the emotions of shame and humiliation have received a great deal of attention. Shame is defined by Tangney and Fischer (1995) as a painful emotion in which the self, not just the behavior in the event, is found wanting. Shame is often accompanied by a sense of shrinking and being small, and by a sense of worthlessness and powerlessness. Often when people feel ashamed they try to hide themselves with their hands or literally try to physically escape the situation.

The emotion of humiliation comes from an appraisal that someone has lessened your dignity or pride and put you in a lower power role. For Lindner (2006) "humiliation means the enforced lowering of a person or group, a process of subjugation that damages or strips away their pride, honor or dignity" (p. 3). While shame is something you see as a fault in yourself, humiliation is something you see being done to you by someone else.

Table 5.1 Basic Emotional Definitions from Appraisal Theory	
Goal Incongruent Emotions (Negative emotions)	
Anger	Someone has committed a demeaning offense against us or those close to us.
Anxiety	We are facing an uncertain threat; we cannot make sense of the situation.
Disgust	We want to get away from someone or something that we find offensive.
Envy	We want something that someone else has.
Fright	We face an immediate physical danger.
Guilt	We have done something or we want to do something that we find morally wrong.
Jealousy	We hold a third party responsible for the threat of the loss of someone's affection.
Sadness	We think we have experienced an irrevocable loss.
Shame	We perceive that we fail to live up to our expectations in someone else's eyes.
Goal Congruent Emotions (Positive emotions)	
Compassion	We are moved by others' suffering and want to help them.
Happiness	We are making progress toward our goals.
Hope	We think something bad is going to happen but we want something better to happen.
Love	We have affection for other people.
Pride	We are able to take credit for something we did that we value.
Relief	We have been experiencing a negative emotion and the situation changes for the better.

(Adapted from Gudykunst et al., 1995, pp. 135–140)

As Albertsen, Connor, and Berry (2006) discuss, guilt is an uncomfortable emotion, occurring when a person believes one has done or considers doing something wrong. Guilt motivates people to make decisions they judge to be morally right. The tendency to feel guilt is a fairly stable trait, but some people are more sensitive than others (Tangney et al., 1992). There is an important difference between guilt and shame; where guilt is a negative emotion resulting from a negative judgment about one's behavior, shame results from a negative judgment about the self. Because of the focus on the self, both guilt and shame (as well as embarrassment) are known as *self-conscious emotions*.

Physiological Element of Emotion

Emotions are called "feelings" because when we have an emotion there is a physical sensation that lets us know we are having an emotional experience. For instance, when you have strong emotions your heart may race, your blood pressure may rise, you may sweat or blush, and you may feel knots in your stomach or aches in your muscles. Some of these changes, like increased heart rate and adrenaline flooding, are noticeable to the person having them; other changes may not be recognized (like pupils dilating) but can still impact the overall experience

---

PUT IT INTO PRACTICE   **5.1**

Your Experience of Self-Conscious Emotions

For each of the following feelings place a number from 0 to 4, reflecting how often you experience the feeling.

4—Very often   **3**—Often   **2**—Some of the time   **1**—Rarely   **0**—Almost never

_____   1. Feeling embarrassed

_____   2. Feeling ridiculous

_____   3. Feeling self-conscious

_____   4. Feeling humiliated

_____   5. Feeling "stupid"

_____   6. Feeling "childish"

_____   7. Feeling helpless

_____   8. Feeling that you are disgusting to others

(Adapted from Harder & Zalma, 1990)

---

of emotion (e.g., by signaling another person that you are happy or upset). Your feelings are "embodied," as Denzin (1984) suggests in his book *On Understanding Emotions.*

Brain research is explaining how the emotion centers in the brain affect us as communicators and decision makers. In past generations, philosophers wondered where the emotions were housed in the human body. In medieval times, doctors and philosophers thought emotions were part of the liver and spleen, and they tried to cure illness by balancing the "humours" of the body. Generations ago, people thought that emotions resided in the heart, and even in our language today we talk about "the heart of the matter," meaning the emotional side of an issue or situation. More recently, largely because of sophisticated medical technology, scientists can prove that emotion is felt in the body but starts in the emotion centers of the brain. Antonio Damasio, a neurologist at the University of Iowa in the 1990s, studied how some areas of the brain are responsible for basic emotions, while others are responsible for reasoning processes. Through his research and the work of other emotion scholars, we understand that the limbic system (or the lower part of the brain) controls instinctive, basic emotional experiences like fear and rage. Reasoning, logic, and analysis depend on the cortex. This higher part of the brain gives us conscious thought, processes new information, and controls higher-level cognitive tasks. And we know that when emotion centers are activated in the brain, our perceptions, decision making, and sense of wellbeing are affected.

Because emotion is triggered in the brain and has a physical impact and manifestation, we can become "carried away" or "flooded" emotionally. Emotional flooding is system overload—being swamped by emotion to the extent that one cannot think effectively. When we experience intense emotion, our brain focuses on the limbic system and reduces our ability to access information from the neocortex (Perry et al., 1995). In other words, emotional flooding switches on simplistic, instinctive, fight-or-flight reactions and makes it difficult to think in a cognitively complex way to make decisions, plan what to do, or reflect on options. Our brain acts much like an engine that has been flooded; it doesn't run well and won't run well until we give it time to "unflood."

A distraught Arabic woman praying.

Expressive Element of Emotion

The expression of emotion is so essential to people they even try to make their possessions emotionally expressive. Anyone who saw the movie *Castaway*, starring Tom Hanks as a FedEx executive marooned on a deserted island, will remember Wilson, the volleyball who became Hanks' "friend." Hanks' character identified with the volleyball after using a bloody handprint to create a "face" with a slightly smiling expression. How could Hanks consider it only a volleyball without the face, but see it as a "someone" with the face drawn on? We have been raised to identify humanity through a collection of emotional expressions. In Chapters 6 and 7 we discuss how culture affects the verbal and nonverbal expression of emotion.

Emotion Is a Process

Sometimes it seems you are suddenly in the middle of an emotional experience. We're likely to think of our emotional experience once it's full blown, once we realize we're sad, happy, angry, or disgusted. In reality, however, we have gone through several steps before we get to that point of "feeling." Sally Planalp (1999) articulated her model of this process in her book *Communicating Emotion: Social, Moral and Cultural Processes*. The following is a paraphrase of that model:

1. The process begins with something that gains our attention. It may be a person's behavior, an event, or encountering an object—it is the something that emotion is about. Seeing a child being bullied, witnessing a friend making a strong presentation, or listening to a report of an attack on America can all stimulate emotion.

2. Once we focus on the event, we make an appraisal, an evaluation, or a judgment of that thing. As we've already explained using Lazarus' theory, the appraisal results in an emotional experience.

3. Once we have appraised the situation, we have a physical reaction to it. The emotion produces physical changes in the body. Many scholars think the physiological changes are the body's way of preparing for the next step of the process—action tendencies.

4. *Action tendencies* are the motivation to express the emotion. Our action tendencies are not just biologically primed, they are socially constructed as well. For example, when you see a family member at the airport you may have the urge to shout out across the crowds to show your happiness.

5. *Emotional regulation* is our decision of whether or not to engage in the action tendencies. Often we regulate our emotions unconsciously, but sometimes we do it very consciously. In the example above, instead of screaming with joy in the airport, you limit yourself to a strong wave since it is less intrusive to others in that public place.

In the "emotional moment" you probably don't recognize all of the stages of an emotional process occurring. Still, those processes are happening and result in the totality of the emotional experience—the physiological, cognitive, and expressive elements of emotion. And that emotional experience is definitely influenced by culture, as we discuss in the next section.

Cultural Influences on Emotional Experience

To say that emotions are culturally influenced means our emotions are, to some extent, socially constructed. Our culture influences the emotions we feel, when we feel them, and how we show those emotions to others.

There are many ways we can see cultural influence, from the macro-historical level as well as the micro-social level (the ways that individuals respond to certain situations due to cultural rules for emotion). For example, we can think about culture's influence across time by realizing that the "basic" emotions we take for granted today (e.g., anger, sadness, contempt) have not always been the emotions "of the time" (Stearns, 2008). If we were living in the 3rd to the 11th century as Hindus, we would have a different list of basic emotions. While there is no direct English translation of the Sanskrit, we could summarize them as: (1) *rati*—sexual passion, love, or delight; (2) *hasa*—amusement, laughter, humor, or mirth; (3) *soka*—sorrow; (4) *krodha*—anger; (5) *bhaya*—fear or terror; (6) *utasha*—perserverence, energy, or heroism; (7) *jugupsa*—disgust or disillusion; (8) *vismaya*—wonder, astonishment, or amazement; and (9) *sama*—serenity or calm (Shweder et al., 2007).

What would you say if we suggested, as has the noted anthropologist and expert on love, Helen Fisher (1992), that the notion of romantic love (being "in love" with someone) was a creation of the modern era? Most of us have grown up believing in, as Cole Porter would say, "that thing called love." We wait to fall into it, hopefully finding "true" love. But if we were living in the Middle Ages and talked to someone about romantic love they would have no idea what we meant. They might understand chivalric love, platonic love, or maternal love, but not romantic love. As a concept, it simply did not exist for them.

Bharatanatyam, a classical Indian dance, shows a variety of emotions while being performed in Tamil Nadu.

Arlie Hochschild (1983), a sociologist at the University of California, talks about rules on feeling that societies develop to help people understand how they are supposed to feel about things. In 19th century America, the feeling rules for the South said that free people were supposed to feel contempt for slaves because slaves were subhuman. Some cultures have feeling rules that create emotions unknown in other cultures. For example, in Greece they have an emotion called *philotimo*, which is understood as an "honor" emotion. A *philotimo* person can be a person who is honorable (*éntimos*), honest (*tímios*), generous and hospitable (*filóxenos*), good (*kalós*), or worthy (*agios*). Despite its tendency to elude precise definition, *philotimo* is valued in Greek society more than status or wealth (Koutsantoni, 2007).

Once people recognize the "feeling rule" and know what emotion they are supposed to feel, they engage in what Hochschild (1983) calls "emotion work" or showing the emotion in the right way (Saarni, 1985). You can think of this as you would a scene in a play. Each scene in a play is about something; all the actions and dialogue in the scene serve to enact the content. For example, if a person criticizes or insults us, our minds revert to an "I'm being threatened" script, which has a series of expected responses and behaviors associated with it. Both feelings rules and *emotion scripts* are culturally influenced. In America, for example, when someone is afraid, the emotion script is usually to scream and yell or to run away. But the Balinese have a very different emotion script for fear; they fall asleep in the face of something frightening. In Balinese culture, falling asleep is seen as good way to avoid the terror—they "play possum" (Niedenthal, Krauth-Gruber, & Ric, 2006).

Rituals are formalized emotion scripts; the more relevant the emotional experience the more a culture develops rituals concerning that emotion. For example, the Navajo have a strong fear of dead bodies (Niedenthal, Krauth-Gruber, & Ric, 2006). They believe the dead body houses evil spirits and if the body is not handled in elaborate ritualistic ways, the spirit will come back to do harm. When someone dies, the family does not come into contact with the body but hires four mourners to wash and formally dress the body. The mourners put the moccasins of the dead person on the wrong feet to ensure that the dead person will have trouble walking back to the village from the burial site.

Mesquita and Albert (2007) report a particularly powerful ritual among the Philippine Ilongots. In the Ilongot community, ingroup harmony was essential for survival of the group. But *liget*—an emotion indicating energy, passion, and anger simultaneously—was an emotion that could threaten the ingroup harmony, so the Ilongot had special ways of dealing with this emotion and re-establishing harmony:

> A ritual of headhunting was in place, should *liget* arise. When one or more Ilongot men experienced the heavy feeling of *liget*, a group of them would go out to kill an outsider. After the beheading, the Ilongot men came home purged of violence, and the community celebrated the overcoming of *liget* by singing together. (p. 499)

As we explore culture and emotion, it will be most useful to concentrate on concepts that are foundational in the peacebuilding model in Chapter 2. As you recall, the model begins with an emphasis on cultural identity, leading to intercultural interactions, taking place in intercultural contexts, with the potential for creating intercultural community. As we will see in the next section, culture dimensions related to identity (e.g., individualism and collectivism) are strongly linked to emotion (Lewis, Haviland-Jones, & Barrett, 2008); who we "are" affects how we feel. We will also explore how cultural rules for identity-related emotions are a form of social control, with specific consequences when ignored.

Identity Dimensions of Culture and Emotion

> "A single hand clapping, though fast, makes no sound."
> — Chinese Proverb

> "The nail that stands out gets pounded down."
> — Japanese Proverb

> "The squeaky wheel gets the grease."
> — American Proverb

We get emotional about things that matter to us. If something is not important to you it won't make you happy, sad, angry, fearful, etc. Emotion tells the "truth" about what we value, what we think is bad or good, and what we believe is right and wrong (White, 1994). From a cultural standpoint, the values underlying cultures operate to highlight or extinguish certain kinds of emotional experiences. In Chapter 3 we discussed how identity concerns are the foundation of cultural orientations; issues of identity are paramount in determining what is important or valued. Thus, as we begin to discuss specific emotional similarities and differences in culture, we will use those underlying dimensions of cultural difference (e.g., individualism and collectivism) as our conceptual template.

Throughout this book we have repeatedly referred to the dimension of the individual versus the collective as the prime dimension of cultural difference. Researchers have discovered clear distinctions between individualists and collectivists in several domains including: the meaning of the self, the structure of goals, norms and attitudes, ingroup needs, and affect (Markus & Kitayama, 1991). For example, Kitayama et al. (1993) found that in Japan, feeling good is associated with success in maintaining *interdependence* with others, whereas in the United States, feeling good is associated with success in maintaining *independence* from others (Aizawa & Whately, 2006). Hence, collectivists are more likely than individualists to be involved in situations that produce ingroup harmony and individualists are more likely to be involved in situations *they* perceive as "fun" or "self-serving" (Triandis, 1994).

Markus and Kitayama (1991; 1994) contrasted the experience of Westerners and East Asians in terms of **ego-focused emotions** and **other-focused emotions**. Ego-focused emotions are centered on the individual and involve such experiences as self-affirmation. An emotion like anger is ego-focused to the extent that it reflects an affront or threat to one's personal integrity. Other-focused emotions have the "other" as the primary referent. Cohen and Gunz (2002) argue that people from collectivist cultures actually see themselves from the other's point of view. They see themselves as they think others see them. In their study of Chinese and

The power of expression displayed in a mask at Kadammanitta Temple in India.

Americans, they found that Easterners were more likely than Westerners to take a third-person perspective on themselves when asked to remember situations in which they, as individuals, were the center of attention. Westerners saw situations in terms of how they felt and assumed others in the situation would feel the same. Easterners first identified the expected emotion, what a general member of their culture would assume should be felt, and then saw their own emotions as an instance of that general, cultural emotional expectation.

Happiness: An American Institution?

Happiness is highly valued in American culture because "being happy" signals success in standing out, being unique, and/or fulfilling one's goals. You can see the American emphasis on happiness in American schools where activities like show-and-tell, smiley-face stickers, student of the week, etc., are geared to make students happy with themselves and build self-esteem. Researchers have explored how the quest for happiness and life satisfaction differs across cultures. In one study, 8,557 people from 46 countries were asked how often they experienced positive and negative emotions and how satisfied they were with their lives (Kuppens, Realo, & Diener, 2008). The results showed that people in individualist countries have a heightened sensitivity to negative emotions, and that cultures which value happiness (like Americans) are more influenced by being unhappy by not attaining their goal of happiness than are cultures that de-emphasize happiness.

But the goal of happiness is definitely not universal—not all cultures value happiness:

> During her stay with the Ifaluk (on a Pacific atoll), the anthropologist Catherine Lutz was reprimanded for smiling at a girl who acted happy. The Ifaluk condemn this emotion because it is thought to lead to a neglect of duties that are central to the social organization of Ifaluk life. (Mesquita & Albert, 2007, p. 486)

Happiness is de-emphasized in cultures following Confucian traditions since being happy may cause jealousy in others. For example, the Japanese, emphasizing the obligation to accommodate to others, practice *hansei* (self-reflection or self-criticism). *Hansei* involves focusing on one's shortcomings and on possible improvements. *Hansei* is institutionalized in Japanese elementary schools where children, at the end of each day, are encouraged to search for their inadequacies and weaknesses so they can find ways to improve (Mesquita & Albert, 2007).

And, it may surprise you to think that the flip side of happiness, sadness, is also not universally experienced or valued. The whole concept of sadness so common to American and European cultures is not even recognized as an emotion in many languages of the world (Wierzbicka, 1992).

Anger: A "Useful" Emotion?

> "Usually when people are sad, they don't do anything. They just cry over their condition. But when they get angry, they bring about a change."

—Malcolm X

A CLOSER LOOK   **5.2**

The following are selected excerpts from the article "Depression: Should we be rid of it?" that originally appeared in the *Philadelphia Inquirer* on March 4, 2010.

> Am I as happy as I should be? We've become so obsessed with that question that it's making us miserable, says psychotherapist Gary Greenberg. . . . He asserts that recent advances in psychiatry, which have redefined "depression as a medical disease caused by a biochemical imbalance in the brain" and treatable with drugs such as Prozac, have convinced many Americans that there's a "magic bullet" that can make our suffering disappear.

> In 1987 . . . 44.6% of adults treated for depression were prescribed medication. A decade later, the proportion had grown to 79.4%. By 2005, it had become virtually unthinkable to treat depression without drugs. In 2005 . . . 27 million, or 10% of the adult population, were on antidepressants. . . .

> Bala Cynwyd psychiatrist Elio Frattaroli agrees. "Our culture has a problematic attitude toward disturbing emotions," he says. "We have this idea that the proper way to be is to be happy and that if you have any variety of unhappiness, you are not right."

(Derakhshani, 2010, p. E01)

Americans are a relatively angry people; they often see anger as productive and are not shy about showing their anger. Americans think in terms of "channeling your anger into something constructive," which portrays anger as energizing and motivating (Kovecses, 2000). But, other cultures see anger as useless or counterproductive:

> A Zulu expression translates into English as "to grind rotten mealies." The expression refers to the pointlessness of anger. It derived its meaning from the staple food of the Zulu, mealies, or maize corn. It relates to the idea that one should not expend energy on a useless activity—no one would spend energy grinding rotten corn nor should anyone spend energy getting angry. (Kovecses, 2000, p. 168)

We see similar resistance to anger in other collectivistic, tribal cultures. The expression of anger, for example, is strongly disapproved of by the Utku Eskimos (Eid & Diener, 2001).

Love (Makes the World Go Around?)

Scholars have examined the nature of passionate and companionate love (Kim & Hatfield, 2004) and found that certain cultures emphasize one more than the other. Passionate love, emphasized in individualistic cultures, has the connotation of romantic love, and companionate love, emphasized in collectivistic cultures, infers feelings of friendship. Think of the role that passionate love plays in American and European marriage and the role that companionship plays in arranged marriages in more collectivistic cultures.

CULTURE SHOCK

Shower Me with "Appropriate" Gifts

My husband is Nigerian, and we met in college. When you're in college, you never really think about the long- term implications of your differences. It wasn't until we started planning a wedding that I realized how, even though we were both "brown" I'd probably have more in common culturally with someone who was white. In his culture, their wedding showers are very religious. We didn't know that! My mom and grandmother showed up with a gift of lingerie at a bridal shower hosted by my future mother-in-law. It was kind of embarrassing when I pulled out this pink nightgown and fabulous slippers.

—Shenielle from Philadelphia

Notions of love also influence how culture influences the way we show intimacy. Seki, Matsumoto, and Imahori (2002) studied expressions of intimacy between Americans and Japanese. The participants described where, when, and how they expressed intimacy to parents, friends (opposite- and same-sex friends), and lovers. Americans reported openness, expressiveness, and physical contact more often than the Japanese. Another study looked at American, Russian, and Japanese tendencies to fall in love. Surprisingly, the Japanese reported more love experiences than either the Americans or Russians, but they held less romantic beliefs than the Americans or Russians (Sprecher et al., 1994). Love means different things to different cultures and, correspondingly, people from different cultures think and act differently when "in love" (Kline, Horton, & Zhang, 2005).

Guilt

For people from cultures that emphasize guilt, it is difficult to imagine that not all people or cultures have similar experiences. Suh et al. (1998) analyzed four national groups in their study on emotions in 41 countries. In more collectivistic cultures guilt is more important, whereas in individualistic cultures pride is of greater relevance. The importance of guilt for collectivist cultures may explain why a culture like China has more types of guilt in their vocabulary (Eid & Diener, 2001). Bedford (2004) found that three types of guilt can be differentiated in Mandarin language: (1) the guilt felt from failure to uphold an obligation to another (*nei jiu*), (2) the guilt felt in a case of moral transgression (*zui e gan*), and (3) the guilt felt in a case of legal transgression (*fan zui gan*). In a study of 246 college students, Albertsen, Connor, and Berry (2006) found significant differences between ethnic groups, with Asian Americans higher in guilt than European and Latin Americans. But guilt does not seem relevant for some cultures. Fessler (2004) studied guilt in American and Bengkulu cultures. He found that guilt was a prominent emotion for Americans but was almost completely absent from Bengkulu culture.

Shame: A Core Emotion

Shame is an emotion that we will discuss in the next section because of its centrality in conflict and reparation. Here, we focus only on the general question of whether cultures differ on their experience of shame. Shame is a "self-conscious" emotion (Lewis et al., 2010), more relevant for individualistic cultures because it results when a person, through his or her own behavior, loses face or falls short of their own expected standards of behavior. Yet, people in collectivist cultures can experience shame. Bedford and Hwang (2003) remind us that, when someone from a Western culture experiences shame he focuses on "self," which is construed individually (i.e., a self that does not encompass others). However, when a person from an Eastern culture experiences shame, the self extends to family members and significant others (Tang et al., 2008). This is close to the idea of *transferred shame*, where your shame is my shame (Dost & Yamaguri, 2008).

Even though different cultures experience shame, and perhaps experience it in the same way, they may respond to shame in different ways. Fischer, Manstead, and Rodriguez-Mosquera (1999) conducted a study with samples from Spain and Holland, which they characterized as honor-based and individualist cultures, respectively. Spanish people interpreted shame as an indication of honesty and vulnerability and thought that shame should be shared. But Dutch people interpreted shame as a threat to self-esteem, and felt it should be concealed. Bagozzi, Verbecke, and Gavino (2003) studied Dutch and Filipino salespersons who reported being shamed by customers. Dutch salespeople responded by withdrawing from customers while Filipinos responded by working harder to engage with customers and increase their relationship-building efforts, degree of courtesy, and general work efforts. The Dutch saw shame as a signal to end relationships and Filipinos saw shame as a signal to repair the relationships (Goetz & Keltner, 2007).

Differences in Appraisals Leading to Emotions

Just how similar are cultures in the appraisals that lead to emotions? Scherer's (1997) research of students from 37 countries asked them to recall situations in which they felt certain emotions. He found very similar patterns of appraisal for the emotions of joy, disgust, fear, anger, sadness, shame, and guilt. Matsumoto, Nezlek, and Koopmann (2007) also analyzed data from the International Study of Emotion Antecedents and Reactions. They wanted to see whether emotions were due more to individual differences than to cultural differences. Using the data from 2,921 participants across five continents they found that less than 5% of the variance was due to nationality. To determine whether the proposed dimensions of appraisal are consistent across cultures, 973 people from the United States, Japan, Hong Kong, and the People's Republic of China were asked to describe emotional experiences. The researchers examined the extent to which emotions differed across cultures on each of 10 dimensions: pleasantness, anticipated effort, attentional activity, control, coping ability, certainty, goal/need conduciveness, legitimacy, norm/self compatibility, and responsibility. The results revealed that the same findings describe the cognitive appraisal data across all of the countries studied (Mauro, Sato, & Tucker, 2002). These studies remind us that, while cultural

CULTURE SHOCK

Caught Cheating

The dean of students could not fathom why Thanh persisted in denying his pla-giarizing. The evidence was unmistakable and the university was prepared to treat the incident leniently. Thanh needed only to admit wrongdoing and rewrite the copied passages. He appeared strangely unable to acknowledge his error and was needlessly fearful. It wasn't until a colleague suggested that Thanh might see it as threatening to expose not only his own misbehavior, but the moral failure of the parents whose responsibility it was to raise him, that the dean began to grasp the emotional significance of this seemingly benign scenario for Thanh.

(Adapted from Liem, Lim, & Liem, 2000, pp. 13–14)

differences exist, there is notable consistency across cultures in the ways people appraise situations and trigger emotions.

Yet, when we look at research on how specific cultures appraise situations differently, we do find some interesting cultural variations. As we have mentioned earlier, Americans have a penchant for the emotion of happiness. However, other cultures feel happiness as well, just not necessarily about the same things that trig-ger happiness in Americans. Mauro, Sato, and Tucker (1992) found that different antecedents caused happiness for Americans, Northern Europeans, and Japanese. Americans were likely to see things like births as events that "caused" happiness, but Japanese were less likely to. Similarly, these cultures differed on key anteced-ents to sadness. Death, seen as an antecedent event for sadness among Ameri-cans and Europeans, was much less likely to cause sadness for Japanese—perhaps because many Japanese believe that death allows the person's soul to rejoin the long-lost and much-loved ancestors.

Emotion as Social Control in Cultures

Social control happens when someone sees a person committing a behavior that is socially unacceptable, and openly communicates to the "perpetrator" that they are transgressing and should stop. Social control concerns whether people in a culture become upset enough about someone else's violation of a cultural norm that they signal disapproval. Fessler (2007) provides an entertaining example from his studies of the Bengkulu tribe:

> In Bengkulu, individuals who fail to exhibit shame when others become aware of their wrongdoing are termed "thick-eared," as they are unaffected by gossip or excoriation. Being thick-eared is a form of higher-order norm violation as it indicates that one does not value cultural standards. Thick-eared people are viewed as dangerous and may even be killed if they persist in their thick-eared behavior. (pp. 180–181)

To understand how social control operates, people from eight countries were presented with a description of 46 uncivil behaviors and asked to rate each behavior on: (a) how deviant it was, (b) how frequent it was, and (c) how likely it was that they would express their disapproval to the perpetrator (Brauer & Charand, 2010). In all eight countries, the deviance of the behavior was very important in whether social control was used. Collectivistic cultures were more likely to use social control than individualistic cultures.

Obstacles and Challenges to Peacebuilding

"If we have no peace, it is because we have forgotten that we belong to each other."

—Mother Theresa

In the previous section we showed how emotions differ across cultures. Now, we explore the tendency for cultural differences in emotion to create community-building obstacles in our interactions with persons of other cultural groups. Intercultural interactions can result in misunderstandings, either caused by emotional differences or resulting in emotional consequences that can fuel conflict and relational damage. After discussing the relationship between culture and emotion, we introduce *intergroup emotion theory* to explain how people from different cultures appraise others in ways that increase the potential for conflict. And finally, we articulate how several key emotions (e.g., shame, contempt) escalate intercultural conflicts and further harm communal ties.

Emotion and Conflict: Basic Principles

Emotion is so important in conflict that we define conflict as the expression of an *emotionally relevant* disagreement between two or more interdependent people about what should be done and/or how it should be done. A brief overview of the links between emotion and conflict will set our discussion for how this emotion-conflict dynamic is further influenced by culture. Jones (2000) has provided a much

An Amboseli tribe woman in Kenya.

more in-depth discussion of the relationship between emotion and conflict. The following is a brief review of her major points:

1. *Conflict is emotionally defined.* This is the chicken or the egg question of what triggers conflict and what conflict triggers. Most conflict theory looks at conflict as the cause of emotional reaction. Jones (2000) argues that emotional experience occurs first and acts to help us define a situation as a conflict. If we find ourselves in a conflict, it means we have already been emotionally triggered—and usually in a negative way.

2. *Conflict has levels of emotional intensity.* Conflicts are a little like emotional roller coasters. There are frightening free falls, laborious climbs, and soothing stretches of level inactivity. Emotional intensity flows through a conflict, sometimes high and sometimes low. The more we recognize shifting levels of intensity the more we understand why we become more emotional about some aspects of the conflict. Canary, Cupach, and Messman (1995) have noted that, in conflict, there is a strong propensity for emotional contagion and reciprocity of emotional displays. Our emotional intensity can affect the intensity of others in our interaction and vice versa.

3. *Emotion in conflict reveals our values.* In the last section we discussed how cultural values (like individualism and collectivism) influence emotional experience. Similarly, we have conflicts about things we value, which are often culturally determined or influenced. Sally Planalp (1999) helps us understand that emotions reveal our moral ideas about the world and what is happening at the moment. We perceive a conflict because we see something that is "not right," which means that all perception of conflict is from our particular moral point of view. Because of your morality, you may see something as a conflict when others don't. And we assess what we believe is a just and fair outcome for a conflict based on what we feel is "right and wrong, just and unjust" in the larger scheme of things. When people feel that their basic values are threatened or that their basic sense of justice has been attacked, they are potentially at their most emotional and most primed for action in a conflict.

4. *Emotion in conflict is strongly tied to our identity.* Again, in the previous section we highlighted cultural values related to identity in our examination of culture and emotion. The importance of identity (or face or social image) in conflict cannot be overstated. Threats to identity are among the most powerful emotional triggers to conflict. When you challenge or disrespect someone's identity, it adds an issue to the conflict that must be dealt with before other issues can be addressed. A professor and student may be in conflict over the "fair" grade in a course. But, if the student calls the professor inept, incompetent, and racist, you can assume that the discussion will focus on the justification of and arguments against that insult rather than on any other aspect of the conflict. The professor's culture may also be one that is highly sensitive to certain kinds of insults and demands certain kinds of retaliation—a culture where revenge for insult is expected. Suddenly, the student has a much more serious and complex conflict. Even if revenge is

not forthcoming, the threat to identity creates a defensiveness that may cue the professor to perceive the student with disfavor and distrust, creating a relationship tension that is ripe for explosion in future interactions.

Intergroup Emotion Theory

As Smith and Mackie (2008) explain, "intergroup emotions" happen when people identify with a social group and respond emotionally to events that affect or reflect on the group. The more the person identifies with the group (draws their sense of self from membership with that group), the more prone she is to intergroup emotion. The group member depersonalizes and reacts as a member of a group rather than as a unique individual. One of the authors remembers a personal experience that illustrates this concept:

> My mother and I were on a trip to Dublin for a professional meeting I was attending. The meeting, ironically about peace initiatives in the European Union, was happening shortly after the U.S. invasion of Iraq. My mother, a generally peaceful person, had lived through World War II and I knew her to be a patriot, but not supportive of war or violence. That morning in the hotel lobby I met her for breakfast. She was very angry, which was uncharacteristic, and intensely upset about a story she had just read in the *International Herald Tribune* about the beheading of four American soldiers in Afghanistan in retaliation for the U.S. invasion in Iraq. Her reaction, fueled by her identification as an American citizen, was to call for the most violent and brutal possible treatment of "those people." I had rarely seen her so publicly upset. In response, I suggested that being angry at the Iraqis didn't seem right; the Iraqis had not done the beheadings and had not been involved in the World Trade Center bombings. My comments made her angrier. She would not hear it. I remember thinking that I could barely see "my mother" in the woman across the table from me.
>
> But, I hoped the event was a passing situation and would be forgotten by evening when I returned from my meeting. I was wrong. Later that night when I returned from the meeting (where the beheadings had been a major topic of conversation), I found my mother in the lobby talking with a group of American senior citizens from Iowa who were in Dublin for a tour. Being of my mother's generation, many of them had lived through World War II and had the same emotional reaction that my mother had had that morning. The group was reinforcing and escalating the anti-Iraqi discourse to an alarming level. Instead of entering their conversation I listened until it was time for my mother and me to leave for dinner. As we walked away from the group she asked if I now understood how right they were to seek retaliation against the Iraqis. I realized sadly that we would never see eye-to-eye on this issue and, indeed, the following years have confirmed that.

As this story suggests, in intergroup emotion theory the group membership component becomes a major factor in how a situation or person is appraised and thereby affects emotional experience. One test of whether an emotion is an intergroup emotion is to ask this question: "Would the emotional response be similar if the same event happened to some other ingroup member?" In the case above, the answer was clearly "yes"—the mother and Americans of her generation had similar reactions to that event and collectively fed each other's negative appraisals of an outgroup (Iraqis) and fueled emotions of anger and vengeance.

Research shows that when people's group-level emotions are socially shared and are shared more strongly by people who identify more with the group, there are three processes that contribute to the convergence of individual and group emotions: (1) people may converge because of emotional contagion—people may take on the emotions of the people with whom they interact; (2) people may conform more to ingroup norms (e.g., celebrating patriotic symbols), and (3) people may attend more to some cues when making appraisals because those cues or elements are of heightened importance to their group membership (Rohmann et al., 2009).

Intergroup emotion theory helps explain the emotional power of the ingroup/outgroup dynamic. For example, when an outgroup is appraised as threatening the ingroup, negative intergroup emotions such as fear or anger may result. These can become part of an overall configuration of prejudice against the outgroup that may motivate discriminatory behavior as discussed in Chapter 2.

However, thus far our example about intergroup emotion theory has only been negative. A positive effect can also happen. When outgroups are appraised in positive ways, positive emotions including sympathy or pride may be evoked. These positive emotions lead to more favorable overall reaction to the outgroup as well as to more favorable behaviors. The core idea of intergroup emotion theory is that negative emotions can be aroused by intergroup interaction, so certain types of intergroup contact can effectively reduce prejudice by reducing those negative emotions. Blascovich et al. (2001) demonstrated that intergroup contact with African Americans decreased Euro-American students' physical reactions usually associated with perceived threats. Pettigrew (1998) found in a large sample from several European countries that people who have an outgroup friend were generally less prejudiced against that group. Once again, a personal example from one of the authors makes this critical point:

> In 1995, right after the election of President Mandela and the overthrow of apartheid, we were involved in a project of American and South African educators to develop peace education programs in the Johannesburg area of South Africa. The first stage of the project had a team of South Africans come to the United States for the introduction to U.S. peace education efforts. The South African team consisted of Afrikaners, British South Africans, and black South Africans from Soweto and Thokoza (the two largest Black South African townships outside of Johannesburg). The South African team members had never worked together or met before they joined at the airport to fly to America. For all of them it was their first experience with Americans. For two weeks on that initial trip (and for two years in the entire project) the team shared meals, space, work, challenges, and successes. At the beginning, each group had fairly strong, incorrect, and largely negative opinions about the others. This was especially true for the attributions made between the white and black South Africans. However, as they saw each other succeed, saw how they were treated and respected by others, saw how they were valued by Americans as South Africans who had accomplished the incredible end of apartheid, they began to see each other more positively. Contact, positive emotion, and perseverance worked together to create friends from the most unlikely circumstances.

In conclusion, we know that not all outgroups are treated, seen, or perceived the same way. Outgroups who are the targets of anger may be attacked while outgroups that are the target of disgust may be avoided. Outgroup emotions do not have to be negative, and can be the target of sympathy or envy. What we do know is that when intergroup emotion dynamics are in play, we need to be more consciously attuned to how we can create positive emotion and productive intergroup contacts to avoid the negative spiral into discrimination and prejudice that can happen.

Emotions Related to Escalation in Intercultural Interactions

In conflict, and especially in intercultural conflict, some emotions are more damaging to relationships. Emotions like contempt and shame usually escalate conflict. When we remember that cultures differ on their use of these emotions and their reactions to them, we can appreciate how complex it is to build emotionally positive intercultural communities.

Contempt

Contempt is an emotion we feel when we see the other as inferior; it can be the emotional core of the dehumanization of others based on their culture. As Ortony, Clore, and Collins (1988) explain, contempt may be a response to the action of another or a response to an inherent characteristic of the other. In some cultures there are unique emblems of contempt, and some cultures are more expressive of contempt than others (Miller, 1997).

As A Closer Look 5.3 indicates, we may find ourselves denying the humanity and suffering of others if we look at them with contempt and only as members of an outgroup we devalue (Rohmann et al., 2009). Unfortunately, we know

---

A CLOSER LOOK   **5.3**

Shell Shocked

On his home ground, back in Afghanistan's embattled Helmand province, Pay-anda Mohammed refuses to give up his sidearm. He wore it proudly as a sign of his rank when he led a Taliban combat squad, and his family members still allow him to carry it—after they quietly and prudently made sure the firing pin was removed. They never know when he'll fly into another unprovoked rage, or when he'll experience another violent flashback to the battles he fought against the US. . . . But right now the weapon is hundreds of miles away. His family made him leave it home when they sent him across the border to Pakistan for medical treatment.

Among American troops, post-traumatic stress disorder has become one of the signature injuries of the wars in Iraq and Afghanistan. . . . Yet for all the millions the Pentagon has spent on studying and treating PTSD, and figuring out ways to prevent it, no one has given much thought to whether the enemy suffers it as well.

(Moreau, 2010)

that in intergroup contexts individuals ascribe an essential humanness to their own group and deny the outgroup this same essence (Leyens et al., 2003). This "emotional side of prejudice" has been labeled *infrahumanization* and increases when the out-group is fundamentally different on some valued characteristic, like race. Thus, the outgroup is judged to have an incomplete human essence or an *infra-human* essence.

The expression of contempt escalates conflict. Canary, Spitzberg, and Semic (1998) reported that aggressive behavior is often precipitated by anger and one of the primary causes is "the perception that one's self concept or public image is under attack" (p. 194). Displays of disrespect or intentional demonstration of perceived superiority can be linked with explosive, destructive escalatory cycles (Jones & Remland, 1993; Remland, Jones, & Brown, 1994). Basically, people do more extreme forms of the same behavior to communicate contempt, especially when contempt is directed toward an outgroup perceived as "deserving" of that behavior.

Kemper's (1978; 1993) theory of emotion and power relations further explains why contempt may be so destructive in cultures where identity issues are key. Kemper isolates two underlying relational themes: control of one member by another (power) and degree of positive social relations (status). In a dyadic relationship, four possibilities exist for each member: a person can feel that they have (1) an excess of power in the relationship, (2) an excess of status in the relationship, (3) insufficient power in the relationship, or (4) insufficient status in the relationship. Kemper (1978) explains, "deficit of own power (or excess of other's power) is the social relational condition for fear or anxiety, and . . . loss of customary, expected, or deserved status (other as agent) is the basic relational condition for anger" (p. 37).

Challenging status and power through contempt displays may generate different responses depending on the culture of the target. Research suggests that, in general, collectivist cultures are more sensitive to insult or face loss, especially when communicated intentionally through displays of contempt (Ashton-James et al., 2009). The most prominent finding of Tokunaga's (2008) research is that cultures that value group harmony are influenced by hurtful messages to a greater degree than those who value internal goals—an insight critical for the quality of intercultural relationships and intercultural communication competence with members of collectivist cultures.

An *honor culture* is a collectivist culture that sees response to collective insult as necessary to restore honor. Beersma, Harinck, and Gerts (2003) investigated the impact of insults on emotional response and conflict behavior in workplace conflict among people who are sensitive to threats to identity (discussed as honor sensitivity). In honor cultures, reputation is extremely important. According to Rodriguez-Mosquera (1999, p. 13) honor "has to be socially claimed and recognized in order to have any value." When the self is humiliated or offended during a conflict, "a person's claim to honor and to be treated with respect is denied." In honor cultures, honor can be defended or restored through actions such as aggression or expressions of anger. Therefore, individuals who attach much value to honor react to conflicts in a more aggressive manner than those who attach less value to honor (Rodriquez-Mosquera, Manstead, & Fisher, 2000; 2002).

Similarly, a strong predictor of whether people use avoidance or assertive conflict management strategies is how much they value independence or interdependence (Kim, 2002). Collectivists, with the exception of honor cultures, suppress inner desires and emotions that conflict with the larger group's goals. Personal agendas are de-emphasized. Collectivists are thus more nonconfrontational, using avoidant conflict styles—especially when the conflict occurs with others from the same cultural group (Cahn, 1985). Individualism asserts individual needs, so individualists assume achieving individual goals requires explicit, direct communication and confrontation (Markus & Kitayama, 1991).

Shame

When contempt results in shame, *shame reparation* cycles are usually triggered. Retzinger and Scheff (2000) suggest when someone is shamed and signals that he has been shamed, the other must acknowledge the shame and try to repair it. If the shame is not repaired, the person who has been shamed will retaliate or withdraw. The shame-repair model describes the following process: (1) the social bond is threatened, usually by some disrespectful behavior; (2) shame signals disrupt the bonding; (3) shame is denied (not acknowledged), leading to feelings of alienation and perceptions of the other as attacker; and (4) anger or withdrawal, depending on cultural tendency, follows as a signal of degree of threat and as means of saving face and perhaps repairing the bond (Lewis, 1976). The cycle is exacerbated if the anger or withdrawal signals are ignored. This lack of attention is seen as further disrespect. However, if anger is answered, shame can be reduced and bonds repaired (Retzinger, 1991).

While Retzinger's approach assumes that shame is dysfunctional for conflict, Keltner, Young, and Buswell (1997) take a slightly different view, seeing shame as potentially functional appeasement behavior. Appeasement is the process by which we pacify or placate others in situations of potential or actual conflict. A person anticipates aggression and displays appeasement behaviors (apologetic or submissive behavior) that prevents or reduces another's aggression. The use of appropriate appeasement displays may encourage reconciliation because the appeasement displays generate positive emotions toward the appeaser.

Chun-seng and Bond (2008) argue that for some cultures, open shaming serves a cohesive social function within groups, but not between ingroup and outgroup members. For example, shame plays a distinctive role in China and is even considered a socially appropriate emotion because it may discourage inappropriate behaviors (Li, Wang, & Fischer, 2004).

Emotion and Intercultural Communication Competence

Building peaceful communities with diverse cultures requires attention to the emotional considerations we have discussed. In this final section of the chapter, we present insights from three areas of scholarship: emotional competence, emotional support, and reconciliatory processes (Verbeek, 2009) with special attention to forgiveness and apology.

Emotional Competence as the Foundation of Peacebuilding

In her prologue to *The Development of Emotional Competence*, Carolyn Saarni (1999) explains that

> emotional competence sounds straightforward and simple, but in fact is subtle, complex, and sometimes downright elusive. This is because the ideas behind each of these concepts, namely, emotion, competence, resilience, self-efficacy, character, emotion elicitation, and social transaction, represent whole sets of theories and assumptions, all of them very much anchored in cultural context. (p. 2)

Saarni's work has served as a theoretical foundation for emotional competence and emotional development processes, and she is very sensitive to the need to recognize Western bias in any theories of emotional intelligence or emotional competence.

Matsumoto, LeRoux, and Yoo (2005) developed a "personal growth" model that is an emotional competence analogue for intercultural conflict situations. The four main ingredients to personal growth in relation to dealing with cultural differences are Emotion Regulation (ER), Critical Thinking (CT), Openness (OP), and Flexibility (FL). They argue that the key to achieving successful intercultural adjustment is the engagement of a personal growth process model where ways of thinking, person perception, and worldview are constantly being updated by sensitivity to cultural differences. Similar to the personal growth model, the literature on emotional competence can be summarized in terms of four basic principles of emotional competence. We present our list of these principles with brief discussions of the connection to cultural context.

Principle #1: Emotional Competence Requires Awareness of One's Own and Other's Emotions (Emotional Awareness)

Emotion competence requires the ability to identify, label, and articulate one's own emotions; to decode the emotional expressions of others; and to assess the intensity of their emotional experience. The most basic ability is identifying what you are feeling and why you are feeling it. Sound simple? Sadly, there are many people who are not able to do this easily. It may be because they have not had an opportunity to talk about their feelings. They may not have heard other people talking about emotions. For intercultural interaction, it is essential that you are aware of your cultural norms and rules with respect to emotional experience. And, of course, other-awareness is essential—do you have a sense of their culture vis-à-vis emotion?

Principle #2: Emotional Perspective Taking is the Root of Empathy and Caring, the Bedrock of a Caring Community (Emotional Perspective Taking)

In many ways, this entire book is about building emotional perspective taking and acting upon it in intercultural situations. Emotional perspective taking is the ability to recognize and understand what someone else is feeling and the kind of emotional experience they are having. To appreciate emotional perspective taking is to understand it in relation to a series of related terms: cognitive perspective taking, empathy, and caring.

Cognitive perspective taking is understanding how a person sees a situation, what their needs and interests are in that situation. Emotional perspective taking, or empathy, is understanding how someone feels about what is happening and why. The development of empathy is so very critical to emotional competence and the development of a moral society, as both Saarni (1999) and Greenspan (1997) agree. Only with emotional perspective taking can one "care" by trying to reduce the negative experience of the other.

Principle #3: Emotional Competence Requires Awareness of How Culture Influences Emotional Experience and Expression (Cultural Sensitivity)

Cultural sensitivity is the ability to understand cultural influences on appraisals leading to emotion, feeling rules and emotion scripts, and display rules for the expression of emotion. Cultural understanding extends perspective taking; it requires awareness that situations may not elicit the same emotions in others and that people experience emotion differently. As with perspective taking, these factors influence the inferences about how the other is feeling and attributions for the other's behavior.

Principle #4: Emotional Competence Requires the Strategic Expression of Emotion (Strategic Expression)

Strategic expression is the ability to regulate your emotional experience and expression in adaptive and beneficial ways. Emotional regulation means you learn to control your impulses to respond emotionally. In Adam Sandler's movie *Anger Management*, Jack Nicholson plays a psychologist who has problems with impulse control. In one scene, his car is blocked by another in a garage. He releases the brake on the other car and rolls it off the garage roof. Nicholson's character has work to do on impulse control. Another skill associated with strategic expression is delay of gratification. Like impulse control, delaying gratification requires that one not act immediately on one's feelings.

To the extent that we can increase our emotional competence, we can prevent communication that can damage intercultural relationships. It's a tall order, but one that we should aspire to.

Providing Culturally Sensitive Emotional Support

Cultural sensitivity and empathic perspective taking, two of the principles of emotional competence just discussed, are the foundation of competent intercultural caring. A critical way to show one cares is to provide emotional support to someone in need (Keele & Hammond, 1988). Sometimes, the person needs someone to listen and to allow the person to express their emotions without judgment, condemnation, or impatience (Rime, Corsini, & Herbette, 2002). But showing emotional support has to be culturally appropriate or the best intentions can fall quite short of the goal. Knapp and Vangelisti (1996) suggest the following:

> When the need for comfort has been determined and the helper is committed to providing comfort, it is important to find an environment conducive to comforting, to initiate the comforting when the recipient is ready, and to adapt the message to the history and capabilities of the person as well as the nature of the hurt. (p. 278)

The sensitive interaction systems theory (Barbee, Rowatt, & Cunningham, 1998) looks at providing emotional support and how the emotions of the support-seeker and the support-giver influence the process:

1. When people need support they may ask directly or indirectly, but the supporter has to be able to discern these requests in order to respond.

2. Once someone knows that the other person is seeking support, he has to decide whether to respond. Responding may be perceived as causing more harm or embarrassment depending on the culture of the other.

3. If a response is given, the supporter has to consider the best type of response. For example, problem-solving responses provide support by trying to solve (or suggest a solution to) the underlying problem without dealing with the other person's feelings about the problem. Solace behaviors support the person in pain by expressing closeness and trying to elicit positive emotions from the person (make the person feel better). Dismissive behaviors make the problem appear trivial or nonexistent. The person who is asked to be supportive may even use escape behaviors that make fun of the problem.

4. And then there is the question of how the support seeker responds to shows of emotional support or lack thereof. In the 1990s, Kathy Bates starred in *A House of Our Own*, a film about a poor widow struggling to build a home for her children. The woman was extremely proud and saw the emotional support of her well-meaning neighbors as further damage to her pride and honor. She rejected their help. Her rejection was offensive and almost inexplicably rude—a typical American response to someone refusing an offer of help. Yet, someone from an "honor culture" would more readily understand, endorse, and actively support Bates' response as the only "honorable" behavior.

Cultures differ in seeking emotional support. For example, several studies have found Asians to be less willing to seek support in times of stress than Americans (Burleson & Goldsmith, 1998). Burleson and Feng (2005) summarize several cultural factors that shape the giving and receiving of social support among African American, Hispanic American, Asian American, and Native American families.

Most cultures value responses that are more person-centered, where the sender adjusts the message to the relational, social, and cultural context of the receiver. For example, one study (Samter et al., 1997) examined person-centered responses in African Americans, Asian Americans, and European Americans. All of the groups found comforting messages low in person-centeredness as the least sensitive and least effective; and comforting messages high in person-centeredness as the most effective.

At universities, faculty and staff are often concerned about providing appropriate emotional support to international students (Mortenson, 2006). Students from other nations (who are studying in the U.S.) often refrain from seeking emotional support due to cultural norms and, as a result, suffer from stress-related illnesses significantly more than their American counterparts. Ironically, even though they may not request emotional support, research shows they value it as much as American students (Burleson & Mortenson, 2003) and prefer emotion-focused support messages over both problem-focused and emotion-avoidant support messages.

Reconciliation: Repairing and Rebuilding Relationships

When rifts between cultural groups occur, we need to find ways to reconcile and heal in order to rebuild community. In the literature on conflict resolution, especially in the later development of the field that identifies with "conflict transformation" and stresses the goal of reconciliation between parties formerly divided by deep-rooted conflict, the concepts of apology and forgiveness loom large (Avruch & Wang, 2005). Lederach (1995; 1996; 1997) suggests that conflict transformation is essentially a change of perceptions of issues, actions, and others on both the personal and systemic level. Lederach describes conflict transformation as the following: "to envision and respond to the ebb and flow of social conflict as life-giving opportunities for creating constructive change processes that reduce violence, increase justice in direct interaction and social structures, and respond to real-life problems in human relationships" (Lederach, 2014, p. 14).

Conflict transformation is not a decision-making process; rather, it concentrates on developing empathy and awareness of the other to enable coexistence and even shared community. Lederach (1995) and like-minded colleagues also argue that conflict transformation is inherently honoring the cultural dimensions of the conflict because to transform successfully requires understanding of the shared assumptions and underlying values of the party, the cultural foundation of their conflict. Instead of transferring outside knowledge—knowledge developed in a different setting, or expert knowledge disconnected from the cultural vernacular—the transformation of a conflict needs to put to use the resources, including the cultural forms, available within the conflict setting itself.

Dietrich's (2013) analysis of conflict transformation centers on the energy of conflict and how transformative approaches unlock that energy to enable change. As Sutzl (2016, p. 5) explains:

> Conflict transformation thus goes beyond a movement on the surface of a conflict that Lederach calls an "episode" in which "physical violence is suppressed, the extremes of structural violence mitigated, and a new narrative form, a compromise, the famous win-win solution, is found" (Dietrich, 2013, p. 8). As a result, the energy of the conflict is not transformed, it is merely shifted elsewhere. Using a musicological term, Dietrich calls this a "conflict transposition." The score (or conflict) remains the same, but being rendered in a different pitch, the mood changes: "A melody is perceived differently and gives rise to different feelings when rendered in A major as opposed to F major. It is precisely this, and nothing more, that is done in conflict transposition" (p. 8). Conflict transformation, by contrast, claims to alter the dissonant melody itself, "utilizing its urgent energy creatively in order to form a new harmony based on what exists" (p. 9).

Conflict resolution/management is a process of decision-making, often with the support of a neutral third party (e.g., conflict coach, facilitator, mediator, factfinder, arbitrator) who helps parties arrive at agreements about actions, definition of relationships, distribution of resources, etc., that are driving the conflict (Sutzl, 2016). Chris Mitchell (2003) argued that conflict transformation focuses more on healing and long-term plans for integration of conflicting parties where conflict resolution concentrates on the immediate and short-term issues and deeper interests that keep parties at an impasse. Transformation focuses on conflict aftermath because parties must deal with conflict "residues"—traumas, fears, hurts, and hatreds—that can lie dormant, waiting to re-emerge and poison the social fabric.

Reconciliation is the result of healing and the commitment to relationship. Reconciliation is an inherently emotional experience and accomplishment, emotionally created and emotionally resonant. In conflicts it is marked by a redefinition of a relationship or a return to relationship based on mutual interests and respect. Kriesberg (1998) viewed reconciliation as a "relatively amicable relationship typically established after a rupture in relations involving one-sided or mutual infliction of extreme injury" and outlines the steps taken by former rivals on their way to reconciliation: "They acknowledge the reality of the terrible acts that were perpetrated; accept with compassion those who committed injurious conduct, as well as acknowledging each other's sufferings; believe that their injustices are being redressed and anticipate mutual security and well-being" (pp. 351–352). Reconciliation requires a number of elements to be in place and to be publicly performed in many cases of conflict.

When transformative conflict is enacted, how can we understand the levels of reconciliation that build toward the apex of healing and reconnection? Auerbach's (2009) Reconciliation Pyramid was developed to analyze and direct reconciliation and transformation in identity-based, intractable, and escalated conflicts—conflicts that are often intercultural conflicts. Shown in Figure 5.1, Auerbach's (2009) theory "presumes that partners in an identity conflict will not be able to reach reconciliation unless they become acquainted with each other's narratives, acknowledge their legitimacy, and be ready to incorporate them into their own" (p. 298).

The starting point of the reconciliation process is becoming acquainted with the clashing narratives relating to the core issues of the conflict. It is absolutely foundational that conflicting parties engage in some process that educates them about the experience of the other and their perspectives on the conflict. Becoming acquainted leads to enough familiarity with the parties' narratives that parties can openly acknowledge and then empathize with the "other's" lived experience of the conflict. Empathizing with the other optimally promotes an understanding of the conflict as a shared responsibility so parties can see their role and responsibility in the experience of the other(s). The restitution, responsibility, and apology stages all involve understandings and actions that publicly take responsibility. Ideally all three components are enacted. One repairs tangible harm by performing restitution, explains their responsibility for harm against the other and takes responsibility, and asks forgiveness through an apology. The process of reconciliation reaches its apex when the two sides seriously and honestly consider replacing their old narratives with new, integrated narratives, based on the mutual acknowledgment of past miseries and a joint vision of the future.

Figure 5.1   The reconciliation pyramid was developed to analyze and direct reconciliation and transformation in identity-based, intractable, and escalated conflicts. (Based on Auerbach, 2009)

Forgiveness

Worthington (2005) views forgiveness as two distinct but related processes. *Decisional forgiveness* is a choice to reduce negative behavior toward the offender and (if possible) restore positive behavior toward the offender. However, one can make a sincere decision to forgive yet still be emotionally unforgiving (e.g., angry, resentful, hurt). *Emotional forgiveness* is the internal experience of replacing negative emotions with positive other-oriented emotions (e.g., empathy, love, compassion). When we talk about forgiveness in this section, we mean both the decisional and the emotional aspects of forgiving. Forgiveness is the emotional component to reconciliation. It is the ability to feel differently, more positively, about someone who you perceive to have harmed you, either intentionally or not (Hargrave, 1994).

Cultures differ on willingness to embrace and express forgiveness. One study (Paz, Neto, & Mullet, 2008) assessed forgiveness among Chinese and Western Europeans. Although the initial expectation was that Chinese, as a collectivist culture, would be more prone to forgive, it forgot to consider whether the harm was coming from a member of the ingroup or outgroup. As a result, the study found that although the cultures were equally likely to forgive, the Chinese had longer-lasting resentment than Americans and felt the offense was more serious when the offender was from the outgroup. Similarly, Watkins and his colleagues (2011) found that collectivist cultures in Nepal were much more likely to forgive than their Western counterparts. For the Nepalese, forgiveness was necessary to reintegrate transgressors into society.

Not surprisingly, collectivist cultures tend to see forgiveness as more than an individual emotion; they see it as a social process. For example, the Maori (the indigenous people of New Zealand) see forgiveness as requiring an explicit inter-action that shows commitment to healing the relationship from both the victim and the transgressor. Without this ritual enactment of forgiveness, the relationship remains unbroken and the harm remains present (Rata, Liu, & Hanke, 2008).

Similarly, the Hmong regard transgressions as against the family or social group rather than against the individual and, as such, feel the extended family has to be involved in the offering and acceptance of forgiveness (Sandage, Hill, & Vang, 2003). In Hmong society, forgiving is related less to the offense than to the sincerity in the emotions and behaviors of the perpetrator following the transgression. The act of forgiveness and the act of repentance has to meet certain standards.

Perhaps nowhere in recent history has the standard of forgiveness been more eloquently enacted than in South Africa, where the Truth and Reconciliation Commission modeled for the world the importance of social and public forgiveness to heal a fractured society and build a future community.

Apology

> "Having looked the beast of the past in the eye, having asked and received forgiveness and having made amends, let us shut the door to the past—not in order to forget it but in order not to allow it to imprison us."
>
> —Bishop Desmond Tutu

While Hargrave acknowledges that forgiving can heal relationships, he also points out that it is very risky, as it requires someone to enter back into a relation-ship with someone who has hurt them badly. That is not likely to happen unless the other person takes responsibility through the form of apology (McCullough, Pargament, & Thoresen, 2000). In a *Psychology Today* article on apology, Aaron Lazare states:

> A genuine apology offered and accepted is one of the most profound interactions of civilized people. It has the power to restore damaged relationships, be they on a small scale, between two people, such as intimates, or on a grand scale, between groups of people, even nations. If done correctly, an apology can heal humiliation and generate forgiveness. (1995, p. 40)

Several examples of apologies for significant national or international conflicts are presented by Linda Stamato (2008), who notes that "in restorative justice programs and truth and reconciliation commissions . . . purifying memory seeks to open the mind and heart to a future, while being aware of, but not burdened or immobilized by, the past" (p. 389).

There are general standards for apology that cross cultures. An apology should (1) acknowledge that some moral, norm, or rule in a relationship was violated; (2) accept responsibility for that violation; (3) provide an explanation for the offense; (4) communicate that the behavior was not intended as a

personal affront or, if intended, make that clear; and (5) make an offer of reparation. These basics of apology have been found to be fairly consistent across
cultures (Byon, 2005).

Yet, as Kasanga and Lwanga-Lumu (2007) note, there are enough differences
in the performance expectations of apology across cultures that a culturally insen-
sitive apology may cause even more conflict or disharmony. The following two
stories show how the performance of apology elements can make a huge difference in their effectiveness:

> When American president Bill Clinton went to Kigali, Rwanda, in 1998, to apol-
> ogize for the world's failure to intervene in the Rwandan genocide, observers
> noted that the engines of Air Force One were never turned off.
>
> Clinton was there for less than two hours and never left the airfield. One
> African observer turned to another and offered this telling explanation for why
> the apology "didn't work." "If you go round in the car to say sorry to a neigh-
> bor, it's always good to turn off the engine. Just for a minute at least. Don't you
> think?" (Stamato, 2008, p. 392)
>
> Consider, in contrast, the following example. When Willy Brandt was Chan-
> cellor of West Germany he visited Warsaw in December 1970. A newspaper ac-
> count shows a photograph with the following description appearing alongside
> it, "A man is outdoors, kneeling on the ground at the top of a short flight of
> broad steps, his body stiff and upright. His hands are clasped in front of him,
> very pale against the blackness of his raincoat. His head . . . is bowed so that his
> gaze appears to be fixed on a spot on the ground perhaps two feet in front of
> him. He appears oblivious to the large crowd that surrounds him at a respect-
> ful distance. Many in the crowd are holding cameras . . . recording the scene
> at the memorial to the half-million Jews of the city's ghetto murdered by the
> Nazis. . . . A seminal moment for West Germany. . . . There's not been a gesture
> like it since." (Stamato, 2008, p. 393)

Summary

Intercultural communication has emotional underpinnings that require serious attention. Intercultural communication competence requires an appreciation
that cultures have similarities and differences in the ways they value and express
certain emotions. While many cultures use the same appraisals to trigger positive
and negative emotions, there are strong differences in the experience of "self-conscious" emotions depending on the individualism or collectivism of the culture.
The role of identity, as we have seen in so many other chapters, is paramount.
Whether construed individually or collectively, identity issues are one of the most
important determinants of the nature and degree of emotional experience. We can't
assume that others will feel the same way we do in a situation. This is a significant
barrier to empathy. When we feel as others do, we find it much easier to understand their motivations and their behavior. Without this "natural" connection, we
have to work harder to appreciate how they are emotionally responding to intercultural interaction.

PUT IT INTO PRACTICE   **5.2**

Imagine Your Cross-Cultural Apology

Think of a current or recent situation in which you had a conflict with someone who was from a different culture than you are. It is best if you think of a conflict where your behavior was less than ideal and where you may have done something that was seen as offensive to the other party. Perhaps this situation involved a fellow classmate, roommate, or employee. It may even be a situation where the conflict was with a neighbor or a professor.

1. Write a brief description of the conflict and the behavior you feel you should apologize for.

2. How do you think the other party felt about the situation? Why do you think it may have been offensive?

3. How did you feel about the conflict? How are your feelings affecting your ability to apologize to the other?

4. Looking at the guidelines for an effective apology, write out what you would say and do to apologize to the other party. Be as specific as you can.

5. If you have the opportunity to enact this apology, reflect after the fact on how the experience of apology affected you and the other party.

Intergroup emotion theory offers one way of understanding how feelings about ingroups and outgroups can escalate or de-escalate conflicts between cultures. The more we identify with our own ingroup, the stronger our emotional reactions are to an outgroup. But those emotional reactions can feed prejudice or respect.

We also explored the power of reconciliatory behaviors that produce forgiveness and acceptance of others and enable repair of emotional tears in the social fabric. Emotional competence provides the foundation for empathic perspective taking and cultural sensitivity in emotional analysis and response.

QUESTIONS

1. How does the definition of emotion presented in this chapter differ from the ways that you have previously thought of emotion? Is it difficult for you to see emotion as a form of rationality?

2. The chapter contains research about how cultural differences affect emotional appraisal and emotional experience. What about the influence of a multicultural background on emotional experience? What are your assumptions about this?

3. To what extent is it possible for someone from a culture that does not experience certain emotions strongly (like shame) to truly empathize with a person who has that emotion? In your opinion, what are the realistic limits of emotional perspective taking?

4. What is the role of the media in intergroup emotional responses? Do the media make it more difficult or less difficult for people to feel positively or negatively about another culture?

5. Sharing emotional experience is often facilitated through the arts. What are some ways that we might use the arts to help people from different cultures understand the emotional range and emotional significance in other cultures? Can you think of specific examples where drama, dance, music, etc., helped you tap the emotional perspective of someone from another culture?

6

Culture and Nonverbal Communication

KEY TERMS

backchannels
body modification
communication accommodation
  theory
contact cultures
context differentiation

onvergence
cultural display rules
dialect theory of facial expressions
divergence
emblematic gestures
high-context communication

KEY TERMS (CONT.)

iconic gestures
immediacy
low-context communication
masking smiles
paralanguage

primary expressions of emotion
proxemics
turn-taking signals
word

During the Gulf War in 1991, Paul was stationed in Turkey and then in northern Iraq. He recalls one particular trip to division headquarters:

> Once I was there, I went into a tent where some leaders of Kurdish refugees were assigned. I walked in, bowed politely and then found a chair, sat down and propped up my feet to relax. The three Arab men who were there began to chatter and soon bolted from the tent. After about 30 minutes, a lieutenant colonel came in and explained that I had just insulted the Arabs by displaying the bottoms of my boots in their presence. As he said, by my actions I had told them that I felt superior to them. (Remland, 2017)

Trying only to get comfortable, Paul meant no disrespect. But as you will see in this chapter, much of our face-to-face communication takes place without the use of words, and all too often with little or no conscious intent to send a message. That these intercultural exchanges can have significant and long-lasting social and political consequences for our peacebuilding efforts underscores the need for competence in nonverbal communication. In fact, a growing number of incidents such as the one reported above have led to the adoption of overseas training programs that include educating military and civilian personnel about cultural differences in nonverbal communication. In one such program, adopted by the Pentagon, soldiers in Iraq use a video game that places them in simulated, three-dimensional social situations and then evaluates how well they understood and responded to the language, gestures, and expressions of the local population (Associated Press, 2006). Another program trains US soldiers in Iraq to recognize indigenous emotional cues that could lead to confusion and misunderstandings (Rosenthal et al., 2009).

A recent example that further illustrates the importance of understanding nonverbal cues so we can avoid confusion and misunderstanding occurred at the Tokyo Summer Olympics in 2021. The American silver medalist in the shot put, Raven Saunders, raised her arms in an X gesture above her head while standing on the podium. The International Olympic Committee (IOC) immediately considered whether this gesture violated its rules banning all forms of protest on the medal podium. However, after conducting its own review, the US Olympic Committee concluded (and the IOC concurred) that Saunders' gesture was only a peaceful expression in support of racial and social justice and did not violate the rule against protests on the podium during the medal ceremony (Ganguly, 2021).

This chapter examines the nature of nonverbal communication, some important cultural differences in nonverbal forms of communication, the particular obstacles and challenges that arise from cultural differences, and finally, the elements of nonverbal communication competence that facilitate the community-building aims of our intercultural transactions.

The Nature of Nonverbal Communication

In Chapter 1 we noted that nonverbal communication represents a way of exchanging messages without the use of words. In face-to-face interactions this includes the use of clothing, ***body modification*** (e.g., tattoos and piercings), personal space, touch, eye contact, facial expressions, gestures, tone of voice, articulation, pauses, and silence. As we elaborate below, these numerous channels of communication afford us an opportunity to send and interpret messages in ways and for purposes that are fundamentally different from those of spoken language.

What Are the Properties of Nonverbal Communication?

Since nonverbal communication does not involve the use of words, we begin with a simple question: what is a word? A ***word*** represents the smallest "free-standing" unit of meaning in a formal language governed by rules of grammar, punctuation, syntax, and composition. When we use hand signals in place of spoken words, as we do in American Sign Language for instance, the hand gestures function as words. When we send text messages we are also using words. So verbal communication is not limited to speech and includes written as well as oral modes of expression. But a nonverbal signal, even one that is widely recognized and understood such as a handshake or a head nod, is not part of a formal language (i.e., there are no rules of grammar, punctuation, etc.). Moreover, while we need to learn a language, many nonverbal signals comprise a biologically shared, innate form of communication that we generally do not need to learn. Here we briefly consider four basic properties of nonverbal communication (Remland, 2017).

The first basic property is that *many nonverbal signals are universal*; they are used and recognized by all humans. Some examples of these signals are blushing as a sign of embarrassment, crying as a sign of distress, hugging as an expression of comfort, smiling as a show of joy, and glaring as sign of anger. Still, as you will see later in this chapter, our uses and interpretations of these signals are influenced by the cultural context in which they occur. As one example, certain facial features are seen as attractive in males and females, regardless of culture (e.g., facial symmetry), and people all over the world attribute a host of positive qualities to persons who have attractive faces, a beauty bias known as the "halo effect." But the particular qualities we attribute to attractive people differ depending on the values of our culture. For example, Koreans are likely to see good-looking Koreans as having integrity and being concerned for others. This reflects their high regard for these personal qualities—a characteristic of most collectivistic cultures (see Chapter 4). These qualities are much less likely to be part of the "attractiveness halo" found in individualistic cultures such as the United States. Recent studies of undergraduates in Taiwan, a collectivistic culture, confirm this tendency to stereotype attractive faces in a culturally desirable way (Chen & Shaffer, 1997; Shaffer, Crepaz, & Sun, 2000).

Hugging is a universal symbol of comforting a person in distress.

The second property of nonverbal communication is that *many signals are sent and received spontaneously*. Unlike communication with words, which brings the exchange of messages to the forefront of our thinking, nonverbal communication often takes place below the radar, automatically and outside of conscious awareness. For instance, when something frightens us, it triggers a spontaneous expression on our face (sending a signal) that in turn triggers an automatic response in the person who sees our face (reception of the signal). In both cases (sending the signal and receiving it), the brain responds before the exchange registers in conscious thought, the hallmark of a biologically shared, hardwired system of communication. Yet, while we routinely participate in these stimulus-response exchanges involving our physical appearance, facial expressions, body movements, gaze patterns, and vocal intonations, the more conscious we become of the process and the more culture begins to exert its influence, prompting us to modify our actions and judgments. For example, although the facial expression and recognition of fear is often spontaneous, the things that cause us to show fear (or any other emotion) can vary from culture to culture (see Chapter 5). In addition, our attempts to inhibit or exaggerate the expression of fear, and our interpretations of the fearful expression, often depend on the influence of cultural norms, rules, and biases (see section below on facial expressions).

The third property of nonverbal communication is that *many nonverbal signals are iconic*. This means that the nonverbal expression in some way resembles or graphically represents the content of the message (the *referent*). Many tattoos are iconic forms of expression (e.g., tattoo of a snake), as are *iconic gestures* and body movements that mime some kind of action (e.g., drinking from a glass or making a phone call). This property is unique to nonverbal forms of communication because the words in a language do not look like their referents (e.g., the word *chair* doesn't look like a chair). This property also allows us to overcome the language barriers associated with many intercultural encounters. For example, if you are hungry and looking for a place to dine while traveling in a foreign country, and you can't find someone who understands your language, you may still be able to get your message across by miming the act of eating, conveying the message without using words (see Put It Into Practice 6.1). One recent example of how iconic gestures can transcend language barriers also occurred at the Tokyo Summer Olympics in 2021, where it was common to see many athletes use the heart-shape hand gesture to communicate a clear message of love and affection to the millions of fans unable to attend the events because of the COVID-19 pandemic.

The fourth property of nonverbal communication is that *many nonverbal signals occur simultaneously*. Whereas speech is a single channel of communication that conveys messages one word at a time, nonverbal communication conveys messages through multiple channels at the same time. Moreover, verbal communication is a turn-taking activity with participants periodically switching roles of speaker (message sender) and listener (message receiver). In contrast, nonverbal communication lets participants assume the roles of sender and receiver at the same time. One of the many consequences of this property is that we can use nonverbal cues to regulate the turn-taking that characterizes verbal interactions, signaling when a listener wants to speak or continue listening, and when a speaker wants to listen or continue speaking. As with most forms of nonverbal communication, cultural differences in the use and recognition of these simple, taken-for-granted *turn-taking signals* can lead to misunderstandings or uncomfortable breakdowns in the give and take of ordinary conversations.

What Are the Functions of Nonverbal Communication?

Humans, like all other animal species, have developed unique signaling systems enabling individuals to identify themselves, relate to others, express their intentions, and deliver vital information about their environment. These are the *primary functions* of nonverbal communication—the communication-related activities that are necessary for the survival of a species (Remland, 2017). Nonverbal signaling systems evolved to perform these basic functions.

The Identification Function

The most basic and universal function of nonverbal communication is signaling one's identity. Through physical appearance and various behaviors we signal our age, race, gender, ethnic origin, social class, occupation, values, personality, and more. Like other species, we inherit much of this nonverbal repertoire because

---

PUT IT INTO PRACTICE 6.1

Miming Your Own Business

Instructions:

This exercise can be done in small groups or in front of the class. Imagine being in a place where you cannot speak the language of the people and they cannot speak yours. How will you communicate if you must? Try finding out how well you can communicate the following messages without uttering a single word.

Messages:

1. My friend is very sick, where is the nearest hospital?

2. My car just broke down and I need help getting it repaired.

3. I'm looking for an electronics store so I can buy a computer.

4. Is there a zoo here in the city?

5. Where is the nearest restroom?

6. I'm very thirsty. Where can I get some water?

7. I need directions to the hotel I'm staying in.

8. Do you know where the train station is?

(Adapted from Remland, 2017)

---

of its survival value, such as the need to exchange information about gender and group membership. Unlike other animals, however, we have the ability to invent the signals we use for identification, giving rise to all sorts of cultural differences in dress and demeanor, many of which we discuss in this chapter.

The Relationship Function

We also communicate nonverbally to create or discourage attachments with others (relational intimacy) and to intimidate or appease them (relational control). So basic are these nonverbal signals that it is impossible to engage in any face-to-face interaction without expressing some degree of intimacy (i.e., liking–disliking; interest–disinterest) and some degree of control (i.e., dominance–submissiveness; high status–low status). For instance, we exchange messages of intimacy through physical contact, eye contact, close proximity, smiling, and tone of voice. Of course, much of this communication is universal, but that shouldn't obscure the reality of cultural differences. As we point out later in this chapter, cultural norms regarding public displays of affection, conversational distances, and the meanings of same-sex touching, for example, vary considerably (see the Culture Shock box on the next page for an example).

We also rely on nonverbal communication to exchange messages of relational control, addressing questions of authority, status, and power. Like other animals, we stare, growl, and puff up when attempting to intimidate our adversaries. Other actions that perform a similar function include invading the space or territory of another individual, such as getting too close, shouting, or touching, and expressing powerful emotions such as anger, disgust, and contempt (Remland, 2017). In contrast, many of our appeasement displays are the opposite: avoiding the gaze of another, speaking softly, shrinking our bodies, backing away, smiling, and expressing weak emotions (e.g., fear, shame, embarrassment). As with messages of intimacy, messages of control often vary across cultures. For example, the value orientations of some cultures encourage its members to behave in ways that affirm differences in status and power between people (see Chapter 4). In these *high power-distance* societies, persons are more likely to act according to their relative status in a relationship (e.g., a young person might show respect to an older person by avoiding eye contact or speaking softly) than they are in *low power-distance* cultures.

The Emotion Function

Another primary function of nonverbal communication is emotional expression. Some of our facial expressions are innate signals of emotions or social motives. Researchers Mark Knapp and Judith Hall (2008) reviewed numerous studies on the facial expressions of children deprived of hearing and sight, infants, nonhuman primates, and persons from both literate and preliterate cultures. Given the remarkable similarities observed in the expressions of these groups, they concluded, "A genetic component passed on to members of the human species seems probable for this behavior" (p. 72).

Exactly how many emotions we express nonverbally is not known, although the general consensus is that the number of primary emotions—those that are

---

CULTURE SHOCK

Holding Hands

When I was in high school there were two new girls in my gym class who were friends and transfer students from China. Every day in my gym class we would go straight to the locker room, change, and go to the bleachers to sit and wait for the two teachers to begin with roll call. When we were all sitting there, the two new girls emerged from the locker room and they were holding hands as they walked over to the bleachers. Everyone assumed they were lesbians, and there was a lot of murmuring and gossip going on about the incident. It wasn't until the next class period, after our teachers had gotten word of the rumors, that they informed us that in China women often hold hands as an expression of friendship.

—Kaitlin

(Remland, 2017)

---

signaled and recognized similarly by all humans—is probably in the range of six to ten. Based on their groundbreaking cross-cultural work, researchers Paul Ekman and Wallace Friesen (1976) identified these *primary expressions of emotion as anger*: happiness, sadness, surprise, fear, disgust, and contempt. Other researchers also include emotions of shame, guilt, and interest (Izard, 1977; Tompkins, 1962).

Following rules we learn at a relatively young age about how and whether to reveal our feelings in social situations, our emotional exchanges may reflect the influence of culture. These *cultural display rules* can lead us to misrepresent our true feelings (Ekman & Friesen, 1969). Cultural taboos against showing anger in public, for example, are very common. Someone who feels enraged might show only mild disapproval or might even cover up the anger with a social smile. This seems to be especially true among Asian populations, where people routinely use *masking smiles* to conceal negative feelings. Cultural differences in smiling may in fact reflect actual differences in how people relate to the challenges of everyday life.

The Delivery Function

When we send a text message, we don't use our voice, face, or body to get the message across. When we talk to someone over the phone we use our voice but not our face or body. When we speak to others face to face, we use our voice, face, and body in ways that not only reinforce the verbal content of our message but often in ways that alter the meaning and impact of our words. The delivery function of nonverbal communication is a *speech-related* function that includes the many ways in which nonverbal behavior replaces and facilitates speech (Remland, 2017). Ekman and Friesen (1969) identify six basic ways:

1. *Nonverbal signals can emphasize our words*. We use gestures, facial expressions, movement, changes in vocal volume or speech rate, and deliberate pauses to highlight the text of our message.

Researchers have identified seven universal facial expressions of emotion. Top row, left to right: anger, surprise, happiness; bottom row, left to right: disgust, contempt, sadness, fear.

2. *Nonverbal signals can repeat what we say*. We can say yes to someone while nodding our head; we can order three drinks in a restaurant while holding up three fingers; if someone asks us where the telephone is, we can point to it while saying, "Over there."

3. *Nonverbal signals can substitute for words*. Instead of speaking we can shake our head to indicate no, or use a thumbs-up sign to say "nice job." We sometimes use nonverbal signals to express things that we can't afford to say in words. Coaches and players on a football team, for example, use a secret code of nonverbal signals in place of words so they can exchange messages that won't be understood by opposing players and coaches. And as we noted earlier, we can use iconic gestures to overcome the language barriers associated with many intercultural encounters (i.e., miming).

4. *Nonverbal signals can regulate speech*. We use gestures and vocalizations to alternate the conversational roles of speaking and listening, without the need for verbal declarations (e.g., "It's my turn to talk").

5. *Nonverbal signals can contradict what we say*. We often send contradictory messages on purpose. One way is through the use of sarcasm, putting a negative nonverbal spin on a positively worded message. Carl tells Jackie that he thought the service at the restaurant was truly exceptional, but he rolls his eyes when he says it. We can also use nonverbal signals to say things facetiously, for example, teasing someone by saying you had a lousy time, with a grin on your face (to signal that you really had a good time).

6. *Nonverbal signals can complement the verbal content of our message*. One of the special features of some speech-related gestures is that they

sometimes provide information that is not contained in the text of the message. For instance, if you were telling some people about something you saw while you were alone eating lunch in a restaurant the previous day, and as you spoke you used your hands to mime the act of eating a sandwich, but you didn't *say* you were eating a sandwich (maybe you just said you were eating lunch), listeners who saw your gesture would have some idea of what you ate for lunch.

The Impact of Culture on Nonverbal Communication

Because much of our nonverbal communication is universal—signaling key elements of our identity, building relationships, expressing our emotions, and delivering verbal messages—it is easy for us to overlook the influence of culture on this basic form of communication. Yet as you will see in this chapter, the influence of culture can at times be quite profound. In this section, after briefly discussing the overall cultural context in which nonverbal communication takes place, we consider the impact of culture on the various *channels* of face-to-face nonverbal communication: physical appearance, dress, personal space, touch, eye contact, facial expressions, gestures, vocal intonation, speech accent, pauses, and silence. Of course, as we address these cultural differences you should bear in mind that continuing trends toward globalization (bringing diverse groups of people into regular contact) are making it less likely that some of the differences observed in the past are still true today.

The Cultural Context of Nonverbal Communication

In Chapter 1 we explained that cultures create the *symbols* as well as the *rules and rituals* that shape the way we communicate with others in various situations, determining the meaning of a gesture or dictating how to behave properly with the parents of a new friend or the clients of a new employer. Many culture-bound rules and rituals grow out of the divergent worldviews we discussed in Chapter 4. For example, display rules governing the appropriateness of showing certain emotions in certain situations often differ according to the individualistic or collectivistic orientations of a culture (see section below on expressions of emotion). Many expressions of culture also emerge from the unique customs and conventions of a particular society or social group (e.g., traditional costumes, greeting rituals, symbolic gestures), but there are also other, perhaps more subtle manifestations of culture as well.

According to one such account, nonverbal communication carries more weight in some cultures than in others. That is, the amount of information conveyed through nonverbal channels of communication compared to the verbal text of a message varies from culture to culture. As we discussed in Chapter 4, Hall (1976) wrote extensively about the many differences between what he called **high-context** and **low-context** cultures, the former using a different type of communication than the latter. As he explains:

A high-context (HC) communication or message is one in which most of the information is either in the physical context or internalized in the person, while very little is in the coded, explicit, transmitted part of the message. A low-context (LC) communication is just the opposite; i.e., the mass of the information is vested in the explicit code. (p. 90)

The context of communication, which includes who we are addressing, where we are, what we are doing, what our prior experiences are, and so forth, is always an important element in determining the meaning of a message. But it also refers to a style of communication that differs systematically from one culture to another. Low-context cultures typically embrace an individualistic orientation that puts a premium on self-expression, unlike high-context cultures that are more collectivistic and therefore much less self-centered. The list of low-context countries includes Canada, the United States, Australia, New Zealand and most of Europe (not Spain and Portugal). Arab, Asian, South American, and African countries belong to those classified as high-context cultures.

Social psychologist David Matsumoto and his colleagues offer a related, though distinctly different way of classifying cross-cultural differences in communication: the degree to which a culture encourages members to change their communication behavior from one context to another, a cultural (and also individual) trait they refer to as *context differentiation* (CD) (Matsumoto et al., 2009). People in high-context differentiation (HCD) cultures are more likely to vary the way they dress and their emotional expressions from one situation to another than are people in low-context differentiation (LCD) cultures. Thus, inconsistency in behavior is the norm in HCD cultures whereas consistency in behavior is the norm in LCD cultures. In a recent study of 32 countries around the world, Matsumoto and his colleagues found that CD was positively related to power distance and negatively related to individualism. In other words, persons in high-power distance and collectivistic cultures—such as Mexico, Egypt, and Japan—are more likely to change their communication behavior according to the situation they are in, compared to persons in low power distance and individualistic cultures, such as America, Israel, and Sweden.

Cross-Cultural Differences in Nonverbal Communication

Thinking about the cultural context of our everyday interactions draws our attention to the dynamic and complex interplay between nonverbal signaling as an evolutionary product of our biology (inborn, universal, and spontaneous) and nonverbal communication as a fundamental product of our environment (learned, cultural, and deliberate behavior). In this section we consider some of the specific ways that nonverbal communication varies across cultures.

Physical Appearance

Our racial and ethnic identity is closely tied to our physical appearance (e.g., skin color, facial features). Some physical features we attribute to differences in race are the natural by-products of geography, as Nancy Etcoff (1999) points out in her book *Survival of the Prettiest*:

The features that signify our identity and ancestry evolved partly as adaptations to climactic conditions, just as body shapes and skin tones did. Noses carry air into the lungs. They evolved into long narrow shapes in climates where the air was cold or dry and needed to be warmed and moistened before reaching the lungs. People of northern European or Middle Eastern ancestry often inherit long noses with narrow nostrils (perfect for restricting air flow). In humid environments, the short wide noses common to many African and Asian people are more efficient. (p. 134)

An attractive appearance in one culture may look odd or even repulsive to people in another culture. Exotic ritualistic practices such as neck stretching, lip enlargements, earlobe plugs, and teeth filing represent the beautifying practices common in some parts of the world. Of course, liposuction, hair implants, face-lifts, laser surgery, and the like, while not the least bit extraordinary to many Westerners, may seem abhorrent to people in other parts of the world. Some forms of body modification, such as tattooing, can serve any number of functions and typically are not intended to make someone more attractive. For example, people can get tattoos for cultural identity (e.g., ethnicity, religion, race, group membership), delivery (e.g., values and beliefs), or relationships (e.g., the face of a partner, relative, or idol). Some surveys indicate that tattooing has become a worldwide practice although overall frequencies vary from one study to another. For instance, one survey of different countries found that Italy, Sweden, and the United States had the largest percentages of people with at least one tattoo (48%, 47%, and 46%, respectively (Armstrong, 2018). Another study of more than 11,000 participants with fewer but some different countries found that about 18% of the respondents said they had at least one tattoo (Kluger et al., 2019). Both studies found that the proportion of respondents saying they had tattoos differed by country. For example, in the survey of 19 countries noted above, those with more than the average percentage of people saying they had tattoos (more than 38%) included (in rank order) Italy, Sweden, the United States, Australia, Argentina, Spain, Denmark, and the United Kingdom. The countries with fewer than the average were

CULTURE SHOCK

Different Shades of Black Identity

If you are a light-skinned Black person, you are looked upon as "uppity" or thinking that you're too good. This is something I have come across a lot. For my first year of college, I attended the first historically Black college, Lincoln University. It was my first time being around that many African Americans (the high school I attended was mostly Caucasian). I am naturally shy, so I would walk around not speaking to anyone. In many cases I would walk around looking at the ground or just with no expression on my face whatsoever. I was viewed as the "uppity" light-skinned girl who thought she was too good for everyone else.

—Ami

(Remland, 2017)

Brazil, France, Germany, Greece, South Africa, Russia, Canada, Mexico, Turkey, and Israel (Holmes, 2018). In this particular survey, however, while suggesting cultural differences, the differences between countries were quite small and no doubt may be changing from one year to the next. There may also be cultural differences in the meanings and motivations for getting tattoos. For example, the primary motivation for respondents in China was expressing love and affection;

[Top] Women from the Padaung Tribe in Loikaw, Myanmar (Burma), display the brass rings on their necks. [Bottom] A group of women attend the Desert Festival in Jaisalmer, India. Traditional forms of dress and body modification are often distinctive signs of one's cultural identity.

in Russia the primary motivation was embellishment; in France, Brazil, and the US, the primary motivation was representing some important milestone in one's life (Kluger, Seite, & Taieb, 2019).

In many Arab and West African societies, obesity signifies wealth and wide hips in women signal fertility and sensuality. There are also cultural differences in how people choose to modify and adorn their bodies. Kenya's Maasai women not only pierce their ears, they stretch them. After piercing, a young girl's ears are hung with heavy pendants. Over the years, the weight gradually pulls the lobes down nearly to her shoulders. In Ethiopia, girls have their lower lips pierced and implanted with baked clay discs. Larger discs are inserted to increase the size of the lip hole and improve their chances of finding a mate. The size of a girl's disc also indicates how many cattle her family demands as a wedding gift. In Melanesia, men find toothless women more babyish and therefore more appealing. Women in parts of Angola knock out their front teeth and some women in the Congo file their teeth to a point (Remland, 2017).

In addition to physical features, clothing often communicates culture. Although Western dress has spread in popularity throughout much of the industrialized world, we still can see the traditional costumes of many religious and ethnic groups (e.g., the Japanese kimono, the Indian sari, the Scottish kilt, the African dashiki). Most of us have also seen the clothing associated with any number of well-known co-cultural groups that are spread across the United States (e.g., the Amish). People all over the world alter their appearance to celebrate important life events. Ceremonies and rituals typically prescribe certain forms of dress. A particular costume thus becomes a symbol of the occasion (e.g., wedding, graduation). Rules of proper attire also differ. For instance, it is customary in many Asian and Middle Eastern cultures to remove shoes when entering a person's home, and customs that dictate modesty require covering up parts of the body, as women do in many Muslim cultures. Other rules and norms emerge out of respect for authority and encourage individuals to dress in a way that symbolizes their relative status in a society. In many cultures, attire is an unequivocal symbol of where one stands in the hierarchy. Among the Kalabari in Nigeria, men's style of dress corresponds to their position in society, indicating whether one is a young worker, "gentleman of substance," corporate chief, or ruler of state (Michelman & Erekosima, 1992).

Nonverbal Immediacy

As originally conceived by social psychologist Albert Mehrabian, *immediacy* refers to the degree of mutual sensory stimulation between people, resulting from their use of interpersonal proximity, eye contact, and touch. For example, a shy person tends to stand farther away, use less eye contact, and touch others less than does a person who is not shy. Thus, shyness produces a collection of behaviors characterized as low in immediacy. In his pioneering studies of nonverbal communication, Hall (1959; 1966) observed cultural differences in these immediacy behaviors, particularly in the use of personal space and touch.

Using the term *proxemics* in reference to the way people use space in their everyday interactions, Hall classified as **contact cultures** those places where people use relatively closer distances, more touch, and more eye contact than they typically use in lower-contact cultures. In his view, contact cultures exhibit a relative preference for interaction that stimulates the olfactory and tactile senses whereas low-contact cultures prefer interaction that stimulates the visual and auditory senses. The list of contact cultures includes countries in South America, southern Europe, the Middle East, and the Mediterranean region. Lower-contact cultures include North American, northern European, and East Asian countries. Keeping in mind that many factors influence our use of personal space, touch, and eye contact with another person (such as our relationship with the person or our personality), there is nevertheless considerable support in the social science literature for Hall's basic premise (Remland, 2017; Sicorello, Stevanov, & Hecht, 2019).

Yet while these cultural differences between high- and low-contact societies seem to exist, there is little research about why they exist, except for the assumption that they emerge from different cultural norms about what is appropriate in various social interactions. For instance, studying the data produced from a number of focus groups in Finland (low-contact culture) and France (high-contact culture), Isosavi (2020) found that the Finnish participants in the study were more likely to regard close interpersonal distances as impolite than the French participants were. So, one possible explanation for differences between high- and low-contact cultures may derive from socialization experiences about polite and impolite interaction with others. Another study comparing Australian and Korean passengers' tolerance for personal space intrusions at airports highlighted traditional differences between individualistic (Australia) and collectivistic (Korea) cultures (see Chapter 3 on cultural identity). As expected, Australian passengers' focus on their individual needs and desires led them to express more dissatisfaction with crowded conditions that invaded their personal space than were the Koreans. The researchers noted that the Korean passengers' greater tolerance for crowded conditions was consistent with the norms of collectivistic cultures that place the needs of others ahead of the needs for themselves. But there was an exception: age. Younger Australian and Korean passengers were equally tolerant of personal space intrusions and young Australian passengers were no more dissatisfied with crowded conditions than were Korean passengers. This finding may suggest the need for a more nuanced comparison between individualistic and collectivistic cultures and the need to consider a shift away from traditional cultural norms. But differences in the norms of a culture is not the only explanation for proxemic behavior and personal space preferences. Another explanation offered by some researchers is that differences between high- and low-contact cultures may be attributed to the temperature of a region. For example, in a study of interpersonal distance preferences in 42 countries around the world, Sorokowska et al., (2017) found that preferences were predicted by average temperature. These results suggested that the higher the annual temperature of a country, the closer participants preferred to interact with people they did not know. Although these results are not fully explained, they are consistent with the idea of high- and low-contact cultures. Perhaps the increased noise and distractions of interacting outdoors, which may be more commonplace in warmer climates, encourages people to interact at closer distance with strangers than they would indoors in colder climates.

Cultural norms also vary regarding public displays of affection. While taboo in many Muslim communities, these affectionate touches are tolerated and encouraged in many others. For example, one of the leading researchers on the social and cultural implications of interpersonal touch, Tiffany Field (1999), observed peer interactions among adolescents in Paris, France, and Miami, Florida. She found that American adolescents spent less time leaning against, stroking, kissing, and hugging their peers than did the French adolescents. In another study, researchers observed male-female couples walking on a college campus. They found no differences in hand-holding when comparing Latino couples with Asian couples, but arm embracing was much more prevalent among the Latinos than it was among the Asians (Regan et al., 1999). Researchers in another study observed the most male-female affectionate touching (hugging, kissing) in Italian dance clubs and the least in American dance clubs (DiBiase & Gunnoe, 2004).

Cultural differences are particularly striking when we see individuals participating in rituals, such as greetings and departures. Handshaking is common throughout much of the world but greeting rituals differ across cultures (e.g., the Japanese bow). Other forms of touch, like hugging and kissing, are more common in some cultures, particularly among friends and acquaintances (e.g., South America, Italy, France, Russia). In many Latin American countries, hand-kissing is still a widely performed greeting. Customs in other parts of the world also differ. For example, placing the palms together in prayer-like fashion and bowing (the *wai*) is a common greeting gesture in India. In Arab countries people touch their forehead and chest (the *salaam*) when meeting someone. In other cultures (e.g., the Maoris in New Zealand, Lapps in Finland, Bedouin in North Africa, Eskimos, Polynesians, and Malays) people may rub their noses together or against the other person's face when greeting (Morris, 1994).

The meaning of touch often depends on one's culture. For some countries in the Middle and Near East, shaking hands is an act of bargaining rather than a form of greeting. In much of the Middle East, holding hands is a sign of friendship (unlike in the West, where such an act between men implies homosexuality) and is a common practice among male friends. In fact, same-sex touching in public is more acceptable in many Asian and Middle Eastern countries than is opposite-sex touching (Jones, 1994).

In some cultures, making eye contact is a sign of respect while in others avoiding eye contact and casting a downward glance has a similar meaning. People from many Asian, Latino, and Caribbean cultures avoid eye contact as a sign of respect, and many African Americans, especially from the South, adhere to this custom as well (Dresser, 2005). When comparing the eye-contact patterns of individuals from Canada and Japan as they answered an interviewer's questions, researchers in one study found support for this cultural difference. The Japanese participants were more likely than the Canadians to avoid eye contact and look down while answering the interviewer's questions (McCarthy et al., 2006; 2008).

Expressions of Emotion

In their pioneering studies documenting cross-cultural similarities in the facial expressions of emotion, Ekman and Friesen (1969) also found a cultural difference, which led to their discovery of cultural display rules. They observed that in the

President George W. Bush and King Abdullah of Saudi Arabia hold hands during the latter's visit to the United States in 2005. In much of the Middle East, hand-holding among men is a common sign of friendship.

presence of another person, Japanese participants in one of their experiments were more likely than American participants to use masking smiles to cover up negative emotions. They explained that Japanese were following a rule to promote positive relations with others in certain situations (Ekman, 1972). So, although many facial expressions of emotion are spontaneous displays of genuinely felt emotions, many other expressions result from the pressure to follow cultural display rules, such as those identified in Put It Into Practice 6.2 on the following page.

Governor-General Sir Jerry Mateparae and Prime Minister of New Zealand John Key exchange a hongi, the traditional greeting of the Maori people of New Zealand.

PUT IT INTO PRACTICE   **6.2**

What Display Rules Do You Follow?

Instructions:

Indicate the type of emotional display rule you generally follow when with family members, close friends, coworkers, and strangers. Please choose among the following list for each situation noted in the table below.

1. Honestly express your true feelings (spontaneity)

2. Don't show the emotion at all (neutral expression)

3. Cover up your true feelings with a different expression like smiling (masking)

Emotion	Family	Close Friends	Coworkers	Strangers
Sadness				
Anger				
Happiness				
Fear				

(Adapted from Matsumoto et al., 2005)

Building on the idea of cultural display rules, Matsumoto (1990; 1991) developed a theory of emotional expression that incorporates the cultural orientations of individualism-collectivism and power distance (see Chapter 4). According to Matsumoto's theory, because individualistic cultures encourage self-expression, its members are relatively free to display a range of emotions, positive or negative, toward others. In addition, the politeness rules most people follow prompt individuals to be friendly, smiling at others regardless of who they are. But in collectivistic cultures, people learn to put the needs of the group ahead of their own needs. This pressures them to suppress negative emotions (e.g., anger, disgust, sadness) toward ingroup members because the display of such emotions will upset the harmony of the group. Yet there is little pressure to conceal negative emotions or to show positive emotions toward outgroup persons. The lack of group affiliation with such persons lessens the pressure to promote positive relations.

The second part of Matsumoto's theory focuses on the power distance orientation of a culture—the degree to which it promotes the maintenance of status differences among members. High power-distance cultures endorse displays of emotion that reinforce hierarchical relations (i.e., status reminders), such as showing anger toward a low-status person or appeasing a high-status person (e.g., smiling). Low power-distance cultures embrace egalitarian values and teach the importance of treating people as equals. Thus, there is less pressure in these cultures for members to adjust displays of emotion according to the status of another person. Although it isn't always the case, high-power distance cultures tend to be collectivistic, whereas low power distance cultures tend to be individualistic. For instance, high power-distance/collectivistic cultures include most Arab, Latin American, African, Asian, and southern European nations. Low power-distance/individualistic cultures include South Africa, North America, Australia, and northern Europe (Hofstede, 1980; 1983).

There are also cultural differences in the recognition and interpretation of emotional expressions. For instance, numerous studies have shown an ingroup bias—a tendency to recognize the emotional expressions of ingroup persons more readily than those of outgroup persons. A recently proposed explanation for this cultural bias is the ***dialect theory of facial expressions*** (Elfenbein et al., 2007). This theory, while accepting the principle that communicating emotion is universal, rests on two basic propositions: (1) as with other languages, different cultures can express themselves in different dialects; and (2) the presence of dialects has the potential to make recognition of emotion less accurate across cultural boundaries. In a study comparing the posed facial expressions of participants from Quebec and from the West African nation of Gabon, researchers observed significant cultural variations in the participants' facial expressions of contempt, shame, and serenity, and more subtle differences in their facial expressions of anger, sadness, surprise, and happiness. The findings also showed an ingroup bias. Participants were better able to recognize their own facial expression dialect than that of the other cultural group (Elfenbein et al., 2007).

Research also reveals an interesting difference between East Asian and Western cultures in recognizing and interpreting emotional expressions. Persons in East Asian cultures, consistent with their preference for holistic/high-context information processing compared to the West, are more likely to interpret facial expressions taking the *overall context* into consideration. Researchers in two experiments found that when identifying the emotions of individuals, Japanese observers were more inclined to incorporate information from the social context, specifically the facial expressions of surrounding individuals, than were Westerners. Tracking the eye gaze of the participants, the researchers found that the Japanese were more likely than the Westerners to look at the surrounding people (Masuda et al., 2008). But this cultural difference, which depends on an observer's ability to process multiple sources of information, often declines with age, thus explaining the finding of a recent study showing a difference in processing when comparing young adult Koreans with young adult Americans, but not when comparing older Koreans and Americans (Ko et al., 2010). More recent studies have also shown that people in Eastern cultures are more likely than people in Western cultures to make holistic and more nuanced judgments of facial expressions (Fang, Sauter, & Van Kleef 2019).

No other facial expression is more recognizable than that of smiling. Moreover, most of the available research on smiling shows a strong association between smiling and all sorts of positive judgments, such as looking more attractive, being friendlier, appearing more honest, more approachable, more intelligent, warmer, and so forth (Remland, 2017). Yet some research shows that positive first impressions of a smiling face are not universal and may depend on the particular trait being judged, as well as the culture of the person making the judgment. Another factor to consider is that nearly all of the studies on smiling have been done in cultures that are generally Western, educated, industrialized, relatively rich, and democratic. One study did take these factors into account and examined first impressions of smiling faces in 44 countries across 6 continents. While they did find considerable cross-cultural agreement on the positive first impressions of smiling, there were some notable exceptions, primarily on the perception of intelligence. Specifically, when comparing first impressions of the same person either smiling or not smiling, the researchers found no differences in 20 countries. However, smiling persons were seen as more intelligent in 18 countries. But, interestingly, smiling persons were seen as less intelligent in 6 countries (Japan, South Korea, India, Russia, Iran, and France). While there may be cultural display rules in each of these countries that result in such judgments, the researchers also found in an analysis of all 44 countries that there was a positive association between the cultural value orientation of uncertainty avoidance (UA) and judgments of intelligence. As the authors of the study explain, societies that rank high on UA socialize their members to try and make future events as predictable as they can, whereas in societies that rank low on UA, the future tends to be seen as unpredictable and less effort is made to change that. So it may be that people in cultures low on UA see smiling as a bewildering sign of confidence or certainty when little exists and are therefore perceived as less intelligent (Krys, 2016).

Symbolic Gestures

"Why can't Italians talk without using their hands?" Do you share the belief expressed in this question? You may be surprised to learn that, aside from considerable anecdotal evidence that the members of some cultures gesticulate more than the members of other cultures (e.g., southern Europeans compared to northern Europeans), there is little empirical research to substantiate such claims. In fact, it may well be the case that differences exist in the size and type of gestures speakers use rather than in their frequency. For example, in his landmark study of east European Yiddish-speaking immigrants and those from southern Italy, David Efron (1941) discovered that, while both groups made extensive use of hand and arm movements as they spoke, Italians favored sweeping iconic gestures, whereas Jewish speakers preferred smaller and less graphic kinds.

But the meanings of *emblematic gestures* (also called emblems), the kind with relatively clear, agreed-upon meanings, vary from one culture to another more than any other type (Axtell, 1998; Morris, 1977; 1994). For example, a *multimessage gesture* has more than one agreed-upon meaning. Typically, its meaning in one culture differs from its meaning in another. The best example is the forefinger-thumb circle gesture, which means "okay" in America, but can mean "zero" or "worthless" in France, "asshole" in parts of Latin America and the Middle East, and "money" in Japan. Even the well-known thumbs-up gesture has some meanings that could create problems for its users. In Australia it can mean "up yours," in Japan it can mean "five," and in Germany it can mean "one." A simple throat-grasping gesture can mean several different things: "I'll strangle you" (Arab cultures), "I could kill myself" (New Guinea), "I've had enough" (Italy), "He/she has

Emblematic gestures have recognizable meanings, do not require speech, and often vary from one culture to another.

been caught" (South America), "I performed badly" (North America), and "I can't breathe" (North America).

Sometimes different gestures communicate the same basic message. A *multi-gesture message* reminds us of the great cultural diversity that characterizes emblematic gestures. For example, some people use beckoning hand gestures with the palm of the hand facing up, but other people hold the palm facing down. The palm-up version is typical in North America and most of northern and central Europe; the palm-down version is preferred throughout much of southern Europe, Latin America, and Asia. Obscene gestures also vary across cultures. While an angry American might give someone the middle finger, an angry Italian often uses a forearm thrust to express the same message, and an angry Briton might use the palm-back V-gesture.

Unique gestures are exclusive to a single location. Table 6.1 introduces a small sampling of these gestures. Our ignorance of unique gestures can be troublesome in cases where an unintended gesture gets confused with an intended one, when a noncommunicative act in one culture turns out to be a communicative act in another. For example, many self-touching movements fall into this category (Remland, 2017). Do you ever touch your ear lobe? Depending on how you touch it, you could be saying, "I don't like him" (Russia), "He is effeminate" (Italy), "Don't argue with me" (Saudi Arabia), "I don't believe you" (Scotland), or "Good luck" (Turkey).

Paralanguage and Silence

Imagine receiving a phone call from someone who begins speaking to you in a language you do not understand. Even though you cannot understand the text of the message you will probably still form some judgments about the caller's gender, nationality, age, emotional state, and more from the caller's voice alone. Each "non-text" element of speech is often referred to as *paralanguage*. Like other

Table 6.1   Some Gestures Possibly Unique to Particular Countries

Country	Gesture	Action	Meaning	Origin
Indonesia	Armpit tickle	Forefinger tickles gesturer's own armpit	Poor joke	The joke is so bad I'd have to tickle myself to laugh
Greece	Palm thrust (known as "moutza" gesture)	Palm is thrust toward other as if pushing something into person's face	Go to hell	Symbolizes ancient practice of pushing filth into face of chained-up criminals
Saudi Arabia	Ear circle	Forefinger makes a circling motion around the ear	Be good or else	Stylized threat by parent towards a misbehaving child. Threatens to pull ear as punishment

(Adapted from Morris, 1994)

forms of nonverbal communication, paralanguage can indicate one's cultural identity. The most obvious way is through accented speech, reflecting a speaker's native tongue and ethnic roots.

Do some cultures produce louder speakers than other cultures? Researchers claim, for instance, that Arabs prefer loud speech because they regard it as stronger and more sincere than a softer tone of voice (Hall & Whyte, 1966; Watson & Graves, 1966). In contrast, Britons generally prefer a quieter, less intrusive volume than persons from many other cultures, including both Arabs and Americans (Hall, 1966). There is also some evidence that Latin Americans may sound loud when their speech

---

CULTURE SHOCK

The "OK" Gesture Is Not OK Everywhere

I did some relief work in Haiti the summer following the 2010 earthquake. While we were there, we did some work in some orphanages. There, we often played with the kids, played games, and did other various activities to bring some joy to their lives. Oftentimes, if a child did something that was good, like scoring a goal in a game of soccer, we would give them the "OK, good job" signal by making a circle with our thumb and forefinger with the other three fingers sticking up. However, when we did this, we noticed an interesting reaction from the youngsters. They would just look at us, stare, and walk away with a confused look on their faces. Finally, one of our translators noticed what we were doing and explained to us that in Haiti that gesture was the equivalent to our "middle finger" gesture.

—Mike

is compared to that of Asians and Europeans (Watson, 1970). In one recent study, researchers found that participants from Finland were better able to tolerate silences in conversations than French participants. The French were also more likely than the Finnish were to regard silence as an obstacle to rapport (Isosavi, 2020).

Other more subtle elements of paralanguage include the turn-taking cues we rely on to navigate the give and take of conversation. These vocalizations and intonations differ across cultures. For example, English speakers often misinterpret the vocal intonation of Arab speakers, judging the drop in vocal pitch Arab speakers use to seek listener feedback as expressing negative feelings (Ward & Al Bayyari, 2010). There are also cultural differences in use of vocalizations that encourage speakers to keep talking ("uh-huh"). For instance, some scholars claim that Japanese listeners use more of these vocal *backchannels* compared to American and British listeners (Argyle, 1988; Hall, 1959; Cutrone, 2005), and that Germans use fewer than Americans (Heinz, 2003).

Pausing and interruption patterns can also vary according to one's culture. In her study of the Cree people in western Canada, Darnell (1985) observed that they use long pauses between turns to show respect and to think about how to respond. In contrast, interruptions and overlapping speech, as signs of involvement and interest, are common in many Latin American countries. Another study found longer silent pauses in samples of five-minute Japanese interactions than in similar samples of German interactions (Endrass, Rehm, & Andre, 2011).

Cultures also vary in their uses and interpretations of silence. In many low-context or extraverted cultures people are uncomfortable with silence; but silence is more useful and meaningful than speech in many high-context or introverted cultures, suggesting embarrassment, politeness, disagreement, contentment, thoughtfulness, and more. Americans, in particular, have little tolerance for silence. Especially when interacting with nonintimates, Americans act as though speech is always better than silence (Ishii & Bruneau, 1988). This contrasts sharply with many Native American cultures, such as the Western Apache, for whom silence is the norm in many "unscripted" social situations, like encounters with strangers, first dates, times of mourning, greeting people who have been away for a long time, reactions to angry outbursts, and so on (Basso, 1972). As Bonvillain (2000) explains:

> These circumstances have a common theme: that an individual is interacting with someone who is unpredictable, either because s/he is unknown, not known well, has been absent for some time, or is in a distressed psychic state. When interacting with such people, one must take care to observe them silently, in order to pick up clues, and anticipate their likely behavior. (p. 45)

In addition, the introverted makeup of some cultures promotes the use of silence over speech in many social situations. Surveys generally confirm that East Asian cultures tend to be more introverted than Western cultures (McCrae et al., 2010). But even in the West there are differences across national boundaries. For example, studies show that persons in some northern European countries, such as Finland, tend to be more introverted and less inclined to talk in social gatherings compared to persons in America (Carbaugh, 2005; Sallinen-Kuparinen, McCroskey, & Richmond, 1991).

Obstacles and Challenges to Peacebuilding

Take a moment to consider the following description of a meeting that takes place between two college students concerning a class assignment:

> Michael, who is Black, is meeting with Jim, who is White, to begin work on an oral report they will be giving in their biology class. Michael wonders if Jim is prejudiced and Jim worries about appearing prejudiced. When they get together, Michael is attuned to subtle signs of prejudice in Jim's behavior, and Jim is careful not to say anything that Michael could take the wrong way. Jim's self-consciousness and control over what he says makes his nonverbal behavior appear more awkward and less friendly than usual: he makes less eye contact with Michael, fidgets more, exhibits more polite smiles, touches his face more, and so forth. But because Jim is more aware of what he's saying than how he's saying it, he thinks he's making a good impression. Michael, however, is paying as much if not more attention to Jim's nonverbal cues, and therefore gets a different impression. (Remland, 2017)

Given the above description, what are the chances that Jim and Michael will meet in the future, let alone strike up a close friendship? Of course either outcome is possible, but considering the discomfort and miscommunication that occurred, neither outcome seems likely. Intercultural exchanges such as the one described above, offer a glimpse into the obstacles and challenges associated with even the most earnest efforts to build rapport and community with individuals of other cultural groups. In fact, studies of interracial interactions, like the one described above, confirm that both Blacks and Whites are more likely in mixed-race interactions than in same-race interactions to attribute nonverbal signs of discomfort from the other person as proof of unfriendliness (Dovidio et al., 2006). In this section we note several ways in which nonverbal communication can hinder the community-building goals of intercultural encounters.

Threats to Identity

One of the key challenges of intercultural communication is managing potential threats to identity (see Chapter 3). In large part, we signal our cultural identity through physical appearance and dress as well as other nonverbal expressions common among people in our cultural group (e.g., speech accents, clothing, greeting rituals, symbolic gestures). Intercultural encounters often prompt us to alter the way we communicate, knowingly or not, in response to the other person. For instance, according to *communication accommodation theory*, we may adopt the speech accent, intonation pattern, gestures, dialect, and so on, of another person's cultural group in order to blend in or gain their approval, a behavioral adaptation referred to as *convergence*. On the other hand, we may enact behaviors that call attention to the intercultural context of the encounter, signaling different cultural identities, a behavioral adaptation called *divergence*. Whereas convergence heightens the perception of similarity (and closeness) between individuals of different cultural groups, divergence heightens the perception of dissimilarity (and distance). Research on communication accommodation theory usually shows that divergence produces less beneficial outcomes in an intercultural encounter than convergence does. However, convergence results in some loss of one's cultural identity and because pressures to converge tend to be greater for members of marginalized co-cultural groups than for individuals of the dominant culture, convergence does not necessarily enhance intercultural relations (Jackson, 2002; Orbe & Drummond, 2009).

Misinterpreted Signals

An unsuspecting visitor in a foreign country who takes the meaning of a gesture for granted runs the risk of offending his or her host by inadvertently using a gesture that sends the wrong message. Some cases of cross-cultural miscommunication are so far-reaching they become the next day's headlines. For example, when President George H. W. Bush visited Australia in 1993, he drove by crowds of citizens showing what he thought was the V for victory sign from the backseat of his limousine. Apparently not knowing the difference, he gestured to onlookers with the back of his palm instead of the front. The next day, his picture appeared in newspapers alongside the headline "President Insults Australians." In Australia, as in England, the reverse V sign is their equivalent of the American "screw you" gesture (Axtell, 1998).

In her book *Multicultural Manners*, Nora Dresser (2005) explains how in multicultural America misinterpreting the meaning of eye contact can have unfortunate consequences:

> In many urban centers, non-Korean customers became angry when Korean shopkeepers did not look at them directly. The customers translated the lack of eye contact as a sign of disrespect, a habit blamed for contributing to the open confrontations taking place between some Asians and African Americans in New York, Texas, and California. (p. 23)

Dresser continues by offering another example of misreading someone's gaze, but with far more serious consequences:

> Particularly in urban centers, when one teenager looks directly at another, this is considered a provocation, sometimes called mad-dogging, and can lead to physical conflict. . . . In one high school, it resulted in a fight between Cambodian newcomers and African-American students. The Cambodians had been staring at the other students merely to learn how Americans behave. Yet the others misinterpreted the Cambodians' intentions and a fight occurred. (p. 23)

Of course, these misinterpretations are not limited to teens. In Tucson, Arizona, a 22-year-old man died from a gunshot wound police described as a "road rage" homicide that started when the passengers in a nearby vehicle began "mad-dogging" the man (glaring at him threateningly). After the man responded to the glares by making obscene gestures, the passengers in the other vehicle opened fire, riddling the man's car with dozens of bullets (Keen, 2013).

Cross-Cultural Transgressions

Cross-cultural misunderstandings can involve more than the misreading of a single gesture. Failures to appreciate cultural differences in the norms and rules that guide everyday conduct can have disastrous consequences, particularly when a transgression violates the moral code of a society. Consider the tragic case of Sam and Kathy Krasniqi, Albanian Muslim immigrants living in the United States since 1971, who lost their children over allegations of sexual abuse. It began in 1989, when Sam Krasniqi took his five-year-old daughter to a karate tournament in their hometown of Dallas where his son was competing. Witnesses alleged that Krasniqi was touching his daughter, who was sitting on his lap at the time, in a "sexual" way. Based on these allegations, the Krasniqis ultimately lost custody of their two children. Did he touch his daughter in a "sexual way" as the witnesses alleged? The answer, which came during Sam Krasniqi's criminal trial in 1994, was no. It was a cultural misunderstanding over the appropriateness and meaning of touch among family members, which differs across cultures. Unfortunately, however, the Krasniqis were never able to regain custody of their children (Zimmerman, 1998).

Another cross-cultural transgression involved the movie actor Richard Gere, who, on stage during an HIV-AIDS news conference in New Delhi, India, embraced and kissed one of Bollywood's most popular actresses, Shilpa Shetty. A photograph of the kiss made the front page of newspapers across the country amid protests condemning the act as disgraceful and obscene. Outraged protesters beat burning effigies of Gere and set fire to photographs of Shetty. India is one of many countries in the world where large numbers of people frown on public displays of affection.

Nonconscious Bias

While we may be able to avoid incidents involving a misunderstood gesture and the violation of a cultural norm, other obstacles remain unseen, hidden below the surface of our conscious thought, and may therefore be more difficult to confront. One example is the snap judgments we make about individuals who share the stereotypical facial features of a cultural group. In a series of experiments, a team of researchers wanted to find out if the negative stereotyping of African American males in general also occurs in response to any individuals with Afrocentric facial features (i.e., coarse hair, dark skin, full lips, and wide nose). In one experiment the researchers asked participants in the study to match photographs of African American men with written descriptions of African American men. One of the descriptions contained information typical of the negative stereotype: the person grew up in the inner city, was attending college on a basketball scholarship, had failed several classes, had been involved in fights on the basketball court, and was waiting to talk to his coach about a drug charge. The photographs matched up with this description tended to be of men with stronger Afrocentric facial features. In a follow-up experiment, the researchers found that photographs of European-American faces were matched up in a similar way; the faces with stronger Afrocentric features were more likely to be seen as the ones fitting the negative stereotype (Blair et al., 2002).

Another example is the instantaneous judgments we form in response to a person speaking in a "foreign" accent. There are two widely held viewpoints for why this happens. The first is the linguistic perspective, which simply holds that it is harder to understand speakers with non-native accents and this results in negative judgments. The second, the social perspective, explains that we immediately categorize a speaker's accent as representing a cultural identity as that of in-group or out-group membership, with corresponding bias favoring the ingroup. This bias is particularly strong when the foreign accent is associated with a "lower-status" cultural group than it is with a "higher-status" cultural group (Foucart, Santamaria-Garcia, & Hartsuiker, 2019). Numerous studies confirm that, with some exceptions, we tend to judge foreign-accented speakers less favorably and discriminate against them more than we do in comparison to speakers with little or no accent (Cunha et al., 2016; Montgomery & Zhang, 2018; Orelus, 2020).

Cultural and racial stereotypes can also bias our perceptions of facial expressions, particularly in response to the faces of group members we regard as threatening in some way. In one experiment, White undergraduate students viewed a scary scene from the movie *The Silence of the Lambs* and subsequently rated the intensity of emotions expressed on different faces. The researchers hypothesized that arousing fear in the participants would cause them to see more danger in the faces of some people more than others, based on cultural and racial stereotyping. As expected, the participants' perceived greater anger in Black male faces and also greater anger in Arab faces than in the faces of other "less threatening" faces (Maner et al., 2005).

We also exhibit an ingroup bias in recognizing, reading, and responding to the facial expressions of others. Studies show we infer with greater accuracy the emotional and mental states of ingroup members compared to outgroup members from their facial expressions, even from just their eyes alone (Adams et al., 2010b). Amazingly, studies of *brain responses* to facial expressions confirm this ingroup bias for emotion recognition. That is, fundamental parts of the brain responsible for processing fear are more active in persons when they are looking at fearful faces of ingroup persons than of outgroup persons (Adams, et al., 2010a). Recent research also shows an ingroup and outgroup bias that affects preferred interpersonal distances. For instance, in one study participants from Russia interacted with other individuals in a virtual environment that allowed them to move around and establish preferred distances with avatars representing three ethnic groups: Slavic (e.g., Russian), North Caucasian, and Central Asian. The researchers found that the Russian participants maintained closer distances with avatars from their own ethnic group than with the other ethnic groups (Menshikova, Saveleva, & Zinchenko, 2018).

Nonverbal Communication and Intercultural Communication Competence

Cultural differences in nonverbal communication create special challenges that make it difficult to build community across diverse cultures. But all of us can begin the work of meeting these challenges by becoming more aware of how to improve our nonverbal communication skills. In this section we consider the key elements that define nonverbal communication competence in the context of intercultural encounters: learning to negotiate nonverbal expressions of identity and learning to adapt and contextualize nonverbal messages.

PUT IT INTO PRACTICE   **6.3**

The Implicit Association Test (IAT)

Objective:

To assess your "implicit" bias in judging people based on their physical appearance.

Instructions:

The IAT measures your nonconscious tendency to favor some people over others based on their physical attributes, such as race, skin color, age, and body weight. The test presents pictures of people along with positive and negative concepts and asks you to make split-second decisions about which pictures and concepts "belong together." How quickly you make these decisions is a measure of your bias, or inclination to hold a positive attitude or negative attitude toward people with those physical attributes. You can go online and take a demonstration test at implicit.harvard.edu.

Negotiating Nonverbal Expressions of Identity

As we pointed out in Chapter 1, the peacebuilding view of intercultural communication competence places the responsibility for building community on all of the participants involved in an intercultural exchange. In this regard, one key element of nonverbal communication competence is the ability and willingness to negotiate expressions of cultural identity so that one person's loss is not simply another person's gain. We see the impetus for this sort of negotiation with increasing regularity in cases involving the dress and religious symbols of co-cultural groups (e.g., nightclubs letting customers wear turbans and other religious head coverings; the armed forces letting Orthodox Jews wear *yarmulkes*; construction companies letting Amish workers wear their customary black felt hats) (Dresser, 2005). In some particularly noteworthy cases of *mutual accommodation*, the parties in dispute find creative ways of negotiating conflicts over identity and building community. For an interesting example see A Closer Look 6.1 on the following page.

Adapting and Contextualizing Nonverbal Messages

One element of intercultural communication competence is the ability to adapt to the rules, rituals, and practices of another culture, like learning how to dress for an occasion, when to be silent, whether it's OK to interrupt, when not to touch or make eye contact, how to greet someone, and so on. Another element is the ability to comprehend the symbol systems and *nonverbal accents* of another culture, taking the context into account when interpreting another person's actions.

A CLOSER LOOK   **6.1**

Weightlifting Championship: A Case of Identity Negotiation

Kulsoom Abdullah, a Pakistani-American weightlifter, made headlines in 2011 when she requested that the International Weightlifting Federation (IWF) change its rules to allow competitors to wear clothing that covers the legs and arms so that she could compete in accordance with her Muslim faith. The IWF granted the rule change and Abdullah became the first woman to compete in a full body "unitard" under a wrestling uniform. The previous rule required competitors to keep their knees and elbows visible to ensure lifts were performed correctly. "I'm really happy that I got this experience and that there's a lot of support, and I hope that it could encourage other women and people, whether it's weightlifting or another sport, to try competition because it's fun to meet people," Abdullah said.

(Meredith, 2011)

Like learning the words and phrases of a foreign language, learning gestures takes time and effort. Our knowledge of these gestures, like our knowledge of any other aspect of a foreign culture, is a sign of our familiarity with that culture. In one series of studies, researchers wanted to determine whether the ability to distinguish between genuine and phony gestures in a foreign culture indicates how well one is adapting to that culture. They administered a videotaped test of American emblematic gestures, including both real and fake gestures, to a large group of non-native American students. Higher scores on the test predicted length of stay in the United States. In addition, persons who scored higher on the test rated themselves higher and received higher scores from others on a measure of intercultural communication competence (Molinsky et al., 2005).

Being able to *contextualize* a nonverbal message means being able to take various elements of the situation into account when interpreting a message. Even in low-context cultures, the meaning of many nonverbal behaviors depends on the context in which it occurs. For instance, a smiling American salesperson isn't necessarily happy or friendly. The context (her sales job) demands that she smile in order to be successful. In some high-context cultures, the interpretation of a smile depends to a larger degree on elements of the situation. In many Asian countries smiling can express happiness, sadness, disagreement, frustration, confusion, politeness, anger, gratitude, or an apology, depending on the situation (Dresser, 2005).

Becoming more familiar with a culture over time may even improve our recognition of their facial expressions. In their review and summary of these cross-cultural studies, one team of investigators confirmed an ingroup advantage for recognizing facial expressions of emotion. But they emphasized that the advantage was much smaller for cultural groups with greater exposure to one another, such as living in the same nation, having close physical proximity, and having access to telephone communication (Elfenbein & Ambady, 2002).

CULTURE SHOCK

Silence Is Golden

Brian Lande wanted to learn more about the Amish for a research paper he was writing, so he attended Sunday worship in New Holland, Pennsylvania, and spent the day observing and interviewing an Amish dairy farmer named Aaron. Brian found a cultural difference in the way the Amish communicate: "While my family often discusses intellectual topics, feelings, etc., the Amish don't talk much. During and after my interview with Aaron, there was a small group of men sitting with each other. However, these men often just sit without talking for long periods of time. This is cultural; the Amish are not talkers but a people of action."

(Lande, 1998)

Summary

Nonverbal communication represents a way of exchanging messages without the use of words (e.g., clothing, personal space, facial expressions, gestures). There are four basic properties of nonverbal communication: (1) Many nonverbal signals are universal. Some basic facial expressions of emotion, for example, are used and recognized by everyone. (2) Many signals are sent and received spontaneously, with little or no conscious awareness. (3) Many nonverbal signals are iconic; that is, they resemble in some way what they represent, such as a graphic tattoo or a pantomimed action. (4) Many nonverbal signals occur simultaneously, which would happen, for instance, if we expressed anger with a facial expression, tone of voice, and a gesture, all at the same time. Nonverbal communication evolved to achieve four basic functions. The first function, signaling identity, refers to the many ways we exchange information about individual traits (e.g., age, personality, fitness) and group affiliations (e.g., race, ethnicity, gender). The second function involves building relationships, which includes signals related to interpersonal control and intimacy. The third function involves the expression of emotions such as anger, fear, sadness, and joy. The fourth function is delivering symbolic messages and includes the nontextual features of speech as well as the many ways we use nonverbal channels to facilitate or replace spoken language.

Nonverbal communication depends heavily on the cultural context of an interaction. This includes the classification of cultures based on whether they rely on high-context messages as opposed to low-context messages. A more recent attempt at classification, called context differentiation, suggests that some cultures are more likely to adapt their communication to changing contexts than other cultures are. Researchers have uncovered numerous cross-cultural differences in nonverbal communication, including variations in appearance, nonverbal immediacy (e.g., personal space, touch, eye contact), emotional expressions, symbolic gestures, paralanguage, and silence. These differences create special obstacles and challenges to the peacebuilding enterprise in the form of identity threats, misinterpreted signals, cross-cultural transgressions, and nonconscious expressions of bias. Becoming a more competent nonverbal communicator involves skills in negotiating identity conflicts and adapting and contextualizing messages.

QUESTIONS

1. Sign language for deaf and hearing-impaired populations, which relies on the use of gestures in place of spoken words, is a type of verbal communication rather than a type of nonverbal communication. But does sign language contain any of the properties of nonverbal communication? Explain.

2. One of the primary functions of nonverbal communication is signaling our identity. Can you think of how you nonverbally express your own membership in a particular cultural group? How does this type of communication lead to cultural stereotyping?

3. As discussed in this chapter, the delivery function of nonverbal communication focuses on how nonverbal messages can replace and facilitate speech. Specifically, can you think of an example to illustrate how a nonverbal message: (a) substitutes for speech; (b) emphasizes speech; (c) repeats speech; (d) contradicts speech; (e) regulates speech; and (f) complements speech?

4. Because emblematic gestures have agreed upon meanings, many of these gestures may not be used and recognized across cultural groups and some may only be used and recognized by the members of a particular group. Can you think of any emblematic gestures that may not be understood by persons outside of a group to which you belong?

5. This chapter identifies several obstacles and challenges to peacebuilding that result from cultural differences in nonverbal communication. Which of these obstacles and challenges do you think is the most important: threats to identity; misinterpreted signals; cross-cultural transgressions; or nonconscious bias? Why?

7

Culture and Verbal Communication

CHAPTER OUTLINE

I. Language and Cultural Identity
  A. Learning the Rules of a Language
  B. Language as an Expression of Culture

II. Cultural Influences on Verbal Codes and Styles
  A. High- and Low-Context Communication Codes
  B. The Four-Factor Model of Verbal Styles

III. Obstacles and Challenges to Peacebuilding
  A. Limits to Language Learning
  B. Threats to Cultural Identity
  C. Roadblocks to Rapport
  D. Challenges to Civility

IV. Verbal Communication and Intercultural Competence
  A. Linguistic Competence
  B. Conversational Competence

KEY TERMS

affective style
alignment talk
connotative meaning
denotative meaning
direct style
elaborate style
exacting style
foreign language effect

idioms
indirect style
inflections
instrumental style
lingua franca
morphemes
person-centered style
phonemes

phonological rules
pragmatic rules
role-centered style
sapir-whorf hypothesis
semantic rules
speech acts
succinct style
syntactical rules

In 1907, the President of the United States, Theodore Roosevelt, famously declared, "We have but room for one language in this country and that is the English language." Reflecting the same basic sentiment that the citizens of a country should share a common language, many Americans favor the passage of a federal law that would require the use of English in all official government transactions, thereby making English the "official" language of the United States. The most recent example is the "English Language Unity Act," introduced in the House of Representatives in February 2021 (H.R. 997, English Language Unity Act of 2021). At the present time, 30 states have passed laws requiring the use of English in all legal and governmental processes. While certainly not the most pressing matter facing the country at this time, it nonetheless represents an ongoing controversy over the role and impact of language in a multicultural society.

This controversy is fueled in part by increased immigration and the fact that close to 9% of the United States population is not adequately proficient speaking English. Moreover, US Census Bureau data for 2018 estimated that more than 67 million Americans—about 22% of American residents—speak a language other than English at home, which is nearly twice the percentage of American residents who didn't speak English at home in 1980 (Zeigler & Camarota, 2019). In the reading below (A Closer Look 7.1), you will see a brief synopsis of the arguments for and against such a law. How would you describe your position on this enduring controversy?

A CLOSER LOOK   **7.1**

Should English Be the "Official" Language?

The Close Up Foundation—a nonprofit organization based in Washington, DC—lists some common arguments made by supporters and opponents of designating English as the official language of the United States:

Supporters:

1. **It promotes unity**: Making English the "official" language promotes unity and empowers immigrants by encouraging them to learn English, the language of opportunity in this country.

2. **It protects English as the majority language**: English needs constitutional protection because of the unique threat posed by the growing Spanish-speaking population of the United States.

3. **It urges immigrants to assimilate more quickly to American life**: Bilingual education and multilingual [voting] ballots discourage rather than encourage assimilation and encourage separatism and hostility toward American ideals.

4. **There are too many languages to accommodate them all**: There are over 350 languages spoken in the United States. We cannot create government materials for all of them.

Opponents:

1. **We don't need to make English the "official language" because it is not under threat**: While there may be a large number of people who speak languages other than English in the United States, the rate of English proficiency among foreign-born citizens is actually on the rise.

2. **It is at odds with our ideals**: It is a denial of the "essential ideals of tolerance and respect for diversity that underlie American democracy...and a return to racial and ethnic discrimination and the xenophobia that marked much of American history.

3. **It is discriminatory**: H.R. 997 simply discriminates against those who have not yet learned English or those perceived not to be proficient in English, with damaging consequences for society as a whole.

4. **We should be taking an English Plus, not English Only approach**: In an ever-increasing global community more language acquisition, not less, should be encouraged for US residents.

(Close Up Foundation, 2019)

The use of a common language is an important hallmark of any culture. At the same time, the intimate connection between our language and our cultural identity creates special challenges for peacebuilding efforts within and across diverse cultures. This chapter focuses on the development of intercultural communication competence as a prudent response to these particular challenges. In the sections that follow we address the connection between language and culture, important cultural influences on everyday verbal discourse and the challenges that result, and conclude by considering the implications for developing intercultural communication competence.

Language and Cultural Identity

Although language is but one of the many defining features of a culture, when we hear someone speaking a language other than our own (a "foreign" language) we have little difficulty regarding the speaker as the member of some distinctly different cultural group. Language learning is a fundamental part of the socialization process involved in becoming the member of a culture. In fact, our conception of the world's population is closely tied to our understanding of how geography and culture coalesce to shape and sustain the variety of languages used in the world today (see Table 7.1). Differences among the world's languages notwithstanding, the speakers of any language must learn the same basic rules in order to become proficient. What are these rules?

Learning the Rules of a Language

Learning any language means learning to follow four basic sets of rules. *Phonological rules* govern the sounds we make to form words, including rules about the stress and intonation patterns accompanying our words. A *phoneme* is the smallest unit of sound in a spoken language, such as the sound of various vowels and consonants. In English there is only some correspondence between the number of phonemes in the language and the number of letters in the alphabet. For example, distinct sounds such as *sh*, *ch*, and *th* do not correspond to any letters. In some languages, like Danish, the correspondence is perfect. But in other languages, such as Chinese, there is no correspondence at all (Liska & Cronkhite,

Table 7.1 Largest World Languages by the Number of First-Language Speakers

Ranking	Language	Population (in millions)
1	Mandarin Chinese	929
2	Spanish	475
3	English	373
4	Hindi	344
5	Bengali	234
6	Portuguese	232
7	Russian	154
8	Japanese	130
9	Yue Chinese	85
10	Vietnamese	85

(Eberhard, Simons, & Fennig, 2022)

1995). The smallest meaningful unit of sound is called a *morpheme* and includes words and parts of words, called *inflections* or *bound morphemes*, such as prefixes and suffixes. Words can consist of one or more morphemes. For example, the words "happy" and "help" contain one morpheme. The words, "happiness" and "helping" contain two morphemes (*ness* and *ing*). In many languages, converting a word to its plural or past tense form also involves adding a morpheme, such as an *s* to make the word plural or an *ed* to add past tense. Languages of the world vary considerably in their use of inflections to modify the meanings of words. Indo-European languages—such as Spanish, French, Greek, and Italian—are more highly inflected than are English or Chinese, for example.

We also need to learn the *semantic rules* that produce the shared meanings of words. The *denotative meaning* of a word is the objective, agreed-upon meaning that you would find in a dictionary (i.e., the literal meaning). But the meaning of any word runs deeper than its literal translation. The *connotative meaning* of a word is the subjective, highly personal meaning we attach to it, which may differ not only from person to person but from culture to culture as well (e.g., the words "freedom" and "independence" do not have the same positive connotations in all societies). In addition, cultural groups often develop their own distinctive dialects—vocabularies, slang, jargon, and colloquialisms that distinguish them from the language users of the mainstream culture (Thomas & Inkson, 2009).

Learning a language also means learning its *syntactical rules* about how to arrange words in meaningful ways. Learning to construct grammatical sentences involves much more than learning the meaning of words. Proper *syntax* is what makes one statement understandable and another statement with the same words nonsensical, as in the statement "the dog is playing with the ball" instead of the statement "playing the ball with is the dog." Proper syntax can vary from culture to culture. For example, the sentence structure in Japanese follows a subject-object-verb pattern, in contrast with the subject-verb-object pattern in proper English sentences.

In addition to the rules of phonology, semantics, and syntax, we need to learn *pragmatic rules*. These are the rules that enable us to use language in an appropriate and effective manner, what some scholars call *communicative* rather than linguistic competence (Hymes, 1972). Pragmatic rules include the range of social skills we need in order to meet people, make friends, manage conflict, sell ideas, build intimacy, and so on. The core concern among those who study the pragmatics of language is how people use verbal communication in ordinary conversations to express their intentions and achieve their goals. For instance, linguistics scholar H. P. Grice (1975) provided a framework for the study of conversations by offering a set of rules that communicators must follow: *how much to say* (quantity), *telling the truth* (quality), *staying on topic* (relevance), *taking turns*, and *making sense* (manner). Perhaps most importantly, communication competence demands some degree of flexibility and the ability to "say the right things" for the particular occasion, taking into account who we are addressing. The linguistic tools we use to say the right things are referred to as *speech acts*, and include common utterances such as questions, compliments, declarations, requests, promises, threats, apologies, excuses, and the like (Searle, 1969). As we will discuss later in the chapter, the uses and interpretations of speech acts vary considerably across cultures. But in the next section we consider how the languages of a people can shape and reflect their shared experiences and worldviews.

Language as an Expression of Culture

The idea cited most often to explain the interrelation between language and culture is known as the *Sapir-Whorf hypothesis*, crediting the work of linguistic anthropologists Edward Sapir (1921) and his student Benjamin Whorf (1956). Their hypothesis posits a link between the language of a particular culture and how the members of that culture perceive and think about the world. In fact, bilingual speakers often comment that they seem to think differently in one language than they do in another. One interpretation of the Sapir-Whorf hypothesis, known as *linguistic determinism*, asserts that our language determines our thoughts and perceptions. A more modest and widely accepted version, called *linguistic relativity*, asserts only that different languages reflect and promote different worldviews. Some support for this hypothesis comes from knowing that the language of a group often differs in ways that represent the cultural milieu of that group. Additional support comes from the results of studies on the effects of a language on the thoughts and perceptions of its users.

Language Reflects Culture

One line of inquiry examines the features of a particular language—its vocabulary and grammar—to find examples of how that language reflects the culture of the people who use it (i.e., values, thoughts, perceptions, experiences). First, consider some examples of how the *vocabulary of a language* tells us what a culture regards as important. Often, this involves representing aspects of the physical environment related to the survival of a people. It is well known, for instance, that Eskimo languages contain many different words for *snow*. Central Alaskan Yupik, which is spoken by about 13,000 people in the coast and river areas of southwestern Alaska, is one of five Eskimo languages. It contains as many as 15 different terms representing types of snow, including words for fine snow, drifting particles, clinging particles, crust on fallen snow, fallen snow floating on water, and so on (Woodbury, 1991). In his early research, Sapir (1921) observed that the language of Paiute people living in semidesert areas of Arizona, Utah, and Nevada contained numerous words signifying the geography of the surrounding area: circular valley, sand flat, spot of level ground in mountains surrounded by ridges, canyon without water, shaded slope of mountain or canyon wall, and so forth. While the English language can describe each of these topographical features, as Sapir does above, it does not contain specific words for each. The color-coding used in a language can also be revealing. How many words are there in the English language for the color green? The reading below offers an insightful account of the many words available to the Zulu people of South Africa (see A Closer Look 7.2).

The language of a culture can also provide insight into the emotional experiences of that culture. In Greece, for example, they have an emotion called *philotimo*, which is understood as an "honor" emotion. A *philotimo* person can be a person who is honorable (*éntimos*), honest (*tímios*), generous and hospitable (*filóxenos*), good (*kalós*), or worthy (*agios*), among others. Despite its tendency to elude precise definition, *philotimo* is valued in Greek society more than status or wealth (Koutsantoni, 2007). The importance of guilt for collectivistic cultures may explain why a culture like China has more types of guilt in their language. Bedford (2004) found that three types of guilt can be differentiated in Mandarin language: (1) the guilt felt from failure to uphold an obligation to another (*nei jiu*), (2) the guilt felt in case of moral transgression (*zui e gan*), and (3) the guilt felt in case of legal transgression (*fan zui gan*). The emotion of shame and other self-conscious emotions are more important and differentiated in some cultures than they are in others. One study reported as many as 113 terms for shame in contemporary Chinese (Li, Wang, & Fischer, 2004); another identified more than 150 Chinese words for varieties of shame, guilt and embarrassment, with only a few dozen in English.

Words indicating spatial or temporal relations, called *deictic terms*, also differ by culture. In American English, for instance, we refer to things that are "here" or "there" and if at a greater distance, "over there." In the Trukese language of Micronesia, such references are accompanied by location markers that specify the position of something relative to both the speaker and the listener, including words that indicate something is "closer to you than to me." The availability of these terms seems to suggest that the Trukese peoples' experience of spatial relations may be more salient than that of Americans, whose language does not provide so many "spatial boundary markers" and for whom space is therefore a more abstract concept (Stewart & Bennett, 1991).

The grammar of a language can also be a sign of what a culture regards as important. Whorf's own studies of the language spoken by the Hopi Indians (Native Americans who have been living in northwestern Arizona for more than a thousand years) provided some of the first data on this subject. For instance, Whorf demonstrated how the Hopi language reflects a different conception of time than that of English speakers. The Hopi people do not objectify time; they do not regard it as something discrete, measurable in units and counted as though we were counting physical objects. Thus, they do not express time in plural form, such as saying, "I will be there in *10 days.*" Their language also does not use verb tense, as English and many other languages do, to indicate whether something happened in the past, is happening in the present, or will happen in the future (e.g., he *ate*, he *is eating*, he *will eat*). Similarly, the Trukese language does not have any elaborate future tense, reflecting a "here and now" orientation to life (Stewart & Bennett, 1991).

A CLOSER LOOK   **7.2**

39 Words for the Color Green

I was interested in how the Zulus could build up 39 one-word concepts for green, while English has only one, and discussed this at length with a former Zulu chief who had earned a doctorate in philology at Oxford. He began by explaining why Zulus needed 39 words for green. In the days before automotive transport and national highways, the Zulu people would often make long treks across the savannah grasslands. There were no signposts or maps and lengthy journeys had to be described by those who had traveled the route before. The language adapted itself to the requirements of its speakers.

English copes with concepts such as contract deadlines and stock futures, but our tongue is seen as poverty stricken and inadequately descriptive by Africans and Native Americans, whose languages abound in finely wrought, beautifully logical descriptions of nature, causation, repetition, duration, and result.

"Give me some examples of different green-words," I said to my Zulu friend.

He picked up a leaf. "What color is this?" He asked.

"Green," I replied.

The sun was shining. He waited until a cloud intervened. "What color is the leaf now?" He asked.

"Green," I answered, already sensing my inadequacy.

"It isn't the same green, is it?"

"No, it isn't."

"We have a different word in Zulu."

He dipped the leaf in water and held it our again. "Has the color changed?"

"Yes."

"In Zulu we have a word for green shining wet."

The sun came out again and I needed another word (leaf-green-wet-but-with-sunshine on-it!).

My friend retreated 20 yards and showed me the leaf. "Has the color changed again?"

"Yes," I yelled.

"We have another word," he said with a smile.

He went on to indicate how different Zulu greens would deal with tree leaves, bush leaves, leaves vibrating in the wind, river greens, pool greens, tree trunk greens, crocodile greens . . . . He got to 39 without even raising a sweat.

(Lewis, 2018)

Some languages reflect a pattern of thought that differs from other languages. The syntax of Chinese, like English, forms sentences in a subject-verb-object sequence, but avoids the "is or is not" polarity of the English language (e.g., "she is young or not young"). Chinese encourages complementary ordering of relations, which would be opposites in English, such as "young" or "old." Chinese articulates the *middle values*, which in English would represent a continuum stretching between polar extremes (young vs. old). Chinese thinking avoids using the ends of the dimensions to grasp the nature of the things. Instead, Chinese focuses on the quality of the continuum. For example, some emotions that are polarized in English (e.g., love and hate) would be expressed in Chinese through the use of complementary pairs of moderate emotions, such as deference and politeness, social obligations and privileges, and congeniality and despondency, rather than the pairing of extreme opposites. So, Chinese functions more as an *analog* code compared to the more *digital*, binary structure of English (Stewart & Bennett, 1991).

Another revealing difference between English and Chinese is the relative weight attached to nouns and verbs. English speakers are more interested in categorizing things, placing greater importance on nouns than on verbs in their everyday discourse. In contrast, Chinese speakers pay more attention to verbs. For example, suppose a guest finishes drinking a cup of tea and the host wants to know if the guest would like more. A Chinese host might ask, "Drink more?" whereas an American host would be more likely to ask, "More tea?" To the Chinese speaker the action (verb) is more informative than the object (it's obvious the person is having tea), but to the American speaker the object (noun) is more informative than the action (it's obvious the person is drinking). In fact, this difference in focus begins early in a child's development. As Richard Nisbett (2003) explains:

> Western parents are noun-obsessed, pointing objects out to their children, naming them, and telling them about their attributes. Strange as it may seem to Westerners, Asians don't seem to regard object naming as part of the job description for a parent. (p. 150)

In one study, researchers visited the homes of Japanese and American mothers to observe how the mothers interacted with their infants (Fernald & Morikawa, 1993). They gave the mothers several toys (e.g., stuffed animals, a car, a truck) and asked them to play with the toys with their babies as they normally would. American mothers used twice as many object labels as did the Japanese mothers (e.g., "That's a car. See the car? It's got nice wheels."). Japanese mothers spent more time teaching their babies how to be polite with the toys (e.g., "I give this to you, now you give this to me"). Other researchers have found that Korean children generally develop object-naming and categorization skills much later than French- and English-speaking children (Gopnik & Choi, 1990). More recent research supports this cultural bias. One study, for example, comparing the vocabulary acquisition of English-speaking Europeans and that of Mandarin-speaking and Korean-speaking Asians at three different age groups (16, 19, and 22 months) found that the English-speaking children used more nouns in their speech than did the Chinese-speaking and Korean-speaking children (Yee, 2020). According to the researcher, the primary difference between Eastern and Western cultures regarding the emphasis on nouns compared to verbs is the that, "Western cultures are known to favor pointing and labeling in their interaction with young children and thus should produce more nouns overall than Asian culture, which is seen as more event oriented" (p. 40).

Language Shapes Culture

A second line of inquiry into the Sapir-Whorf hypothesis examines the impact of a language on thoughts and perceptions. Some early experiments failed to support the claim that our language influences the way we see the world. For instance, there is no evidence that Eskimos "see" more varieties of snow than others do, even though they have a richer set of snow-related terms in their vocabulary. Similarly, most studies have not confirmed the idea that people who speak languages containing fewer words for colors—some languages contain only the words "black" and "white"—are less likely to see certain colors than people who speak languages that have many color-related words. However, some research suggests that perceptions of *people*, in particular, may be vulnerable to the effects of language because these descriptions (especially "inner qualities") are much more variable and subjective than our descriptions of the physical environment (Holtgraves, 2002).

In one study, researchers presented Chinese-English bilingual speakers with personality descriptions of four individuals. Two of the descriptions were consistent with a one-word label in English, but not Chinese (e.g., artistic) and two of the descriptions were consistent with a one-word label in Chinese but not English (e.g., the word *shi gu* means a person who is worldly, experienced, reserved, socially skilled, and devoted to family). The participants were randomly assigned to read the descriptions in either Chinese or English. Several days later, the researchers asked for the participants' impressions of the individuals who had been described and found that the impressions were influenced by the language used: participants relied more heavily on Chinese stereotypes when they read the descriptions in Chinese and English stereotypes when they read the descriptions in English (Hoffman, Lau, & Johnson, 1986).

Other studies suggest that the verb-oriented language of Asians encourages them to be less focused on putting things into categories than Westerners, but more focused on figuring out how things affect one another. In one study, American and Chinese children viewed pictures of three things (grass, chicken, cow) and then had to decide which two seemed to go together (Chiu, 1972). Americans were more likely to put the cow and the chicken together because they are both animals (category/noun), the Chinese children tended to put the cow and the grass together because the cow eats the grass (action/verb). In another study, researchers compared college students from the US with students from mainland China and Taiwan (Ji, Zhang, & Nisbett, 2002). The students looked at sets of three words and decided which two belonged together in each set. For instance, which two of these words belong together: panda, monkey, banana? Once again, Americans showed a preference for categorizing (panda and monkey go together because they are animals) whereas the Chinese showed a preference for action (monkeys and bananas go together because monkeys eat bananas). Interestingly, one researcher studying the Tongan language (Tonga is a country located in the South Pacific) suggested that their language produces a different conception of "probability" as it is typically understood in Western cultures. This difference, in turn, could influence the Tongan comprehension of the concept as well as how the concept is used in Western languages such as English. As the author says, "Attitudes toward uncertainty, fatalism, free will, obedience, and predetermination combine with a dearth of vocabulary to provide a lens through which probability is understood (Morris, 2021, p. 131). Although more research is needed, these studies provide some support for the linguistic relativity version of the Sapir-Whorf hypothesis, namely that the language of a people reflects and influences the culture in which they live.

Cultural Influences on Verbal Codes and Styles

When we think about the connection between culture and language, we tend to focus on the linguistic differences associated with the phonological, semantic, and syntactical rules of a particular language. Less apparent are the differences that arise from learning the *pragmatic rules* of a language; that is, the rules governing the use and interpretation of various *speech acts* we use in everyday interactions: greetings, compliments, complaints, apologies, requests, refusals, forms of address, self-disclosures, expressions of gratitude, and so on. As a result, we may assume that everyone is following the same set of rules when, in fact, they are not. So how does culture influence this aspect of everyday discourse? We discuss some of these theories below. But first we offer a word of caution. Increased globalization may be complicating, weakening, or eradicating many of these cultural differences. The error of assuming a cultural difference where none exists is no less troublesome than is the mistake of assuming we are all alike.

High- and Low-Context Communication Codes

In the previous chapter we introduced Edward Hall's contention that cultures differ in their use of high- versus low-context communication codes (Hall, 1976). The *context* of communication includes all the elements of an interaction except for the communicators' verbal and nonverbal messages. The contextual elements in an interaction include one's prior experiences, the interpersonal relationship, the occasion, the surrounding environment, and so forth. Low-context cultures rely more heavily on verbal communication to get a message across than do high-context cultures, which rely more on the unspoken messages embedded in a particular context (often silence). Collectivistic cultures tend to use high-context communication whereas individualistic cultures rely more heavily on verbal expression. Richard Brislin (2008) offers the following example:

> People in collectivist cultures do not feel the need to verbalize their appreciation to members of their groups, since everyone already knows they are grateful to each other. In Korea, these phrases are used more often with people who do not know each other well. Once people spend time together and become close, they assume that favors and positive behaviors are appreciated. If they had to say, "thank you" frequently, this would be a sign that the relationship is not particularly close. (p. 44)

Low-context, individualistic cultures place a heavier burden on the speaker to get a message across than on the listener to understand the message. In contrast, high-context, collectivistic cultures are more likely to blame the listener for not understanding a message than the speaker for not being clear enough. To illustrate the difference, and also draw some attention to the potential for cross-cultural misunderstandings, consider the following intercultural encounters:

> An American student shares a dormitory room with a Thai. They get on well. Then, after they have lived together for several weeks, the Thai abruptly announces that he has applied for a transfer to another room. The American is surprised and upset and asks the Thai why he wants to move. The Thai is reluctant to speak but eventually says that he can't stand the American's noisiness, loud stereo, late visitors, and untidiness. The American is even more surprised: all this is new to him. "Couldn't you have told me this sooner?" he says. "Maybe I could have done something about it." (Thomas & Inkson, 2009, pp. 113–114)

> Shortly after arriving from Beirut, Mrs. Berberian breaks her ankle and goes to a doctor who expresses interest in her Middle Eastern background. Consequently, on her next appointment, she brings him homemade Armenian pastries. He falls in love with her cooking, so on subsequent visits, she brings him more treats. One day he asks her if she would be willing to make three hundred spinach *bouraks* (spinach-filled pastries) for a party he is hosting. "I'll pay you for your costs," he says. Flattered, Mrs. Berberian agrees. She labors many hours, spends a lot of money on the ingredients, and even buys a special tray to display the finished delicacies. When the doctor comes to pick them up, he is delighted and asks, "How much do I owe you?" "Oh, nothing," demurs an exhausted Mrs. Berberian. Surprised, the doctor says, "Why, thank you," and leaves with the three hundred pastries. Mrs. Berberian weeps bitterly. (Dresser, 2005, p. 197)

Despite a promising start in both cases, neither of the above scenarios offers much hope of intercultural community building. What went wrong? The answer lies in the cultural context of each interaction. Both scenarios present a revealing exchange between two persons, one from a low-context culture and the other from a high-context culture, who are trying to build a friendly relationship. But in both cases, the cultural differences in their communication styles are striking. In the first scenario, what to the American (low-context culture) seemed like a failure to speak up on the part of the Thai, was to the Thai (high-context culture) a failure on the part of the American to figure out what was going on between them. The second scenario offers a similar misunderstanding based on the low-context orientation of the doctor and the high-context orientation of Mrs. Berberian. The doctor's literal interpretation of Mrs. Berberian's refusal to accept payment for the work she did misconstrued her true intention to accept payment something she believed he should have been able to figure out. In low-context cultures people generally say what they mean and expect others to do the same; if there is a misunderstanding, it's usually the speaker's fault for being silent or unclear. In high-context cultures actions speak louder than words; if there is a misunderstanding, it's usually the listener's fault for not figuring things out.

Aside from differences in the value of speaking up and assigning responsibility to the sender or receiver of a message, there are other notable differences in the verbal communication of low- and high-context cultures (Gudykunst & Matsumoto, 1996). First, when offering information, people in low-context cultures tend to use more words expressing certainty such as "absolutely," "definitely," and "positively." People in high-context cultures, in contrast, use more tentative language, favoring qualifiers such as "maybe," "perhaps," and "probably." Second, speakers in low-context cultures are more likely to avoid comments that are not directly relevant to the topic being discussed. Third, low-context cultures tend to favor honesty over harmony or good relations. People are more likely to tell us what they think, regardless of the consequences. In high-context cultures people consider harmony to be a more important goal than telling the truth. In his book *Language Shock*, Michael Agar (1994) reports that Mexicans, a high-context people, embrace a more "relaxed" attitude about honesty than Americans do:

> The point of conversation is to keep the moment pleasant, to construct a positive sense of life. . . . It's more important to maintain that feeling than to "tell the truth" in some literal sense of the term. If the choice is tell the literal truth or maintain the pleasant moment, you tend to maintain. Forget a "frank exchange of views." George Washington was an inconsiderate fool for telling his parents he chopped down the cherry tree. All he did was upset them. (p. 156)

Mexico is one of many countries that fit the profile of a high-context culture. Other high-context cultures are found in South American, Arab, Asian, and African countries. Low-context countries include Canada, the United States, Australia, New Zealand, and most of Europe (not Spain and Portugal). As Lewis (2018) confirms:

> In Japan, where no one must face exposure, be confronted or lose face, truth is a dangerous concept. In Asia, Africa and South America, strict adherence to the truth would destroy the harmony of relationships between individuals, companies and entire segments of society. (p. 4)

The Four-Factor Model of Verbal Styles

Building on Edward Hall's distinction between high- and low-context cultures and Geert Hofstede's influential work on the dimensions of culture (see Chapter 4), communication scholars William Gudykunst and Stella Ting-Toomey (1988) identified four basic styles of verbal communication that differ across cultures. Table 7.2 presents their model of culture and verbal style, which we examine in this section.

The model proposes that differences in the verbal communication of high- and low-context cultures are modified further by a culture's classification on the dimensions of individualism and collectivism, power distance, and uncertainty avoidance. The *individualism-collectivism* dimension predicts the tendency to use direct or indirect and instrumental or affective verbal styles; the *power distance* dimension predicts the tendency to use a person- or role-centered verbal style; and the *uncertainty avoidance* dimension predicts the tendency to use an exacting, elaborate, or succinct verbal style.

Table 7.2   The Four-Factor Model of Culture and Verbal Style

Cultural Dimension	Low context	High context
Individualistic	Direct style Instrumental style	
Collectivistic		Indirect style Affective style
Uncertainty Avoidance—Low	Exacting style	
Uncertainty Avoidance—Moderate		Elaborate style
Uncertainty Avoidance—High		Succinct style
Power Distance—Low	Person-centered style	
Power Distance—High		Role-centered style

Direct and Indirect Styles

A *direct style* is blunt and straightforward; the speaker says exactly what is on their mind, leaving little doubt about the meaning of the message. With an *indirect style*, the speaker "beats around the bush" instead of saying exactly what

The verbal communication styles of persons in collectivistic societies differ from those commonly used by persons in individualistic societies. Many Asian societies tend to be collectivistic in nature.

they think. Often, the desire for honesty motivates directness, while the desire for good relations (i.e., face-saving, harmony) motivates indirectness. The direct style is most common among low-context, individualistic cultures whereas the indirect style is typical of high-context, collectivistic cultures. We often use indirect language with people in order to avoid confrontations, hurt feelings, imposing, bragging, and unpleasant topics—goals more congruent with high-context, collectivistic orientations than with low-context, individualistic orientations. Indirectness is a form of *nonliteral communication*, where the speaker's intended meaning differs from the literal meaning (Grice, 1968). Any speech act can be indirect (e.g., apologies, insults, compliments, requests). For example, try the exercise below to see if you can use indirect language to transform a blunt criticism into a softer and perhaps less hurtful one (Put It Into Practice 7.1).

Instrumental and Affective Styles

With an *instrumental style*, speakers focus primarily on themselves and the task at hand, using language to accomplish a personal goal such as persuading or making a good impression. This style is consistent with the values of individualistic, low-context cultures. As Richard Brislin (2008) notes:

> In the United States, the person who wants to communicate a message has the responsibility for seeing that this goal is accomplished. The person is expected to be clear, well organized, and should deliver the message in an interesting and enthusiastic manner. . . . Public speaking is a required course in many high schools and in most colleges. People learn to stand on their feet, to be the focus of an audience's attention, and to deliver their messages clearly. (pp. 42–43)

In contrast, when speakers use an *affective style*, they focus as much on the listener as they do on themselves and are more concerned with the process of interacting than with accomplishing a goal. The affective style is consistent with

---

PUT IT INTO PRACTICE   **7.1**

Being Polite with Indirect Language
Can you think of how to use indirect language in order to be polite? For each of the statements listed below, try to find a more indirect form of expression:

1. He's ugly. _____

2. The movie was boring. _____

3. The food was too cold. _____

4. My hotel room was dirty. _____

5. He's a bad driver. _____

6. I don't like her. _____

7. She talks too much. _____

CULTURE SHOCK

Why Can't I Get a Straight Answer?

An American scholar, Jeanne was attending a conference in Romania. Growing slightly impatient waiting for the bus that would take her and several other Americans to the conference, she asks the Romanian hostess, Sylvia, what time the bus is going to arrive. Silvia answers, "The bus will come." A short while later, Lisa, another American, asks Marius, one of the Romanian conference organizers, "Tell me what tour arrangements you have made for tomorrow," He replies, "Yes, but first I must organize the drinking of more plum brandy."

Americans expect precise answers to questions. . . . However, Romanians often avoid direct responses. Sylvia knew the bus would be late, and the truth would have caused complaints from the Americans. Sylvia's dodge kept them hopeful. Two hours later, when the bus finally appeared, the conventioneers were so relieved they forgot their impatience. Likewise, Marius knew that details of the next day's tour were not yet fixed. He shifted the topic to a Romanian hospitality custom, the serving of tuica, a strong plum brandy. After a few rounds of this libation, Lisa's anxiety about travel arrangements disappeared.

(Dresser, 2005, p. 184)

the use of an indirect style and is common in high-context, collectivistic cultures. In Thailand, for example, the responsibility for successful communication is shared among speakers and audiences. Even if the speaker is dull, unclear, and poorly organized, listeners are expected to pay attention and work hard to appreciate and understand the message (Brislin, 2008).

An instrumental style is more likely to employ various speech acts in the service of personal goals than is an affective style. For instance, complaining about one's personal problems and requesting help from others is more characteristic of an instrumental, self-focused verbal style than of an affective, other-focused style. In a study comparing Chinese and European Americans, researchers found that Chinese respondents, consistent with their collectivistic orientation to avoid losing face and upsetting others, were less likely to seek comfort and support from family and friends than were European Americans (Mortenson et al., 2009).

The appropriateness of offering and accepting compliments varies across cultures in a similar way. Compliments that recognize individual achievement are less acceptable in collectivistic cultures. As Dresser (2005) points out, "While Americans place high value on being singled out for achievement, many Asians feel awkward and embarrassed" (p. 185). On the other hand, *apologizing* is more characteristic of an affective, other-focused verbal style. In the United States, for example, people tend to associate apologies with weakness and the admission of guilt. In Japan, however, apologies show modesty and demonstrate that people are not putting themselves above others (Brislin, 2008). Arguing with others and expressing personal opinions also reflect the self- and other-focused orientations of these verbal styles, with clear implications for how one is likely to cope with conflict in everyday situations. In most collectivistic cultures, direct confrontations are generally regarded as more rude and undesirable than they are in individualistic cultures (Hofstede, Hofstede, & Minkov, 2010).

Person-Centered and Role-Centered Styles

A *person-centered style* (also called a *personal style*) emphasizes the personhood of the speaker by relying heavily on the use of first-person pronouns. It is also an informal style that downplays differences in status between individuals, encouraging people across a wide range of socioeconomic classes to engage in friendly conversation. The language itself often reflects this style. For example, in English there is only one pronoun for "you." English speakers say, "How are *you*?" no matter whom they are addressing (higher- or lower-status persons). A *role-centered style* (also referred to as a *contextual style*) is a more formal style that requires a speaker to consider the status of the person being addressed. It incorporates various linguistic devices called *honorifics* that signal respect toward an addressee. For example, the French and Thai languages contain many forms of the pronoun "you" that vary according to status and familiarity. Role-centered speakers are also more likely than person-centered speakers to use formal titles when addressing others, and are less likely to initiate conversations with persons of higher or lower status. Low-context, low-power-distance cultures tend to favor a person-centered style; this list includes North America, northern Europe, Australia, and New Zealand. High-context, high-power-distance cultures favor a role-centered

---

CULTURE SHOCK

Call Me Mrs. Rao

Sandy, a bubbly American in her twenties, meets Mr. and Mrs. Rao, a lovely older couple from India. They have such a good time together that the Raos invite Sandy to their home for supper. Soon after her arrival, Sandy goes into the kitchen to chat with her hostess as Mrs. Rao puts the finishing touches on the food. The mood is relaxed and congenial, so Sandy asks, "By the way, what's your name, Mrs. Rao?" Coolly, the hostess answers, "Mrs. Rao." The tone and response stun Sandy and she falls silent, feeling embarrassed and rebuffed. For her, the visit has lost its flavor. She can hardly wait for the evening to end.

Americans pride themselves on their informality, but people from Asia and most other places in the world do not see this as a virtue. Instead, informality often equals disrespect. Mrs. Rao believed that Sandy was impertinent. The major issue was age differences. Since Sandy was younger, she should not have taken liberties by wanting to call the older woman by her first name.

(Dresser, 2005, p. 188)

style; examples of these countries include those in South America, the Middle East, Asia, and West Africa.

In many parts of the world, even when they are well acquainted, young people must show their respect by addressing older persons as "aunt" or "uncle." In some Chinese families, the members themselves may not address each other by their first names and must call each other by their family relationship (e.g., "sister" or "brother"). In some cultures, people avoid using names entirely and describe the social relationships instead. For example, a friend of a Palestinian woman's daughter might call on the phone and say, "Hello Karen's mother."

Exacting, Succinct, and Elaborate Styles

There are three styles that deal with the quantity of talk a culture favors in most situations. An *exacting style* uses language that expresses neither more nor less than what it takes to get a message across. This "economical" style tends to predominate in low-context, low-uncertainty-avoidance cultures, where people value honest, straightforward communication and where they are not apprehensive (i.e., avoidant) about speaking their mind in unpredictable situations. An *elaborate style* refers to the use of rich, expressive language, including hyperboles, similes, and metaphors. To outsiders, the speaker using this style may seem to be going overboard in most situations, creating an impression that he or she is overly

---

A CLOSER LOOK   **7.3**

Too Friendly or Not Friendly Enough: Culture Matters

In the United States, there is often the informal norm that people acknowledge each other every time they come into contact. In Russia, the norm is that "once is enough." People greet each other and exchange pleasantries the first time they see each other, but they are not expected to do this upon a second or third meeting during the same day.

In China and other Asian countries, people can be charming and animated in their interpersonal interactions. However, they often limit these behaviors to a smaller number of people. When they behave in an enthusiastic manner, they are signaling a willingness to form a special relationship. . . . In the United States, people learn to meet others in an enthusiastic manner as part of social skills development. While growing up, they are taught to meet people quickly and to put them at ease, to show interest in what they have to say, to keep up conversations on a variety of topics, and to tell them how much they enjoyed the interactions.

In many other parts of the world, enthusiastic reactions when meeting others for the first time are not expected. Rather people are more wary and careful and want to get to know others well before communicating special interest and a clear desire for future interactions. . . . To Americans, many Asians seem like "cold fish." . . . To Asians, many Americans seem superficial.

(Brislin, 2008, pp. 39, 51, 52)

CULTURE SHOCK

Don't Talk to Strangers

Monica and her Ethiopian husband, Teshome, attend a concert, and at the intermission Monica begins chatting with the woman sitting next to her. Before long, Monica has told her that she is a teacher, the name of her school, and the kinds of CDs she collects. Going home, Teshome criticizes her habit of talking to strangers. He cautions that Monica has given away too much of herself. "People may use the information against you." He believes it is undignified to reveal oneself to a stranger.

(Dresser, 2005, p. 186)

---

emotional, or even confrontational. According to Gudykunst and Ting-Toomey (1988), high-context cultures classified as moderate in uncertainty avoidance are more likely to embrace this style than other cultures are (e.g., Arab countries). The *succinct style* involves the least amount of talk, and includes the deliberate use of understatement and silence. This style is most compatible with high-context, high uncertainty avoidance cultures, where people do not stress verbal communication and where they are likely to use silence and/or terse statements in situations that cause anxiety. Cultures that fall into this category include Japanese, Chinese, and Native Americans.

Up to this point our focus has been on the connection between one's cultural identity and one's use of language in everyday interactions. Cross-cultural differences reflect the fact that different cultures require language users to learn different sets of rules governing the correctness as well as the appropriateness of communication in a wide range of circumstances. In the remainder of the chapter we address the peacebuilding implications of this important connection. We identify a number of factors, arising from the use of verbal communication in intercultural encounters, that present special obstacles and challenges to peacebuilding. We conclude the chapter by discussing the verbal interaction component of intercultural communication competence.

Obstacles and Challenges to Peacebuilding

Consider the following scenario describing the communication breakdown between two people:

> Sean Seward crams all night for his medical school exams. At 3:00 a.m., he gets hungry and drives to a supermarket to pick up some snacks. Tae-Soon, a Korean man, is the only other shopper in the market. Sean walks down the aisle, where Tae-Soon seems absorbed in studying a canned soup label. Since Sean is a friendly fellow, he says to Tae-Soon as he passes, "Hey, how's it going?"

> Tae-Soon looks at Sean bewilderedly, then turns away and ignores him. Tae-Soon didn't understand the expression "How's it going?" because he didn't know what "it" referred to. Many immigrants share Tae-Soon's confusion about this common American greeting. (Dresser, 2005, p. 191)

As this episode illustrates, communication breakdowns in even the simplest verbal exchanges between persons of different cultures can challenge our most earnest efforts to build community. In this section we examine four such challenges: limits to language learning, threats to cultural identity, roadblocks to rapport, and challenges to civility.

Limits to Language Learning

There is little debate about the benefits of learning a second language, particularly as they relate to the task of promoting cross-cultural understanding. But learning a new language is no simple task. As intercultural communication scholars David Thomas and Kerr Inkson (2009) point out:

> Learning a new language carries major costs. Becoming fluent in another language takes substantial study and practice, particularly if that language is unlike your own in pronunciation, grammar, and conventions. Language learners expend considerable time and effort in learning, and find that when using the language they feel stressed and you may even be distracted from other aspects of the situation. Also, lack of fluency may unfairly undermine credibility in the eyes of fluent speakers. (pp. 121–122)

Have you ever taken a college course in a foreign language? If so, you have some idea of the work and time it takes to learn a new language. Estimates indicate that, while the typical college course contains no more than 180 hours of instruction, it takes at least 600 hours of instruction to achieve speaking and listening proficiency in a new language that is relatively similar to one's native language (e.g., English speakers learning Spanish). Those numbers go up to 1,300 hours of instruction for new languages that are moderately different (e.g., English speakers learning Russian) and 2,200 hours for new languages that are very different (e.g., English speakers learning Chinese). Putting in the time and effort needed to learn a new language requires a great deal of motivation. But research confirms that successful outcomes also depend on the age of the learner (young children generally learn more easily than adults do, particularly with respect to pronunciation), the level of exposure to the language, and various factors related to a learner's general aptitude for language learning that directly influence the ability to learn the sounds and syntax of a new language. For example:

> In a study of immigrants who spoke Korean or Chinese at home but English outside, those who came to the United States between the ages of 3 and 7 had average English grammar test scores as adults equal to those of native English speakers. Those who arrived at later ages had less mastery of grammar as adults. (Zurawsky, 2006, p. 3)

Language learning also involves understanding a culture's *idioms*, the figurative and nonliteral expressions or speech acts that characterize much of our informal everyday discourse. It takes considerable time and effort beyond formal language instruction to become proficient in using and understanding these culture-bound expressions. And, as we saw in the verbal exchange between Sean and Tae-Soon, the taken-for-granted use of these idioms (e.g., "How's it going?") and the inability to understand their nonliteral meanings, constitute a barrier to intercultural relations. How familiar are you with the idioms of different cultures? Take the quiz in the exercise on the following page (Put It Into Practice 7.2).

PUT IT INTO PRACTICE	7.2

What Do They Mean?

Instructions: In the blank spaces to the right of each idiomatic expression, translate what you think is its nonliteral meaning. Can you figure out or find the meaning of the Chinese, Dutch, and Hindi idioms?

AMERICAN IDIOMS	MEANING
1. "Tongue-in-cheek"	Statement not meant to be taken seriously; lighthearted; sarcasm
2. "Chip on his shoulder"	Holding a grudge; easily provoked
3. "That's the last straw."	The last in a series of bad things that can be tolerated
4. "Back to the drawing board."	Starting over again
5. "He has an axe to grind.".	Doing something for selfish reasons such as getting revenge
6. "Going out on a limb"	Taking a risky chance despite the consequences (thinking it's worth it)
7. "I'm pulling your leg."	Kidding with someone; a practical joke intended to fool someone

CHINESE IDIOMS	MEANING
1. "Three liars make a tiger."	
2. "Don't supply feet to a painted snake."	
3. "Plugging your ears while stealing a bell"	

DUTCH IDIOMS	MEANING
1. "Carrying water to the sea"	
2. "A flag on a mud barge"	
3. "High tees catch lots of wind."	

(continued)

PUT IT INTO PRACTICE (continued)	7.2

INDIAN (HINDI) IDIOMS	MEANING
1. "He walks like an elephant."	
2. "A monkey doesn't know the taste of ginger."	
3. "Thieves are cousins."	

GERMAN IDIOMS	MEANING
1. "You have tomatoes in your eyes."	
2. "I only understand the train station."	
3. "To buy a cat in a sack"	

POLISH IDIOMS	MEANING
1. "Did an elephant stomp on your ears?"	
2. "Did you fall from a Christmas tree?"	
3. "It's a roll with butter."	

Despite language learning as a significant obstacle to cultural assimilation, the United States lags behind other industrialized countries in removing some of these obstacles. As Khazan (2021) has noted:

> [T]he U.S. has an unusually laissez-faire attitude toward immigrant integration. Other industrialized countries do more to integrate immigrants and refugees into their society. In Sweden, foreigners get unlimited Swedish lessons at no cost; sometimes these lessons are built into job-training programs. France requires a short indoctrination session on "French values," but afterward offers 400 hours of language instruction with free child care. Canada offers extensive free language classes to newcomers, some of which provide free child care and transportation.

Another obstacle to learning a nonnative language has been a likely consequence of the global pandemic, which has forced people indoors where they interact more in their native language than they otherwise would. The linguist John McWhorter (2020) explains that:

> conditions under the coronavirus have created something ominously close to just that kind of isolation for the time being. Children whose Bengali or Danish

was slipping have now been spending infinitely more time with parents (and especially in immigrant communities, grandparents) and have been able to use the home language all day every day for the first time since toddlerhood.

Threats to Cultural Identity

Another formidable obstacle stemming from cultural differences in verbal communication is the damage to one's cultural identity that can result from intercultural encounters. As we have seen in this chapter and in the previous chapter on nonverbal communication, our cultural identity is inseparable from the symbol systems we use in everyday life: language, speech acts, gestures, emotional display rules, and so forth.

On a national scale, public debates over the need for an "official language" represent a fundamental tension between the desire to respect the linguistic identities of co-cultural groups and the desire to defend the linguistic identity of the mainstream culture. As linguistics scholar Barbara Seidlhofer (2009) explains:

> On the one hand, language use is influenced by the cooperative imperative: We need to continually modify and fine-tune our language in order to communicate with other people. On the other hand, we adjust our language in compliance with the territorial imperative to secure and protect our own space and sustain and reinforce our separate social identity, either as an individual or as a group. There is, of course, room for maneuver between these two options, but in principle one imperative urges us to lower our defenses and reduce our differences in the interests of wider communication with other people, while the other urges us to close ranks and enhance our differences *vis* à *vis* others to keep them out. (p. 196)

In a multicultural society, members of the majority culture may resist efforts to accept or accommodate the language practices of minority cultures if they feel threatened by such efforts, as may be the case with some proponents of the "Official English" movement in the United States. For members of minority cultures in particular, the choice of either facing criticism for using less acceptable "lowerstatus" dialects or criticism for abandoning one's cultural group is often what they perceive as a no-win situation. In a study of language criticism among Hawaiian speakers, Marlow and Giles (2010) cite numerous instances of reported criticism directed toward Hawaiian speakers who use the local Pidgin language, a lowerstatus dialect compared to Standard English. For instance, one person reported: "Speaking Pidgin is heavily discouraged by my father and his side of the family. Whenever we spoke Pidgin in the house, we were corrected. School teachers discouraged it as well, especially when speaking to the class" (p. 243). Non-English speakers in the United States often speak their native language because doing so enhances social solidarity with their peers; but not doing so labels them as outsiders or worse for adopting the speech patterns of the dominant culture. For example, Mexican Americans seeking to elevate their socioeconomic status by speaking English instead of Spanish risk being labeled as a *vendido* (sellout) by their peers (Edwards, 2010).

Roadblocks to Rapport

One of the primary challenges in building the foundation for a good relationship with someone is being able to interact with that person in ways that reflect and facilitate a sense of common ground. This feeling of "being on the same page" and "connecting" with another person, the essence of conversational rapport, may be more difficult to achieve in intercultural interactions. Less familiarity with persons from other cultures leads to verbal interactions that take more work, create more stress, and are more likely to go awry. Moreover, the very anticipation of these difficulties can lead to a *self-fulfilling prophecy*; we expect things to go wrong (e.g., saying something stupid, being distracted, or misinterpreting something), which makes us become overly tense and self-conscious, which in turn increases the likelihood of something going wrong.

It takes more conscious effort to initiate, sustain, and end a conversation with a nonnative speaker than it does with a native speaker. Not surprisingly, studies confirm that in America, for instance, immigrants who speak English are judged more positively than immigrants who do not (Khazan, 2021). Some studies show that when interacting with a nonnative person, Americans introduce more explicit and accessible topics, engage in more information exchange, elaborate more often, and go along more with incoherent comments from the other person than they do when interacting with a fellow American (Chen, 1997). The extra work it takes to navigate the unfamiliar terrain of intercultural encounters includes the use of *alignment talk*, specific verbal devices speakers and listeners use to show understanding, lack of understanding, or misunderstanding; to display interest or noninterest in a topic; and/or to reveal intent in the conversation. In a study comparing the conversations of American students paired with nonnative English-speaking East Asian students and American students paired with other American students, communication researcher Ling Chen (1997) found that the Americans engaged in alignment talk significantly more often with East Asian partners than they did with American partners. In particular, the American students used more verbalizations to clarify what they said, seek clarification about and agree with something their partner said, rephrase or repeat a partner's comment, finish a partner's sentence, and so forth. One of the unintended consequences of alignment talk in intercultural conversation, as Chen observes, is that its use (or perhaps overuse) may foster the impression that the user hasn't been paying enough attention during the conversation; an impression that could also damage efforts to build rapport and good will.

Listeners may also have to work harder to understand the "foreign accent" of nonnative speakers, which can impede efforts to build rapport. In addition to the negative stereotypes we hold about many nonstandard speech accents, new research suggests that some negative judgments have less to do with the impact of stereotyping and prejudice than they do with the impact of having to work harder to comprehend accented speech. In one study, researchers asked listeners to judge the truthfulness of trivia statements that were recited by either native or nonnative English speakers (i.e., a giraffe can go without water longer than a camel can). The nonnative speakers had mild or heavy Asian, European, or Middle Eastern accents. Even though the participants were told that the researchers wrote all the statements, listeners still tended to doubt the veracity of the statements more when they were recited with an accent than when they weren't (McClone & Breckinridge, 2010).

Building rapport may also be impeded by what some researchers call the *foreign language effect*, or the idea that people react differently to things when communicating in their native language than they do when communicating in a nonnative language. Some research among second language learners bears this out. For example, one study found that native speakers of Chinese were willing to take more risks in a gambling game when they received positive feedback in their native language when they won, than when they received negative feedback in their native language when they lost. This effect was not present when they were communicating in English. According to the researchers, this effect implied that the Chinese participants in the experiment were less emotional and impulsive when getting positive or negative feedback from persons communicating in their nonnative language (Thierry, 2018). But in terms of rapport, the experiment also implies that the gamblers and the persons offering the feedback were more "in sync" when they were interacting in the native language than when they were not. More importantly, other studies reveal that people show less empathy and consideration for others when the communication is in a nonnative language than when it is in the native language. (Thierry, 2018). Studies such as these add to the sizeable body of research reinforcing the idea that similarity build rapport.

Challenges to Civility

Cultural differences in verbal codes and styles can lead to negative interpersonal judgments that hamper efforts to build community. Consider the following case:

> An American student listens with growing impatience to a Nigerian student, who is responding to a simple question about his religion with several long stories about his childhood. Finally the American breaks in and makes her own point clearly and logically. The American evaluates the Nigerian as being stupid or devious (for talking "in circles"). The Nigerian evaluates the American as being childish or unsophisticated (for being unable to understand subtlety). The American urges the Nigerian to state his point more clearly, and in response the Nigerian intensifies his efforts to provide more context. (Stewart & Bennett, 1991, pp. 165–166)

In the incident above, it is easy to see how each person misjudged the competence and motives of the other because of a mutual failure to appreciate a cultural difference in verbal style: the indirect and affective style of the Nigerian as opposed to the direct and person-centered style of the American. In many intercultural exchanges, such misperceptions contribute to an escalating cycle of negative judgments, a "regressive spiral" that becomes difficult to reverse (Stewart & Bennett, 1991). See A Closer Look 7.4 for more on regressive spirals.

A CLOSER LOOK   **7.4**

The Danger of Regressive Spirals

The ethnocentric impression that one's communication style is natural and normal predisposes Americans to evaluate other styles negatively. Such evaluation is likely to elicit a defensive reaction, forming a *mutual negative evaluation* that stems from blindness toward differences. . . . For instance, Americans may evaluate Japanese indirect communication style as "ambiguous," while American directness may be received by Japanese as "immature." When communicators engage in mutual negative evaluation, the recriminatory interaction may be enough to block communication. If the communicators then attempt to overcome the difficulty through ethnocentric procedures, the communication event may deteriorate even further. The American, sensing Japanese reluctance to confront a problem, becomes even more personal and aggressive. The Japanese, reacting to an embarrassing social indiscretion, becomes even more formal and indirect. With each turn of this regressive spiral, negative evaluations are intensified; "ambiguity" may spiral to "evasion," "deviousness," "deception," and finally to "dishonesty." On the other side of the culture curtain, "immature" may spiral to "impolite," "brash," "impertinent," and finally to "offensive." In this pattern of mutual compensation, the actions of each person intensify the reactions of the other.

(Stewart & Bennett, 1991, p. 165)

Verbal Communication and Intercultural Communication Competence

We began this chapter by exploring the close connection between people's cultural identity and their use of language in everyday interactions. We then examined how cultural differences in verbal codes and styles create obstacles and challenges to building community. In this section we identify the two core elements of verbal communication competence that people need in order to meet the challenge of building peaceful communities: linguistic competence and conversational competence.

Linguistic Competence

As we noted earlier, learning a new language takes considerable time, effort, and motivation, along with the general aptitude and instructional methods that facilitate language learning for different age groups. Linguistic competence varies according to one's level of proficiency in speaking, listening, reading, and writing. The American Council for the Teaching of Foreign Languages identifies five levels of proficiency (novice, intermediate, advanced, superior, and distinguished) and specifies at each level the kinds of communication functions, vocabulary, degree

Learning a new language takes considerable time, effort, and motivation, along with the general aptitude and instructional methods that facilitate language learning for different age groups.

of accuracy, and flexibility that language learners need for each of the four major language skills (listening, speaking, reading, and writing). For example, new foreign language speakers at the intermediate level can handle a limited number of interactive task-oriented and social situations, such as introducing oneself, asking for directions, ordering a meal, and making purchases (ACTFL, 2012). But acquiring language skills at any level can be advantageous. According to Thomas and Inkson (2009), "Most people appreciate the efforts that others may have made to learn their language. So even though your fluency in another language may be limited, the fact that you have made the effort may generate goodwill" (p. 121).

Today more than a quarter of the world's population speaks a reasonable standard of English, somewhere between 1.5 and 2 billion speakers, making it the most widely spoken language in the world. Recent estimates have nonnative speakers of English well outnumbering native speakers. The growing use of English worldwide reflects the choice of English as a preferred *lingua franca* (shared language among native and nonnative speakers). It is the de facto language used for business meetings, academic conferences, science, diplomacy, international news media, social media, and the internet (McGovern, 2019). But this does not necessarily mean that the use of English as the dominant language faces no challenges. The increased use of computerized translation technology, the spread of hybrid languages (e.g., Hindi-English, Spanglish, etc.), and the rise of China as an economic superpower represent some of these challenges. As

Robin Lustig (2018) of the BBC puts it, "If you are an ambitious young job-seeker in sub-Saharan Africa, you might be better off learning Mandarin Chinese and looking for work in China than relying on your school-level English and hoping for a job in the US or UK."

Competent language use with lingua franca speakers usually entails some degree of adaptation and accommodation. For instance, the native speaker of a language has an obligation to ensure clear, simple communication by communicating in relatively standard terms, by avoiding jargon, idiomatic expressions, and other obscure language, and by not making too many assumptions about the other person's comprehension. As Thomas and Inkson (2009) emphasize, "Culturally intelligent people will consciously adapt their language to be in harmony with the vocabulary and style of the other person" (p. 123). Focusing on speakers using English as a second language (ESL), they propose some useful guidelines for native speakers:

- Use clear, slow speech; enunciate carefully; and avoid colloquial expressions.
- Repeat important points using different words to explain the same concept.
- Use active verbs and avoid long compound sentences.
- For oral presentations, use visual restatements such as pictures, graphs, tables, and slides; hand out written summaries of your presentation.
- Pause more frequently and do not jump in to fill silences.
- Take frequent breaks and allow more time
- Be careful not to attribute poor grammar or mispronunciation to lack of intelligence.
- Check for understanding and comprehension by encouraging ESL speakers to repeat concepts back to you.
- Avoid embarrassing ESL speakers, but encourage and reinforce their participation. (p. 123)

As we discussed earlier, native speakers often use a variety of verbal techniques to enhance mutual understanding with nonnative speakers (alignment talk). When not used in excess, these meta-communicative techniques contribute to the success of intercultural encounters. As Chen (1997) explains:

> By commenting on others' talk, on one's own talk, or on the conversation as a whole to secure mutual understanding of an event, alignment talk generally helps partners get in tune. It provides feedback on how accurate and clear the messages in the immediate past talks were, whether they should be taken literally or figuratively (as in apologies or warnings, etc.), what should be taken into account in interpretation, in what direction the conversation is going, and how well the participants have understood each other up to the current point. (p. 303)

Research indicates that linguistic competence builds community. For example, in a survey of Japanese sojourners in America, one team of researchers found that the Japanese respondents' perceived linguistic competence with English, and their perceptions of Americans' communication accommodation, positively predicted their relational solidarity with their most frequent American contact (Imamura, Zhang, & Harwood, 2011).

Conversational Competence

Of course, it takes more than the language skills noted above to become competent in verbal interactions with people of other cultures. Conversational competence includes the pragmatic uses of language, particularly those that enable us to say the right things in the right situations. Zhao and Throssell (2011) report studies showing that programs teaching English as a foreign language in China often focus on linguistic competence without paying much attention to the elements of pragmatic (conversational) competence. They conclude that these programs tend to produce many Chinese learners with a good mastery of English grammar and vocabulary, but often lacking in the knowledge required to make use of appropriate speech in their interactions with native English speakers. So, conversational competence requires a knowledge of the *rules and scripts* associated with contextually appropriate and inappropriate communication in different cultures and a willingness and ability to employ various *accommodation strategies* as needed to obtain positive communication outcomes.

As we noted earlier, although globalization may be lessening cultural differences in verbal communication codes and styles, being competent means being aware of these potential disparities. In specific instances where people rely on verbal scripts, as is often the case in greeting and leave-taking rituals, not knowing the script can be awkward and embarrassing. As mentioned earlier, one of the unfortunate consequences of the global pandemic has been the lack of social interaction outside the home so that learning these social rules takes more time and effort than would otherwise be the case. No doubt, regular daily in-person conversation makes it easier to develop conversational competence.

Summary

Differences in language and verbal styles of interaction contribute to conflict and misunderstandings in a multicultural society. Language is an expression of cultural identity. Learning any language requires one to learn the phonological, semantic, syntactical, and pragmatic rules of a language, which differ from one culture to another. Phonological rules govern the sounds we make to form words; semantic rules create the shared meanings of words, which include their objective (denotative) as well as subjective interpretations; syntactic rules address the meaningful arrangement of words; and pragmatic rules enable us to use language in an appropriate and effective (i.e., socially competent) manner.

Different languages reflect and promote different worldviews. Language reflects culture through its vocabulary as well as its grammar. Language also shapes culture by influencing the thoughts and perceptions of its users. There are also many cultural differences in verbal codes and styles of interaction, reflecting fundamental differences in the pragmatics of language. These differences draw on Edward Hall's distinction between high- and low-context cultures as well as Hofstede's classification of cultures. The four-factor model of verbal styles focuses on a culture's preference for communication that is direct or indirect; instrumental or affective; exacting, elaborate, or succinct; and person-centered or role-centered.

The strong connection between verbal communication and cultural identity creates significant obstacles and challenges to peacebuilding, which include limits to language learning, threats to identity, roadblocks to rapport, and challenges to civility. Successful intercultural communication requires both linguistic and conversational competence.

QUESTIONS

1. As noted in this chapter, the denotative meaning of a word is the objective, literal interpretation whereas the connotative meaning of a word is its subjective, highly personal interpretation. Connotative meanings can differ considerably, not just from person to person but also from culture to culture. Can you think of some words that may have a very different connotation in one culture than in another?

2. The language of a culture may reveal what a culture regards as important. For example, members of a culture may have access to a richer set of terms when describing places, events, or things that are important in their culture. Think of a cultural group that you identify with. How does the language of that cultural group reflect the values, beliefs, and/or customs of the group?

3. Explain the potential for misunderstanding and conflict that exists when someone from a high-context culture interacts with someone from a low-context culture. Can you give a specific example?

4. Think of a situation in which a friend solicits your feedback about something he or she has done. How would you respond if you had a negative opinion of what the person did? Would you tell the person how you felt even if that would hurt their feelings? How does this situation reflect a cultural difference in verbal communication styles?

5. In your opinion, how much of a roadblock to peacebuilding is the lack of a common language? In multicultural communities where people speak different languages, what is the best way to improve communication?

3

Contexts of Intercultural Communication

Intercultural Communication and Friendship

KEY TERMS

friendships
intercultural alliance
intercultural friendships
intercultural relationships
intracultural friendships
long-term and short-term reciprocity

relational learning
service learning
social penetration theory
targeted socializing
volunteer vacations

"What is a friend? A single soul dwelling in two bodies."

—Aristotle

"Peace is a daily, a weekly, a monthly process, gradually changing opinions, slowly eroding old barriers, quietly building new structures."

—John Fitzgerald Kennedy

The bedrock of peacebuilding is the construction of positive and powerful relationships. Throughout history, as aptly suggested in Aristotle's quote above, friendship has been one of the most important forms of interpersonal relationship. In this chapter we examine the advantages of developing intercultural friendships, the "new structures" that John Fitzgerald Kennedy identifies as the cornerstones of peace. Such friendships cross borders, religions, and cultures. Becoming friends with someone from another culture is a gradual process of breaking through stereotypical images.

The goal of this chapter is to appreciate communication processes that are critical in developing intercultural friendships, and consider strategies for becoming actively involved in building intercultural friendships—especially in a university environment. We begin with an overview of the nature of intimate relationships, introduce a general definition of friendship, consider cultural differences in understanding and enacting friendships, and explore research on the impact, challenges, and processes of building intercultural friendships. We conclude the chapter with suggested opportunities for contact and dialogue and strategies for creating and maintaining healthy intercultural friendships. Opportunities to develop intercultural friendships are all around us; sometimes we don't realize it until a teacher gives a suggestion in class or until an event on campus catches our eye, like becoming aware of student organizations on campus that are multicultural or volunteering with organizations that promote intercultural exchange that are part of the fabric of your college campus. Being part of a community such as a college campus can open unexpected doors of opportunity to explore *intercultural relationships* and develop friendships that might not have been possible or available during high school. Friendships between students whose ethnic or cultural backgrounds are different from our own background allow us to contribute to one-on-one peacebuilding efforts on our campuses and in our classrooms. Peacebuilding can start with domestic friendships and expand to international friendships that will last a lifetime and contribute to global peacebuilding efforts.

The Foundations of Relationships

What does it mean to be in a relationship with someone else? How does a relationship differ from a casual acquaintance? Millar and Rogers (1987) wrote a classic article about the three dimensions of interpersonal relationships: intimacy, trust, and control. They defined intimacy as the extent to which we let the other person know who we are. Fehr (2000) defined intimacy in terms of qualities that increase as a relationship becomes more intimate: (1) interaction increases in terms of frequency and duration, (2) partners gain knowledge of each other's innermost thoughts, (3) partners become more skilled at predicting each other's behavior, (4) partners increase their own investments (time, money, concern) in the relationship, (5) interdependence and a sense of "we-ness" increases; partners feel that their separate interests are linked to the wellbeing of the other, and (6) positive affect and trust increase.

Long-term, intimate relationships are marked by a commitment that the relationship is important enough to work at and protect. Knapp and Vangelisti (1996) make a distinction between "want to," "have to," and "ought to" commitment to a relationship. The "want to" commitment is voluntary and something that fulfills our needs, like forming a friendship because you share a common interest in sports. "Have to" commitment is dictated by legal or normative pressures; for example, a relationship between an instructor and a student that is dictated by the policies of the university. An "ought to" commitment is a grudging commitment because pressure to continue the relationship is too great to deny. An "ought to" commitment may be the obligation to care for in-laws even when there has been little contact between the families. It is in friendships where we have our first opportunity to emphasize the "want to" rather than the "have to" or "ought to."

The ability to know one another is essential for intimacy and that requires that we openly share about ourselves through communication. *Social penetration theory* argues that communication, and particularly *self-disclosure*, is the only way to move toward true intimacy in relationships (Altman & Taylor, 1973). As we see in the later discussion of friendship development processes, self-disclosure is an important element of relationship development in all cultures.

A General Understanding of Friendship

Friendship, more than any other kind of intimate, interpersonal relationship, is *voluntary*—people are born into families and marriages have legal and economic factors that influence their formation, maintenance, and possible dissolution. Even across cultures, a common characteristic of friendships is that they do not have these kinds of constraints (Sheehy, 2000). *Friendships* are voluntary relationships we enter into with people with whom we share common traits, shared experiences, or joint goals. Thus, friendship is *deliberate*. We are able to choose our friends and our friends are able choose us.

Friendship is both a *social* and *personal* relationship. While friendships are personal, our friendship interactions and expectations are shaped and shared by our cultures. Thus, we act within socially accepted parameters of behavior for people who are "friends" in our culture. Because there is an obligation of companionship and mutual support, close friendship is considered a scarce resource

---

PUT IT INTO PRACTICE   **8.1**

Defining Friendship

Often we take our friendships for granted because it seems like they have always been there for us. This exercise will help you to think about how your closest friendships developed and what makes them "tick". On a sheet of paper, write down the names of your two closet friends and then answer the following questions:

1. How long have you known these friends?

2. Where did you meet them?

3. How did you meet them?

4. What types of activities do you engage in together?

5. Why did this person become a close friend as opposed to an acquaintance?

6. Was there a turning point in the relationship where you realized your friendship would be less superficial and deeper and more meaningful?

7. How do you keep this friendship going?

8. If this friendship were to end suddenly, what would you miss the most about the qualities of this person and your relationship?

(Stewart & Bennett, 1991). Research across cultures found shared characteristics in definitions of "close" friendship:

> Someone who helps, someone who does not judge you, someone who does not need to be physically with you all the time, someone who knows how to keep in touch, someone who is like family, someone you can share with and trust, someone who shares your interests, someone who is truthful to you, someone who shares the same sense of humor or who can laugh with you, someone who can accept changes through life and grow with you and someone who has a similar personality. (Lee, 2006, p. 11)

A General Process of Friendship Development

Communication scholar Bill Rawlins (1992) has spent his career studying friendships and how they develop. Based on his qualitative interviews with thousands of people about their friendships, he suggests that there are specific stages of development in friendships and that these differ from the usual stages identified for romantic relationships. Rawlins' model gives us a general framework for how friendships form (later in the chapter we will explore processes for how intercultural friendships develop):

- **Role-limited interaction:** In the first stages of friendship the initial interactions are characterized by the use of standard social roles and rules—general politeness behaviors.

- **Friendly relations:** People move from a "civil stranger" mode of interaction to a "friendly acquaintance" stage. This acquaintance stage is marked by some more personal knowledge and generally pleasant interaction.

- **Moves toward friendship:** One or both partners invite the other to engage in brief interactions or activities that fall outside the other role relationships in the previous stage. People engage in more self-disclosure and start to compare basic views of the world.

- **Nascent friendship:** There is a point in every friendship when the partners actually start thinking of themselves as "friends"—perhaps not close friends or best friends, but friends nonetheless. This internal labeling is critical because it signals that they believe they should be acting toward the other in a "friendly" manner, a manner distinct from how they treat acquaintances or strangers.

- **Stabilized friendship:** When the friendship stabilizes it has progressed to the greatest degree of closeness that it will achieve, and energy is used on maintaining that degree of closeness. In addition to openly talking about their friendship, the friends also put greater emphasis on trusting behavior and trustworthy behavior.

- **Waning friendship:** When the friendship has been violated, reasons for the friendship have decreased, or challenges to the friendship have increased, friendships may wane and/or terminate. Argyle and Henderson (1985) found that certain offenses are often cited as reasons that friendships in American culture wane or are terminated. These offenses include acting jealous or being critical of your relationship, discussing with others what your friend said in confidence, not volunteering help in ties of need, not trusting or confiding in your friend, criticizing your friend in public, not standing up for your friend in his or her absence, not being tolerant of your friend's other friends, and/or not showing emotional support.

Cultural Influences on Friendship

Our definitions of "friend," our expectations of appropriate friendship behavior, and our understanding of the processes involved in developing and maintaining friendships are all influenced by our cultural affiliations.

National Differences in Friendship Orientations

Countless surveys of people from various countries show that national cultures can have vastly different ideas of what it means to be a friend.

The word "friend" in English can range from someone you just met to a best friend to a "friend with benefits" (Rubin, Palmgreen, & Sypher, 1994). In contrast, some languages make clear distinctions between types of "friends"—an indication of the relative importance of the idea of friendship in the culture. The Spanish language has different words for female friends (amiga), male friends (amigo), close friends (e.g., compañero), and serious girlfriends/boyfriends (novia/novio).

One of the most influential studies of nationality and friendship was done by Elizabeth Gareis:

> In her case studies of German, Indian and Taiwanese students in the USA, Gareis mapped some of the subjective components of friendship, and made suggestions about how cultural differences influenced notions of friendship and its obligations within and across cultural groups. She developed an incipient model, or at least a taxonomy, of 12 key factors involved in friendship formation among American and foreign students: culture, personality, self-esteem,

---

PUT IT INTO PRACTICE   **8.2**

Friendships in Film

It is easier to "see" the development of a friendship by watching one develop that is not necessarily your own. Watch a film in which a cross-cultural friendship develops and match the terms from the section above to various scenes in the film. Pay particular attention to verbal and nonverbal communication that indicates a change. Terms: role-limited friendship, friendly, move towards friendship, nascent, stabilized, waning friendship.

Film suggestions: *Gung Ho* (1986), *Mississippi Masala* (1992), *The Color of Friendship* (2000), *Bend It Like Beckham* (2002), *Gran Torino* (2008), *Loving* (2016), *The Upside* (2019), *Zola* (2020), *Boogie* (2021).

CULTURE SHOCK

"I made a new friend today!"

"I made a new friend today!" Adriana shouted happily in Spanish as she entered the house. My daughter Adriana and I, who were born and raised in the United States, were visiting her Ecuadorian Grandmother Teresa in Guayaquil for the summer. My mother-in-law and I reacted completely differently to Adriana's announcement. I was glad that Adriana had found a new friend on her first day of classes at the local university but Adriana's grandmother was horrified. She grew more horrified as Adriana explained that she had just invited her new friend to come for dinner that evening to her grandmother's home. The situation got worse as she included the news that she was going out later on with her new friend. As an American, I was surprised at my Ecuadorian mother-in-law's reaction and asked her to explain her negative response. She replied with a series of questions: "Why is Adriana calling a stranger, a new acquaintance, a 'friend'?" "Why would Adriana invite a person without 'confianza' into the home?" "Why would she even consider going out with a person that the family does not know?"

—Dolores

friendship elements, expectations, adjustment stage, cultural knowledge, communicative competence, external variables, proximity, U.S. (host) elements, and chemistry. (Kudo & Simkin, 2003, p. 93)

However, cultural differences in ideas of friendship are not only a function of nationality, but are also influenced by co-cultures. What characterizes friendship differs across ethnic groups in the United States: (a) Latinos stress relational support; (b) Asian Americans emphasize positive exchanges of ideas; (c) African Americans place emphasis on respect and acceptance; and (d) European Americans value recognition of individual needs (Collier, 2002).

Another significant difference in orientation to friendships is emphasis on *long-term reciprocity* vs. *short-term reciprocity* (Yum, 1988). There is a saying in Ecuador, "Today for me, tomorrow for you." It means that today you are helping me (for example, lending me money or listening to my problems) and tomorrow I will do the same for you. There is an expectation of reciprocity and that there will be time for that to happen because there is an expectancy that the friendship will not be short-lived and will grow and deepen with time.

American Orientations to Friendship

Making friends easily and quickly has always been a hallmark of American culture. American friendships are based on spontaneity, mutual attraction, personal feelings, and proximity. To a large extent, they are also founded on the knowledge that such friendships can end as quickly as they began when mutual need has dissipated. For example, think of college freshmen who are "best friends" during their first year of studies but who grow apart when the friends move during their sophomore year.

Americans primarily engage friends for socializing, activity-sharing, and fun-seeking (Argyle & Henderson, 1985). Unlike other countries, Americans are very open and receptive to contact with strangers and tend to have many friends, but not necessarily intimate friends (Barlund, 1989; Triandis, 1995).

American friendships often revolve around shared activities such as work, shared interests such as politics and sports, or shared relationships such as neighbors or family. In the case of college students, friendships often develop from classes, academic majors, proximity of living spaces, and participation in college organizations such as sororities, fraternities, and on-campus clubs.

Compared to other cultures, American friendships prioritize self-concerns, interests, and have few expectations of long-term reciprocity (Yum, 1988). These relationships are more vulnerable to dissolution due to fewer expectations, lack of institutional ties, and the ease of making new friends (Blieszner & Adams, 1992; Cramer, 1998; Sias & Cahill, 1998). Major reasons for ending friendships include a lack of time to share activities and/or a physical move that inhibits regular contact (Johnson et al., 2004).

American orientations to friendship often appear too casual to members of other cultures. International students sometimes complain that an American student may say, "We should hang out together sometime" and the international student waits for an invitation that never comes. The willingness of Americans to strike up conversations with strangers and to engage in small talk that discloses very personal information may give international visitors the impression that we are very friendly people. What visitors may not understand is that sounding friendly and striking up conversations with strangers does not usually indicate an interest in forming a serious friendship.

International students are surprised that Americans say they have so many "friends." Of course the number of friends that someone has may also include cyber friends. Social networking sites have resulted in widespread "friendship" formation, but the e-friendships formed by Americans are very different from the deeply personal relationships found in many other cultures. This may change as other nations become more increasingly "wired."

Asian Orientations to Friendship

Individualism/collectivism has a huge impact on social relationships in general and friendship in particular (Parsons, Shils, & Olds, 1951). A hallmark of some collectivist cultures is that friendship is considered a group/family responsibility with obligations that can span generations.

Another characteristic of collectivist cultures is the expectation that there will be fewer friendships and that those friendships will be more intense and longer lasting (Yum, 1988). In fact, research suggests that these expectations are passed on from parent to child. For example, a survey of 521 parents from four cities (Oslo, Norway; Lincoln, Nebraska; Ankara, Turkey; and Seoul, Korea) looked at differences in how parents taught children expectations of friendships. North American parents placed greater emphasis on fostering personal autonomy and independence in their children while Koreans placed greater value on family or community affiliation and on long-term, serious friendships (Aukrust et al., 2003). Another study of approximately 3,000 Americans and Japanese looked at the relationship between family-relationship quality and friendship quality. Associations between family relationships and friendships were stronger in Japan than in the United States (Piller, 2010).

In collectivist cultures, there are greater expectations that friends will always support and be there for each other; "true" friendship takes considerable effort and, as a result, fewer friendships can be sustained by any one individual. Further, members of collectivist cultures identify very strongly with their friends.

Confucianism, a foundational value system in South Korea, Japan, and China, strongly affects orientations to and practices of friendship. Confucianism is a philosophy of human nature that upholds proper human relationships as the building block of society. Confucianism is based on four principles: *jen* (humanism), *yi* (faithfulness), *li* (propriety), and *chih* (wisdom) (Yum, 1988). Three of the four deal with relationship building. For example, *jen* (or warm human compassion) is reserved for people who are familiar or intimately related to you. Think about the difference in US relationships in which familiar and unfamiliar people alike might receive the same treatment. While standing in line at a movie theater, an American might strike up a conversation with a total stranger and share a story to "pass the time." Talking to a stranger in public and sharing personal information or stories would seem very strange in Confucian cultures.

In direct opposition to the American model of carving up friends into categories for different activities, East Asian cultures focus on the idea of lifelong

CULTURE SHOCK

"I'm stuck at the airport!"

A Japanese friend of mine was unexpectedly grounded overnight at Philadelphia International Airport. Even though I was living in Japan at the time, he called my parents who lived 20 minutes from the airport wondering if they might pick him up. This friend and I flew to Japan together a few months before and he was incredibly helpful as I prepared to start a teaching position in Tokyo. My parents were aware of the great deal of support my friend lent me, including an invitation to stay with his aunt and uncle during my first weekend. Nonetheless, my parents told him that they had plans for the evening and could not help him. They were actually annoyed that he would ask for help when they had only met him a few times. From their individualistic perspective, Aki was my friend, not theirs, and they felt no need to reciprocate. I explained that if the situation had been reversed, my Japanese friend's family *would* have picked me up at the airport. They would have considered me a friend not just of Aki, but of the family. They would have felt an obligation to help out and would have reciprocated for the kindness and attention I had shown him.

—Dolores

friendship. But, as the following Culture Shock box demonstrates, this focus is not exclusive to Asian cultures. Other collectivist cultures also have this orientation.

Co-Cultural Friendship Impacts

Thus far we've explored the influence of select nationalities on friendships. But, as we have stressed throughout this book, culture is more than national distinctions. Friendships are also affected by other levels of culture or group affiliation, such as gender and sexual orientation. While an American friend may be male or female, in other cultures cross-gender friendships are frowned upon or strictly forbidden by custom.

The idea of expressing affection in same-sex friendships can be very different in other countries. For example, in Korea it is not uncommon to see women holding hands as they walk down the street. In India men show their affection to their male friends by holding hands (Gareis, 1995). This is an indication that they are very close friends, not lovers, as might be assumed in the United States. Turks tend to express friendship openly; men and women often kiss each other on the cheek in greeting and departure, and men supporting the same political parties may greet each other by making their temples touch (*The Istanbul Insider*, n.d.).

While we should bear in mind that different cultures may have norms for who can be friends with whom, it is important to consider the impact cross-cultural friendships may have on groups of people. Allport's (1954) intergroup contact hypothesis posited that "equal status between majority and minority groups in pursuit of common goals" could reduce prejudice. This means volumes for

CULTURE SHOCK

The Pandilla

While studying abroad in Spain, Sherry went to the cafeteria in the Facultad de Filosofía y Letras to buy a snack in between her classes. A group of about 10 Spanish students saw her sitting alone and invited her to join them. They referred to themselves as the "pandilla." During her semester-long stay in Valencia, the pandilla integrated her into their group. The pandilla had been friends since middle school; they were all from the same neighborhood and all lived at home with their parents while they attended the University of Valencia. They were studying different disciplines but each person frequently made time to spend together as a group. They had two favorite tapas bars to gather at regularly and took turns paying the tab depending on who had some Euros. They also traveled together on university breaks, usually going camping, and hung out together every weekend in an apartment that no one lived in but they all shared. Twenty years later, Sherry went back to Spain with her own daughter and was surprised to learn that all the members of the pandilla were still friends. They no longer got together weekly because of the stress of full-time work and families, but they did vacation and spend holiday time together in the summer as often as possible. In fact, their children had become friends.

A CLOSER LOOK   **8.1**

Bluetooth Friendships

The restaurant, like all Riyadh eateries, has taken precautions to prevent its male and female diners from seeing or contacting each other. . . . Yet despite the barriers, the men and women flirt and exchange phone numbers, photos and kisses. They elude the mores imposed by the kingdom's Wahhabi version of Islam—formulated in the 18th century—by using a 21st-century device in their mobile phones: the wireless Bluetooth technology that permits users to connect without going through the phone company. Unrelated men and women caught talking to each other, driving in the same car or sharing a meal risk being detained by the religious police. But connecting by Bluetooth is safe and easy. Users activate the Bluetooth function on their phone and then press the search button to see who else has the feature on within a 30-foot range.

(Abu-Nasr, 2005)

---

minority groups such as people of color and LGBTQ+ individuals. Many research studies have shown that as people from different social groups get to know each other and form friendships, prejudice reduction does occur (Barbir, Vandevender, & Cohn, 2017; Pettigrew, 1998; McKinney, 2008; Pettigrew & Troop, 2016; Galupo et al., 2014). Pettigrew et al. (2007) even concluded that indirect contact, such as when one's ingroup friends has outgroup friends, also has an effect in reducing prejudice toward the outgroup overall. In addition, there are corollary positive effects among those who have cross-group friendships, including better academic and social skills (Denson & Chang, 2009), increased satisfaction with college (Page-Gould, Mendoza-Denton, & Tropp, 2008), and increased multicultural competence and volunteerism (Smith et al., 2010). Liu, Wang, & Nuttall (2020) furthermore followed Asian Americans from adolescence to adulthood and found that cross-race friendships promoted adolescents' psychological well-being, especially when they were in schools where there were few same-race peers or where prejudice was widespread.

Individuals who identify as lesbian, gay, bisexual, transgender, or questioning (LGBTQ+) particularly benefit from cross-cultural friendship. In the book *Gay Men's Friendships: Invincible Communities*, Peter Nardi (1999) discusses the familial nature of gay friendships. Many gay men, as well as women, are ostracized from their families and communities, so new families are constructed. In this respect, gay friendships play a significant role in LGBTQ+ communities. Scholarly research studies have also affirmed the value of friendships among those who identify as sexual minorities (LGBTQ+) and those who identify as cisgender (Barbir, Vandevender, & Cohn, 2017). Galupo et al. (2014) emphasize that friendships between sexual minority and heterosexual or cisgendered individuals allow minorities to feel understanding and acceptance, with the following benefits (p. 200):

1. It helps minorities feel "normal."

2. Transgender and sexuality issues do not take up the majority of conversation or the friendship.

3. Validation from a person with normative identity is more powerful.

4. The larger population group offers a greater opportunity for friendship.

5. Emotional stability for minorities.

6. Helps minorities present as their identified gender.

7. Allows exposure to diverse perspectives and interactions.

8. Offers the opportunity to discuss the transgender experience.

These friendships helped transgender individuals feel "safe" when out in public and helped them feel connected to mainstream society. They also gave cisgendered individuals mutual support, a sense of "family," and an understanding of nonnormative experiences.

This being the case, what are some of the factors that could encourage cross-cultural friendships? There are quite a few which might yield some influence on where cross-cultural friendships could occur in a given environment, and here we present a few that play significant roles. One factor is **homophily**, or the likelihood by which people tend to want to be with people who are similar to themselves,

Friendships among sexual minorities and cisgender individuals are valuable. These friendships help provide mutual support, a sense of family, and an understanding of nonnormative experiences. (Shutterstock/Marcos Castillo)

with whom share a salient identity (Wimmer & Lewis, 2010; Gillig & Bighash, 2019). Another relates to **structural diversity**, or the relative representation of diverse groups in the institution (Bowman & Park, 2014). A third factor pertains to whether individuals value diversity, in other words, their attitude toward diversity could be a strong predictor of whether or not they establish diverse friendships (Bahns, 2019).

Gillig and Bighash (2019) studied the role of inclusive spaces in adolescent friendship network patterns. In their research, they observed adolescents in a summer camp that featured gender-inclusive housing and concluded that a camper's assigned cabins was significantly related to their friendship ties. This means that a camper's gender and sex was not the main driver of friendship formation, but the physical proximity with their cabinmates was a stronger driving factor. The authors conclude that providing inclusive spaces could play a role in counteracting the tendency toward homophily, allowing for greater likelihood of cross-cultural friendships.

Bowman and Park (2014) and Hudson (2020) highlight the importance of structural diversity, underscoring that if there is no demographic availability of different-race peers in institutions, then cross-race friendships cannot occur. Not only do they emphasize the importance of diversity in recruitment and retention, they also state that institutions should make it a priority to reduce tendencies toward homophily by promoting workshops and activities that allow cross-cultural contact.

Bahns (2019) looked at how beliefs toward diversity affected diverse friendship formation. She concluded that valuing diversity was a strong predictor of having diverse friendships. Among pairs of students who were studied, those who said they thought diversity was important were more likely to have friends from different races, religions, and sexual orientation.

We can conclude, therefore, that there are distinct advantages to having cross-cultural friendships. We now look toward other challenges brought about by intercultural friendships.

Challenges of Intercultural Friendships

The topic of friendship has been studied since the late 1970s but the research has concentrated on relationships within cultures rather than across cultures. According to Cargile (1998) and Gareis (1995), the focus has been on middle-class European-American friendships and the development of friendships across the lifetime (e.g., Rawlins, 1992). This is problematic since we live in a global community where our neighbors, friends, and co-workers will probably not share our values or speak the same native language (Lee, 2006); where opportunities to meet others from different cultures have increased dramatically and where intercultural relationships are becoming more prevalent and influential (Chen, 2002; Dainton, Zelley, & Langan, 2003; Gaines & Liu, 2000).

As we noted earlier, one of the reasons intercultural contact may reduce prejudice is the potential for contact to create friendships. In Chapter 13 we show that international cultural exchange has great potential to bring young people of

The number of international undergraduate students on U.S. campuses is growing annually throughout the nation, with the majority coming from China.

different nations together. However, positive facilitation of friendship requires more than just increasing the possibilities for contact. The contact can result in strong and lasting friendships when both parties learn to embrace differences and notice similarities (Gaines & Agnew, 2003).

The movie *Gran Torino*, starring Clint Eastwood, provides a moving portrayal of the challenges and beauty of creating a friendship between people from very different cultures, and the power of that friendship in building peace in a community. In the beginning it seems like there is no hope for civility, much less friendship, between the harsh and apparently racist Mr. Kowalski and his neighbors, a Hmong family. Events lead to a need for the neighbors to support one another against the gang violence in their community and they slowly develop an appreciation for their cultures and backgrounds that leads to real friendship.

While you may not have the need or opportunity to develop such life-changing intercultural friendships at this point in your life, you can do a great deal to explore the possibilities of the university context for these relationships. As you read the next sections, think about how these insights are related to your own experiences with intercultural friendships in your university life.

Research on cross-cultural friendship indicates that international students complain about their friendships or what they perceive as the lack of friendship with Americans. Complaints center on the perception that friendships with US students are too superficial and lack personal concern and care from the point of view of the international students (Mao, 2007).

There are some basic communication differences linked to cultures, as discussed in Chapters 6 and 7. Some of these communication patterns may "get in the way" of intercultural friendship, such as: How well do both prospective friends speak a common language? Which topics of conversation are appropriate? Is it more important to talk or to listen in a conversation? How much disclosure is too much? What can silence mean? How are emotions communicated?

International students as well as other foreign nationals can experience language difficulties when they move to the United States. Many who thought their language skills were sufficient soon realize that idioms, slang, nuances, and accents make them feel different, foreign, and misunderstood (Urban & Orbe, 2007). Nonnative accents, even for those whose first language is English, can affect communication. For example, a South African female once noted that even though her words were in English, they were alien to American ears and communication was more difficult than she imagined.

The level of self-disclosure is critical in intercultural friendships and consistently increases as friendships move from superficial to important personal relationships (Chen, 2006). Non-western cultures have a greater depth of disclosure, while western cultures have a greater breadth of disclosures (Chen, 2006). High-context communication styles do not place great value on verbal openness and verbal communication (Yum, 1988). Gudykunst and Nishida (1983) found that American friends talk more about marriage, love, and emotions while Japanese friends talk more about interests/hobbies, school, and physical activities. Japanese will discuss more superficial topics when establishing intercultural friendships, so Americans should respect the need to slowly increase self-disclosure as the intercultural relationship develops (Cahn, 1987).

Another aspect of self-disclosure is how we talk about ourselves. In the European-American context, boasting (positive self-disclosure) is a way of affirming the self as independent. In Japanese culture, the inclination is to self-criticize (negative self-disclosure) as a way of affirming the interdependence with others improving one's self by maintaining harmonious relationships (Miyahara, 1986).

Relational Development in Intercultural Friendships

Developing an intercultural friendship has unique aspects (Chen, 2002). In this section we review themes of relational development in intercultural friendships and processes of relational development.

Themes of Intercultural Friendships

Collier and Thomas (1988) stated that intercultural competence is the continuing match between appropriate respect for the other's cultural identity, appropriate level of curiosity, continuing interest in the other's culture, and the ability to adapt when inevitable mistakes are made. Collier (2002) refers to this as forming intercultural alliances. An *intercultural alliance* gives both friends the space to question, learn, and make cultural blunders that the other will notice but forgive. An intercultural friendship is an intercultural alliance—one that may be challenging to create and difficult to maintain.

An important question for intercultural friendships is how well they can weather the pressures against them. Intercultural relationships are more likely to be vulnerable because the dyad's relational identity is not well developed (Gaines & Liu, 2000). Relational identity (also termed "relational culture" or "third culture") is an abstract concept that might best be defined as the values, rules, and processes of the friendship (Wood, 1995). If intercultural friends can create a strong relational identity their relationship tends to last longer.

Relational identity helps us understand the links between friendship development and third-culture creation:

> The relational process emphasized in Identity Management Theory is close to the Third-Culture Building Model. . . . The focus of the current research, relational identity, to some extent, can be seen as a third-culture. The central

---

A CLOSER LOOK   **8.2**

Many Foreign Students Are Friendless in the US

More than one in three foreign students in a new survey say they have no close U.S. friends, and many say they wish they had more, and more meaningful, relationships with Americans. Students from China and elsewhere in East Asia report fewer friendships and greater dissatisfaction than do other international students.

The study of more than 450 students at 10 public universities in the South and Northeast supports what educators have observed anecdotally: Many students from abroad, and especially the recent influx of undergraduates from China, are struggling to integrate in American classrooms and dorm rooms. That's troubling, college officials say, for both foreign students and their American counterparts. "Where else can people meet and have the time and the freedom to make friends across cultures than at college?" said Elisabeth Gareis, an associate professor of communication studies at Baruch College, part of the City University of New York, and the study's author. "But we're not fulfilling that promise." . . .

The participants, who included both graduate and undergraduate students and were evenly split between men and women, were asked to report their number of close American friends. Although 27% said they had three or more close U.S. friends, 38% said they had no strong American friendships. Seventeen percent reported one such friend, while 18% said they had two. . . . Participants from English-speaking countries were most likely to report having three or more close American friends, while more than half of the students from East Asia said they had no Americans in their circle. . . . Half of the East Asian students surveyed said they were not happy with the number of American friends and 30% criticized the quality of their friendships. Overall, 38% of international students surveyed were not satisfied with the number of American friends, and 27% said they were unhappy with the quality of those relationships. Most of the students in the survey had been in the United States between one and three years.

(Fischer 2012)

assumption of the third-culture approach . . . is that members in intercultural relationships have a need to engage in a process of understanding and negotiating differences. This process involves adapting and converging different cultural values and identities. The activity of third-culture building allows all participants to gain an appreciation for and an understanding of others through negotiating standards, goals, and satisfaction in a conversational process. The third-culture represents a mutuality, which is understood and supported by people who are involved in its development. (Lee, 2006, p. 4)

Activities that promote the development of an intercultural relationship include being positive and providing help for a friend, rituals and activities, self-disclosure, networking, exploring each other's culture and language, emphasizing similarities and exploring differences, and competent conflict management (Lee, 2006). Providing help and being positive for a friend might include offering support during the culture shock period that accompanies living in a new culture. Rituals and rules might include "hanging out" together on a regular basis and either correcting the other person's language mistakes or agreeing not to "pick on language" (Lee, 2006). Self-disclosure and sharing personal information bring friends closer because there is an understanding that the other is trusted to keep confidences. Networking involves meeting the significant others in your friend's life. Exploring cultures and language means learning about each other to eradicate stereotypes and misunderstanding. *Relational learning* occurs through these experiences. For example, learning firsthand from a Japanese friend what impact the nuclear bomb had on the Japanese nation in 1945 is quite different from reading a textbook from a US perspective. Exploring differences and not ignoring them is critical in the process; however, emphasizing the role that similarities play in the relationships is also critical. Last, but certainly not least, competent conflict management is crucial to relational development and deeper understanding.

In *intracultural friendships* (those of the same culture, language, and background), factors such as perceived similarity in interests, values, and attitudes trigger the initial development of a friendship (Sias & Cahill, 1998). In intercultural friendships, however, "difference" may be the defining factor that sparks interest in a friendship. Cultural differences can serve as conversation starters. Prior international experience can also be a gateway to initiating a new relationship.

Some people are more receptive to meeting people from a different country or culture (Kudo & Simkin, 2003). The more receptive the person, the more likely he or she will initiate an intercultural friendship. Other favorable factors include frequent contact, similarity in personal characteristics and age, language skills, the willingness to disclose, and the openness of the host country to "outsiders."

Yet, it is also true that ethnocentrism is a strong inhibitor of initial intercultural interactions (Arasaratnam & Banerjee, 2011). To facilitate intercultural friendships we need to think about how to prevent or counteract ethnocentrism—a process that requires reflection, awareness, and action.

Models of relationship development between friends of the same cultural background focus on the increase of the depth and breadth of self-disclosure as an indicator of relational growth (Altman & Taylor, 1973; Knapp & Vangelisti, 1996).

A study of self-disclosure in intercultural friendships between American and East Asian (Chinese, Japanese, Korean, and Taiwanese) college students supports previous findings of the need for self-disclosure:

> First, there was consistent and steady increase in the participants' self-disclosure in intercultural friendships. . . . Second, regarding the six topic areas of self-disclosure in intercultural friendships, two categories emerged: Superficial Topics and Intimate Topics. Superficial Topics included attitudes and opinions, tastes and interests, studies or work, and personality while Intimate Topics were concerned with money or financial matters, and body and appearances. Third, the participants self-disclosed slightly more in close intracultural friendships than in intimate intercultural friendships. However, there was no clear difference between the amount and positive-negative self-disclose in those two types of intimate friendships. (Chen, 2006, p. 45)

The realization that all friendships depend on self-disclosure has practical implications. If you are interested in initiating a friendship with someone from another culture, you know that your ability to disclose information about yourself will be important. You may want to meta-communicate about the nature and levels of self-disclosure they are comfortable with in order to have the friendship develop as smoothly as possible. Meta-communication is "talking about the talk" and can be helpful in removing the guesswork about what seems culturally appropriate and personally comfortable for you or your friend to discuss or disclose. It also sends a strong message of respect that is likely to be well-received by any potential friend. For example, it is not uncommon for Japanese friends to ask how much money you make or how much your car is worth. An appropriate response would be to say that those questions are unusual for you and explain why you feel uncomfortable. It could be a way to start a conversation about what is considered comfortable to discuss and what topics are taboo in a developing friendship.

Processes of Relational Development in Intercultural Friendships

In the previous section we identified several themes or characteristics of intercultural friendships. Now we consider the stages of intercultural friendship development by reviewing insightful research in this area. As we present Lee's (2008) insights, think about whether these stages resonate with your own experiences of forming intercultural friendships.

Lee bases her expectations of stages of intercultural friendship development on relational identity theory created by Cupach and Imahori (1993), who argued that intercultural relationships in general follow three phases that are interdependent, sequential, and cyclical.

The first phase, "trial," represents the initial encounter of intercultural relationships. Successful trial phases demonstrate that relational partners support and confirm each other's cultural identities. At the same time, the possibility for social or cultural gaffes is high, so partners need to be tolerant of mistakes and willing to coach the other in a better understanding of their culture's norms. For example, is it appropriate to use the familiar form of *you* with your friend's parents or is that considered inappropriate? What does it mean if you are invited to a new friend's home for a meal? Does it signal something significant in terms of relational building or is it the norm in the culture to invite friends home for a meal?

The second phase, "enmeshment," involves the integration of their cultural identities into a mutually acceptable relational identity by which their relationship can grow and evolve. The new friends create a new relational identity and begin to specify the behavioral and normative expectations for that identity. For example, consider students who have joined a conversation partner program where they exchange time speaking each other's languages to improve their proficiency. The friends may decide that they always correct each other's pronunciation if needed or that it is the message that is important and not the way the language is pronounced.

The third and final phase, "renegotiation," represents a truly interdependent and personal relationship. At this point, the relational identity is fully developed. Competent members in an intercultural relationship at this stage renegotiate their different cultural identities based on their preliminarily defined relational identity, which emerged in the second phase.

Lee investigated whether relational identity theory explains the actual process of intercultural friendship development by interviewing partners in intercultural friendships at American universities. She discovered three stages of development that also involved some important turning points.

In the "initial encounter stage," friends tend to have light and general conversations discussing school or work-related issues. This is a starting point to explore each other's cultures and clarify some cultural stereotypes. There was an important transition at the end of the initial encounter stage. This transition had to do with the realization of whether continuing to build the friendship would fulfill basic needs and interests. If that was seen to be the case, the friendship continued to develop into the "interaction stage."

The interaction stage is when friends begin to realize that they have roles, rules, and rituals that they engage in on a regular basis. They increase frequency of contact and start to bond over activities such as eating, shopping, and playing sports. Friends reported being drawn to their friend's culture via celebrations (e.g., Chinese New Year, Christmas, Passover) and unique cultural activities (e.g., creating origami). In this stage, friends emphasized similarities and did not view differences as impediments to their friendship. On the contrary, in this stage they viewed cultural differences as positive. Another hallmark of the interaction stage is a turning point or a particular incident that stood out in the minds of the friends as something that moved their friendship to another level. For example, a student from Argentina recalled how her American friend stayed in touch with her when she had to return to Argentina for her brother's funeral: "I consider [Brent] as a good friend after the trip home when my brother died. The calls I received from him were something I did not expect. I never expected it from anybody because people were so far away. I received so many emails. People were so far away and so for me that was a surprise. And it made me feel good in many ways" (Lee, 2008).

The last stage of development in Lee's research is the "involvement stage," where the emerging rules (e.g., confidentiality) and roles (e.g., the peacemaker) for both members in the intercultural friendship were much better understood. In this stage, participants built trust and saw the other person truly as a lifelong friend. Participants revealed that they found their lives were overlapping with their intercultural friend's lives. Because of further interactions in the involvement stage, participants came to a deeper understanding of the other's culture. In other words, involvement is a stage in which intercultural friends truly learned to respect the other's cultural perspective.

Opportunities for Contact and Dialogue

"International education promotes the relationship building and knowledge exchange between people and communities in the United States and around the world that are necessary to solve global challenges. The connections made during international education experiences last a lifetime. International students enrich classrooms, campuses, and communities in ways that endure long after students return to their home countries. We encourage US schools to continue to welcome more international students to their campuses and to do more to make study abroad a reality for all of their students."

—Evan M. Ryan, Assistant Secretary of State
for Educational and Cultural Affairs

Leading up to the Lunar New Year in China, homes are decorated with fruits, flowers, and fragrance bags to bring good luck and happiness. (Shutterstock/Lee Charlie)

In 2020, the Institute of International Education (IIE) released the latest annual Open Doors Report on International Educational Exchange, which presents the latest trends on international education. Thousands of international students enter the United States every year to study at American universities. There are more international students studying in the United States now than ever before. Undergraduate international students continued to outnumber graduate international students in the United States. In the 2019–2020 academic year there were 1,075,496 international students studying at US universities, representing 5.5% of all students in US higher education (IIE, 2020). East Asian countries are among the top for sending their students to study in the United States, with China being the top country of origin for several years in a row (IIE, 2020). Based on this information, be aware that you have opportunities on your campus to meet students from all walks of life and from every part of the globe. A university campus serves as an excellent site to meet and develop an individual's first intercultural friendship. Research indicates that most students form their first intercultural friendship during their college years (Lee, 2006).

A key step in the path to building peace through intercultural relationships is to identify opportunities to create such friendships. You may be surprised to learn just how many ways there are to meet like-minded individuals who want to sow seeds of peace.

Seek out student organizations that are involved in building bridges between US students and international students studying at your university. Look for "targeted socializing" events. *Targeted socializing* refers to opportunities to interact with those from another culture through planned social gatherings such as a Chinese New Year celebration, international night, and Kwanza (Sias et al., 2008).

International students also benefit from opportunities to participate in formalized programs that promote interaction (Urban & Orbe, 2007). Many international students are more familiar with US culture than US students are with other cultures. By sharing "teachable moments" with US friends, it is possible for both to gain insight. When US students express interest in understanding a particular way of doing things, the international person becomes the cultural educator and advocate for international understanding (Urban & Orbe, 2007).

For many college students, the best way to build global understanding and forge intercultural friendships is through the experience of living in and taking college courses in another country. Using a study abroad program as a vehicle to make lifelong friendships will be examined in Chapter 13. Other ways you can get involved are through governmental organizations that promote sustainable peace and transformation. Non-Governmental organizations (NGOs) with these foci abound. *Service learning*, volunteering abroad, and *volunteer vacations* are organizations that promote positive peace through the creation of international relationships and networks. For many college students, you can combine study abroad with service learning for credit and student exchange programs.

The organizations listed below will give you the opportunity to work side by side with local people to achieve important community objectives. Projects can take place in orphanages and childcare centers, schools, health clinics, hospitals, homes for the elderly, centers for people with disabilities, and other vital community organizations.

- Volunteer opportunities, such as through Global Crossroad (www.globalcrossroad.com) and Operation Crossroads Africa (www.operationcrossroadsafrica.org), offer programs abroad in places like Asia, Africa, and Latin America. Organizations such as these enable the volunteer to become involved from the grassroots level to the administrative level of working towards sustainable peace.

- One organization that brings together young delegates from all over the world to exchange views, share experiences, and detect common preoccupations and problems is the United Nations Educational, Scientific and Cultural Organization (UNESCO, www.unesco.org). The UNESCO Youth Forum strives to create ideas for action. The Youth Forum allows young people to voice their ideas and concerns and make suggestions directly to the UNESCO General Conference.

- Service-learning opportunities abroad are plentiful for students who are interested. There are organizations that train and provide opportunities for service in Latin America, such as Amigos de las Américas (www.amigosinternational.org). Peacework (www.peacework.org) is an organization that promotes sustainable solutions to world poverty and disparity through global partnerships in development, education, health, and service. It offers projects throughout the world in countries such as Belize, China, Ghana, Honduras, India, Russia, Thailand.

Volunteers in Bangkok, Thailand, help bag food for families struggling after tropical storms caused major flooding in different parts of the country. Volunteering is a great way of giving back to your community and the world.

PUT IT INTO PRACTICE   **8.3**

Your Intercultural Friendship Behavior

How would you assess your comfort level with initiating, sustaining, and deepening your intercultural friendships? Which of the following statements most accurately reflects your personal choice in friendship matters?

1. I would seek out friendships with people from different cultures in order to learn more about their cultures.

2. I find it difficult to pursue a close friendship with someone from a different culture.

3. Even though I enjoy interacting with people from other cultures, I am most comfortable sharing close friendships with people from my own culture.

4. I would be comfortable pursing a romantic relationship with someone from a different culture.

5. My most satisfying relations are with people from my own culture.

6. I find it difficult to share deep personal feelings with someone from a different culture.

7. I have many acquaintances from other cultures, but my closest friends are from my own culture.

8. All of my close friends are from my own culture.

9. I find it easier to pursue close friendships with people from other cultures than with people from my own culture.

10. I don't have many friends or acquaintances from other cultures.

11. I don't mind talking to someone from a different culture, but I would prefer them to start the conversation.

12. I enjoy starting conversations with someone from a different culture.

13. I am always concerned that I might offend people from other cultures by saying the wrong thing.

14. My most satisfying relationships are with people from other cultures.

15. I find it boring to always associate with people from my own culture.

16. I always like to experience new things, including meeting people of different cultures.

(Adapted from Morgan & Arasaratnam, 2003)

- Have you ever imagined taking part in a volunteer vacation? Check out this slide show outlining the volunteer program in Portugal offered through the Global Volunteers Program (www.globalvolunteers.org). Global Volunteers is an example of an organization that combines volunteerism in a country with visits to sites of historical and cultural importance. Another volunteer vacation organization is Globe Aware (www.globeaware.org). They offer 1–2 week vacations that highlight culture awareness and sustainability. Participants have compared this experience to being involved in a "mini Peace Corps."

As the world settled into the reality of the COVID-19 pandemic, one communication pathway remained open and has become more relevant in friendship formation and maintenance. Social media offers exciting opportunities for communicating and engaging with others, especially for the phone-call averse Gen Y (those born approximately from 1981–1996) and Gen Z (1997–2012) (Dimock, 2019). As of January 2023 the United States and China accounted for the most widely used social media platforms (ranked by the number of monthly active users) (Statista, 2023). Facebook has the most uses with over 2.9 billion. It is followed by YouTube (2.5 billion), WhatsApp (2 billion), Instagram (2 billion), and WeChat (1.3 billion). TikTok, which only started in September 2016, has experienced phenomenal growth, with around 1 billion active monthly users. Other major platforms include Duoyin (715 million), Telegram (700 million), and Snapchat (635 million).

Several researchers have studied how social media has facilitated intercultural friendships. Chang (2021) did an in-depth analysis of the interaction between two individuals using WeChat; one person was in the United States and the other was in China. She concludes that WeChat enabled them to have interactive communication that created a "third culture" (Casmir, 1999) that was co-created and mutually beneficial. WeChat allowed them to have informal and personal interactions, enhanced their expressions of affinity and liking toward each other, and helped learn about each other's cultures. Mas'udah (2017) examined the use of social media in intercultural friendship development among foreign students in Turkey. Students shared that social media was useful when they could not meet face-to-face with their friends and allowed them to find out more information about other foreign students. In terms of use, they used social media platforms to share information such as news, jokes, and photos, as well as information that would have been sensitive if conveyed face-to-face. WhatsApp was used more for personal messaging than Facebook and Instagram, since WhatsApp was perceived to allow more privacy. One limitation mentioned by students was that personal problems were difficult to solve only through social media, and therefore they tended not to use these venues for this purpose. They also usually discontinued interactions when they found that others were not very similar to them, which implies that while it was easy to begin friendships using these platforms, it was also relatively easy to drop the friendships. Turistiati (2020) echoed Mas'udah's findings, adding that a WhatsApp private group maintained intercultural friendship by exchanging information about their families, expressing birthday wishes, congratulating achievements, fundraising, and coordinating reunions. However, the group found it important to impose unwritten rules governing interactions, specifically avoidance of politics, religion, and anything pornographic or demeaning to women. Interestingly, they also imposed rules regarding discussions about football that might result in enmity among members. One criticism of social media is that it could generally mirror friendship development outside its confines, in the sense that it encourages interaction among those who are similar to each other more successfully than among those who are different. For example, Shiau (2016) explored how social media enhanced friendships among people from East Asian countries in the United States who were learning English as a second language (ESL). It was concluded that the platforms allowed users to connect easily but hampered deeper levels of friendship. ESL learners ended up becoming closer friends with other East Asian students rather than North American friends through social media use, primarily driven by language proficiency barriers, as well as a lack of shared common interests with the latter. Communication styles also differed, with East Asian students preferring to send visual messages (photos, stickers, emojis) and American students preferring to send verbal texts.

Social media is not without its problems. More research is needed regarding its ability to nurture deep, long-term friendships beyond the "likes" and information-sharing capabilities. As discussed, groups have had to create rules of interaction in their friend groups. Certainly, the immediacy and breadth of social media's reach could pose dangers to those who post negatively when friendships go awry.

Students use social media platforms to share news, jokes, photos, etc., as well as information that would be sensitive if conveyed face-to-face. (Shutterstock/EF Stock)

Nonetheless, it does offer opportunities for cross-cultural friendship development that was not available even a decade ago.

The path to world peace can be paved with intercultural friendship, mutual respect, and understanding. With all these opportunities to build intercultural friendships, find the one that's right for you.

Summary

This chapter began with Aristotle's quotation about friends being two bodies who share the same soul. Throughout, we've helped deepen appreciation for how important and difficult forming friendships can be, especially when people are coming to that friendship from different cultures. The very idea of friendship is culturally based; what "friend" means depends on your cultural perspective. How we understand friendship is part of our cultural programming. How we understand who can be a friend and who is outside of the circle of choice is also a cultural choice. In addition to a difference in the general understanding of the term "friendship," the process for friendship development would not be identical in each culture. As discussed, there are national as well as co-cultural differences in friendship orientation, and societies often make it more difficult to create and sustain friendships. But intercultural friendships are a very valuable aspect of life and are especially beneficial to minority communities. We therefore encourage you to explore ways that you can increase your involvement in these relationships. You have great opportunities to form these friendships on your own college campuses, but you must seek out these opportunities. Being aware of your own comfort level in initiating, creating, and sustaining intercultural friendships will guide you in the process.

We also reviewed models of friendship development and how that process changes when the prospective friends are of different cultural backgrounds with varying expectations for what the term "friend" means. Friendships develop through stages and the better we understand these stages the more we can track our progress in where we are and where we want to go with them.

QUESTIONS

1. What benefits come from creating friendships with a person from another culture?

2. How would you handle a conflict situation with a new friend from a cultural orientation that is very different from your own? For example, what important aspects of face-saving/face-giving would you have to keep in mind?

3. Even though there are many international students who come to US college campuses to obtain undergraduate degrees, not all of these students make friends with the domestic students. What challenges do the international students face in making domestic friends on campuses in the United States?

Intercultural Communication in the Family

KEY TERMS

arranged marriage
biracial
extended family
face negotiation theory
family subsystem
family system
identity-affirming communication
identity-supportive responses

interracial children
LGBTQ+ parenting
love match
multicultural family
structural definition
traditional family
transracial
work-family interface

In the United States, marrying outside one's racial group was illegal in some states until 1967! In the landmark *Loving v. State of Virginia* case, the United States Supreme Court overturned laws preventing people from marrying a person of a different race (***interracial marriage***). Indeed, what was once a "scandal" is today something often not worthy of note, much less derision. According to the Pew Research Center, approximately one in six new marriages in the United States is interethnic or interracial (Livingston & Brown, 2017). Intermarriage differs for males and females in some minority groups. In 2015, for example, 24% of all Black male newlyweds married outside their race, compared with just 12% of Black females. Among Asians, 36% of females and 21% of males married outside their race. But, there were not significant differences between White males and females or Hispanic males and females on marrying outside their race or ethnicity (Livingston & Brown, 2017).

As these statistics show, the American family is becoming increasingly diverse. Beyond race, in 2020, for the first time, the US Census Bureau counted married same-sex couples. While less than 1% of all married couples in the United States are same sex, the numbers are increasing. This chapter considers intercultural communication in the context of the family. We begin by briefly discussing the basic characteristics and types of families, and in the sections that follow we

Interracial marriage was still illegal in some U.S. states until 1967, when anti-miscegenation laws were ruled unconstitutional by the Supreme Court. (Shutterstock/Rawpixel.com)

consider the influence of culture on family orientations and family systems. We conclude the chapter by addressing some of the many opportunities for contact and dialogue that are available to intercultural families today.

Family Characteristics and Types of Families

Families are a constant in every human society, although culture affects their different forms and functions. Cultural influences on the family are the focus in this chapter. We begin with a general definition of "family" based on structural and functional characteristics. We then examine cultural differences in orientations to family, emphasizing differences between individualistic and collectivistic cultures. Consistent with our peacebuilding view, we explore how cultures handle family conflict. Since families are complex systems, we use a brief overview of family systems theory to look further into the subsystems of marriage, parenting, and grandparenting—again with an eye toward the influence of culture. We also acknowledge that external systems (like work and social contexts), along with culture, exert a significant influence on family orientations. In the final section of the chapter, we introduce some resources that can help culturally diverse families find more peaceful ways of living together.

There is no universal definition of family. Scholars argue for definitions of "family" based on biological, sociological, or legal factors (Fitzpatrick & Caughlin,

2002; Galvin, Bylund, & Brommel, 2003; LePoire, 2006). Communication scholars Chris Segrin and Jeanne Flora (2019) clarify that we can define family in terms of structures, functions, and/or transactions. The most common is a *structural definition* of family—seeing family in terms of the structure of relationships among family members. The structural definition is also the most reinforced (at least in the United States and other Westernized nations) since government agencies, like the United States Census Bureau, use structural definitions, as we see in Box 9.1.

Other family structures are also important. *Extended families* are families with biological or social ties extending across generations. Extended families can include many forms, like grandparents raising their grandchildren or cousins living together.

We can also define family in terms of functions, by what they do for their members. For example, Fitzpatrick and Caughlin (2002) suggest that "family" is a small, kinship-structured group with the basic function of nurturing and socializing children. More modern views recognize *family functions* as including the care and nurturance of all family members. Families are the people who provide basic care, emotional and financial support, and help socialize members to help them be productive members of society.

Both structural and functional aspects of families are critical, thus, we use the following definition of family:

Box 9.1   Definition of Family Types

The US Census Bureau (USCB) defines "family" structurally, laying out who is in the family and who is not. According to the USCB, a family "is any two or more people (not necessarily including a householder) residing together, and related by birth, marriage, or adoption" (United States Census Bureau, 2021). Segrin and Flora (2019) provide the following examples of structural definitions for family types:

- **Nuclear family:** two parents and one or more children. According to the USCB, the number of families with their own children under age 18 in the household declined from 48% in 2001, to 44% in 2011, to 40% in 2021.

- **Single-parent family:** a parent, who may or may not have been married, and one or more children.

- **Stepfamily:** spouses, at least one of whom was previously married, living with the child(ren) of at least one of the spouses (also referred to as a "blended" family).

- **Family of orientation:** the family one chooses and/or creates (e.g., mate, child).

Segrin and Flora note that "just as the simplicity of structural definitions and labels seems useful, limitations are apparent. People get left out. Common structural definitions have not been adequate enough to encompass some family forms, for example nonresidential stepfamilies, foster families, or intimate partners or caretakers without a legally recognized relationship" (p. 6).

Family is any group of persons united by the ties of marriage, blood, or adoption, or any sexually expressive relationship in which (1) the adults cooperate financially for their mutual support, (2) the people are committed to one another in an intimate interpersonal relationship, and (3) the members see their individual identities as importantly attached to the group with an identity of its own. (DeGenova & Rice, 2002, p. 2)

Cultural Influences on Family Orientations

Family therapist Renee Singh (2009) explains, "when we use the word 'family' we may be referring to something quite different from the way in which somebody from another society or culture uses it" (p. 360). The norms, values, and practices of families can vary considerably across cultures; for example, family orientations differ in Native American, Pacific Islander, African, Caribbean, Latino, Asian, and European cultures (McGoldrick, Giordano, & Preto, 2005).

Families in cultures within the United States (e.g., Latino or African American) may deal with family relationships differently. Barbara Penington (2004) interviewed African American and European American mothers and teenage daughters about how they handled the age-old tension between connection and independence. African American mothers and daughters favored more connection and closeness while European American mothers and daughters favored more autonomy and independence. In Latino families, researchers have studied parenting behavior concerning sexual socialization of Latina girls. Consistent with traditional cultural views, female romantic involvement outside of marriage was described as potentially dishonorable to the family (Raffaelli & Ontai, 2001), leading to a great deal of parental involvement and monitoring of their teenage daughters. Box 9.2 gives a quick exposure to the varied ways that cultures around the world think about family.

Even general studies of cultural differences have found that basic definitions of what constitutes a family differ by culture. Mexican children think that a family where either the mother or the father is missing is not a family while French children see single-parent families as just as legitimate as two-parent families. Mexican children see biological bonds as more relevant to understanding families while French children saw emotional or affective bonds as more relevant (Day & Remigy, 1999). The reading below offers a look at two unique family traditions in Nigeria (A Closer Look 9.1).

Collectivism and Individualism

Throughout this book we have commented on the influence of the cultural dimension of individualism and collectivism. Several studies confirm the importance of this dimension when understanding cultural differences in families.

The first two studies compared families from collectivist and individualist cultures. Initially, Georgas and his colleagues (2001) looked at cultural differences in communication in the nuclear family and the extended family in Britain, Germany, the Netherlands, Cyprus, and Greece. All of the cultures had

---

Box 9.2   Cultural Differences in Family Configurations

Fictive Kin Networks

In African American families, individuals who are not related by blood but who are considered part of the family are important in terms of involvement and function served. These family members, referred to as "fictive kin," might include numerous people who are "mamas," "papas," aunts, uncles godmothers, babysitters, and neighbors.

The Nayars

The Nayars were a group in southwestern India in whose culture the birth of a child did not obligate the man in any way to the mother and the child. The man's strong ties were to the family in which he grew up; his obligation was to his female relatives—his mother, his mother's mother, and his mother's siblings. As far as children were concerned, his responsibility was not to his own children but to his sister's children.

Israeli Kibbutz

A kibbutz is an agricultural collective in Israel. Among its other features is the rearing of children by the community as a whole rather than by the parents alone. In many kibbutzim, children are raised by nurses and teachers and they eat and sleep in areas away from their biological parents. The children often experience one another as brothers and sisters and, when older, tend to form sexual bonds with individuals outside their kibbutz.

(Fisher, 1996, p. 316)

---

similar family communication in nuclear families. But, collectivist cultures were more likely to have and communicate with the extended family. In the Greek and Greek-Cypriot societies, indicative of collectivist cultures, the family network was more extended (with grandparents, uncles/aunts, and cousins) and the extended family regularly communicated with each other. In contrast, the individualistic cultures, the three Northwestern European family groups, limited regular communication to parent–child networks. Based on these results, the researchers expanded their research to 16 countries and gathered questionnaire information from 2,587 people. They found very significant differences among the cultures in terms of emotional distance, geographical distance, meetings, and telephone communication. As anticipated, collectivistic cultures, despite geographical distance, were much more likely to maintain emotional closeness and communication.

Another study (Keitner et al., 1990) looked at how families from different cultures assessed their own strengths, using the six dimensions of the McMaster Model of Family Functioning: problem-solving, communication, roles, affective responsiveness, affective involvement, and behavior control. They compared

A CLOSER LOOK   9.1

Parenting and eating often display cultural values. In Nigeria, two traditions—postnatal care and Sunday Rice—highlight the collective nature of Nigerian culture.

Postnatal Care

Extremely significant among many Nigerian ethnic groups is the traditions in which the extended family helps to care for a newborn baby. For at least three months beginning immediately after a mother gives birth her mother-in-law comes to the home to take care of the new mother and child. The nursing mother is not required to lift a finger as everything is done for her—including bathing the baby, massaging the new mother's tummy, performing household chores, cooking special meals, and so on.

Sunday Rice

Sunday rice is a weekly fixture in many Nigerian homes. Sunday rice is usually plain-white rice and stew (made with tomatoes and pepper) with chicken, beef, or fish. However, on special occasions, it could be jollof, fried, concoction, or any other variation of cooked rice. Rice was seen as a relatively pricy option, so it was most appropriate for special occasions, like Sunday, after church. Leftovers can also be used for Monday lunch. Rice becomes a signal of comfort and love. Many traditions vary throughout Nigeria, but Sunday rice seems to be shared across most.

families in Hungary and North America. Hungarian families perceived their problem-solving and communication practices more positively than the North American families who rated themselves as superior in roles and behavior control. But when it came to emotion—affective involvement and affective responsiveness—there were no differences between the cultures. Both cultures thought their families were emotionally strong and responsive.

In the studies reported above, data were collected from adult family members. Would similar results be found from comparing adolescents in individualistic and collectivist cultures? In one study, adolescents in Arab countries, India, France, Poland, and Argentina completed the Family Connectedness Scale (see Put It Into Practice 9. 1 on the following page). Teenagers from collectivist and individualist cultures differed in their answers to this questionnaire. Adolescents in France, Poland, and Argentina were less connected to their parents than adolescents in Kuwait, Algeria, Saudi Arabia, Bedouins in Israel, Jordan, and India. Despite the diversity among them in historical, economic, political, and geographical factors, the Western countries were homogeneous in terms of adolescents-family connectedness, suggesting that it may be legitimate to consider the West and East as two major cultural clusters with respect to family connectedness, at least from teenagers' perspectives (Dwairy & Achoui, 2009).

Culture and Family Conflict

Face negotiation theory explains cultural differences in family conflict (Oetzel et al., 2003). As you recall from Chapter 4, "face" is someone's desired identity (Ting-Toomey, 1988; 2005) and culture affects desired identity and how we present and protect it. And, as we discussed in Chapter 5, being from a collectivist or individualistic culture will impact face negotiation.

Barber (1994) examined 1,828 White, Black, and Hispanic families to explain conflict and face negotiation between parents and adolescents and found that White families had more conflict than Black and Hispanic families. Oetzel and his colleagues (2003) studied face concerns and facework behaviors during

---

PUT IT INTO PRACTICE   **9.1**

Your Family Connectedness

How much do these statements apply to you?

Emotional Connectedness

1. I feel upset when family members do not approve of people I am intimate with.
2. When family members disapprove of something I have done, I feel obliged to change my actions.
3. If I did not follow advice that a family member offered, I would feel guilty.
4. When family members ask me to do certain things, I feel guilty when I have to say no.
5. When I am told I have done something which hurt other family members, I feel guilty.

Financial Connectedness

1. My family pays for my own clothing.
2. Family members help me pay for major life expenses.
3. Family members give me money to spend on pleasurable things for myself.
4. When I need money, I ask my family and get what I want.
5. Family members buy me things I need in my life.

Functional Connectedness

1. Family members watch TV and go to the movies with me.
2. Family members spend leisure time with me.
3. I help family members with everyday household duties and cleaning.
4. I take vacations with members of my family.
5. I ask for family members' advice when I am dealing with difficulties.

conflicts with parents and siblings from 4 national cultures (Germany, Japan, Mexico, and the United States). People using more independent self-construals were more protective of face and tried to dominate others' face, but interdependent self-construals were associated with other- and mutual-face strategies and with use of integrating and avoiding facework behaviors. Basically, when families from individualistic cultures were in conflict, they were concerned with how they looked and were treated as individuals. But family members from collectivistic cultures were more careful to protect the face of others in the family since any face damage to a member of the group was face damage to all members of the group.

The conflict dynamics of the extended family can be very important. One study looked at how in-law conflict creates conditions for the abuse of Chinese women (Choi, Chan, & Brownridge, 2010). Conflict between a daughter- and mother-in-law is common in Chinese families and in other Asian families as well. For example, for some Japanese families where the son married a foreign wife, the parents-in-law control the family finances, and that may lead to conflict. In Japan, the housewife traditionally has the authority to make decisions about housework, so conflict about housework management between daughters- and mothers-in-law can be significant, especially when these two housewives are living under the same roof (Choi, Chan, & Brownridge, 2010).

People in collectivist cultures do not consider themselves separate individuals but parts of a larger group. Collectivist cultures are more likely to have and communicate with extended family.

The Effects of Culture on Family Systems

When referring to a family as a system, we mean that we see the family as an interdependent unit of people, whose behavior impacts everyone else in the system. We also mean that the *family system,* as an open system, exists within a larger environment and interacts with that environment through a constant flow of resources and information. We also mean that the family system is continually changing and dynamic; it alters its activities in response to the information or feedback it gets from the environment. Families can be divided into a number of subsystems, and three subsystems will be given attention in our discussion: parent-parent relationships (marriage/partnership), parent-child relationships, and grandparent-child relationships. Families are also continually affected by the larger social systems—the suprasystems in which they live.

Family Subsystems

Following World War II, the image of the *traditional family* as White, nuclear, Christian, heterosexual, and suburban was iconized in popular TV shows such as *The Adventures of Ozzie and Harriet, Leave It to Beaver,* and *Father Knows Best* (as suggested in the Culture Shock box on the next page). But the images of families so common to older people in the United States are not very descriptive of families and their subsystems today, in this country or in others.

Marriage

First, let's look at marriages. Cultures differ greatly in how they understand the purpose of marriage and how marriages happen.

Medora and colleagues (2002) explored romantic courtship and marriage in the United States, Turkey, and India. The researchers found that individualistic cultures like the United States focus on romantic images and expectations of marriage are high. Americans are more sexually permissive and adventuresome in courtship in a search for the "perfect match." Conversely, in India the romantic element may be devalued, even discouraged, because it threatens tradition. Turkey has elements of both westernized individualism and collectivism and their attitudes toward romantic courtship and marriage fall between those of the Unites States and India. In their investigation of communication strategies in Latino marriages, Harris, Skogrand, and Hatch (2008) found that Latinos living in the United States see strong romantic marriage as an extension of family more than European Americans. They also found that friendship preceding romance is an important element articulated by successful Latino couples. So, just in this short collection of studies, we see that we have real differences in cultures that emphasize marriage as a romantic love match and those that see marriage as a traditional commitment of continuing cultural values.

A *love match* is a prominent theme in American popular culture but is just one perspective on marriage. Many cultures (even within the United States) use *arranged marriages* to one degree or another. Gupta and Singh (1982) asked the basic question: "Is the amount of love different in arranged marriages or

Television sitcoms of the 1940s and 1950s helped establish a view of the traditional American family as White, nuclear, Christian, heterosexual, and suburban.

love matches?" They found that love in arranged marriages increases over time but love in romantic matches decreases over time. After five years, love in the arranged marriage surpasses that in romantic matches. In the book *First Comes Marriage* (2008), journalist Reva Seth presents findings from over 300 interviews with people happily wed in arranged (not *forced*) marriages. Seth says the wisdom of arranged marriage has something to offer a culture where television shows, like those in *The Bachelor* franchise, portray the need for commitment and marriage.

Whether based on love matches or arranged meetings, couples in many countries are putting off marriage, and often childrearing, until they are older. According to US Census, the average age of first marriage in the United States in 1950 was 23 for men and 20 for women. By 2021, the ages were 30.6 and 28.6. In South Korea, New Zealand, Japan, Australia, Singapore, and China (Hong Kong) the mean age is into the 30s, with men marrying several years older than women. In Sweden the average marriage age for men is 36 and for women 34 (Organization of Economic Co-operation and Development, 2023).

Given so many cultural variations, what factors contribute to successful cross-group relationships? Research on Black-White interracial couples found that couples traverse stages of interracial relationship development (Foeman & Nance, 1999; 2002). These stages include *racial awareness*, *coping*, *identity emergence*, and *maintenance*. In the first stage (racial awareness) the partners experience both an interpersonal attraction and a new consciousness that the society around them may make judgments about their partnership. In the second (coping stage), the couple develops strategies for discussing their interracial relationship and negotiating situations that may be threatening. Foeman and Nance (2002) find that success of these partnerships is based more on the partners' ability to reach agreement on their strategies rather than any particular approach they select. In the third stage (stage of emergence) couples begin redefining their partnership in their own positive terms and not accepting negative views of others. Partners see themselves and their relationship as special, unique, or a natural product of a diverse society. During the final stage (maintenance) couples put race in a larger context, dealing with it as needed and learning to "evolve as an interracial couple" (Foeman & Nance, 2002, p. 247). Further they will revisit stages at different points in life as they make decisions, especially about children.

Subsequent work on a wider range of interracial couples (Lawton, Foeman, & Braz, 2013; Lawton, Foeman, & Brown, 2013) explored sensibilities that partners from different ethnicities bring to decisions regarding their children's education. In her book *Battle Hymn of the Tiger Mother*, author Amy Chua (2011), a Chinese American wife and mother, describes the "compromise" reached by herself and her husband (a Jewish American). She says that she plans to rear their children Jewish and educate them Chinese. While her practices can be considered

CULTURE SHOCK

Whose Family Counts?

I recall the first time I realized that my family was not the family of the American mind when I was about 11 years old in 1966 and a television news program decried the movement of illicit drugs "from the Black inner cities into White suburban neighborhoods." I didn't really understand the term "inner city" or really even that I was Black, but I do remember wondering why it was okay for some people to suffer from drugs but not others. Only later did I notice that the TV shows that I loved and related to as a child were not about me at all, as a Black urban child with a mom, dad, grandparents, aunts, uncles, and cousins all living under one roof in our "inner city" Philadelphia home. I was more aware of the cultural dynamics by the time the first Black family appeared on television—made up of a single mother and son. My favorite shows included:

- *The Adventures of Ozzie and Harriet* (1952–1966): A real life family including Ozzie and Harriet Nelson and their sons David and Ricky.

- *Father Knows Best* (1954–1960): The television family included parents Jim and Margaret Anderson and children Betty, Bud, and Kathy.

- *Julia* (1968–1971): A widow and mother of six-year-old Corey, nurse Julia moved to Los Angeles following the death of her husband, a pilot killed in Vietnam.

—Anita

CULTURE SHOCK

An Arranged Marriage in Japan

Omiai, or the tradition of Japanese arranged marriages, is still practiced in modern Japan. As a university lecturer in Tokyo, Dolores was horrified to learn that one of her best students was planning to let his parents set up an arranged marriage for him because he was being transferred to the United States by his full-time employer. His family did not want him to be alone in a new country. Dolores's idea of an arranged marriage was one where your parents or extended family chose your partner and you see them for the first time at the altar on the day of your wedding. She told him that she wanted to choose her own life partner when she decided to marry. He asked why she would want to make such an important lifelong decision all by herself—why wouldn't she want the help of friends and family? He explained that the English translation of the word "omiai" into arranged marriage was not accurate. In Japan, "omiai" means "meet and see." A *nakodo*, or professional matchmaker, makes suggestions to both interested parties. Should the young people be interested in a prospective match, then the nakodo sets up a meeting in a public location with both sets of parents present. If the young couple thinks they would like each other, they are encouraged to begin dating.

---

controversial (no sleepovers, intensive studying, and even demeaning her children to push them toward achievement), they are endorsed by many people of Asian background. Lawton, Foeman, and Braz (2013) found that in successful interracial relationships, divergent styles are managed and cultural attitudes tend to be moderated to create what the couple believes is the best of both worlds in service to their children's education.

Interracial marriages among Indian Americans and European Americans have been studied as well (Inman et al., 2011). Successful interracial couples develop skills to negotiate everything from how to address unsupportive in-laws, to which traditions they observe, to what language(s) to speak and in which contexts. Soliz, Thorson, and Rittenour (2009) studied a variety of interracial/interethnic families (Asian, Hispanic, European, Native American, and African American) to discover communication characteristics associated with relationship satisfaction. They found that quality of communication—open and satisfying communication—de-emphasizes ingroup and outgroup identifications. The better the family communication, the more they can develop a shared family identity that embraces and merges the respective cultures.

Parenting

The role of culture in parenting practices can be very important, especially if the cultures of parents and children differ. In this section we discuss the challenges faced by parents who are members of minority or marginalized cultures and then discuss issues when families have children whose culture differs from those of their parents. Because of space limitations, we have chosen to concentrate on examples of specific minority groups rather than a comprehensive review of all cultural differences in parenting practices.

LGBTQ+ Parenting and Adoption

LGBTQ+ families have two adults of the same sex parenting one or more children. While a family including one or more transgender parents may or may not fit technically into this category, since it is often social attitudes that weigh on the family, their challenges will be relevant here. Attitudes toward families that are sexual minorities are changing rapidly. Popular myths that perpetuate stereotypes and unfair judgments, like the idea that these parents will create homosexual children (which in itself is a bigoted attitude), are becoming less relevant. Millbank (2003) points out that "the persistent misconception that homosexual parents raise homosexual children [is] genuinely silly given the number of lesbians and gay men with heterosexual parents" (p. 568). We also need to consider the benefit of having these parents as role models for their children who are LGBTQ+.

Although the research on LGBTQ+ families is more limited than research on other family forms, it has been increasing since the 1970s (Allen & Wilcox, 2000). LGBTQ+ couples face similar parenting issues and tend to have a similar division of labor as heterosexual parents. In one study "both lesbian and heterosexual couples reported a relatively equal division of paid employment, housework, and decision-making. However, lesbian couples reported sharing childcare tasks more equally than did heterosexual partners" (Peplau & Beals, 2004, p. 239). Lesbian and heterosexual mothers parent similarly and their

A gay couple participates in the annual San Francisco Gay Pride Celebration with their children.

children show no differences in important areas of development such as gender identity or levels of self-esteem (Millbank, 2003). Still, there is resistance to such parenting by some. Many people assume that these couples simply cannot be good parents, and certainly not as good as heterosexual parents. One of the arguments raised against lesbian families is the "father absence" argument: children do worse if they don't have a father or father figure in the home. But Silverstein and Auerbach (1999) suggest that these arguments are very simplistic, assuming that all fathers are good fathers and to the same extent. They did a study of 200 fathers and concluded:

> Our data on gay fathering couples have convinced us that neither a mother nor father is essential. Similarly, our research with divorced, never married, and remarried fathers has taught us that a wide variety of family structures can support positive child outcomes. We have concluded that children need at least one responsible, caretaking adult who has a positive emotional connection to them and with whom they have a consistent relationship. (1999, p. 397)

The bottom line in the research is clear—there is no evidence that LGBTQ+ parenting is inferior to heterosexual parenting (Lambert, 2005). In a meta-analysis, Allen and Burrell (1996) gathered results from 18 earlier studies on outcomes for children of LGBTQ+, and heterosexual parents and found no differences for children in terms of their sex role identification, level of happiness, level of social adjustment, satisfaction with life, and moral and cognitive development. Research going back 30 years has supported that LGBTQ+ parents rear children who are as well-adjusted as the population at large (Johnson & O'Connor, 2001). For many children of LGBTQ+ parents, their challenge is the poor adult behavior they experience outside the home in the form of homophobia (Laird, 2003).

Parenting Interracial Children

Social images of *interracial children* have, fortunately, shifted from that of the "tragic mulatto" portrayed in the film *Imitation of Life* (the story of a light-skinned Black girl who passes for White rather than acknowledge being the daughter of a Black maid). Today, attitudes about interracial children tend to be much more positive, aided by more supportive media depictions such as in the independent film *Rachel Getting Married*, where the interracial couple's marriage and pregnancy is greeted with unequivocal joy. Celebrities like the Kardashians have multiracial children who are celebrated.

Early research on interracial children profiled them as emotionally disturbed, racially confused, and alienated (Brown, 1990; Herring, 1995) and suggested they exist within families that are culturally homeless (Vivero & Jenkins, 1999). Much of the early research came out of counseling fields and the children studied were a population of youth who had been identified with problems, some associated with their racial background.

More current literature reports that people who identify as *biracial* (of two racial backgrounds) have unique problems, such as not identifying as one race in a racial society. But they also have unique strengths, like having less racist attitudes, the ability to get along with a wide range of people, and an ability to integrate well with more than one race (Harris, 2000; 2004). *New York Times* reporter Susan Saulny (2011) comments on student attitudes toward race, stating that "many young adults of mixed backgrounds are rejecting the color lines that have defined Americans for generations in favor of a much more fluid sense of identity" (p. 1). Identity development of minority and majority people, covered in Chapter 3, addresses some of the developmental themes of majority and minority people.

Parenting with Disabilities

The term "disability" encompasses a broad range of conditions including both physical and psychological diagnoses (although many scholars are beginning to speak of psychological conditions in terms of physical brain functioning). Disabilities can be episodic, progressive, hidden, curable, and/or static (Shapiro, 1993).

Specialists in the area of disability studies offer a different view of people with disabilities than the typical image of "weakness, limitation, and even suffering." An alternate view offers an opportunity to see people and families living with disabilities in new ways and our relationships with them as more equal and functional (Cypher, 2008).

Two unique articles present a different view of disabled parents. These works address the concerns of disabled parents without presenting them as needy, selfish, or exceptional relative to other parents (Cypher, 2008). One article is by Sandra Gordon (2001), who writes in *Parenting* magazine about discrimination against mothers with disabilities that prevent them from getting adequate pre-natal and obstetrical care and the subsequent improvements in systems to meet their needs. The second piece is a response printed in *Baby Talk* magazine to a deaf parent's write-in question about concerns for her hearing son Toby. Psychologist

According to the National Council on Disability, roughly 6.2% of all American parents with children under the age of 18 are disabled.

Anita Sethi (2002) presents an evenhanded, educated perspective that addresses the parent's special concerns without exaggerating them.

The book *No Pity* (Shapiro, 1993) documents the movement of people with disabilities who fought successfully for the Americans with Disabilities Act (passed in 1990 and later amended in 2008) and who continue to seek to be treated as valued members of a community. The most radical and important thing the community can do for families with disabilities is to include them in every element of life and integrate their needs into larger efforts to create services for everyone, allowing them to give as much as they receive. It is a liberating view for anyone who is not perfect (that is all of us!) and allows more people to reach for their very best and to contribute in a myriad of ways.

Multicultural Adoption

Adoptions and marriages can result in **multicultural families** (Galvin, 2003). According to the 2010 US Census, 2.3% of children in the United States are adopted (Kreider & Lofquist, 2014). This statistic remains the approximately the same in 2021. In 2013, 7,092 children were adopted by families in the United States from outside the country. The largest groups of children were adopted from China (2,306), Ethiopia (993), and Congo-Kinshasa (311) (Bureau of Consular Affairs, 2013). Since 2004, when intercountry adoptions peaked at 22,991 children, it has been in a steady decline, with the COVID-19 pandemic having a further impact, leading to a total of 1,622 (down from 2,971 in 2019) (United States Department of State, 2021).

Multiracial adoption has unique challenges. Families who adopt multiracially struggle with "privacy regulation" or how to manage the psychological and physical boundaries between themselves and others, because the nature of their family is on visual display to be remarked upon or challenged by any outsider. Parents who adopt children of another race face challenges about how to best socialize their child. They struggle to balance the goal of creating a positive connection to the child's country and culture of origin and the goal of developing a biculturally competent person with a "strong sense of . . . ethnic identity . . . able to function within both cultures without having to choose" (Friedlander, 1999, p. 47). Socialization frequently involves conversations about the birth culture, opportunities to participate in cultural events and rituals, development of relationships with persons who represent the birth culture, and travel to the country of the adoptee's birth.

Any adoption brings a number of variables that distinguish it from families in which children are the biological offspring of two parents. In the case of older children, kids who look different than their parents, kids from stigmatized groups, and those who have been in foster care, families may face more challenges of identification, connection, and integration.

But despite challenges of multiracial adoption, the vast majority of parents are happy that they adopted and would do it again (US Dept. of Health & Human Services, 2007). A longitudinal study of cross-racial adoptions found that cross-race adoptions can be successful. Over the course of 20 years, researchers tracked 204 White families who had adopted minority children. They interviewed adopted children and adoptive parents at different times during the 20-year period and found that the children's self-esteem levels were almost identical to levels of children raised by birth parents or adopted into same-race homes (Simon & Altstein, 1996). In another study, an extensive review of literature concluded that most families who adopt multiracially do so successfully and that disruption of adoption is rare (Barth & Miller, 2000).

In step with more open attitudes toward multiracial adoption, President Clinton signed The Multiethnic Placement Act of 1994 on October 20 of that year (MEPA, 1994, p. 1). The Act permits adoption agencies to consider a child's racial and ethnic background in determining if adoptive parents "meet the needs of a child of this background" but prohibits agencies from "categorically denying to any person the opportunity to become an adoptive or foster parent solely on the basis of the race, color, or national origin of the adoptive or foster parent or the child."

But, multiracial and cross-cultural adoption is still a hotly debated issue. Recently, international adoptions from countries including China, South Korea, Russia, Rumania, and Malawi have been stopped or limited for political reasons (Russell, 2009). In 1972, the US National Association of Black Social Workers announced that it was opposed to White families adopting Black children. Their position still stands today. From their perspective, *transracial* (cross race) adoptions "are harmful to black heritage" and are tantamount to "cultural genocide." Similar fears on the part of the Native American community led to the Indian Child Welfare Act of 1978 (ICWA). This is a federal law giving preference to family and tribal adoptions of Native American children.

Grandparenting

Arthur Kornhaber (2002), in his book, *The Grandparent Guide*, reminds us that grandparents can be critical transmitters of ancestral knowledge and family history. Grandparents are a child's link to a time before the child was alive. And children need to see themselves as part of a bigger connection and a larger tradition. In some cultures, the role of the grandparent is so revered that grandparents are seen as possessing magical abilities, like the Tupian tribe of South America where "the grandfather is associated with thunder" or among the Yurok Indians where "every grandmother has her own song that has the power to drive away evil spirits" (Kornhaber, 2002, p. 62).

Most of the research on grandparental roles and communication has come from the study of European American cultures. But enough information exists to convince us that cultural differences in grandparenting are fascinating and important.

Research exists on differences in grandparental roles and behaviors in African American, Maori, Latino, Apache, and Taiwanese cultures, to name a few. For example, Burton and Dilworth-Anderson (1991) have highlighted the importance of the grandparent role in African American families. Historically these grandparents have acted as surrogate or coparents. Another study found that African American grandparents are more likely to be classified as active (63%) than White grandparents (26%) or other minority grandparents (33%) (Cherlin & Furstenberg, 1985).

Worrall (2009) has written on the Maori culture and grandparenting. The New Zealand Children, Young Persons, and Their Families Act of 1989 was a leader in international child welfare legislation mandating extended family placement for children in need of care and protection. The Act, formulated on Maori concepts of family/*whanau* decision-making, follows the cultural value held by Maori and Pacific Island cultures that children belong to the wider family/*whanau* group. Maori children needing care and protection are now almost twice as likely to be placed with grandparents or other extended family members as European children.

In recent years, scholars have begun to look at the role of grandmothers among other ethnic groups in the United States. Hispanics, like African Americans, play a more active role in caring for grandchildren and live in extended families and function as cultural teachers (Facio, 1996). Bahr's (1994) work looked at Anglo-American and Apache models of grandmothering. The Apache family sees the role of the grandparent as very important in the socialization and care of the children, as is true for most Native American cultures. Among the Sioux, a new child is called "little grandmother" or "little grandfather" to help impress on them the important role of the grandparent. When a grandparent disciplines a child, the parent does not interfere; they leave the matter entirely to the grandparent.

There is a long and valued tradition of grandparenting, specifically grandmothering, in Asian cultures. Sandel and colleagues (2006) studied the folk theories of European American and Taiwanese grandmothers concerning their roles, discipline, and advice-giving. While grandmothers in both contexts were engaged in similar tasks and perceived their roles as distinct from that of mothers, their interpretations of these tasks differed. European American grandmothers saw themselves playing a valued, but relatively minor, role in the lives of their young grandchildren. They were willing to step in to play a more substantial role only if problems arose in their daughters' families. In the European American case, grandmothers were deferential to their daughters in discipline and advice-giving and were reluctant to suggest they were more knowledgeable and experienced in the task of childrearing. More than anything, European American grandmothers saw their roles as companions to their grandchildren.

Taiwanese grandmothers saw themselves as temporary caregivers. They played a major role in their grandchild's first few years of life, when caregiving needs are presumably the greatest. As the child aged, attended school, and required less care, the grandmother's role diminished and the mother's increased. Taiwanese grandmothers readily disciplined misbehaving grandchildren, advised their daughters-in-law, and expected their advice to be followed.

Family Suprasystems

In Anne Tyler's (1985) wonderful book *The Accidental Tourist*, she tells the story of a family of siblings so enmeshed that they try to pretend the larger world doesn't exist for them. As a family, they draw boundaries so tightly that they are smothering themselves, and as Tyler shows in her story, ultimately the family cannot refuse the influence of the larger world that it must interact with at some level. This fictional family tries to be a closed system, cutting off information flow and interaction with the environment.

No matter how we might desire it, we cannot refuse to interact with our suprasystems. Families are continually influenced by their communities, cultures, and institutions (e.g., governmental, educational, religious, media). Here, we briefly consider how work-family interfaces and changes in social context (e.g., through immigration) impact families, and the cultural differences in the work-family interface.

Work–Family Interface

Anyone who has struggled to balance work and family responsibilities can appreciate the challenges. Many of us spend more time in our workplace than with our families. Let's look at some scholarship that investigates whether cultures differ in their management of the work-family balance.

Galovan and her colleagues (2010) compared the work-family interface in two nationally representative samples from the United States and Singapore. Initially the expectation was that more individualistic cultures (the United States) would be more negatively affected by conflicts with work and family. They found that family-to-work conflict was negatively related to marital satisfaction in both Singapore and the United States, although the effect was stronger in the United States. Similarly, family-to-work conflict was positively related to job satisfaction in the United States but was negatively related in Singapore. Basically, in more individualistic cultures it is more likely that work pressures will result in family sacrifices rather than family protectionism.

In recent years, the growing number of multinational companies and a more diversified workforce on both national and international levels has contributed to increased investigation of work and family across cultures (Mortazavi et al., 2009). In a comparison of work-family conflict across three different countries and cultures (Ukraine, Iran, and the United States), no differences were found with work and family demands and work-family conflict across Ukraine, Iran, and the United States. But, more collectivistic cultures were more negatively impacted.

Immigration and Its Impact on the Family

One reality is that families sometimes have to move to new cultural systems because of immigration or other factors. How do these larger suprasystems affect the family? In this section we see that these changes can be quite important and that we should give greater consideration to how social contexts impact family culture.

Immigration is a growing trend that affects many families, especially those from developing countries who immigrate because of political or economic reasons. Kacen (2006) was involved in evaluating an experimental program to prevent spousal abuse among immigrants from Ethiopia in Israel (Kacen & Keidar, 2006). Immigration has been found to increase spousal abuse because of the unsettled roles within the family. Spousal violence is more common among people who immigrated from traditional to modern societies, a correlation that rises in intensity when the original culture was fundamentally patriarchal.

Similar effects of immigration were observed on Iranian immigrants who moved to Sweden (Darvishpour, 2004). Iranian men and women were asked if they wanted to return to Iran if the political situation changed. Almost all of the men said "yes" while almost none of the women did. The women's power had increased drastically since they had been out of Iran. They had more financial, professional, and personal freedom; more access to education; and more freedom to leave their marriages if they wanted. Iranian women did not want to go back to more power-imbalanced relationships.

But, we also see changes to families when Westerners move to more collectivistic cultural contexts. Studying Western women who followed their husbands to Pakistan, Kahn (1998) identified four categories of cultural adaptation—the extent to which each spouse embraces the partner's culture. Initially, all foreign wives were found to be insecure in their identity; they felt a loss of "who they were." After a period of time some women moved on to complete assimilation, compromise, or total rejection. Women who completely assimilated gave up Western values and practices, fully embracing Pakistani values. Some women tried to compromise and retain some Western ways while adopting new Pakistani ways. Other women completely rejected Pakistani values and practices and usually left their marriages to return home. Though she did not interview the husbands, Kahn (1998) claimed that the move to Pakistan had influenced the husbands' attitudes. According to the wives, the husbands used to be liberal and broad-minded, but they became more traditional with the move and they gave up much of the couple's independence in favor of the wishes of their extended family. Imamura (1990), who studied adaptation patterns of foreign women in Japan and Nigeria, argued that foreign wives are always marginalized, especially if there are political tensions between the cultures. Abu-Rayya (2000) found that Arab-Jewish couples used one of four coping mechanisms to deal with the effect of the political conflict on families: identification with the oppressed, greater unity between the couple, avoidance of accusation, and political amnesia (ignoring anything that has to do with politics).

A CLOSER LOOK   **9.2**

A Case Study of How Immigration Affects Families

In her study of Ethiopian Jews immigrating to Israel, Kacen (2006) found a series of ways that Ethiopian family relationships were undermined:

> On their immigration to Israel, efforts were made to preserve the communities intact, but their exposure to a Western lifestyle in Israel led to many changes in their traditional way of life. Their dream of spiritual fulfillment was shattered. The *Kessim* (clergymen, singular: *Kes*) were not recognized by the Israeli establishment, and their status was weakened. They found themselves unlike others because of their culture, dress, and dark skin color. The community's traditional institutions declined in status and were no longer effective in solving problems. For example, the *Shmagaleh* (elders), who were involved in solving families' conflicts in Ethiopia, lost their standing, especially among the younger generation, who preferred the Israeli establishment to the traditional one. Balance was disrupted in both nuclear and extended families: Children, who learned the language and norms of the surrounding society quickly, became the "foreign ministers" and thereby were empowered and stopped respecting their parents. Young men and women began acquiring higher education and leaving home while still unmarried. They married at a later age and by free choice. (p. 1279)

Opportunities for Contact and Dialogue

This section explores the insights and initiatives that have been effective in meeting the needs of families, which includes: multicultural family therapy, and support systems for interracial, adoptive, and LGBTQ+ families.

Multicultural Family Therapy

Beyond counseling for families in crisis, having families share stories of their histories can be a very healing and uplifting experience. In A Closer Look 9.3 on the following page, one African American woman learns what her family has survived to be what they are today.

Support for Interracial Families

Family communication improves relational satisfaction and increases shared family identity and appreciation of ethnicity (Soliz, Thorson, & Rittenour, 2009). *Identity-affirming communication* is important for satisfaction in multiracial/multiethnic families who might easily find themselves unattached to any particular cultural community. Since they are more likely to have less external support, it is more important for these families to have a strong sense of who they are as a family. Supportive communication and self-disclosure helps to develop a strong family identity that is more relationally satisfying. When multiethnic families have stronger identities, they minimize perceptions of differences among their various ethnic groups. So, the ability to support the identity of family members and secure an identity as a family unit are key factors in communication success and satisfaction, and tend to lead communicators to see groups as more similar than different (Soliz, Thorson, & Rittenour, 2009).

Foeman and Nance (2002) noted that successful interracial families found family identity vital for creating a positive family experience. Family members spoke of home as "a safe place" or "a rock" and a place where they always and completely felt they belonged. Another study found that culturally appropriate expressiveness and ethnic identity predict family satisfaction and family strength, in general (Pearson et al., 2010). Together these findings suggest that the ability to openly talk about identity, support ethnic and family identity, and create a safe space for being and expression are all factors associated with multicultural family success.

One of the challenges of accomplishing the goals of openness and expression is the ability of the family to negotiate how that works best for them. The level of openness across families of different cultural backgrounds may differ so different levels of disclosure may work better or worse in any particular family context (Soliz, Thorson, & Rittenour, 2009). Research suggests that in multicultural families these levels may have to be negotiated (Foeman & Nance, 2002; Pearson et al., 2010). Cheng and Tardy (2009) find that the use of silence can be functional in some family conflict situations. Silence serves different purposes, both positive and negative, in Eastern versus Western cultures. Thus, negotiation of appropriate levels of expressiveness and restraint may have to be explored.

Finding a Lost Past Enriches a Family

Michelle Marsden is a middle school teacher who works with her students on diversity issues. Her passion for her work is fueled by research that has led her back to ancestors from the time of slavery. Michelle writes:

I was a sophomore in college when I became interested in learning about my family's history. An elderly coworker of mine regularly discussed his genealogical research with me and volunteered to locate any census information he could find on my family. After one of his visits to the National Archives, he returned with a copy of a page from the 1920 census that listed my grandmother, Estella, as a young child living with her parents and siblings in Georgia. Excited about the document, I arranged a family meeting and we poured over the details.

During our conversation and review of the census, we discovered that her father, Peter Vaughters, was a literate, Black farmer and a land owner. In addition to this, my grandmother explained that he built a school on their property which she and other local children attended. Although his occupation was listed as a farmer, she revealed that he was primarily a minister who eventually started his own church. Impressed and proud of my great-grandfather, my level of respect for him deepened when I calculated his birth year as 1852. Suddenly, his accomplishments seemed even greater as I realized that perhaps he was born a slave.

This discussion became the catalyst for my new passion. From this point on it was important for me to make the time to sit down and talk with my grandmother about her past and our family. After eleven years of interviews, library research, and document gathering, I finally had an opportunity to travel with my sister to our grandmother's birthplace. It was a life-changing experience. In a matter of days we met some of our elders for the first time, talked to a 97-year-old former student of the Vaughters School, stood on the land that was still owned by our family, saw the remains of our grandmother's childhood home, and learned a host of new information about Peter.

At the probate courthouse and the Georgia State Archives we were fortunate enough to locate his will, marriage records, and a very rare file. On the last day of our visit we sat in a dark room, reeling through dozens of pages of microfilmed handwritten documents. Despite the challenge of this dizzying experience, my sister spotted a single line in an estate inventory that read "1 Negro Woman Clary and child Peter . . . $800."

At first we stared at the page in disbelief. We accomplished the task of finding Peter listed by name as a slave on the plantation of his previous owner. . . . Later that year, my sister and I presented our findings at a special family reunion.

This experience has changed the way I look at the past. The institution of slavery now feels personal. Whether I am reading about the topic or watching a documentary, I remember the names and faces of people from my family. The pain of the era is more real, but the victory of our survival is even more amazing.

One model organization for supporting multiracial families is the Biracial Family Network (2004) that began in 1980 in Chicago. It is one of the oldest organizations providing services and information to biracial, multiracial, or transracially adopted children. The organization has a mission to connect multiracial families and fight racism. Countless social media sites are dedicated to topics from interracial dating to rearing interracial children. A simple search can connect people to both formal and informal networks.

Support for Adoptive Families

In her work on identity negotiation in US families with adopted Asian children, Suter (2008) found that families have to deal with threats to their identity on a regular basis. For example, strangers may ask a family if their two adopted Asian children are "real" siblings or people may gush that the adoptive parents are "saints" for taking in "such children." Family responses to these offensive comments included some strategies that the families themselves saw as problematic and not identity-supportive: sarcasm, walking away, or an ambiguous response. But families also developed *identity-supportive responses*, including directly answering the questions, educating the other person, or asking if the person was considering adopting from China. Having a cache of responses can be useful for any family that feels on display, as do many multiracial families. Having effective, identity-affirming strategies can work to support the family and build its strength at the same time it protects from assault.

The website of *American Adoptions* (www.americanadoptions.com) offers suggestions for families who adopt cross-racially and suggests reading material to help perspective parents make informed decisions. They suggest that families who adopt cross-racially or internationally should cultivate a diversity of friendships and make sure that the children are exposed to experiences related to their biological background as well as those of other cultures.

Another multiplatform resource for adoptive families is the magazine *Adoptive Families*. With a readership of over 100,000, this bimonthly publication and associated peripherals, including a blog and website, provides information resources for families before, during, and after adoption. Topics covered in every issue include preparing for adoption, health issues, school and education, family, friends, and community, birth families, talking about adoption, parenting tips, and guidelines.

PUT IT INTO PRACTICE   **9.2**

Support for Adoptive Families

Locate a local agency that conducts adoption, foster care, or parenting training and get permission to attend a training session. How do the standards presented in these sessions compare to your personal standards for good parenting? How would you train prospective parents?

Support for LGBTQ+ Families

One of the oldest support networks for LGBTQ+ families is PFLAG. The PFLAG website (www.pflag.org) reports that the organization began in 1972 when Jeanne Manford marched with her gay son in New York's Pride Day parade. After many gay and lesbian people approached her to talk to their parents, she decided to begin a support group. The first formal meeting took place in March 1973 with approximately 20 people in attendance. Several years later when "Dear Abby" mentioned PFLAG in one of her advice columns, more than 7,000 letters requested additional information, and in 1981 PFLAG launched their national organization. PFLAG was involved in the earliest Safe Schools legislation and is responsible for the Department of Education's ruling that Title IX protects gay and lesbian students from harassment based on sexual orientation. Civil rights, antibullying work, and building safe spaces are key elements of their work on inclusion.

Summary

The most important social unit in any culture is the family, however the nature and function of "family" is culturally influenced. A "family" in one culture may not be like "family" in another culture. In this chapter we reviewed various definitions of family, such as structural definitions that describe families from nuclear to extended, and how certain cultures enact being a family. One way to understand family similarities and differences is to examine families from a systems perspective. We also delved into family subsystems exploring new choices, such as whether or when to marry. We considered families that are by their nature a blend of cultures, such as adoptive families and interracial families, and families that are often marginalized, like LGBTQ+ families and families with disabilities. We also discussed the role of grandparenting to illustrate how people are managing diversity and reinventing the meaning of family in modern society. In addition, we explored family suprasystems, such as work-family relations and immigration patterns, to show how cultures manage these larger social realities. Finally, this chapter examined some current developments in helping culturally diverse families deal with internal and external pressures. Several organizations that support these families are discussed and examples of their programs are included. Social media as a source of support is also mentioned.

QUESTIONS

1. Do you believe that the increasing numbers of interracial couples, families, and children in the United States will change our view of race over time? Why or why not?

2. There are extensive rules and regulations in place for people who wish to become parents via adoption. Should there be rules for people who want to become biological parents? If you were to identify 10 qualities that are important for good parenting, what would they be? Would you exclude some people from becoming parents?

3. Should grandparents be able to sue for legal access to their grandchildren, even if parents do not want them involved? How vital are grandparents to the healthy development of children? What factors would ever lead you to limit grandparents' access to their grandchildren?

4. When you think of the word "family," what individuals come to mind? What is your relationship to those individuals? How does your list compare to the list of classmates?

5. Is there an ideal age to marry and/or have children? What are the benefits of marrying or parenting at younger ages versus older ages?

6. To what extent do you see family as the central support system versus friendship networks, other types of social support groups, or private or governmental agencies?

10

Intercultural Communication in the Classroom

KEY TERMS

antibias education	conflict resolution education
bilingual education	constructive conflict community
bilingual students	culturally responsive teaching
bullying	curriculum infusion
bullying prevention	cyberbullying
circles	digital divide

KEY TERMS (CONT.)

group conferencing
human rights education
ijime
marginalized child
monocultural education

multicultural education
peace education
restorative justice
social and emotional learning
victim offender mediation

Educational settings are one of the frontline contexts in which we need to develop intercultural peacebuilding, for "the hand that rocks the cradle is the hand that rules the world." How critical it is to have children learn peacebuilding. The younger the pupil, the more extensive the education, the more likely the application, and the more change for society.

Initially we review increasing diversity in educational contexts that provides opportunity for intercultural community. Too often diversity is a trigger for prejudice rather than an opportunity for peace, especially when children from cultures with different orientations to education share the same classrooms. Parents and community members may be in conflict with educators and administrators about educational values. In the last section, we show how, around the world, peacemakers and educators are creating programs in multicultural education, peace education, and conflict resolution education.

Diversity in Educational Settings

In the United States, there is increasing diversity in our schools. Recent U.S. Census Bureau data suggests that by the year 2040, White non-Hispanics will make up less than half of the school-aged population. The Hispanic student population is predicted to increase by 64% over the next 20 years; the Asian non-Hispanic student population is projected to rise to 6.6% by 2025; and the percentage of African American and Native American student population will remain stable. (Drexel.edu, 2023; Smith 2009).

Increasing Diversity in Schools

According to the U.S. Department of Education, more than 4 out of 10 public school students are racial and ethnic minorities. In addition, in 2000, 2 out of 5 children in the United States came from racial and ethnic minority families, immigrant families, or both, and by the year 2035 the numbers will be close to 50% (Rogers-Sirin, 2009). The number of **bilingual students** has increased from 1 in 10 students in the late 1970s to 1 in 5 students today. At current rates of growth, a majority of Americans will be bilinguals by 2044 (Scanlan, 2011).

However, the increasing diversity in our schools is occurring in a troubling context. A recent Government Accountability Office (GAO) report shows that

CULTURE SHOCK

Being Taught

Darla was getting ready to start her first semester of student teaching in a Philadelphia area high school. She had finished her content classes and was confident in her ability to teach history to 9th graders. But when she met with her supervising teacher, he asked her whether she'd gone to school in an urban setting and what she had experienced of diversity in the classroom. Having gone to elementary, middle, and high school in a small rural Pennsylvania town, Darla felt a little anxious about her ability to relate to her students, but still ready. When she met her students on the first day of class, she was amazed to learn that several of them had only recently come to the United States, almost half of them spoke English as a second language, and less than 10% of them were, like her, Caucasian American. She was about to teach history to a group of 9th graders whose lives had little in common with her own in terms of her experience as a student. In every sense, her history was not their history and she realized she would need to learn more about them before they could learn from her.

public schools remain highly segregated along racial, ethnic, and socioeconomic lines (Carillo & Salhotra, 2022). More than a third of students (about 18.5 million of them) attended a predominantly same-race/ethnicity school during the 2020–21 school year; 14% of students attended schools where almost all of the student body was of a single race/ethnicity. Schools with large proportions of Hispanic, Black, and American Indian/Alaska Native students—minority groups with higher rates of poverty than White and Asian American students—are also increasing. Jackie Nowicki, the director of K–12 education at the GAO and lead author of the report states, "What that means is you have large portions of minority children not only attending essentially segregated schools, but schools that have less resources available to them." The GAO analysis also found school segregation across all school types, including traditional public schools, charter schools, and magnet schools. Across all charter schools, which are publicly funded but privately run, more than a third were predominantly same-race/ethnicity.

The conflation of essentially segregated schools and resource deprivation was experienced significantly during the COVID-19 pandemic, as disruption of in-person learning highlighted the inequity often discussed as the *digital divide* (Brown, 2022). The digital divide means students without modern devices or internet lack access to the same up-to-date resources and learning opportunities that technology provides. Education in digitally divided communities is unable to reach the same high quality and level of rigor that areas with access to the latest technology have made their standard. The Public Policy Institute of California (Starr, Hayes, & Gao, 2022) summarizes how COVID-19 made digital access an educational necessity and also revealed gaps in access. Before COVID-19 about 71% of California households had internet access; but significantly fewer low-income, Black, or Latino households had internet. The need for online learning did spur states like California to close the digital gaps and some strides were made, but not enough. As they report, full digital access remains lower among low-income, Black, and Latino households by a significant percentage.

During the COVID-19 pandemic, minority students were more disadvantaged by schools' reliance on online learning processes that these students could not access. The result was less learning and a larger learning gap to make up when schools reopened to in-person learning. Students who spent the least amount of time learning remotely during the 2020–21 school year—just a month or less—missed the equivalent of seven to 10 weeks of math learning, says Thomas Kane of the Center for Education Policy Research at Harvard University. High-poverty schools spent about 5.5 more weeks in remote instruction during the 2020–21 school year than low- and mid-poverty schools. This learning deficit will impact students long after the 2020–21 school year, with extra work required to make up for lost learning (Brownlee, 2022).

Majority Teachers and Minority Students

Lynn Olson (2023), author of the FutureEd.org report on teacher diversity in U.S. schools, concludes that while students of color comprise more than 50 percent of public-school enrollment nationally, nearly 80 percent of teachers are White. Additionally, only 58 percent of the teachers surveyed think their school district is "committed or very committed" to teacher racial and ethnic diversity. In many states, the lack of teacher diversity means that many students attend schools and districts that do not employ a single teacher of color.

As Erica Frankenberg (2009a) explains, one of the keys to educational success, especially with diverse student populations, is to have teachers who are diverse and culturally sensitive. In 2009, Frankenberg (2009b) reported results of a survey of over 1,000 teachers in K–12 public schools:

> White teachers comprise an overwhelming majority of the nation's teachers. Yet at the same time, they were the least likely to have had much experience with racial diversity and remain remarkably isolated. The typical African American teacher teaches in a school where nearly three-fifths of students are from low-income families while the average White teacher has only 35% of low-income students. . . . Teachers who teach in schools with high percentages of minority or poor students are more likely to report that they are contemplating switching schools or careers. (p. 4)

However, more recently, the FutureEd research paints a brighter picture. Mounting research on the importance of a diverse teaching force combined with the recent surge in support for racial justice has spurred a wide-ranging commitment to increasing teacher diversity. A new national survey of K–12 teachers conducted for FutureEd by the RAND Corporation found that 81 percent of the nation's teachers think it is "important or extremely important" for students of color to be taught by teachers of diverse racial and ethnic backgrounds, and 79 percent think it is "important or extremely important" to have colleagues of diverse racial and ethnic backgrounds (Olson, 2023).

The difference between teacher and student/parent cultures can have critical impact on perceptions and expectations in education. When teachers are different from their students, the teachers are likely to have lower expectations for those students. When significant differences exist between a student's home culture and his/her school culture "teachers can easily misread students' aptitudes, intents, or abilities" (Delpit, 2006, p. 167). When teachers thought their values differed from their students' parents' values, they saw those students as significantly less competent even though there was no real difference in the students' academic ability. The more familiar a teacher is with their students' cultures, the more comfortable they are teaching those students (Thomas & Kearney, 2008).

The impact of teacher diversity on student performance and outcomes is critically important, as shown by the following research:

- Black students who had at least one Black teacher by third grade were nine percentage points more likely to graduate from high school and six percentage points more likely to enroll in college than their peers who were not assigned a Black teacher.
- In North Carolina, Black students were less likely to experience exclusionary discipline (office referrals, suspensions, expulsions, etc.) when they had Black teachers than when they had White teachers, even within the same school.
- In North Carolina and Tennessee, matching Black and Latino students with same-race teachers increased long-term outcomes, including high school

graduation, college aspirations, and college enrollment rates. It had roughly the same impact as a significant reduction in class size.

- Increased exposure to same-race teachers is also associated with improved course grades, attendance, grit, and self-management, and the likelihood of being selected for gifted-and-talented programs (Olsen, 2023, pp. 2–3).

COVID-19 has made it even more difficult to accomplish goals in the area of teacher diversity to secure the academic and social advantages the above research demonstrates. Education Week (Will, 2020) published a summary of the ways that COVID-19 ground teacher diversity efforts to a halt. Many school districts were forced to layoff teachers during the COVID-19 pandemic; some estimates are in the thousands of teachers laid off. An unintended consequence of these layoffs was a disproportionately high number of minority teachers losing their jobs because layoffs are often done based on seniority and many less-senior, diverse teachers were among the first to go—a practice that seriously undercut teacher diversity initiatives in many school districts.

In their book, *Teacher Diversity and Student Success*, Seth Gershenson, Michael Hansen, and Constance A. Lindsay (2021) argue that promoting more racial diversity among teachers is good for everyone and disproportionately benefits students of color, helping to narrow longstanding educational gaps. And they note that the COVID-19 pandemic and the consequent fallout for schools and students has made these goals less attainable:

> Students of color were both more likely to attend schools that had extended periods of remote instruction and more likely to fall behind academically during the pandemic. Thus, the problem motivating the need for a diverse teacher workforce has grown more acute . . . The higher-than-normal turnover among teachers could even be viewed as an opportunity for vanguard states and districts to make quick progress on teacher diversity—if they prioritize recruiting and supporting teachers of color (p. 1).

They argue that research published over the last few years since the COVID-19 pandemic strengthens their case for why teacher diversity matters now more than ever. The book discusses the evidence that having a same-race teacher improves test scores, a student's likelihood of being selected for gifted and talented programs, graduating high school, and intending to enroll in college. More recent evidence adds a variety of other student benefits to this list: Increased exposure to same-race teachers is also associated with improvements in course grades, student attendance, student grit and interpersonal self-management, their working memory, and the likelihood of taking an advanced math course. Blazar's (2021) research used randomized assignment for teachers in 4th and 5th grades to explore how teachers of color teach differently from White teachers. He found that teachers of color spend significantly more time preparing lessons and differentiating instruction for students. They were also more likely to hold growth mindset beliefs about students and spend more time developing relationships with students and families.

Immigrant and Refugee Students

More and more, teachers will be working with students from immigrant and/or refugee populations who may come from cultures with different educational values than "mainstream" American culture. Educators and policy makers are trying to provide opportunities for immigrant and refugee students. Nationally, among undocumented young adults ages 18–24, 40% have not completed high school, and among high school graduates only 49% are in college or have attended college. Although undocumented young people who arrive in the United States before the age of 14 fare slightly better (72% finish high school and 61% of high school graduates go on to college), these figures are still much lower than for residents born in the United States (Gonzales, 2010).

As with teacher diversity issues, COVID-19 has damaged efforts to create supportive educational environments for immigrant and refugee students. Santiago and colleagues (2021) found that COVID-19 has exacerbated the challenges that newcomer refugee and immigrant families face. In addition to education-related challenges, many newcomer families have been disproportionately impacted across financial, employment, and health contexts and reported difficult social-emotional adjustment and significant academic difficulties.

Immigrant and refugee populations can be targets of xenophobia, which sometimes leads to violence:

> The deadly killing of Marcelo Lucero, an Ecuadorean immigrant, in Long Island in 2008 revealed a whole youth subculture of violent behavior directed at undocumented immigrants or people who look undocumented. *The New York Times* reported: "Perhaps once a week, seven young friends got together in their hamlet of Medford, on eastern Long Island, to hunt down, and hurt, Hispanic men. They made a sport of it, calling their victims 'beaners.'" They called their sport "beaner hopping," and it is clear from reports by police investigators and reports from the Southern Poverty Law Center who track hate crimes nationally, these teenagers were far from alone in their violent attacks on immigrants. (Hale, Kransdorf, & Hamer, 2011, p. 317)

Even when prejudice does not rise to the level of xenophobia, it can have devastating effects. A serious challenge for immigrant students is that educators and policy makers often have strongly negative attitudes toward them, assuming that immigrant students will pull down the performance of the entire school. However, data from an international survey with responses from over 60 countries found that both native and immigrant students have better academic performance when immigrant students are a part of the school community (Konan et al., 2010).

Refugee students often face the same challenges of acceptance and have already experienced the trauma of having to flee their country and leave their cultural homeland. Imagine being a young refugee student coming to the U.S. because your family was escaping warfare or natural disaster (Hollenbeck, 2008). Now see yourself going to a new and strange school where you may not speak the language and where teachers and peers may marginalize you.

Rummens and Dei (2010) define a *marginalized child* as a child who is socially isolated, whose identity is attacked, whose voice is not heard, and whose protest is ignored. Newcomer immigrant and refugee youth grapple not only with learning a new language but also with numerous resettlement stresses. Their families are often isolated, uncomfortable interacting with government and official sources, and usually face unemployment and/or other economic difficulties. Immigrant children may have to take care of the household or younger children in addition to dealing with their role as student.

The European Union, experiencing many more immigrant students than before, has focused on teaching multiculturalism in schools. Kowalczyk (2011) argues that the economic prosperity of the EU will depend, in part, on this success. The logic is simple; students who are not integrated and educated are less likely to be economically stable and more likely to create drains on the system.

The experience of immigrant and refugee students is often the same regardless of the country in which they are integrating, whether Turkish immigrant students and their families in the United States (Isik-Ercan, 2010) or Chinese immigrant students in Canada (Li, 2010). Some school districts, like in Tukwila, Washington, are working hard to meet the needs of immigrant students and their families:

> The 2,500 students at Tukwila's five schools speak 65 different languages, including Bosnian, Somali, and Russian. Sixty percent are English language learners (ELLs). . . . 71 percent of students are eligible for free or reduced-price lunch, and up to 40 percent leave the district in a year. Cultural, financial, and language barriers have made educating students more difficult, but school officials aren't wasting time. Instead, they organize cultural celebrations, reach out to immigrant families, and provide English instruction that caters to students at all stages of comprehension. . . . [P]artnership also has produced after-school and summer courses for parents that complement similar district classes. Tukwila now offers after-school classes for parents four nights a week. There, they can learn English and computer skills, study for citizenship tests, and prepare to get a GED. . . . While parents learn, tutors assist their children. . . . The Tukwila Community Schools Collaboration, a partnership between the district and the city, provides after-school care and family liaisons who speak Spanish, Russian, Somali, and Bosnian. (Hollenbeck, 2008, pp. 42–43)

The television program *All-American Muslim* was based in Dearborn, Michigan, which has one of the largest Muslim populations in the United States. Dearborn has a school district with exemplary programs for English Language Learning (ELL) and cultural diversity. The following is a description of these programs:

> About 4 in 10 students across the district currently have limited English skills. . . . Many of the district's newest students are arriving as refugees, often from war-torn countries, and many lack any formal education in their native lands. . . . Yet Dearborn is succeeding, as well and perhaps better than any district in the country. Immigrants are acquiring English and achieving academic proficiency more quickly than the five to seven years studies indicate is common—an average of three to four years to reach a 40% proficiency rate on the Terra Nova English reading test. (von Frank, 2008, p. 13)

According to the same article, the success in the district is due to (1) student progress being continually monitored at school and district level; (2) teachers being trained in Sheltered Instruction Observation Protocol (SIOP), a framework for organizing instruction; (3) Dearborn helping teachers gain ESL or bilingual cer- tification; (4) teaching cultural awareness in the orientation for new teachers; and (5) Dearborn opening a Newcomer Center to help students from different cultures adjust to American life (von Frank, 2008).

Cultural Differences in Education Expectations

Cultures place different value on education and have different expectations for how education should happen through the processes of learning, the behavior of students, and the involvement of parents and families. Such differences can be serious when cultural expectations clash and lead to conflicts.

One cultural difference can be found between Japanese and American edu- cational practices and orientations. As Akimoto (2008) describes, the Japanese Traditional Model emphasizes a lecture format. The teacher, especially at higher education levels, doesn't use examples and anecdotes and doesn't invite student comment and discussion. Students assume that the instructor will tell them what they need to know and any comment they might make would be inappropriate and presumptuous.

Traditionally, teachers in Cambodia are seen as absolute authority figures for academic issues and moral development (Akiba, 2010); Cambodian parents assume teachers will act as substitute parents. So, Cambodian parents in the United States typically don't consider it appropriate to play a role in their children's formal edu- cation. Adding to this, Cambodian Americans are usually Khmer Buddhists who see fate as a guiding principle of human development. Their religion discourages parents from being proactive about their children's education. In this belief system a parent should not push the child to achieve—fate determines the child's future

---

PUT IT INTO PRACTICE   **10.1**

Your Cultural Values About Education

Think about the following questions and what they say about the ways that you have been influenced to think of education.

1. How important was education to your parents? Grandparents? How did they show this?

2. In your family, is education seen as a right or a privilege? How has that influ- enced your involvement with your education?

3. In your experience, who had the authority over your education—your parents, grandparents, larger community, or government? In what ways?

4. What would you describe as the "American" values of education?

5. Have you ever gone to school in a different country? A different culture? How did this compare with your experience in American schools?

(Akiba, 2010). You can imagine the potential conflicts between this philosophy and an American emphasis on a "teach for success" mentality.

Shifting to a Native American example, Navajo society presents an interesting challenge in education. Navajos still successfully preserve and practice their traditional cultural values and speak their own language (68% of the Navajos use their own language at home and about 26% of Navajos do not speak English well). Parent–child socialization within Navajo Indian families is predominantly nonverbal. Elders and parents often use firm looks to communicate and they tend to ignore inappropriate behavior during interactions. Children are expected to learn by observation, respect their elders, and take responsibility for themselves. When these children go into "traditional" American classrooms, they seem to be responding inappropriately to the teachers' highly verbal and directive behavior (Hossain & Anziano, 2008).

Parents' culture may affect their attitudes about special needs issues. Some parents just don't understand labels such as autism, ADHD, etc. In immigrant cultures where education is highly valued and seen as the primary means for economic advancement, a disability may be misinterpreted as a lack of cooperation rather than a genuine impairment. Basically, the child is seen as "bad" rather than in need of specialized help. In this case, parents are much less likely to seek help, give input, and support suggested interventions (Tincani, Travers, & Boutot, 2009).

Examples of Diversity-Related Conflicts in Schools

In the previous sections we have given examples of conflicts that can happen when cultural difference is used as a trigger for prejudice and discrimination. Here, we talk about two examples of conflict in schools that are often diversity-related: sexual harassment and bullying prevention.

Sexual Harassment

Gender-related and sexual orientation-related discrimination in schools occurs more frequently than you might imagine: 4 out of 5 students report experiencing sexual harassment at all levels of education—even elementary schools. The American Association of University Women's survey found that approximately one third of their sample of 2,064 public school students recalled first experiencing harassment prior to the sixth grade (Lichty et al., 2008). The study also reports that almost half of 7th to 12th graders experienced sexual harassment in the last school year; 87% of those harassed had negative effects like absenteeism, poor sleep, and stomachaches. Girls reported being harassed more than boys and boys were more likely to be the harassers (Anderson, 2011).

The most targeted groups of students are Lesbian, Gay, Bisexual, Transgendered, Queer and/or Questioning (LGBTQ+) students, and it is clear that being targeted has serious mental and physical health consequences (Hatchel, Espelage, & Huang, 2018; Hill et al., 2022). Sadly, the research also reveals that there is serious under-reporting of these incidents by LGBTQ+ students due to their fear of further retaliation, the lack of trust they have in schools and health services, and

A CLOSER LOOK   10.1

School Violence Is Global

School Violence in Context: Culture, Neighborhood, Family, School, and Gender
. . . reports on a study of Jewish and Arab students in grades 2 to 12, and compares it to data about U.S. schools from the California School Climate Survey at the University of California at Santa Barbara. . . . Astor and Benbenishty surveyed three sample groups totaling 51,500 people between the years of 1998 and 2003.

It will probably come as quite a large surprise that the incidence of physical assault shows very little national and cultural variation. Rather, the incidence of physical assault is mainly affected by gender and age . . . boys are twice as likely as girls to be victimized physically, most often in elementary school. The rates of victimization decline with age across cultures, the researchers said.

It was the area of sexual harassment that was found to be the most different from culture to culture. "The more patriarchal the cultures—ultra-Orthodox Hasidic, fundamental Islam—the more sexual harassment we saw," Astor said. But that sexual harassment was not found to be occurring in the ways in which the researchers had been expecting that it would take place. "In most fundamentalist Muslim and Orthodox Jewish samples, the girls were least victimized, while the boys were off the charts."

(Schroeder, 2005)

the lack of awareness that many educators have of the nature and severity of the abuse they are experiencing (Tillwein et al., 2020).

Sexual harassment is not just a problem in the United States. Attar-Schwartz (2009) surveyed 16,604 students in grades 7 through 11 in 327 schools in Israel. The survey found that 25.6% of students were victims of at least one act of harassment by peers (such as being touched or pinched in a sexual manner) in the prior month.

Recognizing the seriousness of sexual harassment in schools, U.S. Supreme Court rulings have established school liability for known instances of sexual harassment under Title IX of the Education Amendments of 1972. Federal guidelines established by the Office for Civil Rights of the U.S. Department of Education mandate schools to develop sexual harassment policies (Lichty et al., 2008). And, although more school sexual harassment policies have been put into place, sexual harassment in schools is still increasing (Agger & Day, 2011). Lichty and colleagues (2008) evaluated 784 primary and secondary school sexual harassment policies and found they had problems in clarity and how they were communicated to parents. Only 14% of sexual harassment policies were available online; the majority of policies incorporated only 5 of the 10 critical components, and elementary school policies contained significantly fewer components than all other educational levels. Bottom line: schools are not doing as much as they can or should to address sexual harassment.

Bullying and Cyberbullying

Bullying is repeated, intentional behavior that is used to create power imbalances and to inflict physical and/or psychological harm on another. Since the vicious shootings at Columbine High School in April 1999, there have been volumes written about bullying in schools and the best practices for preventing or counteracting bullying behavior. In this section, we concentrate more on the cultural links with bullying behavior.

Research on ethnicity- or race-based bullying has been going on at least for three decades (Kuldas, Dupont, & Foody, 2021) and has an increased importance with awareness of migration movements and xenophobic attacks across the globe. As Schultze-Krumbolz, Pfetsch, and Lietz (2022) note, Europe has seen a constant increase of migration since 2000. Thus, many of the students today which are ascribed a migration background are actually second- or even third-generation immigrants. In 2020, almost 27% of the population in Germany had a migration background in the broadest sense, i.e., they were immigrants themselves or their parents or grandparents were immigrants, making them so-called first-, second-, or third-generation immigrants. However, this number increases significantly when considering only the younger age groups: among children 0–5 years old, about 40% were immigrants or descendants of immigrants. For children with a migration background being targeted by peers based on ethnic, racial, or cultural characteristics may be especially detrimental because adapting to a country with a different culture, language, or tradition already requires extensive psychological and social investment.

Culture may affect what kind of behavior is seen as bullying. One study found that African American youth who were frequently victimized by peers were less likely than their White peers to report that they had been "bullied" (Bradshaw & Waasdorp, 2009). "Hazing" explanations may mask the reality of bullying. In one incident that received considerable media coverage, a drum major in the Florida A&M Marching 100 was beaten to death; the explanation of the physical violence was "hazing" as a means of proving the fitness of a student to be a member of the band. This incident prompted not only discussion of possible cultural differences in orientations to bullying but potentially biased media reporting of such incidents.

Bullying can differ in terms of gender and social status. The movie *Mean Girls* portrays a series of relationally aggressive girls in economically advantaged schools. These girls use rumor, slander, innuendo, and ostracism to bully others into joining them or at least not challenging the power hierarchy that is being established. Sarah Sparks (2011), in an editorial in *Education Week*, reports that the research into relational aggression is showing an increase in popular, socially astute students who use rumors and social isolation to control others. She notes that students who physically fight tend to be avoided by peers but students who use relational aggression actually become more socially acceptable, especially as students get older. The bully gains more if the relational aggression is performed publicly. Sparks continued:

> The investigation into the 2010 suicide of Massachusetts bullying victim Phoebe Prince suggested students had spread rumors that the 15-year-old was sexually promiscuous before she was allegedly raped by fellow students.

Researchers led by Karin S. Frey, a research associate professor of educational psychology at the University of Washington, found relational aggression on the playground was "semi-public" and episodes could go on for quite a while, even with adults present. "This kind of social aggression is much more painful than many people realize," Ms. Frey said. "When you talk to individuals about being excluded, ostracized, they often say it would be less painful to be beaten up." (Sparks, 2011, p. 2)

Another study found ongoing bullying, especially against racial and ethnic minorities in the Netherlands. It looked at 2,386 adolescents from 117 school classes and found bullying was more common in classes with a mix of ethnicities. Classes in which at least 25% of students were from ethnic minorities had more bullying compared to classes with fewer minority students (Vervoort, Scholte, & Overbeek, 2010).

Cultures with high power-distance orientations that encourage status distinctions often condone bullying. Japanese have a form of bullying called *ijime* (Hokoda, Lu, & Angeles, 2006). Verbal teasing and social exclusion are the most common forms of ijime in Japanese schools, with 42% to 56% of students reporting verbal and indirect ijime and about 23% reporting physical ijime. Ijime has been deeply rooted in Japanese collectivism. Bullying in Japan often involves the whole class or a small group within the same classroom leading the bullying behavior. Ijime is often supported by victims and bystanders, including adults who witness this behavior. Bystanders may not intervene when they witness bullying because they seek a sense of security within the group, and may also be afraid of being perceived as different from the majority (Hokoda, Lu, & Angeles, 2006). School bullying appears to be a prevalent problem in Taiwan as well, with as many as 27.7% of the students victimized by direct bullying and as many as 49.7% by indirect bullying (Hokoda, Lu, & Angeles, 2006).

Access to communication technology has escalated the incidence of *cyberbullying* everywhere, and the harms of cyberbullying are well-documented. Kwan et al. (2020) summarized 19 existing meta-analyses and literature reviews from 2007–2018 on how cyberbullying affects mental and psychological outcomes for children under 25. Cyberbullying is significantly related to depression, anxiety, aggression, self-harm, substance abuse, loneliness, low life satisfaction, and suicidality.

In the United States, growing cyberbullying problems have led several states to pass anti-bullying laws with specific cyberbullying components. For example, Georgia's House Bill 927, passed in 2010, expands the definition of bullying to include cyberbullying and applies to students in grades K–12 (Diamanduros & Downs, 2011). Cyberbullying is easy to do and very tough to stop. As Naomi Dillon (2008) comments, "The Internet offers the illusion of anonymity, and adult supervision is absent, leaving children open to predators, hate groups, harassment, and infamy" (p. 14).

Cyberbullying has been studied in many countries and one consistent finding is that students are unlikely to report cyberbullying to adults. In Canada, data show that only 10% of students would inform adults if they were cyberbullied. They fear loss of access to communication technology more than the bullying behavior (Qing, 2010). In Turkish middle schools, students reported that bullying victims did not communicate with adults when they were exposed to harassment (Yilmaz, 2011). In Serbia, one study of middle school students reported that 10% of students have cyberbullied others online, and 20% of them had been victims of cyberbullying (Popović-Ćitić, Djurić, & Cvetković, 2011).

Australia, a country with strong bullying prevention initiatives, is trying to keep up with technology issues to prevent cyberbullying (Goff, 2011; Pearce et al., 2011). The Victorian Department of Education and Early Childhood Development (DEECD) demands that all public schools must develop and implement a Student Code of Conduct that incorporates and deals with cyberbullying, and includes anti-bullying and anti-harassment strategies. The outcomes of a recent comprehensive meta-analysis of school-based bullying programs concluded whole-school programs are effective in reducing bullying and being bullied, and have achieved reduction in rates of bullying on average by 20% to 23%, and being bullied by 17% to 20% (Ttofi & Farrington, 2011).

Opportunities for Contact and Dialogue

Betty Reardon, the founder of the Peace Education Center at Columbia University, once said, "Education is that process by which we glimpse what might be and what we ourselves can become." All over the world, educators are working to develop programs that will allow children to realize Reardon's vision. In this section we introduce you to an array of educational efforts that are helping students learn about building peace and tolerance: *multicultural education, peace education, restorative practices, and conflict resolution education*. These programs overlap in their dedication to tolerance and peace, but each has a unique focus as the following sections explain.

Multicultural Education: Developing Awareness and Tolerance

The first step to acceptance is awareness. Multicultural education is built on three pillars: helping students learn about other cultures (and through that learn more about their own), increase tolerance and appreciation for other cultures, and create "shared" cultures (McDonough, 2005). Multicultural education efforts are found in a number of countries and regions and are often considered the underpinning of democratic education for better citizenship (Fujikane, 2003). They are significant departures from *monocultural education* programs that present students with a very narrow perspective of history and culture in an effort to develop students as supporters of a national or racial/ethnic culture (Ben-Porath, 2005). Unfortunately, history is replete with examples of how monocultural education has been used in this manner. From the "reform" of schools in Nazi Germany to the "education" of Native American children on U.S. Indian reservations, we know that education can be used to destroy awareness and tolerance. In the United States we are facing increasing challenges with efforts to restrict education of race and ethnicity.

Sigal Ben-Porath (2005) argues that multicultural education can expand students' understanding of their nation's history by connecting it with the histories of subgroups and with other cultures in the region and around the world. Nieto (2004), in her groundbreaking book that introduced the goals and ideals for multi-cultural education, explained it this way:

> It challenges and rejects racism and other forms of discrimination in schools and society and accepts and affirms the pluralism (ethnic, racial, linguistic, re-ligious, economic, and gender, among others) that students, their communities, and teachers reflect. Multicultural education permeates the schools' curricu-lum and instructional strategies, as well as the interactions among teachers, students, and families, and the very way that schools conceptualize the nature of teaching and learning. . . . [M]ulticultural education promotes democratic principles of social justice. (p. 346)

Multicultural education can and should move beyond the celebration of cul-tures by infusing into school practices and school curricula, an approach that has been called the *transformative approach* (Smith, 2009). Obviously, teachers are a very important part of such a transformation. Leonard and Patricia Davidman sug-gested guidelines for ***culturally responsive teaching*** that involves (1) guaranteeing that the gift of education be available to all regardless of culture, (2) empowering students and their caretakers to access education, (3) promoting intergroup har-mony, (4) expanding cultural knowledge bases, (5) valuing cultural pluralism, and (6) embracing linguistic diversity (Smith & Batiste, 1999). Drexel University's Gradu-ate School of Education has six key strategies for promoting diversity and multicul-turalism in the classroom and in schools: (1) get to know your students; (2) maintain consistent communication; (3) acknowledge and respect every student; (4) practice cultural sensitivity; (5) incorporate diversity in the lesson plan; and (6) give students freedom and flexibility (Drexel University School of Education, 2023).

Curriculum infusion is a technique that brings the study of cultures into the lessons of regular curriculum content. For example, students studying the history of apartheid can learn about cultural values and practices of the Zulu, Sothu, Afri-kaans, and British cultures involved in that historical event. The Voices of Ameri-can Teens Project (Linder, 2009) helps 7th grade reading students learn reading and cultural awareness through multicultural stories. The teacher chooses a story based on a student's reading ability and the student then focuses on a character from a different culture and prepares a project about that character's culture.

The last component of culturally responsive teaching just mentioned embracing linguistic diversity—is absolutely foundational for a school that wishes to model educational access, respect for cultures, and nonoppressive prac-tice. Powerful examples can be seen in the use of integrated ***bilingual education*** (Arabic-Hebrew) in Palestinan-Jewish schools. Zvil Bekerman and his colleagues (Bekerman, Habib, & Shhadi, 2011; Bekerman & Shhadi, 2003) have researched how bilingual education in very high conflict situations changes children's percep-tions of ethnic and national identities and impacts how they think about building a future together rather than a future against the other. They conclude that the practice of using the languages of the children's cultures in their learning is a deep infusion of respect for difference.

In multicultural education, cultural awareness and appreciation is encour-aged as a means of preventing bias and prejudice. Some educators identify more with the label of *antibias education* than multicultural education for the latter focus. One excellent example of antibias education is the Children's Creative Response to Conflict (CCRC) program (Prutzman & Johnson, 1997).

Modesto, California, faced a challenge in the last several years around religious bias in the community and how that was impacting intolerance of people who were LGBTQ+ . The response of the community, implemented significantly through the Modesto schools, shows how an entire community can pull together to support multicultural education work:

> Modesto Public Schools became the first public school district in the USA to require all high school students to take an extended and independent course in world religions . . . Modesto has always struggled with the challenges posed by diversity. . . . [The course on world religions] focused on seven major world religions in the following order based on their appearance in history [sic]: Hinduism, Buddhism, Confucianism, Sikhism, Judaism, Christianity and Islam. . . .

A CLOSER LOOK   **10.2**

Learning from the Oglala Lakota

Susan Pass describes how she and her elementary school social studies class learned about the Oglala Lakota (Native Americans that you may know better as the "Sioux") and what learning about that culture meant for them.

Oglala Vocabulary

Sioux is considered a derogatory term. The word is a derivative of the Ojibwa tribe's name for snake and was originally coined by French trappers. Instead, teachers and students should call them Lakota or Dakota, both of which mean "friendly people." (*Squaw* is also a derogatory term and woman or lady should be used instead.) *Oglala* means "to scatter one's own." Chief is an honorary title conferred by the tribe to a person who has shown great ability and goodness. Chiefs among the Lakota do not rule; instead they get consensus.

Oglala Rituals

Counting coup is a brave way to show superiority over one's enemies. A coup stick is about twelve to sixteen inches long. Counting coup by riding into battle armed only with a coup stick and using it to touch the enemy (without killing him) is considered very brave and is one of the highest coup. The lowest coup is to cut off parts of a dead, defeated opponent.

As we reached out to the different cultures represented in our classroom, the different cultures seemed to reach back. We discovered that, when a teacher shares an inclusive learning experience, he or she builds a community of learners who respect one another—in our case, this community turned out to consist of both our students and their families.

(Pass, 2009)

PUT IT INTO PRACTICE   **10.2**

Have You Learned a Different Language?

Have you ever been in a learning situation where you did not speak the "majority" language? Perhaps you were an English language learner as a young student in elementary or secondary school. Perhaps you were a student in a school that used a bilingual educational approach and learned the "other's" language while they also learned yours. Maybe you are one of many U.S. students who have never been instructed in a language other than English (and we don't mean a foreign language class).

- What was that bilingual (or multilingual) learning experience like for you?

- In what ways did it make you feel different about yourself? About them?

- To what extent did it change your sense of connection or distance to them?

- Did the language of learning influence how you learned the content itself?

> Students left the course, on average, with a greater knowledge of other religions and increased appreciation for the shared moral teachings found in major religions. . . . Even more impressive has been the acceptance of the course by a broad spectrum of Modesto's residents. In the seven years since the course's implementation, not a single legal challenge to the course has been registered. Parents have the right to opt their children out of the course but only one out of 1000 students on average annually exercise this option. (Lester & Roberts, 2009, pp. 187–190)

Peace Education and Human Rights Education: Valuing Peace and Protecting Rights

Peace education, like multicultural education, attempts to reduce prejudice and bias that leads to poor treatment of others who are different. Yet, it also instructs students (and hopefully their communities) about the dynamics of peace, skills related to creating peaceful conditions, and systems that support or inhibit peace:

> The Peace Education Working Group at UNICEF defines peace education as . . . the process of promoting the knowledge, skills, attitudes and values needed to bring about behavior changes that will enable children, youth and adults to prevent conflict and violence, both overt and structural; to resolve conflict peacefully; and to create the conditions conducive to peace, whether at an intrapersonal, interpersonal, intergroup, national or international level. (UNESCO, 2002, p. 6)

Ian Harris and Mary Lee Morrison (2013) provide a valuable rendering of the peace education field in their book *Peace Education*. Peace education emphasizes understanding the dynamics of social conflict, warfare, and understanding conflict resolution and the dynamics of peace. Peace education can even happen in "partner" programs like the one that the Carolina Friends School has with a sister-school in Afghanistan (Marion, Rousseau, & Gollin, 2009). Students from pre-school through high school from both schools engage in pen pal activities and use a variety of in-class lessons to learn about the other's cultures and explore possibilities for peace.

Peace education programs often differ depending on the context. Gavriel Salomon (2002) suggests that there are three basic types of peace education programs: those in intractable regions, those in regions with interethnic tensions, and those in regions of experienced tranquility. In high conflict contexts, schools are often a place where segments of a warring society are brought together to heal—places like Sierra Leone, Serbia, or Northern Ireland; peace education has a strong element of human rights. These programs argue that peace should be a human right:

A CLOSER LOOK   **10.3**

Facing Our Biases

Founded in New York City in 1972, the organization [Children's Creative Response to Conflict] focused first on themes of cooperation, communication, and affirmation. . . .

[M]uch bias awareness work is based on the theme of affirmation, that is, affirming self as well as others. Activities that help us look for the special qualities of each person are particularly useful in bias awareness work. Such activities can be the basis for potent affirmation of ourselves and others. The first step toward awareness can happen because of an actual experience or by exposure to story or music. The Fred Small song, "Talking Wheelchair Blues," about a disabled friend visiting a restaurant and experiencing one biased experience after another, illustrates how we are often unaware of bias. The waiter asks the able-bodied person, "What will she have?" rather than asking the disabled person directly, and makes several negative comments. As the song ends, the disabled person says that it would be good to have a ramp so she would not have to come in the back door. The waiter responds that there really is not much of a need for that because "the handicapped never come here anyway."

Young people readily invent their own "isms," using words such as "sneakerism," "clothesism," "looksism," "sizeism," "adultism," and "languageism." These biases are often closely related to put-downs of various kinds that are common in schools. In a sense they all relate to a kind of young person's vision of classism, which is often the hardest "ism" for North American adults to define or deal with.

(Prutzman & Johnson, 1997)

> Human rights education addresses injustices brought about by political repression, human suffering, misery, civil strife, and prejudice. This kind of peace education has a literal and broad interpretation. Peace educators are guided by the Universal Declaration of Human Rights. (Harris & Morrison, 2003, pp. 66–67)

In learning for human rights, the focus is on the empowered and active individual. Empowerment means helping the person understand her own needs and the political and social structures that keep her from realizing those needs. HRE focused on learning for human rights puts "the emphasis on social competencies, including solidarity and collective action for the fulfillment of the basic needs of the community. This also entails the discussion and (where necessary) dispersion of power and power-structures" (Lohrenscheit, 2002, p. 177). Negotiation and conflict resolution skills and advocacy skills are an essential component.

One peace education program that is student-based and student-led is the Help Increase the Peace Program (HIPP) developed by the American Friends Service Committee (the Quakers). HIPP was initially a youth-based form of the Alternatives to Violence program (Liss, 2004) and is based on principles of a nonviolent philosophy. The HIPP program includes content on nonviolence with human rights information (specifically economic justice and democracy), and skill development in facilitation, dialogue, negotiation, and mediation.

The Global Partnership for Prevention of Armed Conflict (GPPAC) has a Peace Education Working Group that supports peace education efforts throughout 13 global regions. Gary Shaw (2010) summarizes some of the projects that the GPPAC Peace Education Working Group has undertaken. For example, following the post-election violence in Kenya, peace education was included in the school curricula to respond to the violence. Also, as Shaw (2010) explains:

> In East and Central Africa peace education is a way for individuals and communities to shun a culture of violence. . . . These new attitudes will then see peaceful conflict resolution practiced at the intra-communal level and regionally across countries. (p. 120)

Fiji, an island country in the Pacific, is using peace education to help repair communities after civil conflict. In Fiji the current government was formed following a military coup in 2006 and freedom of speech is restricted. FemLINKpacific is a grassroots organization focused on empowering women, the disabled, and the marginalized by creating an environment for their voices to be heard in Fiji. Mosese Waqa, chair of the Pacific Regional Steering Group for GPPAC, says:

> For emerging, new, and fragile democracies of the Pacific Islands, Peace Education is an ideal entry point to mobilize Pacific communities and their States, which are small by nature, meet their obligations as responsible international community members, where Peace Education can be developed to teach the universal values, standards and principles essential for peaceful futures. (Shaw, 2010, p. 120)

Conflict Resolution Education: Making Peace a Behavioral Reality

Conflict resolution education emerged out of the social justice concerns of the 1960s and 1970s with the work of groups like the Friends Society. Conflict resolution education programs provide students with a basic understanding of the nature of conflict and the dynamics of power and influence that operate in all conflict situations (Jones & Compton, 2003).

An extremely important part of CRE is *social and emotional learning* (SEL) that teaches the following suggested competencies articulated by the Collaborative for Academic, Social and Emotional Learning (CASEL). Some of the basic emotional competencies include the ability to identify emotions, control anger, manage frustration, and respect others' feelings. Cognitively, perspective-taking is critical as is the ability to problem-solve, set goals, and cooperate. Students should learn interpersonal skills including negotiating disputes, taking responsibility for actions, managing time, respecting others' space, and appreciating social norms (Elias et al., 1997).

Thousands of schools within and outside the United States have implemented SEL programs and many U.S. state departments of education have issued, or are in the process of issuing, standards for the development of specific SEL skills at each grade level. So, too, have many federal, state, and local policy makers become willing to provide funding support for SEL programs (Mahoney, Durlak, & Weissberg, 2018).

A CLOSER LOOK   **10.4**

Playing for Peace

Peace Games, an innovative violence prevention program established by college students in 1996 to promote a culture of peacemaking, emerged from the vision of Dr. Francelia Butler, who brought together the power of play with the power of peace. She established a festival that provided the opportunity for children to share games, sport activities, laughter, communication, friendship, and conflict resolution—the building blocks for a peaceful future. In 1992, as a long-term sponsor for her work, Dr. Butler chose Harvard University's centre for social service (Phillips Brooks House Association) and as a result Harvard students ran peace Games until 1996 when it became an independent nonprofit organization. In 2000, Peace Games opened its second office in Los Angeles, and by 2005 became a national organization, doubling its size through partnerships with schools in New York City and Chicago. Peace Games, in its fourteenth year (1992–2006), has grown into a holistic school change model in Chicago, New York, Los Angeles, Boston, and Fairbanks, Alaska. It has worked with over 20,000 elementary and middle school students, recruited and trained over 2,100 college and community volunteers, and worked with nearly 9,000 family members to encourage peacemaking at home.

(Kamperidou, 2008)

Vietnamese students enjoying camaraderie at school.

Still, even more emphasis on social and emotional competencies is needed, especially in middle and high schools. Durlak et al. (2011) summarize:

> In a national sample of 148,189 sixth to twelfth graders, only 29%–45% of surveyed students reported that they had social competencies such as empathy, decision making, and conflict resolution skills, and only 29% indicated that their school provided a caring, encouraging environment. (p. 405)

The research on positive outcomes from SEL is very strong. Mahoney, Durlak and Weissberg (2018) examined four large-scale meta-analyses on student outcomes related to participating in school-based SEL programs. The first meta-analysis synthesized the findings from studies of 213 school-based, universal SEL programs, including outcomes data for more than 270,000 students from kindergarten through high school (Durlak et al., 2011). Two major conclusions are: (1) compared to control students, students in SEL programs had significantly more positive outcomes in terms of enhanced SEL skills, attitudes, positive social behavior, and academic performance, and significantly lower levels of conduct problems and emotional distress; and (2) the higher academic performance of SEL program participants translated into an 11 percentile-point gain in achievement. Three additional meta-analyses have been conducted (Sklad et al., 2012; Taylor et al., 2017; Wiglesworth et al., 2016), all confirming that students who participated in SEL programs saw greater gains in SEL competencies and academic performance relative to students who did not participate. Further, these three meta-analyses also included more international comparisons and more information on both the immediate and longer-term benefits of SEL programs. In short, they provide a useful complement to and extension of the earlier work. The fact that independent research teams from the United States and Europe have replicated positive outcome findings from many experimental-control group evaluations involving several hundred thousand K–12 students offers strong support that well-implemented SEL programs are beneficial for children and adolescents.

One of the central goals of conflict resolution education is creating a *constructive conflict community* in the school and the neighborhoods supporting the school. Creating a constructive conflict community means developing a sense of social justice and advocating for social justice as a cornerstone of a healthy and enriched society. A constructive conflict community is also one in which there is a shared responsibility for social ills and social accomplishments.

Creating a constructive conflict community means actively involving parents and community members in conflict resolution education activities. Parents can and should participate actively in conflict resolution education—receiving training, modeling effective skills for their children, volunteering with program administration, etc. The school can also link with other conflict management and dispute resolution efforts in the broader community like having student mediators work with community mediators to handle parent–teen conflicts in the community or to help defuse gang conflict in the community.

Conflict resolution education has many programs and practice areas like negotiation skills (Druliner & Prichard, 2003), bullying prevention (Title, 2003) and peer harassment (Juvonen & Graham, 2001). The processes in which students and adults are educated include peer mediation (Cohen, 2003), dialogue (Johnson, Johnson, & Tjosvold, 2000), use of expressive arts (Conte, 2001), and *restorative justice* (Ierley & Claassen-Wilson, 2003). And, many CRE programs combine a number of practice areas. While we could identify a long list of excellent CRE

A CLOSER LOOK   **10.5**

Conflict Resolution Education and Social and Emotional Learning Websites

The following websites are excellent resources for information on national and international programs, research, and policies concerning CRE and SEL.

- The Conflict Resolution Education Connection (www.creducation.org) is a clearinghouse website for all CRE/SEL programs. The site was developed to support the Conflict Resolution Education in Teacher Education (CRETE) project and features CRE/SEL developments nationally and globally.

- The website of the Collaborative for Academic Social and Emotional Learning (www.casel.org), a think tank of scholars and practitioners devoted to the promotion of social and emotional learning, provides a wide range of valuable resources and information for academics, parents, and teachers.

- The website of the George Lucas Educational Foundation (www.edutopia.org) provides excellent material about social and emotional learning and character development.

work, we will briefly discuss bullying prevention and restorative justice initiatives because they target conflict that is prejudice-based and use processes that are intended to involve the community in peacebuilding.

Restorative Justice Programs for Schools

Andreopoulos (2002) argues that accountability is essential for peacebuilding, it is a "foundational step towards intergroup tolerance and respect for diversity" (p. 242). Restorative justice programs for schools highlight accountability in a system of nonpunitive reconciliation and community building. These programs help students think in terms of the rights of all and advocate on behalf of community members whose rights have been infringed. A Canadian researcher, Susan Sharpe, has proposed key principles of restorative justice:

- Restorative justice invites full participation and consensus. This means that not only those who are directly involved in the actions but others who feel that they are also affected in some way may voluntarily participate.
- Restorative justice seeks to heal what is broken, not only for the victim but also for the offender.
- Restorative justice seeks to make the offender fully and directly accountable, by not only facing up to their offending but by confronting those who have suffered as a result. (Varnham, 2005)

Evans and Vaandering (2016) identified three core components of RJE that inform the implementation of practices and processes: (a) nurturing healthy relationships, (b) building processes that support the repair of harm and the transformation of conflict, and (c) supporting learning environments characterized by justice and equity.

There are three basic restorative processes: *victim offender mediation*, *group conferencing*, and *circles*. Victim-offender mediation is led by an adult (usually a teacher or administrator) and involves the student who was harmed and the student who did the harm; they are brought together to have the student who did the harm take responsibility and make amends and/or restitution. The mediation is never about whether the harm occurred—the accountability portion is critical. In a group conference the mediation format is expanded to include family and friends of the students on both sides of the conflict so that the "community" can have a chance to share in the discussion and consider how they can help to repair the harm done. Circles are a form of dialogue process that is used for addressing larger conflict issues affecting the school. For example, in 2010 South Philadelphia High School had a series of racial conflicts between African American students and Asian American students that ended in Asian American students leaving school with the support of their families. As one part of the healing process the school had circle dialogue processes about racial tensions in the community; the circles involved students, family, and community members from all the sides.

Restorative justice programs are increasingly common in the United Kingdom, Australia, and New Zealand (Varnham, 2005), and in the United Kingdom a national evaluation of restorative justice practices across England and Wales has provided encouraging evidence (Bitel, 2004). Before the restorative justice programs the schools had high levels of victimization and behavioral problems. Youth Offending

Teams were then given the responsibility of implementing restorative justice practices in the schools. The "post" interviews indicated that 95% of all disagreements, disputes, and conflicts had been resolved through mediation and conferences, and there were significant reductions in the levels of bullying and victimization.

Anne Gregory of Rutgers University and Katherine Evans of Eastern Mennonite University, in their policy brief for the National Education Policy Center (NEPC) (Gregory & Evans, 2020), conclude that restorative justice in schools is playing a positive role, but schools must work hard to avoid the pitfalls that can blunt the programs' impact—usually the result of faulty design and implementation. Their research shows that restorative justice programs have helped reduce exclusionary discipline and narrow the glaring racial disparities in how discipline is meted out in schools. The evidence is a bit more mixed or inconclusive on two other fronts: school climate and student development. Gregory and Evans provide the following guidelines for educators implementing restorative justice education (RJE):

1. **Use principle-based RJE.** Restorative practices must align with values of RJE: respect, dignity, and mutual concern for all members of the learning community; a commitment to justice and equity; and a belief in the value and worth of each person.

2. **Take a comprehensive approach to RJE.** RJE practices should encompass not only student behaviors, but also staff behaviors, policy and practices, pedagogical choices and school-based decision-making practices.

3. **Emphasize the equity focus of RJE.** RJE practices need to explicitly identify opportunity gaps and challenge disciplinary disproportionality as it relates to a range of student characteristics including race, ethnicity, religion, ability, socioeconomic status, language, culture, sexuality, and gender expression. Sole focus on a reduction in suspensions and expulsions will not address the systemic and structural inequalities that impact students' social, emotional, and academic well-being (p. 3).

Bullying Prevention

Bullying prevention is a very popular CRE program (Title, 2003). Many schools are using a systemic approach developed in Norway by Olweus (1991). But as the research shows, bullying prevention programs are most successful when other students who are not targets or bullies become engaged as bystander allies to protect the targets (Orpinas & Horne, 2003). One of the shortcomings of current programs is framing bullying as an incident between students rather than as an offense against the community.

Jones (2006) argues that bullying prevention efforts should consider using a human rights education frame because it would help the entire school see that bullying behavior is a violation of human rights and a violation of students' rights. In many instances teachers and administrators give little tangible support to protecting targets of bullying, especially if those targets are from nondominant groups. If bullying were perceived as a human rights issue, school administrators may be more interested in supporting programs that insure those rights. Students could construct a students' bill of rights that details the kinds of behavior seen as bullying in that school and the kinds of consequences for that behavior (Jones & Compton, 2003).

In some excellent interventions, bullying prevention can be in the form of a curriculum that addresses a current bullying issue. One example is the Columbia University curriculum that helped Muslim students in New York City following the attacks on September 11, 2001 (Kenan, 2005). Muslim and Arab Americans experienced verbal and physical attacks after September 11th. There was a strong anti-Muslim backlash following the terrorist attacks. A team of educators at Columbia University, Teachers College designed a special curriculum called *(Re) embracing Diversity in New York City Public Schools: Educational Outreach for Muslim Sensitivity* from the perspective of peace education for the public schools of New York City, under the supervision of Muslims in New York City Project at Columbia University in 2001–2002. The curriculum obtained the endorsement and support of the New York City Board of Education. The program was learner-centered so students could engage in activities that foster problem solving, critical reflection, and collaborative learning.

Educating Teachers and Administrators to Be Peacebuilders

For the programs we have just described to be effective, we need to help teachers and administrators become skilled and knowledgeable and convince them to be the champions and models for these efforts. The call for such efforts is not new. Over 40 years ago, Smith's (1969) *Teachers for the Real World* called for changes in teacher education to better prepare teachers working with children of the poor. "Smith concluded that most teacher education programs prepared students to teach children much like themselves, and he called for a major overhaul of teacher education programs with respect to diversity and equity issues" (Smith, 2009). The good news is that we now know what elements should be included in teacher education programs to develop culturally responsible champions (Smith & Batiste, 1999). The bad news is that these programs are still too rare and the research on their efficacy is too sparse (Trent, Kea, & Oh, 2008).

School administrators are similarly unprepared to select, implement, and support diversity-related initiatives in their schools. One study (Young, Madsen, & Young, 2010) researched school districts' ability to meet diversity objectives. The findings revealed that administrators did not view their district's diversity initiatives as a priority. The implementation of the plan was hindered by the administrators' inability to apprehend what "diversity" really meant, in the nuts-and-bolts atmosphere of the local school. Similarly, Herrity and Glasman (2010) researched school principals' preparation to understand cultural and linguistic diversity. They conclude that many school administrators lack preparation to develop policies and implement educational programs for diverse students.

Teachers and administrators are too often unprepared to understand and implement the educational programs we discussed earlier (multicultural education, peace education, or conflict resolution education) and, as Bar-Tal (2002) argues, all of these efforts are teacher-dependent. In order for peace education efforts in the form of CRE and HRE mergers to succeed, there must be teachers who are knowledgeable and skilled as CRE/HRE educators (Rogers-Sirin, 2009).

Fortunately, we are seeing developments to support teacher and administrator education in these areas. In the Philippines, President Gloria Macapagal Arroyo signed Executive Order 570, which provided the legislative framework to strengthen peace education in school curriculum through courses for teachers and pre-service teachers. In the United States, the Academic, Social, and Emotional Learning Act of 2009 (House Resolution 4223) proposes to build teacher capacity to deliver conflict resolution skills in the classroom (Shaw, 2010).

A CLOSER LOOK   **10.6**

Enlisting Students in the Battle against Bias

The Student Leadership Project (SLP) used by the Lewiston School System in Lewiston, Maine, is a bullying prevention and antiharassment program initiated to address conflict rising from an influx of Somali immigrants.

Asalaamu alaikum. That's Arabic for "Peace be upon you." . . . In communities all over the country, issues of mistrust, anger, harassment, and bias often accompany the task of cultures learning to live together, and Lewiston is no exception. . . .

Students involved in the SLP learn to "play an active and central role in our efforts to prevent bullying and harassment at school." To accomplish this, the center takes a three-pronged approach. Students first share information and experiences regarding bullying and harassment at their school.

Facilitators then teach students about the short- and long-term effects of such behavior. Finally, students learn about intervention strategies that can be safely used to de-escalate a situation. A group of students meets off campus for one day of training, and a one-period follow-up session is held two weeks later. . . .

A central premise of the training is that bias-related violence almost always begins with words, sometimes weeks or months before a violent act. Students can learn techniques to stop the escalation of violence before it reaches a physical level. . . .

[Another program in this initiative] is Controversial Dialogue (CD), which gives students a chance to learn more about one another and their differences. . . . CDs are organized around specific topics, such as an ongoing controversy between one group of friends and another or when some students appear polarized on an issue of race or religion. . . . Like the SLP, the CD session may start with students writing information on a note card, which is shared with the group. An alternative approach is to begin the session with the facilitator handing out cards from a previous meeting. This keeps the issues discussed close to home and enables students to wrestle with issues bubbling within their own school.

With help from students . . . Lewiston has grown in its understanding of its newest community members. In turn, the Unity Project students have gained greater understanding of their own power and ability to work together to build a school community of which they can be truly proud. . . . *Asalaamu alaikum.*

(Bradley, 2007)

Already well established, however, the Conflict Resolution Education in Teacher Education (CRETE) project, directed by Tricia Jones, has been helping colleges of education infuse conflict resolution education in teacher education programs. CRETE has been funded through Temple University by the U.S. Department of Education's Fund for the Improvement of Postsecondary Education program since 2004. CRETE has also been funded by the JAMS Foundation and the George Gund Foundation. When CRETE began, there were no teacher education programs in the United States that required conflict resolution education as a component of pre-service teacher training (Jones, 2006). CRETE is now a collaboration of more than 25 teacher education programs in universities providing teacher education and professional development in conflict resolution education and social and emotional learning to pre-service and in-service teachers in 12 states and the District of Columbia. CRETE teacher education involves external training programs and semester-long CRETE courses. Thousands of teachers have been taught through CRETE and those teachers are actively teaching their students and colleagues (Jones, 2008).

Summary

The classroom is a place where children can learn about peacebuilding and practice building peaceful relationships across cultures. Increasing diversity in the classroom ensures that the future will be filled with schools where there are many different cultures and backgrounds represented in almost every class. Around the globe education offers the promise of building intercultural competence.

A challenge of this increasing diversity is that cultures have different orientations toward and expectations for teachers and schools. Clashes between parental and school expectations for students may lead to conflicts that stress students. Mixing students from a variety of cultures may generate situations that lead to bullying and harassment, phenomena that are common around the world.

Fortunately, there is an array of educational initiatives, including peace education, human rights education, multicultural education, and conflict resolution education, that offer research-proven ways to build intercultural competence that translate into better academic achievement and healthier school communities. Several of these "best-practice" programs are discussed. It is critical to remember that in order for these programs to work, we need to have better preparation of teachers and administrators. National projects like the CRETE project (Conflict Resolution Education in Teacher Education) at Temple University provide ways for teachers and administrators to learn about social emotional learning and conflict resolution education so they can better develop and support these programs in schools.

QUESTIONS

1. Have you participated in a CRE or peace education program in your school or community? If so, what was the experience like for you?

2. If you had the opportunity to use peace education, conflict resolution education, social and emotional learning, or multicultural education in a conflict in your community, how would you use it? Why?

3. Should all schools use restorative practices? What would it take to make that happen given the realities of education in the 21st century? What would teachers and administrators need to learn in order to support these programs?

4. Can colleges and universities use the conflict education programs that are discussed in this chapter? Are there programs on your campus? If not, where might you start creating some?

11

Intercultural Communication in the Workplace

CHAPTER OUTLINE

KEY TERMS

amae
corporate social responsibility (CSR)
cultural convergence
diversity training
globalization

global work team
glocalized
millennial generation
nemawashi
Title VII

You may be wondering why a textbook on intercultural communication from a peacebuilding perspective includes a chapter on the workplace. One answer is that your career path may lead you to work for a US company that has global partners or a global company that has US partners, branches, or subsidiaries in the United States. At the very least, the changing demographics overall means the workplace has also become more multicultural, not just in racial terms, but also in terms of other identities such as gender, sexual orientation, ability, religion, and age.

> The global company affects every aspect of the way a company conducts business, from sales to consulting to marketing to management. You will find diversity in your workplace. You have to have a level of comfort with your own community because you will also be working with people from all over the world in your daily life. (Director of SAP Global Internal Audit, personal communication, July 2011)

We begin by discussing the current statistics on diversity in the US workforce and reflecting on how different cultures influence the goals and practices of American business. In this section we will also review some of the most current research on diversity initiatives in the American workplace. The second major section of the chapter examines broad cultural differences in orientations to work and work practices including: hiring methods, gender roles, language issues, and conflict management. The chapter concludes with opportunities for dialogue and community, in the contexts of global work teams, global corporations, corporate social responsibility, and intercultural training programs.

Cultural Diversity in the American Workplace

There are compelling business rationales for making diversity a top business priority. One reason cited most frequently is the opportunity to drive business growth by leveraging the talent, knowledge, and resources of a diverse workforce that will make the United States more competitive. To improve marketplace understanding, a diverse workforce with cultural knowledge is critical. Companies can benefit from informed consumers who prefer to spend their money on products produced by a diverse workforce, and it makes sense that a company's workforce should reflect its customer base.

The Changing Workforce

"Seismic changes in the racial makeup of the United States population have led to the American labor force's incoming generation being the most diverse in history" (Maurer, 2011). By 2042 the US workforce will have a completely different composition, with a decline in White working-age employees from 82% to 63% of the workforce. At the same time, ethnic minority employees are projected to double from 18% to 37% of the US workforce, with the Hispanic population projected to triple. Cultural sensitivity and intercultural communication competence among American workers will become even more important. In addition, US employees will also need to have cross-cultural communication skills to work with people of different countries, because more and more companies are forging multilateral and international alliances.

You may have noticed that your cell phone customer service line, your banking customer service operator, and your physician's office now give callers the opportunity to press "1" for English and "2" for Spanish. You may have spotted your favorite ice cream, such as Häagen-Dazs, with new flavors like *dulce de leche*, which is Spanish for caramel. The option to speak to a bilingual customer service representative or purchase a product with a "sabor latino" is indicative of the growing numbers of Latinos in the United States.

The 2020 census shows that almost 1 in 5 individuals living in the United States identifies as Hispanic or Latino (Jin, Talbot, & Wang, 2021). It is projected that by 2060, 28% of the US population will be Latino (US Census, 2018). The buying power of this group will most likely reach $1 trillion. The increasing Latino population has caught the attention of US companies that want to tap into this market. As their buying power increases, so does the need for their perspective and insights into the Latino consumer. This also means that Latinos will be an increasing percentage of the American workforce in all areas. Overall, the trend shows that non-Hispanic Whites will be the minority by 2045, while the strongest drivers of population growth next to Hispanic/Latinos will be immigrants and Asians. Blacks are projected to make up about the same proportion (about 13%) (Frey, 2018).

Social Identities in the Workplace

Not surprisingly, people of color share that they have difficulty integrating into work environments (Varma, 2021). Not only is the United States becoming more diverse racially, it is also seeing increases in how individuals identify on other social categories. Correspondingly, workplaces have had to deal with conflict and discrimination of groups who are not part of the majority culture. One of these domains is gender. For example, in the medical field, female surgery residents commonly report implicit gender bias in the workplace (Ouyang et al., 2021).

As discussed in Chapter 4, Hofstede's (2011) cultural dimension of masculinity and femininity relates to how gender roles are defined in cultures, including organizational contexts. In many countries, more women are obtaining degrees in higher education and seeking work outside the home, increasingly refusing to be limited to traditional female jobs (e.g., receptionists), and are not necessarily leaving work when they get married or have children (Hung, Li, & Belk, 2007). These changes in educational access mean that women in the workforce expect to be viewed in professional roles as equals, not as lower-level employees, which is more of a conflict in some cultures than others (Hofstede, 2001).

An implication of the changing gender presence in the global workplace is the need for change in rules for socialization in the workforce (Cross & Gore, 2003). Gender differentiation, or gender distinctiveness, refers to what men and women do in certain cultures (Hofstede, 2001). In cultures with low gender differentiation, it is not surprising when men and woman have the same benefits and take on similar roles. For example, in Sweden it is not unusual for both men and women to take maternity/paternity leave or for men to stay home and raise children if their partner has a company position that is higher in status and pay. In cultures with high gender differentiation, it is important to consider how actions may be perceived by a person of the opposite gender. Is it appropriate to ask a coworker out for dinner? Does it indicate that you are being friendly? Does it indicate that there

---

CULTURE SHOCK

Just Being Friendly . . .

In my native country, it is polite to greet female coworkers with a kiss on the cheek and to comment on how lovely they look, or their new hairstyle. It is considered friendly and there is no intention of romantic attraction. When I came to the States to work, my boss asked me to stop complimenting the female employees in the company. My boss, a male, noted that calling attention to a woman's looks, dress, or hairstyle was not considered professional behavior. Since that time, I have never commented on the way a coworker looks, I only comment on their work. It feels strange, but I don't want my friendly behavior to be misunderstood as a lack of respect for a female executive or secretary. I think it is a ridiculous rule, but I understand the protocol.

—Julio from Ecuador

is a romantic interest? Can the other person accept or refuse without consequences from family and friends? What does it mean when you are greeted by a coworker who kisses you on both cheeks? Would that behavior embarrass the recipient and perhaps result in a loss of face in front of other colleagues?

Race and gender dominated early research and programs on diversity management; however, other identities have more recently come to the forefront as researchers study workplace discrimination (Triana et al., 2021). The 1964 Civil Rights Act prohibited discrimination based on race, sex, religion, color, gender, religion, or national origin. The 1990 Americans with Disabilities Act protects people with visible (such as physical) and invisible (such as mental) disabilities. The 1967 Age Discrimination in Employment Act protects workers and applicants 40 and over from discrimination. There is no law protecting individuals from the stigma of being overweight; this is one area that needs more focus in the literature on workplace discrimination. Researchers have documented that sexism and ableism exist even in public institutions like Veterans Affairs hospitals (Cencirulo et al., 2021). LGBTQ+ workers around the world, including those who identify as nonbinary and trans, experience negative and exclusionary attitudes from coworkers

More workplaces than ever are actively managing diversity and inclusion, but progress often takes time, especially when hiring for management positions. (Courtesy of Mercer, "Managing a diverse and inclusive mobile workforce." https://mobilityexchange.mercer.com/insights/article/managing-a-diverse-and-inclusive-mobile-workforce)

(Di Marco, Hoel, & Lewis, 2021; Huffman, et al., 2021; Suen, Chan, & Badgett, 2020; Waite, 2021). Neurodivergent individuals also experience differential treatment in many work settings (Coetzer & Gibbison, 2016). This leads us to consider diversity programs implemented by organizations to try and promote inclusion.

Diversity Programs in the Workplace

There is a long history of diversity efforts in US workplaces to encourage inclusion of various groups in organizations. But, these initiatives have not been easy to implement and have not always received strong political or administrative support.

Initial diversity training efforts in the 1960s centered on legislation and compliance. *Title VII* of The Civil Rights Act of 1964 made it illegal for employers with more than 15 employees to discriminate in hiring, termination, promotion, compensation, job training, or any other term, condition, or privilege of employment based on race, color, religion, sex, or national origin. Since its enactment, Title VII has been supplemented with legislation that prohibits discrimination on the basis of pregnancy, age, and disability. In addition, sexual harassment is now deemed to be illegal under Title VII. This landmark legislation spawned an era of training in the late 1960s and 1970s, largely in response to the barrage of discrimination suits that were filed with the Equal Employment Opportunity Commission (EEOC). If the EEOC or state agencies found "probable cause" for discrimination, one of the remedies was typically a court-ordered mandate for the organization to train all employees in antidiscriminatory behavior. During this era, most *diversity training* was imparting knowledge of the law and company policies. During subsequent eras, as explained in A Closer Look 11.1, we have grown increasingly more sophisticated in the way we view and work with diversity in US organizations.

A number of organizations across public and private sectors have begun efforts toward managing workforce diversity. At the federal level in the United States, almost 90% of agencies report that they are actively managing diversity. The Society for Human Resource Management (SHRM) conducted a survey in 2020 among 1,275 human resource professionals and found that more than half (52%) of organizations have provided diversity training (Society for Human Resource Management, 2020).

One example of diversity training that made headlines was Starbucks's decision to close all its locations on May 29, 2018, for racial bias training when employees in a Philadelphia location called the police on two black men who were waiting at a table for a friend before making purchases. The story shone a spotlight on diversity training initiatives and raised the question of what impact these initiatives have.

Some studies question the value of diversity training. For example, one study found that diversity training actually led to a decrease in representation of African American women in managerial ranks (Kalev, Dobbin, & Kelly, 2006). Corporate data was analyzed from 708 companies dating back to the 1970s and progress was measured based on racial composition of the managers group. The negative effect of diversity training was obtained after researchers controlled many other factors, such as existence of a diversity staff, an affirmative action plan, and a formal mentoring program. Dover, Kaiser, and Major (2020) analyzed social psychological evidence on diversity initiatives and concluded that they led to mixed signals at

---

A CLOSER LOOK   **11.1**

Phases of Diversity Management in the US Workplace

Phase 2. Early 1980s

Compliance-oriented training continued into the early 1980s. . . . Some organizations that conducted training during this lull were more likely to present content with the objective of helping women and people of color to assimilate into existing corporate cultures.

Phase 3. Late 1980s

Workforce 2000 . . . shifted the discussion from how to comply with legal mandates to how to assimilate what was thought to be additional large numbers of women and minorities into existing, homogenous corporate cultures.

Phase 4. Late 1980s to Late 1990s

The fundamental shift was from compliance, and focusing only on women and racial ethnic minorities, to incorporating everyone, including White men, under the umbrella of diversity. . . . [T]he content was sometimes squeezed into short time frames or facilitated by internal trainers who lacked subject matter expertise.

Phase 5. The New Millennium

The 21st century variety of diversity training is focused on building skills and competencies that enable learners not only to value differences but also to be able to utilize them in making better business decisions. . . . [T]he assumption is no longer that only certain groups need training (e.g., White men or minorities), but rather that all employees need to be more cross-culturally competent in an increasingly global world.

(Anand & Winters, 2008)

---

best. For example, they found that training could lead to perceptions of unfairness toward overrepresented groups, as well as a perception that underrepresented groups need special treatment because they are less competent than their majority counterparts. They could also lead underrepresented groups to perceive that they are discriminated at higher levels. Dobbin and Kalev (2018) agree, citing several meta-analyses that show diversity training does not have positive effects, had no effect on women's or minorities' careers or managerial diversity, or that they even reduce bias. At best, they show small, short-term improvements; at worst, they say that training activates stereotypes. Similarly, Bezrukova et al. (2016) state that longer training leads to larger effect sizes, but mostly on cognitive learning as opposed to attitudinal of behavioral change.

Overall, the literature therefore shows mixed results regarding the effectiveness of diversity training. But this is not inherent to the *idea* of training, but rather, how training has been provided and its role in the context of wider organizational programs to address discrimination. Some factors that could help achieve better results are the following:

1. One-time or short-term training are generally not successful interventions. Dobbin and Kalev (2018) and Chang et al. (2019) found that one-off sessions have limited effectiveness, especially for groups belonging to the majority which they are often targeted for. Instead, sessions should be framed within a larger program of organizational change that includes careful consideration of hiring, recruitment, and mentorship programs that aim for more inclusion and foster relationships among individuals with different social identities across the breadth of the organization's structure.

2. Allport's Intergroup Contact Hypothesis tells us that the presence of sustained interpersonal contact goes a long way toward reducing biases. Training programs that develop allyships and friendships, perhaps through teams and mentorship, could lead to positive associations between members of majority and minority groups (Dover, Kaiser, & Major, 2020). The potential for reducing prejudice then exists. Certainly, the impact of the COVID-19 pandemic on work relationships is an intriguing question. While most people who have jobs that allow them to work remotely seem to be successful in doing their responsibilities, we do not know how much the pandemic has impacted the development of friendships and relationships in the workplace overall. Of course, leadership cannot mandate friendships, but it could consciously think about removing barriers to friendship formation.

3. There is evidence to show that mandatory training does not work as well as voluntary training, since as Dobbin and Kalev (2018) state, "people react negatively to efforts to control them (p. 50)." Here is where organizations could find that informal strategies and formal programs to develop relationships among employees, instead of those requiring attendance at an event, might work better at fostering more inclusive and accepting environments.

4. Diversity training should consider multiculturalism as an approach, instead of focusing only on the experiences of people in minority groups. Dobbin and Kalev (2018) emphasize that people who belong to majority groups often feel left out of these trainings, leading to a sense of unfairness and a perception that they are not valued. They recommend that curricula should consider including the majority culture in the training and emphasize that the majority and minority cultures are important parts of that organization. Along the same vein, Dover, Kaiser, and Major (2020) suggest that training that focuses on both group commonalities and differences, along with one that tries to generate positive emotions such as empathy, could be more effective at reducing prejudice and allow everyone to feel included. Overall, programs that prioritize relationships rather than judgments and finger-pointing would be more welcome approaches in diversity training efforts.

Globalization and Cross-Cultural Differences in the Workplace

Whether you are working for a local organization with employees and clientele from many cultures and/or nations, or you are working with an organization that has multiple offices in other countries, you are very likely to become a member of a globalized workforce. According to Giddens (2002), *globalization* refers to the reality that we live in a far-reaching interconnected world community that is becoming increasingly homogenized. The world is becoming smaller and strictly national business cultures are becoming obsolete (Blasco, 2004); cultures are converging and becoming more similar rather than more unique. Americans sometimes point to the proliferation in other countries of restaurants like McDonald's, Burger King, and Kentucky Fried Chicken as an indicator that other nations are becoming more Americanized. But these fast-food extensions signal an adjustment on both ends—while American fast food may be attractive to those in different countries, American products are also changing to fit the culture of the host country or region (see A Closer Look 11.2 and decide for yourself).

Globalization doesn't necessarily mean cultural convergence is inevitable. According to political philosopher David Singh Grewal (2008), *cultural convergence* is an increasing intersection and adoption of various forms of culture artistic, culinary, or musical culture—usually moving from the United States to the rest

KFC has become very popular in China because the company has paid attention to cultural preferences in the preparation and presentation of its menu. (Shutterstock/Chintung Lee)

A CLOSER LOOK   **11.2**

KFC's China Success

In 1987, KFC became the first American fast-food chain to open a location in China. Since then, it has continued to annually top lists as the most popular foreign brand in the country.

> The company made some early missteps: for example, KFC's advertising slogan "finger-lickin' good" was mistranslated into Chinese characters that meant "eat your fingers off." But China was opening up to the outside world, and KFC benefited from the curiosity of citizens about all things Western. Its clean, brightly lit restaurants, fast service, and smiling counter help were so unusual that people held wedding parties there. (Adler, 2003)

> Key to KFC's success in the country has been its aggressive catering to Chinese tastes, with menu items that will never make their way to US restaurants. While KFCs in China serve fried chicken, they also serve a variety of local dishes like egg tarts, congee (rice porridge), and the "Dragon Twister." (Jacobs, 2019)

In 2016, KFC's parent company Yum! Brands completed a corporate spin-off of their Chinese business, forming the new Chinese Fortune 500 company Yum China Holdings, Inc. The brand is as popular as ever, with sales in 2020 topping $7 billion (Market Line, 2022).

---

of the world. While cultural convergence is happening, and in a number of directions, diverse workplaces and global corporations have a workforce that becomes "blended" into a global culture rather than Americanized. National cultures of employees, even when there is a strong tie to the organizational culture, are still important in terms of intercultural communication, global teamwork, and intercultural understanding. National cultures do not become obsolete in global organizations; in fact, they affect work practices to such an extent that it is unwise to assume uniform standards are being used across cultures (Ladegaard, 2007).

What makes global workforces so interesting is that, on the surface, a company like Ford Motor Company may appear to be the same in the United States as in Spain. But, underneath the visible similarities are cultural influences that are an important asset to any company and must be taken into consideration.

Orientations to Work

When we discuss orientations to work in an intercultural context, we are referring to how culture influences what work "means" to someone. Is the workplace a context where one can stand out as number one in their field (like in the United States) or is it a place where one expects to join a like-minded and similarly educated group of people for professional success and lifelong relationships (like in Asia)?

We know that cultures seek different rewards from the workplace and assign work different levels of importance relative to family, community, and spirituality. Hofstede (2001) reports that the Dutch and other "feminist" cultures place more

CULTURE SHOCK

Lunch Break in Spain

I had just graduated from university and had accepted a summer job at Ford Motor Company in Valencia, Spain. I assumed that since this was an American company based in Spain, some differences were to be expected. What surprised me the most was lunch time! In the cafeteria at Ford, the lunches were subsidized for all the employees. That in itself was not surprising, but there was a selection of beer and wine for lunch! In addition, some employees preferred not to take a lunch break inside the company plant, but took two-hour lunch breaks in the local town. So, in addition to finding it very strange to see liquor in the employee cafeteria, it was even stranger that the lunch "hour" was two hours long.

—Dolores

value on home and family than on work, while more masculine cultures are the opposite. It is not unusual for Dutch husbands to take paternity leave when they have a new child. In fact, if the wife earns a higher salary than her husband, it is not unusual for the husband to step out of his career for a number of years to raise the child. Although we see some of this pattern in masculine cultures like the United States, it is still not common.

Consider how time is used in the workplace. When cultures are monochromatic, the product will be more important than the process and deadlines are critical (Hall, 1976). Time is highly organized and relationship with coworkers is less important than getting a job done and completed on time. In cultures that are polychromatic, social interaction is valued over the completion of a product. This may mean that a job's deadline is flexible as long as relationships don't suffer for it (Kluckhohn & Strodtbeck, 1961).

CULTURE SHOCK

The Boss Told Me to Speak Up!

When I first started working in the United States, I was very quiet. I never said anything to my colleagues and I never spoke at meetings. One day my boss called me to his office. He was very upset with me. He told me that I would lose my job if I didn't change my behavior. I should talk with my coworkers during break time and I should speak up at meetings. I explained to him that I didn't know that I was behaving improperly. In my native culture, one gained respect from his coworkers by being quiet. I learned that this is not the case in the United States. I had to change my ways immediately. It was not easy at first, but I got used to it. Now I feel very comfortable talking with everyone.

—Haile from Ethiopia

The interface of time, culture, and the workplace is also seen in terms of how people orient to the present, past, and/or future. For example, Americans focus on change, progress, and future actions that are within reach of an individual, so projections may be heavily weighted towards a foreseeable future. But some cultures measure the future in decades or generations, or are oriented to the past and assume that attempts to structure the unknowable future are futile (Stewart & Bennett, 1991).

Interviewing, Hiring, and Firing

Areas where cultural differences impact the workplace include interviewing, hiring, and firing practices. In terms of cultural practices, individualism and collectivism play an important role in understanding the underlying reasons for certain behaviors and expectations in the workforce. In an individualistic culture, for example, the individual is responsible for receiving and setting up a job interview, while in a collectivistic culture the responsibility for finding jobs or getting interviews often belongs to the person's family or close friends. Of course, reciprocity is expected on the part of the individual when it is their turn to assist another family member or close friend who is seeking employment (Brislin, 2008).

The content of an interview is also affected by the individualistic or collectivistic orientation of a culture. Think about how an interviewee might present co-curricular activities in college. If you are a US student, to look well-rounded you might say you belonged to many different student groups throughout your

A bow is a formal greeting between business people in Japan. (Shutterstock/Rawpixel.com)

college career. In Japan, committing to one group and developing and maintaining long-term commitments to that group is more desirable (Brislin, 2008). Culture can also affect the information one decides to share in an interview. For example, masculine cultures like the United States do more bragging and self-promotion to point out their best and most important qualities in an interview (Hofstede, 2011). Members of collectivist cultures are likely to be more modest in their self-presentations. A US interviewer would need to see that a Japanese interviewee was acting on his own cultural knowledge of interview situations if he/she were to say that their contributions to their employer were not important enough to discuss.

Akio Morita (1986), founder of Sony Corporation in Japan, indicated in his memoir that the hiring practice of Japanese companies can be compared to finding "stones" to build the wall of the company, while US businesses look for "bricks." The difference is that in US companies a framework for each job is decided upon. When a candidate is interviewed, if the person is "oversized" or "undersized" for the framework, they will be rejected—the "brick" doesn't fit the wall. But in Japan, according to Morita, recruits are hired from the best universities and the company makes good use of them, combining them, as a mason would build a structure. Management figures out how to put them together and must also think of how the "stones" will change and grow and how they might be better used in another spot in the wall.

Ending someone's employment also differs culturally. Termination of an employee in Spain, according to section 53(1) of the Worker's Charter, includes written communication to the worker explaining the reason for termination. When the written explanation is given, the worker also receives compensation corresponding to 20 days for each year of service up to a maximum of 12 months' pay. And the worker is always given at least 30 days' notice before termination (Monzon, 2007). In the United States, by comparison, workers are not given written communication explaining the reason for termination, nor do they receive a certain amount of compensation by law. Often, termination of employment means a US worker receives a pink slip on a Friday afternoon and is ushered out of their office and out of the building to their car by a company security officer.

Task vs. Social Orientation

Cultures also differ in terms of the degree of task versus social orientation. For example, Americans value individual initiative and personal achievement (a task orientation), which also undergirds American decision-making practices and is deeply implicated in the traditional American definition of success (Wenzhong & Grove, 1991). Individual employees are expected to take initiative, achieve goals, solve problems, and move the company forward. The primary objective is to focus on the task, accomplish goals, and achieve success. Of secondary importance is the strength and stability of personal relationships. Conversely, in China the primary group, and the hierarchy within the group, is more important than the individual or the task (Wenzhong & Grove, 1991).

In cultures that value relationships, issues of face are very important. The Japanese use a communication pattern called *nemawashi*, a "consultation in private." The word means "to smooth around the roots before planting something."

This system works by allowing those in a public meeting to save face because all major ideas/points have been discussed privately in advance.

Developing a business relationship in an Asian culture means understanding existing networks of relationships. In China, workers learn not to underestimate the importance of existing connections. They appreciate the need to deal with a person of influence. If that person feels you are trustworthy enough, and if they can get their network of contacts to trust you, there is a chance you will succeed (this is referred to as *guanxi* in Chinese). Personal contacts are the basis for all human activity; including business connections in China. When relationship building is more important than conducting business, a business partner may decide not to sign a contract, sometimes feeling that a good relationship is built on trust and needs no contract. On the other hand, a signed contract with an American businessperson indicates the beginning of a long serious business partnership. In other words, it may take the Asian partner more time to decide if they want to do business because developing a relationship is their primary goal, which is then followed by business. In the United States it is the opposite; contracts get signed and then colleagues develop relationships because they know they are contractually linked to each other.

In his work on Japanese and American business negotiations, Salacuse (2003) suggests that Asians (and especially Japanese business people) often see Western business people as being in too much of a hurry, rushing to make a deal before the relationship has a solid foundation. Western business people often feel that Japanese are stalling or delaying decisions that cost too much time and money. These findings show us that, while in international partnerships, Westerners should think more about how "haste makes waste" rather than the belief that "time is money" (Salacuse, 2003).

Language Issues

A third area to consider is the use of the English language, both verbal and written, in business transactions. As a result of the Anglo-American business dominance of the 20th century, English became and remains the language among business people who do not share a common language (Thomas & Inkson, 2003). A language that is used as a bridge to communicate between native and nonnative speakers is referred to as a "lingua franca," a term that was previously introduced in Chapter 7. For example, English is a vernacular in the United Kingdom, but is used as a vehicular language (that is, a lingua franca) in the Philippines. Because English is often the lingua franca spoken during business meetings by people from two different countries, native speakers of English have the advantage of conducting business in their first language. Native speakers of English should consider that the other party may have never lived or studied in an English-speaking country. In that situation, it is critical for the native English speaker to make it easier for the non-native speaker to understand what is being said.

Language problems, especially those that result in a poor understanding of the conversation, can be a face issue. Asking for clarification can be interpreted as weakness, especially in a conflict situation (Ehrenreich, 2010). Rather than lose face, an associate may indicate they understood what was said, when in fact they

A market in Cambodia offers fried bugs, spiders, crickets, and little birds. Are these pests, pets, or food in your culture?

did not. Instead of asking them if they understand, it's better to ask open-ended questions and summarize ideas verbally and in writing. While both speakers may be communicating in English, words and phrases can have very different connotations. For example, the grasshopper is considered a pest in the United States, an appetizer in Thailand, and a household pet in China! Making a reference about a "grasshopper" from an American point of view can result in quite different frames of reference and reaction to comments depending on the culture of the audience.

Business Etiquette

Small acts can have huge impacts. Failing to use the correct business etiquette can be devastating. In terms of business etiquette around the world, the key phrase is "Know before you go!" There are a plethora of books, videos, and articles on the topic of business etiquette when interacting with other cultures. Some of the key areas are business introductions, the dynamics of a meeting, and steps to developing a long-term business relationship.

It is a sign of respect to use verbal and nonverbal politeness strategies with an international host or guest. Learning to introduce yourself in a second culture and language is important. For example, in Japan, a polite and culturally competent business professional would know how to introduce himself in simple Japanese, properly give and receive business cards, and bow at the proper and polite angle to his/her business partner. These cultural practices demonstrate you are interested in and willing to learn about another culture. One does not exchange business cards before the bow. If your partner bows to you, you must return a bow as low as the one you received. The depth of the bow signifies the status of the relationships between people. Japanese business people give their business cards, or *meishi*, with both hands. One side of the card will be in Japanese and the other in English. You should also translate your business cards into your partner's language for presentation. Handle the card very carefully with both hands, read it, and do not put it into your wallet or back pocket. Sitting on another person's meishi is very disrespectful. Put the card in a case and slip it into a front jacket pocket. Japanese prefer to use titles and last names upon introductions. They will also use your title and last name as a sign of respect.

While it may seem unusual to give gifts at a business meeting, it may be customary in the country that you are traveling to. In Japan, for example, giving a gift to a future business partner or current partner is considered a sign of good-will. Small and inexpensive gifts from one's company with the company logo are appropriate (Brislin, 2008). The gift should always be wrapped with great care; it is the ceremony of gift-giving that is important. Also, never give gifts of odd numbers or the number four. Odd numbers are bad luck and the word for the number four in Japanese sounds like the word "death."

Expectations about socializing after business hours also differ by culture. In some countries, staying out late to socialize is part of the price of doing business. The socializing may include drinking alcohol as a way to develop closer relationships in relaxed interactions (Brislin, 2008). After a few glasses of sake, business partners may feel more comfortable calling you by your first name or singing songs with you at a karaoke spot.

"Know before you go" is the key. Take the Business Etiquette and Culture Quiz (Put It Into Practice 11.1) and see what you already know.

Leadership and Culture

In the academic literature on leadership, the idea that the leader is an individual agent who can exert direct influence over others is common. But this is a very Western view. Much of what we know about leadership styles is based on research conducted in the United States and assumed to be valid and applicable to other international settings (Thomas & Inkson, 2003; Wu & Stewart, 2005). Other scholars argue that leadership depends on the social context that makes influence possible, like whether the culture is individualistic or collectivistic (e.g., in collectivist settings there is much more commitment to group membership and respect for established leadership hierarchy) (Gomez-Banutu, 2011).

In Japan, all relationships are affected by *amae*. Amae is a Japanese term for the emotion of feeling accepted, cared for, and indulged by others. In Japan, managers are very interested in their employees' personal lives. Leader behavior is embedded in reciprocal obligations. In Korea and other Asian countries, leaders are expected to not only give advice on work-related issues but to be involved on a personal level with employees and their families (Brislin, 2008). If managers are unwilling to take on this role, they lose the respect of their coworkers.

Trust is another factor that is a powerful force in organizational cultures. Along with Emotional Intelligence (EI), leader/member trust is a strong motivational factor that is predictive of employee job satisfaction and commitment (Downey, Roberts, & Stough, 2011). These are intrinsically related to relationships, not just with leadership,

PUT IT INTO PRACTICE   **11.1**

The Business Etiquette and Culture Quiz

For each of the eight statements listed below, try to find out if the statement is generally true or false. (The answers are at the end of the chapter.)

1. In Japan, loudly slurping your soup at a business lunch is considered a sign that you like the soup.

2. In Japan, when sitting down to a business meeting with your Asian counterparts, the seating arrangement will be determined by the status of the participants. As a general rule in Japan, the highest-ranking person from the host side will sit at the head of the table.

3. Confucian ethics dominate Korean thought patterns and this translates in business terms into great respect for authority, age, and seniority.

4. Korean managers are not expected to take an interest in the personal well-being of their staff. It is considered intrusive to ask employees about personal issues that have nothing to do with the business at hand.

5. The rest of "old Europe," which includes Spain, Italy, and Portugal, still has a way of doing business that may seem patriarchal to those from other countries—especially the United States.

6. In China, never underestimate the importance of existing connections. Deal with a Chinese person of influence; if that person feels you are trustworthy enough, and if they can get their network of contacts to trust you, there is a chance you will succeed.

7. In India, women are not expected or respected in business as managers and do not take positions of corporate leadership.

8. Hindi is the official language of India, and one can therefore expect that business communication will not be in English.

but also with co-workers and clients. Individuals with higher emotional intelligence are able to form more effective work teams than less emotionally intelligent ones. Teams with high levels of mutual trust are more successful. Rezvani (2018) looked at 84 project teams in large-scale construction projects. Using the Wong and Law Emotional Intelligence and Cook and Wall Interpersonal Trust scales, they concluded that EI and trust are positively related to team performance. Similarly, Mohanty and Arunprasad (2020) studied Indian power companies' organizational cultures and found that co-worker trust, supervisor trust, and organizational trust led to employee engagement. Teams are essential in today's work environment. Trust and EI are necessary components of team success. But how does one develop these soft skills? Researchers emphasize the importance of interpersonal relationship building. Workplaces are spaces where employees can form emotional bonds with each other. Certainly, we can make the argument that the norms and rituals governing relationship development and maintenance vary across cultures. Our earlier discussion on how Chinese culture values *guanxi*, or relationship building, is an example of how trust can manifest differently in a Chinese vs. a Western organization. According to Chen and Bedford (2022), *guanxi* encompasses a wider range of interpersonal exchanges, both work-related and nonwork-related, compared to Western conceptions of organization relationships. In other words, the compartmentalization of work and nonwork worlds common in many Western cultures is not the way Chinese societies function. Therefore, something like personal favoritism, which might not be acceptable in Western organizational processes, may be expected in a Chinese organization.

Power distance (Hofstede, 2001), which was first introduced in Chapter 4, plays a pivotal role in organizational settings. Status is a signifier of power distance and is often a key component of a leadership position. Cultures have hierarchies in which some people have more status and power than others (Osland & Bird, 2000). The presence of such differentials is universal. However, distinctions between degrees of power and status are different and can be compared to the relative amount of distance between people. Brislin (2008) compares those differences to the rungs of a ladder. In some cultures the difference is two rungs, in others it is eight rungs. Compared to other parts of the world, the United States has a low power distance. For example, bosses and workers might address each other by first name. Also, having a public discussion or disagreeing publicly with a boss in a respectful manner is not considered improper. Workers don't defer to bosses because they hold a specific title but because they are expected to produce certain results and lead. It is not uncommon for today's worker to be tomorrow's boss. Moving up the ladder may not be as difficult in the United States as in other countries.

Countries with high power distance (like in most Asian countries) give great deference to leaders. Employees will rarely, if ever, publicly disagree with a superior because it would make both the superior and employee lose face. Such employees may not envision the possibility of moving up the ladder. In some countries it is considered unconscionable to poke fun at a leader. Respect is given and deference shown in very visible, nonverbal displays, such as bowing lower to a superior or letting a superior walk through a door first. Personal deference may be given to leaders based on the assumption that such a person has wisdom not only about the work, but also life in general (Brislin, 2008). Successful international leaders will need to be able to manage communication in culturally and linguistically diverse contexts in the 21st century as an expectation of employment (Henderson, 2005; Lauring, 2011; Varner & Beamer, 2005).

Culture and Conflict Management

Managing conflict is an essential communication skill, and like everyday conversations, we often assume that everyone plays by the same set of rules. But in fact, cultural differences abound. One model of intercultural conflict focuses on how cultures differ in their perspectives toward conflict, personal constructs, and message strategies (Nadler, Nadler, & Broome, 1985). These cultural differences in conflict have implications for all social contexts—especially for the workplace.

The model begins with the idea that cultures have different perspectives on conflict, which means that their attitudes toward conflict and how to manage it may differ. First, a culture's orientation toward conflict may be generally positive or negative. A positive orientation suggests that people are relatively comfortable with conflict, view it as a normal part of human interaction, and willingly engage in it. Second, a culture's orientation toward conflict resolution, which involves the culturally appropriate ways of dealing with conflict, will determine which conflict management style is chosen. Individualistic cultures are more likely than collectivistic cultures to use competing and problem-solving styles, which reflect a higher concern for self-promotion than other styles do. Collectivistic cultures are more likely to use obliging, avoiding, and compromising styles, depending on the particular situation (Ting-Toomey, 1999). Third, a culture's criteria for conflict resolution, or what constitutes a successful resolution, is important. Some cultures regard success as a short-term gain, while others view success from a long-term perspective. Furthermore, collectivistic cultures are more inclined to consider "protecting the relationship" as a satisfactory outcome. To people in individualistic cultures, "winning" is the preferred result. Ting-Toomey (2002, p. 327) contends that individualistic cultures rely on "outcome-oriented" assumptions of success and collectivistic cultures rely on "process-oriented" assumptions (see Box 11.1 for a list of these different assumptions).

The next element of the model deals with cultural differences in *personal constructs*, specifically our perceptions of fairness, trustworthiness, and power. People may differ in their conception of fairness. For example, when two people are discussing the price of a product, each may have a different idea of what a fair price is. In some cultural contexts, fairness means equality, where equal outcomes or payoffs are due to all parties. In other contexts, the idea of equity, or outcomes judged on the amount of effort put forth, may be more appropriate. In still other contexts, people may believe in balancing the needs of the parties involved. What seems fair to one group may not seem fair to another.

We earlier discussed the importance of trust in the workplace, but it is important to remember that perceptions of trust can differ across cultures. As we mentioned earlier, in some cultures a willingness to enter into binding contracts is a sign of trustworthiness; in other cultures the insistence on contracts suggests untrustworthiness. Imagine sharing an apartment with a friend. Do you both sign the lease? Can one person sign the lease and trust that the other will contribute to the rent as expected? Is an oral agreement sufficient? The power distance orientation of a culture can also make a difference. According to Ting-Toomey (1999), trust in small power distance cultures is often based on charismatic personality traits, personal credibility, reliability, persuasive words, and decisive actions. In large power distance cultures, trust tends to be based on credible roles in a reputable organization, dependable family, and kinship networks, and consistency between words and actions over a long period of time.

The last element in the model suggests that cultures differ in the *message strategies* they prefer. Specifically, they differ in terms of how they regard and use threats and promises, expressiveness, and decision-making styles. What counts as a threat or promise is influenced by culture. In many collectivistic societies the threat of damaging a relationship may be more serious than that of losing material resources. Moreover, cultures differ in who can threaten or promise and when it is appropriate to do so. Violating these norms can have serious consequences. Finally, cultures differ in their decision-making style. Usually these differences focus on who has the right to make the decision and on the kinds of evidence and reasoning needed to justify it.

Box 11.1 Outcome-Oriented and Process-Oriented Assumptions of Conflict

Outcome-Oriented (Individualistic)

1. Conflict is seen as closely related to salient goals of the parties involved.

2. Communication is viewed as dissatisfying when the conflict parties are not willing to deal with the conflict openly and honestly.

3. Communication is viewed as satisfying when the conflict parties are willing to confront issues openly and share their feelings honestly (i.e., assertively but not aggressively).

4. The conflict outcome is perceived as unproductive when no tangible outcomes are reached or no plan of action is developed.

5. The conflict outcome is perceived as productive when tangible solutions are reached and objective criteria are met.

6. Effective and appropriate management of conflict means individual goals are addressed and differences are being dealt with openly, honestly, and properly in relation to timing and the situational context.

Process-Oriented (Collectivistic)

1. Conflict is seen as closely related to face-threat and ingroup/outgroup relations.

2. Communication is perceived as threatening when the conflict parties push for substantive issue discussion before proper facework management.

3. Communication is viewed as satisfying when the conflict parties engage in mutual face-saving and face-giving behavior and attend to both verbal and nonverbal signals.

4. The conflict process or outcome is perceived as unproductive when face issues are not addressed and relational/group feelings are not attended to properly.

5. The conflict process or outcome is defined as productive when both conflict parties can claim win-win results on facework in addition to substantive agreement.

6. Appropriate and effective management of conflict means that the mutual "faces" of the conflict parties are saved or even upgraded in the interaction and they have dealt with the conflict episode strategically in conjunction with substantive gains or losses.

Conflicts in the workplace are increasingly common and complex, due in part to the increasing cultural diversity we have focused on in this chapter (Van Meurs & Spencer-Oatey, 2010). Both Americans and Japanese tend to rely on collaborative conflict management styles, especially in organizational conflicts. However, Americans are more likely to arrive at collaboration through open and direct face-to-face communication in a group setting while the Japanese may do so through indirect communication which allows the group to infer solutions that are workable (Adair, Okumura, & Brett, 2001).

Opportunities for Contact and Dialogue

"Never doubt that a small group of thoughtful, committed people can change the world. Indeed, it is the only thing that ever has."

—Margaret Mead

Consider how many hours people spend in their workplace over the course of a day, a month, a year, or a lifetime. Most of our waking hours, if working away from home full time (40 hours per week or more) are spent with our colleagues, not our families or personal friends. For this reason, our multicultural and global workplaces are ripe with opportunities for intercultural contact, dialogue, and meaningful interaction. There are three intersecting areas in the workplace that afford invaluable opportunities to learn about others through contact and dialogue. They can be found in global teams, through corporate social responsibility programs at our workplaces, and via intercultural training programs offered to employees by their companies.

Global Work Teams in Global Corporations

A *global work team* is a group of people of different nationalities working together on a common project across cultures and time zones for extended periods of time to achieve an outcome or solve problems (Marquardt & Horvath, 2001). Because team leaders change depending on the skills of the group, the idea of a contact hierarchy or chain of command will diminish.

For organizations that have bases around the world, a new type of team has proven to be very successful. In the following case of Marriott Hotel, rather than have a US team assess and make all the recommendations for integrating another hotel chain into their operation, Marriott chose to create a global team:

> Marriott Hotel faced the challenge of quickly integrating the $1 billion Renaissance and New World hotel chain into the Marriott. A global team was formed to complete an assessment of the current status of the new hotels: what branding was needed, what capital expenditures were needed and what design modifications were needed to bring the new hotels in line with Marriott standards. Within 30 days, the global team had developed a strategy and written procedures that enabled all the hotels in different countries to be at operational status and add to Marriott's global growth and prestige worldwide. (Marquardt & Horvath, 2001, p. 3)

The advantage of creating a global team is that Marriott has input from employees around the world who are familiar with culture, customs, and business practices of various locales.

Global teams have the ability to get specialized talent from anywhere in the organization, ensure a greater understanding of local customers, develop global leaders for the organization, and increase the ability to become a global learning organization. If a company has a complex challenge to meet and has ready access to the most knowledgeable employees throughout the system in various countries, there is wealth of vantage points to consider the issue. The most successful organizations are *glocalized*—they have a global reach and a local touch (Marquardt & Horvath, 2001). Employees who are "on the ground" in a particular country can inform a global organization that may be headquartered in another country of the local cultural practices that will influence consumer behavior. This local awareness can avoid cultural missteps like the following mistakes in international advertising campaigns:

- When "translated" into Spanish, the Dairy Association's astoundingly successful "Got Milk?" advertising campaign asked Latino consumers "Are you lactating?"
- During the Pope's visit to Miami, a local T-shirt company printed shirts that read, "I saw the Potato" because in Spanish the article "the" can be either masculine (el papa) or feminine (la papa); on the T-shirt they used the feminine, which describes the tuber rather than the head of the Catholic Church!
- In 2004, Hispanic pop star Thalia Sodi . . . proudly branded a new Hershey's line of "Hispanic Inspired" candy with her name. The new line included a candy bar naively called "Cajeta Elegancita." There wouldn't be an issue if the product was being marketed in Thalia's native Mexico, where the word "cajeta" has the G-rated meaning of milk candy (loosely translated). Unfortunately for Hershey's, in parts of Latin America "cajeta" is also a derogatory slang term for a part of the female anatomy (Tornoe, 2007).

Corporate Social Responsibility (CSR)

In 2016, Colin Kaepernick, a former NFL quarterback for the San Francisco 49ers, "took a knee" when the national anthem was played to protest racial inequality and police brutality. His controversial action generated polarized reactions from both sides of the political spectrum. Since becoming a free agent in 2017, he has not been signed by another NFL team. Kaepernick once again was thrust into the spotlight in 2018, this time by a major sports corporation, Nike, as part of a series of marketing messages that could be classified as corporate social advocacy. Nike's CEO stated in 2018 that their controversial ad with Kaepernick "has driven 'record engagement' with the brand and helped boost sales" (Vizard, 2018).

Since the 1990s, developing corporate social responsibility has become a top priority for the world's largest companies, especially major transnational corporations based in North America or Western Europe (Waller & Conaway, 2011). The notion of *Corporate Social Responsibility (CSR)* can be traced back to the 1940s and 1950s (Bowen, 1953). It requires business organizations to consider their economic, legal, ethical, and philanthropic responsibilities. One of the major responsibilities is that any business must support the educational, religious, artistic, medical, and social welfare of the community in which is it situated and which it serves (Carroll, 1991). More and more, businesses are taking on global issues such as the environment, gender inequality, and poverty, allowing greater dialogue regarding issues affecting countries across the world. Societal expectations about the responsibilities of businesses are also shifting such that it is no longer enough to just be responsible in their business practices, they are expected to take active stances on sociopolitical issues (Overton et al., 2021), in other words, to take on the role of social advocates. This expectation not only comes from consumers, but also increasingly from employees, many of whom are from Generation Y and Z, who are more likely to prioritize purpose over salary. Companies also need to be careful about potential backlash when their CSR campaigns are perceived to be deceitful. One example of this for a multinational company is Starbucks, which received criticism for continuing to serve coffee in single-use cups and promoting a global to-go coffee culture while declaring commitments to sustainability (Harper, 2017). Starbucks was also criticized for making public declarations on racial justice, but refusing to let employees wear Black Lives Matter clothing and accessories. After the fallout, Starbucks backtracked on the policy (Wahba, 2020).

Global corporations are becoming a dominant player in shaping global economic and development agendas (Caprara & Nelson, 2007). Multinational corporations have operations spanning the globe and have capacities and networks that match those of many governments. Because of their economic power, they are taking on challenges that have traditionally been addressed by governmental or public organizations. Global corporations are making it their business to be involved in ways that will contribute to poverty reduction, environmental sustainability, humanitarian relief, and health and human rights (Caprara & Nelson, 2007). Take for example, ManpowerGroup (www.manpowergroup.com), a world leader in the employment services industry. ManpowerGroup was the first global corporation to sign up for the Athens Ethical Principles. They declared a zero-tolerance policy for working with any entity benefitting in any way from human trafficking. "End Human Trafficking Now!" is a partnership of public and private organizations and citizens spearheaded by Suzanne Mubarak's Women's International Peace Movement and endorsed by the United Nations High Commissioner for Refugees (Zarling, 2006).

It will become more and more common for young people looking at potential employers to consider a company's Corporate Social Responsibility (CSR). The Brookings Institute for the Kennedy School of Government reported that the global influence of multinational corporations has significantly increased (Nelson, 2006). As noted in the report, "private enterprises offer the potential to increase innovation, spur wealth creation, transfer technology, meet basic needs, raise living standards, and improve the quality of life for millions of people around the globe" (Nelson, 2006). Responsible leadership of multinational corporations will commit to protecting both market value and social value in the 21st century.

One example of CSR is Starbucks in Colombia, South America, working with Conservation International and local farmers to encourage sustainable coffee development. Another example is Citigroup, one of the world's leading financial institutions, helping develop financial services for the poor, including microcredit and investment opportunities. Such companies will offer their employees socially responsible investment options in the corporate pension schemes to enable them to participate directly with their earning power. Other companies may encourage their employees to become involved in local educational and service-learning opportunities where business is conducted. As can be seen, issues of profits, ethics, shareholders, and human rights are all intertwined in our global economies and workplaces (Collier & Wanderley, 2005).

Environmental, social, and governance (ESG) principles are being used more and more to evaluate how companies invest and manage their resources (United Nations, 2004). For instance, stakeholders, including customers, are increasingly interested in how corporations deal with sustainability issues. Does a company care about its impact in the communities it serves? What types of programs does it have to reflect that it values diversity and equity, transparency, employee engagement, and health? Does the company's management structure promote corruption or is it participatory? These are some of the issues corporations are expected to consider.

Intercultural Training Programs

Preparing employees for intercultural assignments and global relocation is becoming an increasingly important human resource development issue (Osman-Gani & Tan, 2005). Companies have long been aware that many expatriate assignments are unsuccessful. Vance and Ensher (2002) have pointed out "that 16 to 40% of all managers posted abroad return home prematurely either because their performance is inadequate or because they or their families have problems adjusting to the new culture" (p. 491).

Not only is training critical for those moving overseas but training is important for employees who travel overseas frequently and for multicultural teams in international companies (Osman-Gani & Rockstuhl, 2009). A study on the

The environmental, social, and governance (ESG) concept used to evaluate a company's behavior. (Shutterstock/Elnur)

characteristics of companies that have successful international posting identified three key factors in successful outcomes: (1) knowledge creation and global leadership development, (2) intercultural competence, and (3) well-designed reintegration programs (Black & Gregersen, 1999). Hammer (1999) added additional areas that must be addressed. The employee who is working overseas must have the tools and training for their own personal adjustment to the culture. They must be prepared to work well in another culture, prepared to improve their cultural sensitivity about social interactions and ways of doing work in that culture. Training should also include preparation of their family members, who factor enormously into the success and well-being of the employee. Children over the age of 13 tend to have particular difficulties with language and cultural adaptation.

Zhu and Kleiner (2000) argue that training to increase cultural sensitivity is not successful and may create more social unrest than existed previously. Short-term culture-specific training programs have definitely received criticism for these shortcomings (Hammer & Martin, 1992). A supportive work environment that wants to create a corporate culture of diversity awareness must follow through on sustained employee development programs and model the desired behavior at the top level (Sanchez & Medkik, 2004).

Training programs likely to develop intercultural competence should involve communication-focused scenarios where the trainee would not simply read or study about a particular culture and learn the language, but actually participate in and be evaluated on simulated communication situations. For example, a trainee can be assessed in a simulated business encounter such as a staged cocktail party to evaluate the grasp of South Korean social etiquette. Another example would be to read actual business case studies and discuss them with current employees to analyze commonalities and to learn from prior experience of those employees.

Summary

The current statistics on diversity in the US workforce and how our workforce is changing so quickly and dramatically is a driving force in the need to focus on how diversity will impact the way we work together. The values of different cultures in the US workforce will influence the goals and practices of American businesses. The globalization of the US workforce will bring people together whose orientations to work will not be homogeneous. Diversity training has had mixed results, but we discussed some suggestions for improving effectiveness. Taking into consideration that team members in our offices may have differing task orientations or social orientations toward work will help us understand that there are different paths to achieving the same goals. We also showcased flash points where misunderstanding is likely to occur: social identities in the workplace, hiring practices, leadership and culture, language issues, and conflict communication. The chapter concludes with opportunities for dialogue and community in the contexts of global work teams and global corporations. The chapter ends with an emphasis on the importance of corporate social responsibility and programming that is essential for intercultural training in the workplace.

QUESTIONS

1. Imagine that you are working for a global corporation that is sending you to Japan to form part of a global audit team for the next four months. You are a native speaker of English and do not speak any Japanese. All of the team members will be native speakers of Japanese who use English as their lingua franca. Consider the following areas where you will need to take your cross-cultural communication skills into account. What will you need to be aware of in the following contexts?

   a. Team meetings

   b. Working hours

   c. Listening skills

2. Visit Campbell's corporate social responsibility (CSR) webpage and read their Corporate Responsibility Report (www.campbellsoupcompany.com/our-impact), or choose another local company that includes CSR reports on their website.

   a. Read the Executive Summary report for the CSR. What activities are included as examples of CSR? Are they domestic, international, or global activities?

   b. Why is Campbell's rated as one of the top 10 corporations for community citizenship?

3. Will CSR be one of the areas you consider when choosing a company to work for in the future?

4. Discuss how the practice of nemawashi in Japanese companies operates. Then discuss why this communication practice is critical to face-saving and face-giving in Asian countries. Compare and contrast how the types of communication practices would differ in an organizational meeting depending on whether the communication style of the group was more Eastern or Western in terms of their orientation to communication. Consider the following:

   a. Is there a prescribed speaker order?

   b. How would a conflict be managed?

   c. How might leadership styles differ?

5. How would you prepare for an interview with a global company to help the recruiter understand that you have a firm grasp of the intercultural communication skills necessary to work for a global company and on a global team?

ANSWERS TO THE CULTURE QUIZ

1. **True**. Slurping your soup or noodles in Japan, albeit noisy and not considered polite in the United States, is good manners in Japan. Slurping loudly conveys that the food the host has provided is delicious and that the guest is truly enjoying and savoring it.

2. **True.** When you enter the meeting room, wait to be seated. The visitor will always be directed to the seat that has been chosen for them. Seating arrangements are indicative of hierarchy and importance and are prearranged, which can be very different from American-style meeting practices where everyone sits where they want and the seat chosen doesn't indicate importance in the organization.

3. **True.** Respect for age, authority, and seniority are a key component of Korean business practices.

4. **False.** While in the United States employees may not want employers to know a significant amount of personal information about them, managers in Korea are expected to care and be concerned about the personal lives of their employees and their families.

5. **True.** For example, Italy still has a way of doing business that may seem patriarchal to business people from other countries, in particular those from the United States.

6. **True.** Building a relationship before doing business is key. Trust is the primary ingredient for a healthy, long-term business relationship.

7. **False.** Gender issues don't take precedence; the position of the person is more important.

8. **False.** While Hindi is the official language of the government and spoken by the most people, English is considered an associate language and is widely used throughout India, especially in business.

12

Intercultural Communication and Media

KEY TERMS

computer-mediated communication
co-production process
cultivation theory
democratic participation
elite-driven media
Facebook addiction disorder

gaming communities
hate media
intercultural peacebuilding
   programming
media access
online communities

online dialogues
parasocial contact hypothesis
parasocial relationships
peace journalism
peace media

racist ideology
racist media
SIDE model
social networking sites

How we connect with others is a function of how technologically privileged and capable we are. In this chapter, we explore the power of media to influence intercultural communication, and particularly, intercultural conflict. As the examples below suggest, that influence can be powerfully positive or dishearteningly negative. Media can create community, such as that developed through the Soliya Connect Program—a program that has brought together university students from Western and Middle Eastern cultures to increase understanding (see A Closer Look 12.1). Media can also fuel the fires of hatred and xenophobia (see A Closer Look 12.2).

After a basic introduction to concepts of conventional ("old") and contemporary ("new") media, we consider the power of media use and influence in interpersonal relationships; how friendships, courtship, family, and community relationships are increasingly enhanced by computer-mediated technology. An exciting element is media's role in building democratic participation and more participatory foundations of societies and nations. We also discuss basic principles of the role of social media in intercultural conflict; how social media is an increasingly inherent element in understanding how that conflict develops and is managed.

Media can present serious challenges to intercultural communication and peacebuilding, and we explore how the media produce or reinforce prejudice and how media coverage can feed war. Fortunately, the last section of the chapter focuses on more hopeful areas of study. To understand how media can reduce prejudice we introduce the parasocial contact hypothesis, which explains how media develop a form of intergroup contact to overcome prejudice, a process introduced in earlier chapters. We use the example of the television show *Sesame Street*, which entertainingly creates tolerance in a number of countries around the world. We give examples of how media can be used to platform and supplement effective intercultural dialogue processes. We end the chapter with thoughts of the growing field of peace journalism that is devoted to using media to promote peace rather than war.

A CLOSER LOOK   12.1

Soliya Connect Program Builds Understanding Among College Students

Soliya (www.soliya.net) is a nonprofit organization using new technologies to facilitate dialogue between students from diverse backgrounds across the globe. The Connect Program uses web conferencing technology to bridge the gap between university students in the Middle East, North Africa, Europe, and the United States. Soliya recently compiled pre- and post-test results from the participants.

Percentage of students who agreed or strongly agreed that they had a good understanding of the views of people in the United States and Europe/Middle East:

Americans and Europeans:	Before: 35%	After: 72%
Middle Easterners:	Before: 50%	After: 85%

Percentage of students who strongly agreed that they had a lot in common with their counterparts in the United States and Europe/Middle East:

Americans and Europeans:	Before: 45%	After: 75%
Middle Easterners:	Before: 40%	After: 70%

A CLOSER LOOK   **12.2**

Florida Preacher Threatens to Burn Quran

A Florida pastor's plan to burn Qurans at his church on September 11 ignited protests for a second day by hundreds of Afghans, who burned U.S. flags and shouted "Death to America," prompting the top U.S. commander in Afghanistan to say that the pastor could be increasing the threat to his troops. The crowd in downtown Kabul reached nearly 500 Monday, with Afghan protesters chanting "Long live Islam" and "Long live the Quran," and burning an effigy of Terry Jones, senior pastor of the Dove World Outreach Center in Gainesville, who is planning the event.

(Raddatz, 2010)

Media and Intercultural Communication

As Natale (2016) explains, "new media" are dependent on communication technologies related to computers or devices that enable access to the digital. Conversely, "old media" are nondigital or preceded the digital, such as books, newspapers, cinema, radio, and television. Social media can be distinguished from older Web 1.0 forms of digital communication media such as email and text messaging. Web 1.0 platforms tend to be more linear in the way content is distributed and do not easily support large and highly interactive networks (Wei, 2012). Unlike Web 2.0, Web 1.0 technologies do not allow multiple users to access and manipulate posted content (they can only respond to content, or manipulate and then repost it). Thus, what distinguishes social media from other forms of virtual communities and digital communication media is that social media are much more open, interactive, fluid, and dynamic; with a key characteristic being the ability of users to generate their own content (McFarland & Ployhart, 2015). The visual dimension of social media is very powerful (Miguel, 2016). Photos and videos give a sense of immediacy, or being in the moment with another—especially when the images show affection and disclose what is important to the other. In fact, photos act much the same as verbal self-disclosure—an opening up of one to another that almost defines friendship or closeness. Ironically, the fact that the images are consumable by so many others may undermine the sense of impact we desire.

Of course, not everyone has access to communication technology or to the websites we have discussed. An economic reality is that *media access* is very much linked to wealth resources (Straubhaar, 2008). An International Telecommunication Union (2022) report gives a broad outline:

> [S]ome 2.7 billion people worldwide remain totally offline, with universal connectivity still a distant prospect in least developed countries and landlocked developing countries, where, on average, only 36 percent of the population is online . . . . In poorly connected countries, two of the biggest barriers to digital

uptake remain cost and digital skills. . . . For an average consumer in a typical low-income economy, the cheapest mobile broadband basket still costs more than 9 percent of his or her income—over six times the global average. Fixed-broadband service costs over 30 percent, compared with less than 2 percent in the world's high-income countries. (p. iii)

Internet use is not only a function of wealth. National culture impacts the adoption of communication technology and its social uses (Moghadam & Assar, 2008). A study on internet use and attitudes by university students in the United Arab Emirates (UAE) found that Emirati students dedicate substantial time to socializing online, although there were differences due to gender, age, and social status (Sokol & Sisler, 2010). In terms of gender differences, the Emirati women, when online, hid both their identity and gender significantly more than did men. More than half of the women said the internet allows them to communicate without being subjected to prejudice, yet men were comfortable with people knowing their gender online. This research reminds us that technological innovation exists within cultural parameters.

Social media usage has grown dramatically. If we consider that usage by demographic categories like age, race, and gender, we find the following (Pew Research Center, 2021):

- Young adults (ages 19 to 29) use social media the most (84%). However, usage among adults 65 and older rose from 11% in 2010 to 45% in 2021.
- In the past decade, the gap between women and men who use social media has continued to grow (78% for women, 66% for men).
- People with higher education levels use social media the most (college graduates at 77%) Almost two-thirds (69%) of those in the lowest income bracket now use social media.
- Since 2019, a wider gap has started to develop between Hispanic (80%), Black (77%), and White (69%) ethnicities.
- Today, 66% of rural residents, 71% of suburban residents, and 76% of urban residents use social media.

Online Friendships and Interpersonal Relationships

Sherry Turkle, a professor at the Massachusetts Institute of Technology's Center for Computer Technology and Relationship, has argued the potential for social media to be both friend and foe in our quest for constructive interpersonal and intercultural relationships. In her two books, *Alone Together* (2011) and *Reclaiming Conversation* (2015) she articulates the "dark side of social media." Consider the following excerpts:

These days, insecure in our relationships and anxious about intimacy, we look to technology for ways to be in relationships and protect ourselves from them at the same time. . . . We bend to the inanimate with new solicitude. . . . We expect more from technology and less from each other. . . . The ties we form through the Internet are not, in the end, the ties that bind. But they are the ties that preoccupy. . . . After an evening of avatar-to-avatar talk in a networked game, we feel, at one moment, in possession of a full social life and, in the next, curiously isolated, in tenuous complicity with strangers. . . . Yet, suddenly, in the half-light of virtual community, we may feel utterly alone. As we distribute ourselves, we may abandon ourselves. (2011, pp. 162; 166).

A recent Pew Research Center study (Vogels & Anderson, 2020) on dating and relationships in the digital age confirms that people see some drawbacks to their partner's use of social media—drawbacks that can generally be described as distraction and distancing:

- About half of Americans in a relationship say their partner is distracted by their phone when they are trying to talk to them.
- About one-in-three Americans who are in a romantic relationship say they've looked through their partner's phone without that person's knowledge.
- Of social media users who are single and looking, 33% say seeing relationship posts make them feel worse about their dating life.
- Of younger social media users, 70% say they've checked up on their exes via these platforms.
- Younger adults are especially likely to see social media as an important way to show how much they care about their partner.
- About one-quarter of partnered Americans say their partner's social media use has made them feel jealous, unsure about their relationship.
- About half of Americans in romantic relationships say they deal with their partner being distracted by their phone.

PUT IT INTO PRACTICE　　　　　　　　　　　　　　　**12.1**

How Would Your Life Change?

Think for a moment about the implications of this media access issue. What would your life be like if you were suddenly without access to communication technologies that you now take for granted? What if you had never had access to those technologies in the first place? We may be actually creating cultures related to media immersion rather than race, gender, or nationality—the Media rich and the Media poor. Consider the following questions:

1. How much of your connection to other people is dependent on communication technology or media (e.g., cell phone, internet, television, etc.)?

2. How would your life and relationships be different if you could no longer afford access to these media? Would they improve? Be harmed?

3. If you could change something about how you use media to make and keep relationships, what would it be? Why?

4. Choose one of the things that you mentioned as a response to question 3 and try that for one week. At the end of that week, answer the following question: How has that change in behavior affected you? How has it affected the people you are in a relationship with?

Other scholars have also suggested that social media is not a panacea. Fox and Moreland (2015) found that adult Facebook users reported negative psychological and relational experiences in five areas: managing inappropriate or annoying content, being tethered, lack of privacy and control, social comparison and jealousy, and relationship tension and conflict. Facebook users often had negative feelings but felt pressured to access the site for fear of missing out or being seen as a "poor" relational partner. A common complaint was the constant social comparison to other network members, which triggered jealousy, anxiety, and other negative emotions.

In earlier chapters we discussed the influence of culture on verbal and nonverbal communication. So, it should not be surprising that cultures differ in the kinds of communication behaviors used in online relationships.

Cultural variations in individualism and collectivism are related to social media use, with that use generally increasing as the level of individualism increases (Maitland & Bauer, 2001). Tokunaga (2009) explored how individualism and collectivism influence self-disclosure face-to-face (FTF) and in computer-mediated communication (CMC). He found the more someone affiliates with collectivistic values, the more likely he is to self-disclose in greater breadth and depth in FTF than in CMC.

But is frequency of self-disclosure all we need to understand about cultural differences in online friendship communication? Is frequency less important than the relational value of the disclosure? A study of online friendships in Korea, Japan, and the United States found that all three cultures used self-disclosure strategically to build online relationships (Yum & Hara, 2005). In fact, there were no significant differences in the frequency of self-disclosure use across culture. But the cultures did differ in how self-disclosure was related to trust. For Koreans, the greater the breadth and depth of the self-disclosure, the less they trusted their online relational partner! For Japanese, there was no relationship between trust and self-disclosure, but for Americans, the more they self-disclosed, the more they trusted their partner. We can imagine a new online friendship between a Korean student and an American student where both are using self-disclosure and it builds trust for one partner and decreases it for the other. This is a difficult pattern to overcome unless the different ways they react are known and can be openly addressed between them.

Emotional expression may also differ between cultures in online relationships. Internet users in a study of German students reported developing friendships online and expressing emotion through paralanguage (i.e., emoticons such as smileys) (Utz, 2000). The study found that sustained online interaction can overcome the absence of physical displays of affection and lead to a close, meaningful relationship. This research suggests that previous fears about intercultural communication misunderstandings being greater on CMC than FTF are at least somewhat unfounded.

Culture, Marriage, and Dating Online

Dr. Jeff Gavin, a psychology lecturer at the University of Bath in the United Kingdom, compared members of the UK and Japan in online dating sites. The two cultures presented interesting contrasts because in Japan social context plays a bigger role in communication. As we discussed in Chapters 6 and 7, Japanese people tend to express themselves more implicitly through body language and silence (a high-context culture). Being too explicit or up front can actually lead to negative impressions. By contrast, communication in the West is more dependent on content—we express ourselves explicitly through what we say (a low-context culture). In his results, Gavin reports:

> I found that Japanese online daters overcome the lack of social information in CMC by developing their own cues, for example dropping formal language means intimacy is developing between two people messaging on the site, but dropping it too soon is regarded as a sign of social incompetence, and a turn-off. (Tobin, 2010, p. 11)

About two decades ago, Michael Hardey (2004) observed that communication technologies were replacing traditional routes to marriage in many European societies. That pattern has continued. The internet is being used for members from different cultures to contract arranged marriages—a form of courtship still widely unknown in the United States. Chat room visitors from the Third World contract marriages with citizens of the highly industrialized countries, obtain visas, and migrate to the First World to join their cyber spouses. Shunnaq (2009) looked at this process with Jordanians, Europeans, and North Americans. His results shed light on how gender differences and cultural norms affect online behavior of dating men and women. Jordanians, and especially the women from that country, were more likely to create new hybrid identities for the internet in order to attract possible spouses from Europe and North America than the non-Jordanians.

Democratic Participation and the Internet

In late 2010 and into 2011, the world witnessed an amazing social and political upheaval referred to as the Arab Spring. Throughout the Arab world there were democratic uprisings; the movement originated in Tunisia in December 2010 and quickly took hold in Egypt, Libya, Syria, Yemen, Bahrain, Saudi Arabia, and Jordan. There were a complex set of factors leading to this uprising, but one of the things that enabled the ***democratic participation*** was the presence of internet communities. Ironically, experts at a recent Arizona State University conference on the Arab Spring suggested that the internet presence started as an interest in basic social connection that then became politicized (see A Closer Look 12.3). Reaching out to make friends contributed to a movement that toppled governments. More ironically, at least in the case of Egypt, the decision of the government to attempt to suspend access to internet contact actually encouraged people to go to the street, protest, and thus feed the uprising, as *The Canberra Times* reported:

> Last Friday morning, at 12:20, there was an uncanny quiet in Egypt. Not on the streets, or in homes, but online. At that time, most of Egypt's Internet simply stopped. Fearing protests, dissent and embarrassing coverage, the Mubarak Government instructed Internet providers to cut Internet access. . . . Denied the chance to blog, e-mail or contact international news agencies, angry Egyptians took to the streets. . . . Online catharsis became face-to-face, street protest. (February 4, 2011, p. 19)

It's not surprising that challenged governments have realized the importance of media in political unrest. A study of media, power, and political resistance in

A CLOSER LOOK   **12.3**

Did the Internet Help Propel the Arab Spring?

The following is a summary of two of the things that journalist William Saletan (2011) learned while attending a forum about how interactive media and social networks influenced the demonstrations and protests known as the Arab Spring.

- **"The medium can lead to the message."** Ahmed Al Omran, a Saudi blogger, was educated about politics and human rights while communicating with fellow bloggers online. "Merlyna Lim, a scholar of social transformation at Arizona State University, described a similar dynamic in Egypt: Young people went online to keep up with their friends and youth culture. In doing so, they became politicized" (Saleton, 2011).

- **"Online crowd dynamics mimic offline crowd dynamics."** The internet provides a way for people's shared feelings to become known to one another, emboldening their beliefs. "In Tunisia, according to exiled blogger-activist Sami Ben Gharbia, the government blocked YouTube and Flickr but didn't block Facebook because too many Tunisians had already gathered there, and cutting them off seemed too risky. As a result, more Tunisians converged at Facebook, which became the hub for mobilizing the rebellion" (Saleton, 2011).

China examined how the expansion of new information technologies create new forms of online activism. As the authors conclude:

> Today, people protest in many of the same ways they have always protested.... At the same time, a new, online form of activism and protest has appeared.... The posting and cross-posting of messages, a routine part of social interactions in Chinese cyberspace, sometimes turns into radical protest activities known as "Internet incidents." (Guobin & Calhoun, 2008, p. 9)

Many governments have seen the power of the internet in developing a politically active citizenry and have developed initiatives to promote internet use. In the late 1990s, the Government of Canada launched a string of initiatives to usher its citizens into the "information age." Canada has been recognized around the world as the country most connected to its citizens (Fraser, 2007). In Turkey, the government has used the internet to promote parliamentary process and established a website to build the e-participation of Turkish citizens (Sobaci, 2010).

The internet can create a bridge between immigrants and their home culture, as the experience of Taiwanese immigrants suggests (Wang et al., 2009). The internet has become the first channel Taiwanese Americans use for gathering information about Taiwan and has become one of the most important tools to practice their political participation. The British Broadcasting Service (BBC) has developed two websites for Arab subcultures in the U.K. (BBC Persian Online and BBC Arabic Online) and has explored who uses these sites, their demographic characteristics, and their views on global issues (Andersson, Gillespie, & McKay, 2010).

Social Media and Intercultural Conflict

On the evening of George Zimmerman's acquittal from the killing of seventeen-year-old Sanford, FL, teenager Trayvon Martin, Alicia Garza—in an attempt to articulate her pain and frustration with the verdict—posted what she described as a "love letter to Black folks on Facebook." She ended the post writing, "Black people. I love you. I love us. Our lives matter." Garza's friend, activist and prison abolitionist Patrisse Cullors, shared the post with the hashtag #BlackLivesMatter."'BLM' trickled into national discourse after several police killings of unarmed African-Americans. . . . However, the event that propelled it into mainstream popularity was the 9 August 2014 killing of Brown in Ferguson, MO, a suburb of St. Louis. After Brown was killed, many Americans on social media outlets began using the hashtag as a cry for racial justice. Social unrest and protests appeared on the streets of Ferguson, and other cities around the country" (Ince, Rojas, & Davis, 2016, pp. 1818–1819).

The intersection of social media, culture and social conflict is complex, as the story of "Black Lives Matter" (BLM) hashtag demonstrates. The origin of this social media phenomenon reminds us how powerfully the actions of an individual can incite a chain of connection that changes the world. Ince and her colleagues (2016) researched over 66,000 tweets in 2014 to show how other users of social media engaged with BLM by using hashtags that mentioned solidarity with BLM, referred to police violence, specifically mentioned Ferguson, or expressed counter-movement sentiments. In a very short time, a large public engagement was facilitated through Twitter.

Social conflict creates group opposition. This dynamic was evident in BLM. After the initial growth of #BlackLivesMatter, other Twitter users adopted #AllLivesMatter as a counter-protest hashtag that argued that equal attention should be given to all lives regardless of race (Gallagher et al, 2018). Through a multilevel analysis of over 860,000 tweets, Gallagher and colleagues discovered how the protests and counter-protests emerged, each defining the other. One study (Ray et al, 2017) used a Twitter archive of 31.65 million tweets on Ferguson following the fatal shooting of Michael Brown through the one-year mark of his death to answer several questions including: (1) What collective identities (in the form of hashtags) emerged and survived over time as they relate to Ferguson on Twitter? (2) What are the themes that are linked to the surviving collective identities on Twitter about Ferguson?

The following are underlying principles that define the significance of social media in the enactment of intercultural communication and conflict:

- **A contemporary analysis of social conflict must attend to the influence of media** when analyzing the genesis, development, management and post-conflict implications of the conflict. While the field of conflict analysis and management has increasingly noted media applications (Katsh & Rule, 2016), most conflict analysis and intervention pays, at best, a glancing recognition of the role of media.
- **The synergy of various media types requires multilevel awareness.** Granted, some conflicts can be analyzed by examining communication on one

type of media (e.g., examining only Twitter feeds in the BLM movement; content analyzing print journalism coverage of impeachment processes; considering evidence of cyberbullying behavior as modeled in Netflix Teen Programming on streaming TV). However, prolonged, significant social conflict is increasingly likely to play out, be performed on, or be affected by a multiplicity of media inputs. Concomitantly, multiple media sources may be accessed by a conflict party to shape identity and resolution possibilities (e.g., a divorcing spouse who uses email, Facebook, and Twitter to construct a narrative of the relational demise to manage self-presentation and align supporters from friends and family).

- **The media may become a party to the conflict and not necessarily a wanted or manageable one.** Not only are there a variety of media that may become relevant in the conflict; the media users and media purveyors may have their own interests in influencing the conflict process and outcome.

- **Monitoring changes in the mediascape is critical.** Media is changing rapidly, and new media may change the experience of conflict for good or bad. We have little understanding of how advances in virtual reality, artificial intelligence, synchronous dialogue platforms, etc., will expand, enhance, or threaten conflict management. Vigilance of new media, its relationship to existing media, and the potentials for conflict processes is critical.

- **Cultural factors in preference for and utility of media types** may be a factor in creating or managing conflict. Although Helles et al (2015) did not find significant generational differences in media use in their European sample, they hypothesized such given the literature that suggests inter-generational conflicts are often linked to generational preferences for "old" versus "new" media. Issues of accessibility to media types remain a concern in building public space for marginalized communities (Treem et al., 2016).

- **The permanence of certain media types has framing and reframing impact on the narrative of conflict and closure.** A common debate in the conflict management professional community is the appropriateness of terms like "conflict resolution" versus "conflict management," with the former suggesting an "end" to the conflict and the latter suggesting that conflicts may be managed but not truly resolved or ended (Jones, Remland, & Sanford, 2007). Conflict lingers even in non-mediated contexts. The ability of the media to create permanent, publicly accessible renderings and framings of a conflict narrative maximizes the chance that conflicts, once thought "managed," are re-triggered by digging through the media evidence of the conflict episodes. Permanence also means that others may wish to appropriate and use someone else's conflict records on media to alternately frame a new conflict narrative.

- **Patterns of interdependence enable evaluation of the trajectory of conflict interaction.** Media interdependence provides a map for the "who," "what," "when," "where," and "with what impact" of unfolding conflict. While difficult, it provides opportunity for conflict archeology—discovering the nature of the autonomous, sequential, reciprocal, and transactional exchanges that build the scaffold of positive or negative conflict. The BLM research mentioned earlier provides good examples of how intercultural conflict scholars can track interdependence in action.

- **Latency and potential for response becomes an issue in the conflict, a strategic and tactical opportunity.** The phrase "going viral" is not accidental; it signifies the rapidity of spread but also the implication of "dis"-ease. Media vary in how quickly and thoroughly they can disseminate information. Social media is extremely fast and extensive and, in conflicts, that presents advantages of mobilization and building interest and alliance but also threats of damaged identity and strategic disempowerment. When conflict scholars and practitioners consider intervention potential, it is realistically from a frame of media management and control so that strategic, proactive, non-impulsive approaches to conflict management are maximized.

- **The anonymity of media increases the tendency for antisocial and extreme behavior. However, it protects those speaking truth to power.** Anonymity of the media is a double-edged sword. The anonymity afforded to people willing to denigrate or humiliate another on social media is their greatest weapon. As the research suggests, the anonymity often spurs more hurtful and extreme behavior than in face-to-face interaction (Jones, 2012). But, anonymity also provides access to confront oppressive authority from a place of safety.

Influence of Media Representations

Media representations are always multilayered fictions. The portrayal is both revealing and concealing, as Diane Arbus so poignantly suggested, "A photograph is a secret about a secret. The more it tells you the less you know."

In this section we look at ways that media divide cultures through racist portrayals and coverage of war that privileges those in power. Sadly, this section could be quite lengthy if all the examples and research were discussed. But, we will only present an overview, with the recognition that most, if not all, societies can be criticized for these media faults.

Power of the Media to Produce Prejudice

Let's begin with the United States and how our media have engaged in racist or prejudiced portrayals of nondominant groups. Over two decades ago, Rhodes (1993) challenged media scholars to recognize the degree to which *racist ideology* permeated American media portrayals of minorities. Rhodes quoted a noted scholar of African American history, Aptheker (1971), that "a racist society breeds and needs a racist historiography to support and reinforce the ideologies of racial superiority" (p. 9). Rhodes (1993) further argued that a racist society requires a *racist media* to disseminate these values and beliefs to a mass audience.

Graves (1999) showed how American media is overwhelmingly White with visible racial and ethnic groups underrepresented and negatively represented. Coleman (2002) added that "the history or development of the black image on network television reflects a picture of stereotypes, tokenism, paternalism, and neglect" (p. 66).

After September 11, 2001, Arabs and Muslims were framed as "the enemy" in the eyes of far too many Americans. Immediately following 9/11, more than 50% of survey respondents said "Muslims are anti-Western and anti-American" and Muslims topped the "most unfavorable religious group" list (Fuller, 2002). The media were accused (and rightly so) of fueling the negative portrayals of Muslims and Arabs (Anderson, Danis, & Stohl, 2009).

Consider the rumors that attacked President Barack Obama for presumed Muslim connections: that he is a Muslim, was raised as a Muslim, was educated in Madrassa, was sworn into the Senate holding a Quran, and so forth. While most of the responses to these rumors focused on the falsity of the rumors, General Colin Powell's response was a call to action against racist portrayals of Muslims and Arabs. On October 19, 2008, he issued the following endorsement of President Obama:

> Is there something wrong with being a Muslim in this country? The answer is no. That's not America. Is there something wrong with a seven-year-old Muslim-American kid believing he or she could be president? Yet I have heard senior members of my own party drop the suggestion that [Obama] is a Muslim and might have an association with terrorists. This is not the way we should be doing it in America. (Anderson, Danis, & Stohl, 2009, pp. 46–47)

The United States is not the only nation that engages in prejudicial media portrayals of minorities. Examples are painfully present from almost every continent. During the apartheid period in South Africa, the media supported the apartheid ideology. Examples of this bias were provided during the Truth and Reconciliation Commission hearings after the end of the F. W. de Klerk government (Baderoon, 2002).

A peaceful protest by Muslims in Trafalgar Square in London.

As a group, African countries have blamed Western media (European and American) for unfairly portraying the AIDS epidemic in Africa as rooted in the sexual laxity of "natives." British press has been criticized for suggesting that AIDS interventions are wasted on African countries because the sexual behaviors of the citizens will not change (Holohan, 2005). Even liberal Norwegian media have been accused of racist portrayals of the Sami, one of the tribal cultures in the northern areas of the country (Peterson, 2003).

The messages matter—they change people's attitudes and behaviors. George Gerbner, an eminent media theorist, used *cultivation theory* to argue that exposure to media images, especially over the long-term, affects the ways that real-world viewers come to understand the "other" (Gerbner et al., 2002). The more often the messages are sent, the more the view of the "other" as inferior or negative is cultivated (Murray, 2008).

Media images have the power to affect how we see someone of a different culture and whether we are willing to advocate, or have someone else advocate, on their behalf. In Chapter 5 we introduced the concept of intergroup emotion theory that helped explain how emotional orientation to an outgroup can be a very important factor in actions toward that group. Ramasubramanian's (2010) research shows that how people feel about a targeted cultural group determines whether the negative media images result in an increase in prejudice (see A Closer Look 12.4 on the following page).

Media Coverage of Conflict and War

We know that media have the power to create prejudice, so it is especially troubling when governments and media organizations collude to present biased and prejudicial images of reality. In this brief section we summarize the research on media coverage of conflict and war, one arena in which such collusion has taken place. As Anderson noted as early as 1983, with media help, political leaders can use culture and ethnicity as a mobilization device in a conflict:

> Modern communications technology now enables the most atavistic rhetoric of ethnic leaders to reach a far wider audience, with a great deal more vividness than the old tribal chieftain could ever dream of. Ancient prejudices are transmitted through the most sophisticated media, just as ancient vendettas are carried out with the most modern military weaponry. (Bardhan, 1997, p. 79)

In conflict societies, the *hate media* has often been a counter to democracy and peace. For example, hate radio played a key role in the genocide in Rwanda (Gardner, 2001). Privately owned but government-controlled radio secured a listenership through pop music and then broadcast political propaganda and death warrants, encouraging the killing of Tutsis. Radio stations even broadcast names of people to be killed. Media in Nigeria were very much complicit in the ongoing conflict there; with the Nigerian media accused of partisanship and journalists reporting in ethnically biased ways (Omenugha & Adum, 2008).

Many have argued that, in the area of foreign affairs, and especially in times of war, the media can be characterized as *elite-driven media*. Wartime media are often supportive of government war aims, reinforcing elite perspectives (Robinson

A CLOSER LOOK   **12.4**

The Impact of African American and Latino Portrayals in the Media

The following excerpt explores how White viewers' perceived portrayals of African Americans and Latino Americans on television influence their real-world feelings and beliefs about these outgroups, which in turn affect their support for race-targeted policies.

> As perceived negative televised stereotyping of outgroups increased, negative real-world stereotypical beliefs increased, feelings of hostility increased, and support for affirmative action decreased.
>
> In White viewers' minds, the typical African Americans and Latino Americans on television mainly associate with two prominent themes—criminality and laziness. The original hypothesized model suggested that perceived televised portrayals of racial outgroups would influence real-world stereotypical beliefs, which would in turn influence prejudicial feelings toward the groups, which would then influence policy preferences. Real-world perceptions of criminality of racial outgroups did not directly lead to increased prejudicial feelings. Instead, perceived criminality strengthened perceptions of laziness, which led to feelings of hostility.
>
> When televised portrayals of African Americans and Latino Americans repeatedly elicit negative emotions such as fear, anger, dislike, or nervousness, such feelings become strongly entrenched in the memory structure, making them accessible when evaluating feelings toward these racial outgroups in the real world.

(Ramasubramanian, 2010)

et al., 2009). Ironically, even when media are elite-driven, they try to portray themselves as fair and balanced (Liebes & Kampf, 2009).

Elite bias in media coverage of war is not a new phenomenon, nor is it uncommon. In the film *The War We Don't See*, filmmaker John Pilger presents the story of David Lloyd George, Britain's prime minister during much of the First World War, who had a private chat with the editor of *The Guardian*, C. P. Scott, at the height of the carnage. "'If people really knew the truth,' said Lloyd George, 'the war would be stopped tomorrow. But of course they don't know and can't know'" (Baird, 2010, p. 29). American journalists covering Vietnam emphasized "American boys in action" and presented the United States as being militarily successful, even though the facts indicated otherwise (Hallin, 1986). Similarly, a study of the 1991 Gulf War shows UK media focusing mainly on progress of the war with few images of death reaching the evening broadcasts (Morrison, 1992). There have been research reports of elite-driven coverage by the British media in the 2003 Iraq War (Liebes & Kampf, 2009) and studies of the Israeli media coverage of the Gaza War. Orgad (2009) cites one example that typifies the degree of elite-driven coverage there:

> Yonit Levy, one of Israel's most popular news anchors, was accused of expressing what was perceived as excessive sympathy for the enemy in her coverage of

A protester against violence during uprisings in Bangkok, Thailand.

the Gaza War. Channel 2, which enjoys the highest number of viewers among Israel's television stations, was flooded with complaints and demands that she be fired. (pp. 250–251)

Criticism of the U.S. news media's performance in the months before the 2003 Iraq War was profuse. Many argued that the media aided the Bush administration in its march to war by failing to air a wide-ranging debate that offered analysis and commentary from diverse perspectives. Hayes and Guardino (2010) reported a systematic analysis of every ABC, CBS, and NBC Iraq-related evening news story (1,434 in all) in the eight months before the invasion (August 1, 2002, through March 19, 2003). The results indicated that Bush administration officials were the most frequently quoted sources, the voices of antiwar groups and opposition Democrats were barely audible, and the overall thrust of coverage favored a pro-war perspective.

Opportunities for Contact and Dialogue

Recognizing that media may present biased views of minorities or contribute to conflict and war through their portrayals is a first step in changing that dynamic (Murray, 2008). Realistically, changing cultural attitudes may be a much more difficult and lengthy process than changing media behavior. As Stuart Hall commented, "political time is short. . . . cultural time is glacial" (Baderoon, 2002, p. 370).

In this section we suggest three ways that media can be used as a tool of intercultural communication and peacebuilding: (1) by reducing prejudice through positive portrayals of cultures, (2) by considering the use of media in dialogue processes, and (3) by embracing peace journalism and its principles in covering high conflicts. In the discussion of reduction of prejudice, we explore the links between intergroup contact theory and media, discuss the parasocial contact hypothesis, and present media examples where prejudice reduction has been accomplished in youth and adult audiences.

Media Ability to Reduce Prejudice

A central principle of our peacebuilding model is the need to develop appropriate intergroup contact between cultures as one way to build community and increase peace. Media offer great opportunities to develop intergroup contact and greater understanding. In this initial section we discuss how social media helps to provide contact. In the last two sections we look at how television portrayals of cultures can accomplish the same end.

We started this chapter with information about the Soliya Connect Program, a CMC dialogue initiative that brings together American, European, and Middle Eastern college students. This is an excellent example of the potential for media to build community and understanding. Walther (2009) states there are several reasons that CMC might offer benefits in the reduction of interethnic hostilities—benefits that likely surpass face-to-face (FTF) possibilities:

- In a practical sense, FTF contact is often not a realistic option.
- CMC offers the potential to focus collaborators on a task without seeing the physical features of their partners that could arouse stereotypes.
- CMC allows people to interact from the comfort of their own respective homes, which lessens anxiety with meeting members of other groups face-to-face.
- Previous application of CMC to the contact hypothesis has suggested that the *social identity model of deindividuation effects*, or *SIDE model* (Reicher, Spears, & Postmes, 1995) reduces intergroup prejudice in online groups. SIDE argues that CMC's visual anonymity leads users to identify more with their online partners.

Research is mixed on whether CMC creates positive intergroup contact. One study facilitated *online dialogues* between Jewish Israeli and Palestinian students on issues concerning religious practices. Dialogues increased how much groups knew about each other and how positively they felt about the other (Mollov, 2006). In contrast, online encounter groups that focused on Jewish and Palestinian political concerns worsened conflict between the groups (Ellis & Moaz, 2007). Similarly, the results of a review of CMC use among schools in Northern Ireland suggest that mere contact via CMC is insufficient to help intergroup relationships (Austin, 2007).

Walther (2009) reported on the results of his research with Israeli and Palestinians in CMC groups:

> Participants' qualitative responses to these experiences indicate that many of them form strong bonds with their fellow group members. Among their comments, they appear to value their newly developed empathy. . . . [M]any participants emphasized the importance of the initial contact through the Internet, rather than face-to-face meetings, as this allowed them to feel less threatened . . . and enabled them to be more open and frank with each other. (p. 235)

Parasocial Contact Hypothesis

Schiappa, Gregg, and Hewes (2005) have asked a simple but profound question: Can media images of the other groups serve the same purposes as face-to-face contact in reducing prejudice? In their extension of Allport's (1954) contact hypothesis, which they call the *parasocial contact hypothesis* (PCH), they reason that the human brain processes media experiences similarly to how it processes "direct experience"—people typically react to televised characters as they would real people (Kanazawa, 2002). Therefore, when we experience a televised character, we form impressions, make judgments about their personality, and develop beliefs about them. If the television character representing someone from another culture, especially an outgroup, is an attractive or likeable character, we may start to feel more positively toward the outgroup because we like the character.

The literature in intergroup contact theory consistently stresses that majority group members must reach a certain level of "intimacy" or develop "affective ties" with minority group members for there to be sufficient dissonance to lead to attitude change. It follows, therefore, that the possible beneficial effects of parasocial contact with minority characters would be strongest with those viewers with the least direct interpersonal contact with the minority group, and have less or no effect for those with a great deal of interpersonal contact with that minority group.

Two studies were conducted to test the parasocial contact hypothesis. They were guided by two key questions: (1) Can parasocial contact by majority group members with minority group members lead to a decrease in prejudice? (2) Are the effects of parasocial contact moderated by previous interpersonal contact with minority group members? The results found that parasocial contact appears to have yielded the same sorts of judgments about televised characters as people make as a result of direct contact (Schiappa, Gregg, & Hewes, 2005; 2006).

Additional support was provided by another study about the end of such parasocial relationships ("parasocial break-ups") and how recipients deal with the (impending) loss of a media character (Schmidt & Klimmt, 2010). Based on current research concerning parasocial relationships and parasocial break-up, assumptions about the emotional reactions (anger, grief, loss, loneliness) and coping strategies (staying in touch, distraction, positive completion) were formulated and tested with two separate studies in the context of the end of the Harry Potter book series. Their findings reinforce how significantly people can relate to media characters.

Sesame Street as Example of Promoting Tolerance

The children's television show *Sesame Street* has become much more than a beloved American television institution; it has become a worldwide initiative to use media to build tolerance, overcome prejudice, and build community, especially in post-conflict societies (Fisch, Truglio, & Cole, 1999). This is exactly what the creator intended.

Sesame Street debuted on November 10, 1969, following at least three years of preparation and research. The 1965 Watts Riots in Los Angeles set off a progression of urban uprisings that spread across the country and lasted for the rest of the decade. About one year after the Watts Riots, a public television producer named Joan Ganz

A CLOSER LOOK   **12.5**

Chinese Students Embrace Other Cultures through TV: A Parasocial Contact Hypothesis Example

Yanru (2009) reports a fascinating study of the use of TV by Chinese graduate students. In-depth interviews were conducted with 44 Chinese graduate students over a period of time as they viewed television programs from other cultures. Although Yanru never intended his research as a test, the results provide support for the parasocial contact hypothesis. The following are some excerpts from the results of the Yanru study.

Chinese Students and American TV

A female graduate student wrote: "I cannot recall for how many evenings and nights and weekends, my roommates and I gathered in front of the screen to appreciate people's life stories on the other side of the ocean." Watching American TV dramas such as *Prison Break* and *Desperate Housewives* has become a fashion among students. . . .

What about Japanese TV dramas, which have also been popular among Chinese students, most of whom had grown up with stories from books and "orthodox" Chinese movies about the war of resistance against Japanese aggression, in which Japanese soldiers appeared as cruel and wild invaders? . . . The Internet made it possible for the Chinese students of the 21st century to watch the "old" Japanese TV dramas and films imported in the 1980s, which had caused a great stir at that time. What effect do these have on Chinese students today? One of them summarized it well: "The delicate, exquisite, artistic touch to the implicit depiction of fine sentiments in Japanese TV dramas really touched me. I was also impressed by the progressive and sincere life philosophy of the Japanese people. So I found out that after all, Japanese are not savage people; they are also creatures of emotions." . . .

Some Chinese students, especially female students, came up with the initial observation that America may be a chaotic society full of violence and that Americans are too liberal in their approach to male–female relationships. However, when they reviewed the same dramas time and again, their ideas underwent a change. . . . Somehow they felt that what those "crazy Americans" were doing was for the pursuit of personal happiness, which is something above reproach.

(Yanru, 2009, pp. 33–34)

Cooney received a grant from the Carnegie Corporation to investigate the value of an educational program for disadvantaged preschool-aged children. She spent the summer months of 1966 in the United States and Canada interviewing leading educators, psychologists, television producers, and filmmakers, and in October she submitted *The Potential Uses of Television in Preschool Education to Carnegie* (published in 1967). The study launched the development of *Sesame Street* (Mandel, 2006).

Drawing on its long and acclaimed record of providing high-quality educational television to preschoolers in the United States, Sesame Workshop (the nonprofit organization behind the creation and production of the show) has co-produced 20 international programs in Egypt, India, Israel, and other countries (Kibria & Jain, 2009). These international efforts function as a *co-production process* that uses local participation and expertise to honor and reflect involved cultures (Moran, 2006). Following are some examples of international *Sesame Street* productions: (1) *Sisimpur* in Bangladesh features original Bangla-speaking Muppets and has a curriculum that focuses on literacy, math, and science and helps foster values such as self-respect, empathy, and cooperation; (2) *Rechov Sumsum* and *Shara'a Simsim* are Israeli and Palestinian versions, respectively, that have been shown to help children develop better problem-solving abilities and have more positive things to say about the other group (Cole et al., 2003).

Other groups are also supporting this innovation of *intercultural peace-building programming*. Search for Common Ground, an international peace organization, developed the *Nashe Maalo* children's television program to overcome ethnic tension in Macedonia. *Meena*, a popular UNICEF-sponsored animation series, centers on a nine-year-old South Asian girl named Meena and presents prosocial messages on health and education, and ideas that support the education and empowerment of girls (Wucker, 2000).

Dialogue Processes Using Media

In our discussion of emotion and intercultural communication and conflict in Chapter 5, we considered the nature of intractable conflict and the significance of reconciliatory processes. Here we briefly mention some examples of dialogue processes that have used media to engage participants in the transformational change often sought in intercultural dialogue in high conflicts.

Most intergroup dialogue processes involve face-to-face interactions with trained facilitators (Pfeil, 2015). A promising innovation of peace and conflict practice is creating online and mediated dialogue processes for conflict transformation. At a more simplistic level these include online forums, blogs, social networking sites, and instant messaging applications that provide opportunities for intergroup dialogue (Mor, Ron, & Maoz, 2016). However, many of these computer-mediated formats restrict communication between participants to largely text-based, asynchronous and un-moderated exchanges (White, Harvey, & Abu-Rayya, 2015). These platforms allow people who are geographically dispersed to share perspectives; to create equal status between participants that can improve prejudice reduction (Pettigrew & Tropp, 2006); and, through anonymity, can promote greater self-disclosure and reductions in intergroup anxiety compared with face-to-face contact (Amichai-Hamburger & McKenna, 2006). Conversely, these online forums, especially the un-moderated variety, can attract stereotyping and aggressive online behavior that increases division between groups instead of closing the gap (Pilecki & Hammack, 2014).

Selvanathan and her colleagues (2019) implemented a pre–post within-subjects design around a 4-week online dialogue intervention with Bosniaks and Serbs in the post conflict context of former Yugoslavia. They wanted to learn whether dialogue encouraged the discourse of harmony or the discourse of justice and how the discourse was related to participant behavior and attitudes toward the "other." They hypothesized that intergroup dialogue may expose people to the injustice experienced by out-group members, and thereby create an awareness and empathy for those experiences. Increased empathy may reduce the in-group's demands for justice. It's also possible that intergroup dialogue may highlight the need and call for justice; in which case a group could demand a certain type and performance of justice.

They used Wedialog.net, a new text-based, online dialogue platform, in post-conflict, former Yugoslavia, to host dialogue between Bosniaks and Serbs. Students from the University of Belgrade, University of Tuzla, and University of Bihać (representing Bosnia, Herzegovina, and Serbia) were recruited using a snowball sampling method. A total of 54 Bosniaks and 41 Serbs completed pre-test and post-test surveys on their sociopolitical attitudes. Eighty-six participants accepted a subsequent invitation to engage in the online intergroup dialogue for 4 weeks. On the platform, participants created a basic profile with a username and password, read and responded to posted topics, and could introduce their own topics for discussion. Surveys measured the ways in which people identify with their own group (in-group attachment and glorification), their demands for justice (retributive and restorative justice), their preferences for the goals of dialogue (improving relationships and structural change) and their prioritization of different topics (intergroup commonality and justice).

Their findings revealed that the online dialogue increased emphasis on justice rather than harmony. Both Bosniaks and Serbs showed greater group identification and demands for justice after the dialogue compared to before the dialogue and had less support for improving relationships and greater interest in discussions of justice after the dialogue. Exploring the linguistic content of the dialogue during the 4-week intervention, they found that expressions of anger and anxiety decreased, whereas concentration on the present more than the past increased, suggesting that the justice-focused dialogue was not necessarily accompanied by explicit hostility over past atrocities.

The authors identify three important outcomes of their research. First, their research suggests that in post conflict contexts it is critical for reconciliation and peacebuilding efforts to address the issue of justice, perhaps by facilitating discussion around people's recommendations of how to restore justice. Second, they believe a dialogue intervention is unlikely to accomplish both goals of seeking justice and restoring intergroup harmony simultaneously. And third, practitioners are advised to focus on these goals in sequential stages during interventions, given that justice-oriented goals may not always be in tension with harmony-oriented goals but may even serve to facilitate one another (Shani & Boehnke, 2017). There last recommendation raises questions about whether sequential stages could be more effective with some stages occurring offline and some online. For example, (1) are conversations about harmony better done offline to increase immediacy and empathy? Which conversations about justice are better online to manage for more facilitation control?

The Canadian Department of Foreign Affairs and International Trade (DFAIT) Foreign Policy Dialogue was an online policy consultation to develop and enforce rules of civil discourse that promoted consensus building (Hurrell, 2005). The Canadian Department of Foreign Affairs and International Trade (DFAIT) initiated a Foreign Policy Dialogue with Canadian citizens from January 22 to May 1, 2003, which included a significant online component, in addition to town halls, expert round tables, a youth forum, and other offline events. The goal of the Dialogue was to gather citizen opinion on Canada's role in the world. The bilingual Dialogue website consisted of two main sections: in one, citizens were invited to respond to a set of questions posed by DFAIT; in the other, a discussion section, citizens could participate in a less structured set of forums, where they debated foreign-policy issues with one another. The discussion section was organized around the same five themes of "The Three Pillars," "Security," "Prosperity," "Values and Culture," and "Conclusion: The World We Want." Beyond this broad thematic breakdown, however, each discussion forum was completely free-form, and the content was driven by participants. Any participant could initiate a new "thread" or topic of discussion, and messages were displayed in chronological order, grouped by topic. Each forum was bilingual, and participants posted their comments in the language of their choice, although the forums were ultimately heavily dominated by English-language participants.

The success of the project was evident in its ability to attract Canadian citizens to the dialogue. The Civility in Online Discussion site received almost 1.5 million hits and was visited by more than 62,000 unique users. Over 2,000 messages were posted to the discussion forum, and the discussion paper was downloaded over 28,000 times (Jeffrey, 2003).

In the Two Towns of Jasper "Media Dialogue" Project, creators noted the need for integrated media and dialogue processes in conflict. This fascinating project created "media dialogue" and conducted a quasi-experimental study to investigate how the media stimulus impacted citizen's willingness to discuss these issues in dialogue sessions and engage politically on sensitive racial issues. Randomly selected public television members were recruited into various forms of "real world" exposure and discussion about the documentary film *Two Towns of Jasper* that told the story of racial tension in Jasper, Texas, after the 1998 hate killing of James Byrd, Jr., who was dragged to his death behind a pickup truck driven by three white men (Rojas et al., 2005).

"Media dialogue" and intergroup dialogue bring people together to have facilitated discussion on highly contentious issues. However, intergroup dialogue brings in a small number of participants, while media dialogue brings a much larger group together for a much shorter duration, and encourages discussion about media content that stimulates thought on the issue of concern. This media content is a stimulus for reflection, a resource of information and a safe place to offer perspectives about controversial issues.

In this study there were three quasi-experimental conditions: in the first condition some randomly selected participants were asked to attend a media dialogue session focused around the documentary film *Two Towns of Jasper*; in the second condition participants only saw the program; and in the third condition (acting as a control group) the subjects did not watch the program or participate in the dialogue.

Then, 3,000 public television members and members of advisory groups were randomly selected to either attend the media dialogue event or watch the broadcast premiere. More than 300 people attended the event, which included a preview screening of the documentary as well as a facilitated discussion about race and diversity issues in the community. Between the preview screening and the 90-minute facilitated discussion, participants could mingle with representatives from local groups that were working to end racial intolerance. At the event, participants were divided into groups and given a series of questions regarding race, diversity, and prejudice within the community. Many participants shared stories of experiences with racism in the community. Intermittently, representatives from the small breakout groups were asked to express the thoughts shared within their small groups to the other 300 participants. Shortly after the event and the broadcast premiere, a survey concerning media, race, and community engagement was mailed to all initially invited individuals. Controlling for past political discussion and participation, results revealed exposure to the media stimulus, in this case the documentary film, was positively related with willingness to discuss the issue of race and to participate politically on race issues. The dialogue process further enhanced, significantly more than only having watched the documentary, awareness of racism and increased willingness to further discuss and participate on race issues. The combination of media and dialogue yielded the most impact.

Peace Journalism

The media can make a choice to support what Ivie (2009) has called *peace journalism*, or the more comprehensive and independent coverage of conflicts so that the public has a broader understanding of the costs of war. This goal varies from present journalistic practices that, according to Gadi Wolfsfeld (2004), too often and too readily "reinforce ethnocentrism and hostility towards adversaries" (p. 2). Peace journalism proposes a number of ways to compose enriched war stories by addressing questions such as:

- Who is affected by and has a stake in a given conflict?
- What are the power relationships among the various parties to the conflict?
- What circumstances and unresolved issues triggered the conflict?
- What is the geographical reach and political jurisdiction of the conflict?
- What are the rationales (needs, interests, fears) of the conflicted parties?
- What are the potential means, costs, and benefits of resolving the conflict? (Ivie, 2009, p. 8)

Some nations have taken legislative action to mandate aspects of peace journalism. In 2008, Lebanon passed a new media law that requires all media institutions to respect freedom of speech "in a way to ensure equity, balance, and objectivity between all candidates and to abstain from supporting or promoting any candidate or group of candidates in order to remain independent" (Teeple, 2011, p. 2).

Journalists attend a peace education workshop in Pakistan organized by Peace Education and Development (PEAD) Foundation.

Short of legislative action, there are a number of other examples of how media can promote peace in cultural/ethnic conflicts. *Peace media* can be vital to humanitarian aid immediately after a conflict by simply providing information about where food will be distributed, where separated family members can be found, and where medical services can be obtained. Peace media have a vital role in rebuilding civil society. By making space or airtime available for the expression of grievances, media encourage an essential part of the healing process (Gardner, 2001). Media can also empower groups that are disenfranchised and act as mediators. In Macedonia, the Interethnic Team Project brought together journalists from different ethnic news organizations to work together on stories concerning the country as a whole that were then published in identical form in each of the newspapers. Conducting their interviews in mixed ethnic teams, reporters were able to talk to sources they otherwise would not have had access to and avoided stereotyping each other's group (Gardner, 2001).

There are strong opinions on the suggestion of peace journalism. Read Put It Into Practice 12.2 and answer for yourself: "How do I feel about the responsibility of the media to promote peace?"

Summary

Intercultural communication is increasingly mediated communication. In this chapter we discussed some of the ways that media is used to develop intercultural relationships through online social networking sites and even in online

PUT IT INTO PRACTICE   **12.2**

Should the Media Promote Peace?

Amy Goodman and Armstrong Williams are syndicated columnists, political journalists, and hosts of their own radio programs. While both share a common concern with the goals of peacebuilding, each holds a very different view of the media's role in promoting peace. With whom do you most agree?

Amy Goodman:

> I see the media as a great force for peace in the world. Unfortunately, it has been misused; it has been abused; it has been manipulated. We need a media that builds bridges, doesn't advocate for the bombing of bridges. We need a media that is a forum for people to speak for themselves, or we tell their stories until they can tell their own. That is a media that builds understanding between communities, a media that, when someone is blacklisted, their voice can be heard; when someone is imprisoned, their story can be told; when someone is sick, we can talk about the circumstances of their sickness and they can express how they feel. (WACC, 2008)

Armstrong Williams:

> Should the media even consider contributing to the culture of peace? After all, societies have been turned to hell by the efforts of journalists to spread personal messages. For example, the genocide in Rwanda was sped along by the hateful rhetoric disseminated on short-wave radio in that country. . . . Whose morality should the press promote? Yours? Mine? . . . The credibility of the free press depends upon reporters refraining from any sort of individual messages. This impartiality has empowered the press as "the fourth estate," or an honest watchdog of the government. For the democratic journalists, facts, not propaganda, are the goal. That said, I do not believe that the democratic free press ought to completely abdicate its moral responsibility. First and foremost, the media can promote tolerance and multicultural understanding simply by depicting different cultures. (Williams, 2002)

dating and marriage interactions. Not all cultures have equal access to or comfort with computer-mediated communication (CMC) and there is a digital divide related to CMC access and economic resources.

We reviewed the negative power of media to present biased portrayals of cultural groups that fuel the development of prejudice and impact the willingness to support equality and social justice policies. Media have consistently been used to promote armed conflict and war efforts.

However, media can also be used to reduce prejudice and build tolerance. Programs like *Sesame Street* prove how valuable educational television is in helping generations awaken their interests in peace and community. We discussed the parasocial contact hypothesis and related research that proves how positive media images of groups can overcome previous ignorance and negative attributions, even when there has been no real-life contact between groups. We also reviewed research on how online dialogues can create empathy and positive attitudes between cultural groups in high conflict.

Lastly, we covered the controversial issue of the potential for media to create peace through peace journalism. This section summarized how some would define the nature and function of peace journalism, and asked to what extent the media was responsible for helping to develop peaceful communities.

QUESTIONS

1. What are some of the advantages and difficulties of using media to form relationships with people from different cultures? What is your personal experience with this?

2. Throughout this book we've talked about different dimensions of culture. One dimension that has received a lot of attention is individualism and collectivism. To what extent do you believe this dimension of culture will affect how future cultures use social media for connection and collaboration? Do you see different trajectories for individualist and collectivist cultures?

3. How does your experience support the idea of media being racist or ethnocentric? Have you personally experienced examples of media bias against cultural groups? How did that affect your opinions and your willingness to know or be in a relationship with someone from that group?

4. What is your understanding of the parasocial contact hypothesis? Do you agree with the basic premise that "getting to know" someone through the media can reduce your cultural bias? If so, do you think that media vary in terms of their power to help you make a parasocial contact? Do television shows or movies have more parasocial contact power than the internet? Why or why not?

5. As people become more involved with media, what are some of the global implications of having cultures/nations that cannot take part in the media universe? How will it change power, education, social justice, and chances for peace in the world?

13

Intercultural Communication and the Sojourn Experience

KEY TERMS

cultural adaptation	host culture
culture shock	international internship
culture shock curve	sojourn experience
the D.I.E. exercise	sojourner
ethnorelativism	study abroad
expatriate	study away

"The real differences around the world today are not between Jews and Arabs; Protestants and Catholics; Muslims, Croats, and Serbs. The real differences are between those who embrace peace and those who would destroy it; between those who look to the future and those who cling to the past; between those who open their arms and those who are determined to clench their fists."

—William Jefferson Clinton

The commitment to peacebuilding through intercultural understanding means we have to take a first step. The best first step is a literal one: experience another culture personally. This chapter looks at the process of taking that first step through the *sojourn experience*.

A *sojourner* is someone who travels to another country to stay for a particular reason and then returns to their home country (Gudykunst, 1998). Ward, Bochner, and Furnham (2001) define the length of time that defines a sojourner as a stay of more than six months, but less than five years. Staying less than six months is generally classified as a tourist or a traveler. Those who tend to stay longer than five years are often in the category of an *expatriate* or immigrant.

Touristic travel and global tourism makes up the majority of intercultural contact experiences and exposure (Hottela, 2004). Tourists and sojourners differ in terms of duration of stay, range of social encounters, and dependence on a guide who acts as a cultural and linguistic interpreter. Usually, the experience of culture shock for a tourist may be less intense and more limited than for the sojourner (Furnham, 1984).

Sojourners spend enough time in a host country to interact with people on a daily basis in various contexts (e.g., in homes, educational settings, and workplace environments). This allows them to notice different customs, different frames of reference, and different worldviews. An example of a sojourner is a student who lives with a host family in Spain, interacts with the family at home in their native language, takes classes in another language at the local university, and develops and maintains relationships with people from the host country. A sojourner is quite different from a person who visits a country for a much shorter time and often only has interaction with tour guides, vendors, and perhaps other tourists. Through this contact, the sojourners' attention is constantly drawn to compare similarities and differences between the new culture and the home culture (Storti, 1997). For example, sojourners may be students on study abroad programs, international interns working overseas, businesspeople, diplomats, military personnel, immigrants, refugees, or guest workers (Begley, 2003; Nishida, 2005).

A major focus of this chapter will be the sojourn experience of study abroad, which can include both service learning (introduced in Chapter 8) and *international internships*—the two most common experiences of undergraduate students involved in international study. A discussion of cultural adaptation will then enable us to understand the stages and trajectories of change that affect sojourner experiences. Next, we will consider how a particular communication technique of description, interpretation, and evaluation (D.I.E.) can lead to deeper understanding and respect for new cultures. We also discuss the many benefits of study abroad, as well as the numerous opportunities available for intercultural contact and intercultural dialogue. Finally, we will look at a longer-term view of the sojourn experience, briefly touching on how this often translates into a settler or immigrant reality.

Transformation of Worldview through the Sojourn Experience

What is remarkable about the sojourn experience is that it will forever impact your cultural worldview. As discussed in Chapter 4, the term "worldview" refers to your personal perception of what the world is and how it should be (Clark, 2002). One of the true gifts of the sojourn experience is that as you begin to understand a new culture, you in turn begin to receive a deeper understanding of your own culture. The sojourner begins to see that there is more than one way to raise a child, choose a marriage partner, educate youth, care for the old, and venerate the dead.

The alteration of a worldview usually shifts from an ethnocentric worldview (Augsburger, 1986) to *ethnorelativism*. An ethnocentric (or encapsulated) worldview means that a person thinks that their way of seeing the world is the "right" way. They also often view cultural differences as threatening. Being more ethnorelative means a person considers cultural differences as nonthreatening and even welcomes them. This crossover from ethnocentrism to ethnorelativism can only begin when we put aside, at least temporarily, our own values, assumptions, and beliefs to enter the new culture's world (Kauffman, Martin, & Weaver, 1992).

For example, Lisa was a student studying abroad in Spain. One of the things that surprised her immediately was the European attitude toward drinking alcohol. There was no drinking age and, in fact, children were served watered-down wine with their meals. As Lisa became friends with some of the local Spanish students, they invited her to go out with them in the evening. After having a few drinks, Lisa remarked to her friends that she was feeling the effects of the alcohol. Their reaction was quite unexpected by American college student paradigms. They asked if she felt well, if she needed to lie down, and if she needed to go home. Lisa learned that the cultural norms for drinking in Spain did not include getting drunk and that drinking was not the point of getting together.

Your journey into the exploration of other cultures can begin from a variety of experiences, like getting to know someone from another culture who lives in or is visiting the United States, reading about the history and culture of another nation or peoples, or because of the opportunity to be a tourist or a volunteer in another country. Dolores became interested in Japan after being involved in a program that sponsored Japanese high school teachers of English to study in the United States for a summer.

CULTURE SHOCK

Letter Home to Philadelphia from Tokyo, Japan

The following letter was written by Dolores 10 days after she arrived in Tokyo, Japan, to begin a full-time teaching position at a two-year Japanese college.

Dear Mom, Dad, Kath, and Johnny,

First of all, it is so hard to believe that I am so far from home. None of the familiar voices and faces surround me except in pictures. I look at the pictures of family and friends that I brought with me to Japan over and over. They are my link to who I am, but I have no photos of who I will be here in Japan and no photos of the new friends and experiences I will have. I have decided to organize the photos once and for all by years . . . the only problem is I can't find a camera shop with photo albums because I can't read the signs in Japanese!

The first days here in Japan have been euphoric. Everything is interesting and exotic—the Japanese people wearing surgical masks, cars on the opposite side of the street, steering wheels on the right, "pushers" on the train tracks, Japanese bathrooms that separate showers from the toilet, and the neon lights of Tokyo. I feel like I am free-floating and unattached from everything. I don't have my teaching position back home anymore and I haven't started working here, so I feel like I am on the verge of a new life . . . a life in another language, culture, and country.

Love from your daughter in a strange and wonderful new land.

Once beginning the journey, home will never look the same again. The sojourn experience can have a profound effect on the sojourner, in both positive and negative ways. You can become more aware of your worldview before you leave home by using various surveys and questionnaires (Vande Berg, Connor-Linton, & Paige, 2009). Developing a new and positive perspective towards the *host culture* and your own culture is the ultimate gift of the sojourn experience. Not only does the sojourner examine, observe, and question the new culture, but they also begin to recognize what is taken for granted in the home culture.

Study abroad, or education abroad, refers to living and studying in another country. *Study away* takes into consideration that learning about domestic and international diversity are equally important (Sobania & Braskamp, 2009). While it is a relatively new concept, more students from US universities are choosing to study away because domestic study can be as diverse as an international sojourn experience. Throughout the United States, it is possible to uncover and discover the rich co-cultures of those who share our country.

For example, study away could include the experience of spending a semester at a US Indian reservation in the southwestern United States, a semester with an

A Native American man takes part in the 25th Annual Paiute Tribe Pow Wow on May 24, 2014. The visible component of culture includes how people dress and what that dress symbolizes for them.

Amish community in Lancaster County, Pennsylvania, or a semester volunteering with the Chinese immigrant population of Philadelphia.

The sojourn experience has the power to affect growth in intercultural competence, self-understanding, and has long-term implications for both personal and professional life (Brown, 2009). For many university students, study abroad is their first opportunity to travel overseas or their first time to travel overseas as a sojourner rather than a tourist.

The myth persists that study abroad is only for the wealthy, but that is no longer the case (Dessoff, 2006; Lewin, 2009). One of the fastest growing sectors of study abroad involves students traveling in groups led by faculty as part of a course. This travel, which usually is less than two weeks, accommodates students whose schedule, financial responsibilities, or family responsibilities would preclude studying for a summer or semester. In these ways, opportunities to participate in study abroad and study away are expanding rapidly on American university campuses.

Many American universities recognize the role that study abroad plays in providing students with a global perspective. They are encouraging their faculty to include global perspectives in their academic areas of expertise, are inviting international scholars to their campuses, and are encouraging study away and study abroad. Not only are American universities interested in supporting their students to become globally competent, they envision their mission to include the importance of global citizenship as a critical necessity for the 21st century:

> Employers do value both college/university study abroad and completing an internship abroad to a greater extent than all but one other type of experience: majoring or minoring in a foreign language. . . . The greater the firm's internationally generated revenue, the more likely that its employees value all types of study abroad. (Trooboff, Vande Berg, & Rayman, 2008, pp. 20–21)

There is a wealth of databases available to US students and/or permanent residents to take advantage of academic merit scholarships and financial scholarships for studying abroad. The Gilman Scholarship Program is one of the many US programs that offer awards for undergraduate study abroad and was established by the International Academic Opportunity Act of 2000 (www.iie.org). The goal of the award is to diversify the kinds of students who study abroad and the countries in which

---

PUT IT INTO PRACTICE   **13.1**

Websites for Study Abroad Scholarships

Below is a list of scholarship sources for study abroad. Review at least two of the scholarship opportunities and make a list of the criteria for the award.

1. Institute of International Education (www.iie.org/Programs)

2. Boren (NSEP) Scholarships (www.borenawards.org)

3. Study Abroad in Japan: Bridging Scholarships
   (www.aatj.org/japan-bridging-scholarships)

they choose to study. It is sponsored by the US Bureau of Educational and Cultural Affairs with the goal of promoting peaceful relations. To be eligible, students must be receiving Federal Pell Grants. Another US government scholarship, the Boren Scholarship, is funded by the National Security Education Program (NSEP) and focuses on areas and languages of the world that are critical to US national security. Scholarships provide up to $20,000 to US undergraduates. Countries that are excluded from this scholarship are Western Europe, Canada, Australia, and New Zealand.

The Culture Shock Curve

Many first time and seasoned sojourners are surprised to discover that, even though they have been anxiously preparing for their travel abroad, once they arrive they experience new and confusing emotions and reactions due to the sudden transition to a new country or culture that they are not familiar with. This phenomenon is referred to as *culture shock*. This term is used to describe the feelings of sojourners as they enter a new culture and interact with others. People have psychological and emotional reactions to new cultures, in particular when they are very different from their own (Furnham & Bochner, 1986). It has been referred to as culture fatigue, cultural adjustment stress, or cross-cultural adjustment (Anderson, 1994; Befus, 1988; Searle & Ward, 1990).

Culture shock was originally described as a "disease" suffered by individuals living in a new cultural environment. Oberg (1960) noted that culture shock resulted from the loss of well-known cultural signs and symbols that caused individuals to experience anxiety, frustration, and helplessness.

Now, however, there seems to be a consensus that culture shock is not a disease but a defining term for the adjustments that all individuals experience at varying levels when they live for an extended period of time in another culture (Brislin et al., 1986). The new place can be a transition from high school to college, from one city or state to another, or from your country and culture to someplace new.

Culture shock has been studied as a phenomenon in sojourning. The earliest theorist to describe the sojourner adjustment process was Lysgaard (1955) in his study of Norwegian Fulbright Scholars. He noted a three-stage process of initial satisfaction, decline in satisfaction and a subsequent increase in satisfaction over time. Oberg (1960) contributed to this theory by expanding the process to four stages: honeymoon stage, crisis stage, recovery stage, and adjustment stage. Gullahorn and Gullahorn (1963) extended the theory by noting that, upon return, sojourners were again "shocked" to discover that they did not slip back easily into their previous culture, but once again went through a period of adjustment at home.

The Culture Shock Curve (Figure 13.1) is a visual depiction of the trajectories that occur when you live in a new country/culture for an extended period of time. The curve resembles the letter W and should be read from left to right. But remember that culture shock does not occur in a lock-step fashion. Sojourners move back and forth on the curve on their transformational journey.

The sojourner starts out on a (1) "high" filled with excitement and anticipation about the new location. However, it is not long before (2) differences that were once exciting become irritating or confusing. You will probably begin to feel homesick because you miss familiar faces, places, and the way things are done back home. (3) You will begin to develop strategies to cope with the frustration of your new life in a new country. Even though you may feel frustration, you understand that this is how things are and (4) you begin to embrace customs you thought were strange. You will feel excited about returning home and at the same time saddened to leave the life you have created. What is surprising to most students (5) upon return to their home country (6) is that in their enthusiasm to describe their international experience, most family and friends respond by downplaying what happened overseas because they want to talk about what happened at home while you were away. Your friends and family may not have a frame of reference about your experience and don't know how to relate to it. This can be very frustrating to returnees who feel that they have engaged in a life-changing experience that no one seems to be interested in. (7) Gradually life at home will feel more back to normal, but at the same time, you will retain all the experiences of your international travel and you will begin to think about ways to incorporate what you have learned into your life at home. Finally, (8) you will discover ways to give back to your community and share the new and expanded worldview you have developed.

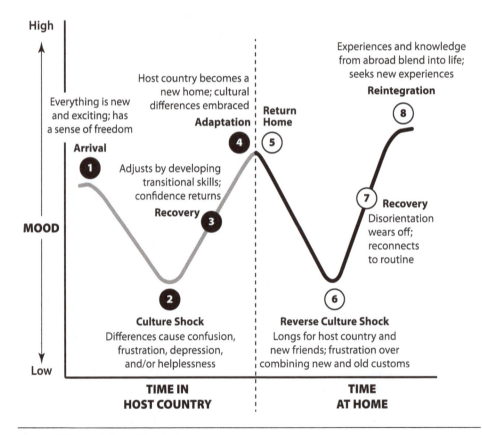

Figure 13.1   Culture Shock Curve

Phases of the Sojourn Experience

Important in the preparation process prior to departure is considering what you can learn before departure that will assist you in the adjustment process. In effect, the sojourn experience can be divided into four segments: pre-departure, arrival and settling in, living in the new culture, and returning home again.

Pre-Departure Phase

In preparation for your life abroad, the best and most important piece of the puzzle is to begin to understand the language and culture of your host country. Many university study abroad programs today have content courses delivered in English for the international students in their programs. Historically, study abroad was considered to be a necessary consideration for language majors who majored in modern European languages, but was not typically considered as part of the academic curriculum in other fields of study. That perception of study abroad is changing dramatically.

According to the 2020 Open Doors Report on International Educational Exchange from the Institute for International Education (IIE):

> For the fifth consecutive year the United States hosted more than one million international students (1,075,496) during the 2019/2020 academic year. Despite a slight decline (1.8%) in the number of international students in the United States during the 2019/2020 academic year, this group still represents 5.5% of all students in U.S. higher education. According to the U.S. Department of Commerce, international students contributed $44 billion to the U.S. economy in 2019. (IIE, 2020)

The report went on to note that in 2018–2019 the leading destinations for Americans in study abroad programs were European countries, followed by Latin America and the Caribbean. The number of US students who study abroad was 347,099, which represents fewer than 5% of all US undergraduate college students. The question remains, why does incoming international exchange far outnumber outgoing US students heading abroad? Let's examine that question by looking at some popular myths about study abroad. Many students think that study abroad is only for language majors and that you have to speak a second language. In addition, many students say that study abroad is too expensive, and are not aware that financial aid, scholarships, and internships abroad can be affordable. The cost of study abroad is an investment in personal, academic, and professional development.

Students in almost any academic discipline can find a program that will fit into their course of study with academic course content offered in English. Still, having a beginner's knowledge of the target language is necessary. Simple gestures such as expressing gratitude, asking for directions, ordering in a restaurant, and basic personal introductions can make you feel much more comfortable in your new home. Learning polite phrases and what constitutes comfortable cultural differences in nonverbal communication is key.

Reading online newspapers (in English) before you travel will give you a glimpse into the topics that are noteworthy at the time you will be visiting. Staying tuned into current events will enable you to find topics of conversation with your fellow classmates. You may be surprised to find that most international students overseas know far more about American history, politics, and current events than you do! In addition to finding out as much as you can about current events, look at websites and books about the culture of the nation you will be visiting.

In Japan, it is not polite to directly refuse offers from the host with a direct "no." This simple direct answer in an English-speaking country is considered extremely rude in Japan. Saying "no" and turning down an offer by a host causes them to lose face (see Chapter 7). One of the authors had such an experience in Japan. She doesn't like fish of any type but in Japan, when a host wants to honor a guest, fish is usually the first choice for a special meal. Knowing this, when she realized that fish was the main meal, she made sure to comment that the fish looked very tasty and that she wished she could eat it, but unfortunately she was allergic to all fish. Both the guest and the host were able to save face gracefully.

Arrival and Settling-In Phase

The pre-departure stage leads into the "arrival and settling-in" phase. In this phase the sojourner is excited, surprised, and interested by differences between their home culture and the new one they are experiencing. The sojourner reacts to new customs and surroundings by comparing them to the home culture and noting how different yet exotic the new locale is. This stage is referred to as the "honeymoon" stage because differences are considered charming and interesting.

Living in the New Culture Phase

In the third phase, "living in the new culture," a sojourner's perspective shifts from outsider to "new inhabitant"—someone living their daily life in the new country. Living in the new culture and being able to function in the new culture can be a long, slow process that takes enormous energy. Being pushed into the overcrowded Tokyo trains every morning was very difficult to get accustomed to (see the Culture Shock box below). The intriguing custom was no longer

CULTURE SHOCK

Japanese Pushers

While I had heard about the professional "pushers" or *oshiya* in Japan, watching them in their white cotton gloves push morning commuters into rush hour trains was strange and fascinating. The morning commuter trains are so crowded that in order to be sure that everyone on the train platform makes it in, the Japanese Railway system employs pushers to exert tremendous force on the backs of the commuters to squeeze them into the railroad cars. Men, women, and children are literally packed like sardines, unable to move their arms once inside the train. (Search for "Japanese pushers" on YouTube for a good visual.)

—Dolores

CULTURE SHOCK

"Doing" the Laundry

I was staying at a university hotel in Shanghai, China. One evening I dropped off my laundry at the front desk. Imagine my surprise when a hotel employee emptied my laundry out on top of the counter, held up each piece high in the air and shook it. I could anticipate that, sooner or later, she would get to my underwear. Just the thought of her waving my panties in front of my friends sent me into a panic. I asked her if she would mind taking care of this behind the counter, but either she didn't understand what I was saying or didn't see what my problem was. I was mortified.

—Natalie

---

interesting, but unpleasant and a little scary. In this phase, students report headaches from listening to a new language, trying to understand TV programs in the native language, trying to read newspapers with an insider's understanding of the issues in the news, and adjusting to new foods, spices, and oils used in cooking.

In some cultures, a sojourner may always feel like an outsider, but in time may come to accept that they are living in two worlds. Japanese will ask an international person (*geijin*) three questions: what is your name, how long have you been here, and when are you leaving? Students in the arrival stage may feel offended that a person is asking them when they are leaving. A student who is settled in may just laugh knowing that these are very common questions that the Japanese ask of all newcomers.

CULTURE SHOCK

Merry Christmas

Having grown up in a country that was 95% Catholic, I never thought twice about how I would greet people during the Christmas season. My first year as a doctoral student changed all that. Wanting to show my gratitude to everyone who had helped me during my first semester in the United States, I bought a box of Christmas cards and proceeded to send them out. Imagine my surprise when several people, including my professor who was Jewish, openly told me how they appreciated the gesture but shared that they had a different religion. I was so ashamed. Nonetheless, when my professor visited the Philippines a few months later, my Chinese-Filipino family insisted on taking him to a favorite dinner place, Chinese hot pot, where everyone cooks raw food in a boiling broth together. I noticed he was barely eating, and then I realized he probably ate kosher. I guess I didn't learn my lesson that first time.

—Bessie

Returning Home Phase

Sojourners return home for many reasons, but it always involves some degree of "return culture shock." Everything strange in the new culture has now become second nature. Going home, seeing family and friends, and sharing the experience can be disheartening. At times, after a sense of euphoria at being home, there is a growing feeling of discontent and feeling invisible. Even though you have changed, it may feel like others just want you to "go back" to being you. Try sharing your excitement with others who plan to participate in a study abroad program.

Understanding Your Cultural Identity

To help you discover more about yourself and how you might respond in novel situations, take time for the following exercise (Put It Into Practice 13.2).

PUT IT INTO PRACTICE   13.2

Values Checklist

Place a "T" beside statements you consider to be true and an "F" beside those statements you consider to be false on a separate piece of paper.

1. Stability, continuity, tradition, and heritage are more important than change.

2. People's problems are generally the result of laziness and an unwillingness to take responsibility to pursue a better life.

3. Keeping busy and not wasting time are very important to me.

4. All people are created equal.

5. Privacy is very important to me; I have to have some alone time every day or I will go crazy.

6. I chose which colleges to apply to and my parents' input was not that important to the decision.

7. My parents sent me to college so that I could have a better life and earn a good living.

8. Today, I am where I am and have achieved what I have through my own hard work and efforts.

9. In my classes, I compete with my classmates for the best grades; we do not collaborate.

10. It is important to work today, plan for tomorrow, and save for the future.

11. I schedule a very full day of courses, co-curricular activities, and work after school because it is important to be productive.

(continued)

12. I have some professors that I call by their first names.

13. I want my friends to tell me if I have done something wrong directly and to my face.

14. Business management, law, and medicine are considered more valuable than careers in philosophy or art in this country.

15. In my home, there is only one TV, hair dryer, refrigerator, telephone, and car.

(Adapted from Kohls, 1984)

Except for the last statement, it is likely that if you are a US citizen or grew up in the United States, the majority of these statements were true for you. All of the statements reflect American cultural values as articulated in the work of L. Robert Kohls (1984). Review the summarized values in A Closer Look 13.1 and see if you agree. If not, how would you articulate core American values? You may not agree completely with these values in particular if you identify as someone from a co-cultural group in the United States such as a Latino American or a Chinese American. There may be different values that are more important to you that are not in line with the larger predominant culture.

What you might consider to be a positive value in the United States may be considered a negative value in your host country and what is considered normal and natural in another country may be frowned upon in the United States (see A Closer Look 13.2 for an example).

A CLOSER LOOK   13.1

American Cultural Values

Does this list resonate with your values; does it describe what you value?

Personal Control Over Environment

"Americans no longer believe in the power of fate, and they come to look at people who do as being backward, primitive, or hopelessly naive" (p. 2). Everyone should have control over whatever in the environment might potentially affect him or her.

Change Seen as Natural and Positive

"In the American mind, change is seen as an indisputably good condition. Change is strongly linked to development, improvement, progress, and growth" (p. 2). Continuity and tradition are not considered very important in the United States.

(continued)

Time and Its Control

Time is vitally important to most Americans. The concern for finishing things on time often takes precedence over developing interpersonal relationships.

Equality/Fairness

Equality is ingrained in American culture and most believe that all people are created equal and should have an equal opportunity to succeed.

Individualism/Independence

Americans view themselves as highly individualistic in their thoughts and actions. Individualism leads to privacy, which is seen as a need and desirable.

Self-Help/Initiative

Americans take credit only for what they accomplish as individuals. They get no credit for rights of birth but pride themselves in having climbed the ladder of success, to whatever level, through their own work and initiative.

Competition

Americans believe that competition produces the best results in an individual and leads to success.

Future Orientation

Americans value the future and its improvements. They often devalue the past and are largely unaware of the present. Present happiness is often overlooked to dream of even greater happiness in the future.

Action/Work Orientation

Action is better than inaction and Americans frequently become overly attached to their work. People define themselves by the jobs they have and the work they accomplish.

Informality

Attire, interactions with authority figures, and greetings are a few of the areas where Americans continue to have some of the most casual interactions in the world. Informality is often seen as a positive quality.

Directness/Openness/Honesty

"Many other countries have developed subtle, sometimes highly ritualistic ways of informing others of unpleasant information. Americans, however, have always preferred the direct approach. They are likely to be completely honest in delivering their negative evaluations" (p. 6).

(continued)

Practicality/Efficiency

"Americans have a reputation of being extremely realistic, practical, and efficient. The practical consideration is likely to be given highest priority in making any important decision. . . . Will it make money? What is the 'bottom line?' What can I gain from this activity?" (p. 6).

Materialism/Acquisitiveness

"Foreigners generally consider Americans more materialistic than Americans are likely to consider themselves. Americans would like to think that their material objects are just the 'natural benefits' that always result from hard work" (p. 7).

(Kohls, 1984)

Identifying cultural patterns that define the United States is not an easy task. Our nation is not homogenous even though we speak a common language. So, which group of people are the real, normal, or typical Americans? Who decides what is typically defined as American? For example, the US film and TV industry exports American culture every day to all over the globe. Is the US film industry a vehicle that accurately depicts who we are as a nation? Do television shows like *The Simpsons, Duck Dynasty, America's Next Top Model, The Bachelor,* or *The Real Housewives of New Jersey* accurately depict how you see life in the United States? Do movies like *Coming 2 America, Top Gun: Maverick, Bullet Train,* and *Nomadland* depict the real America?

Living in a new culture means that the new culture acts as a mirror that constantly reminds you how well you fit in or stand out from your international cohort. What may surprise you is that others may view you as an American and as a representative of the United States and its culture before viewing you as an individual. When faced with confrontations, it may feel as though you are being criticized as "the American" (Dolby, 2004).

A CLOSER LOOK   13.2

Chewing Gum Returns to Singapore

In May 2004, Singapore loosened restrictions of its notorious 12-year-old chewing-gum ban. Brands such as Wrigley's Orbit are now available to purchase in pharmacies and dentist offices, however users also need to provide their names and ID card numbers. "This Southeast Asian city-state, known for its immaculate streets, outlawed the manufacture, import, and sale of chewing gum in 1992 after the country's founding father, Lee Kuan Yew, complained that it was fouling streets, buildings, buses, and subway trains" (Associated Press, 2004).

Models of Cultural Adaptation

How do sojourners adapt to new cultures, languages, and customs? *Cultural adaptation* is the long-term process of adjusting to and finally feeling comfortable in a new environment (Kim, 2005). In qualitative studies of student adjustment and adaptation during study abroad, researchers report that students consider themselves to be completely transformed by the experience (Kauffman, Martin, & Weaver, 1992; McKeown, 2009). How does that change take place? What factors influence the change?

Scholars have looked at adaptation through different lenses by focusing on cognitive, behavioral, affective, and communication variables that influence success. Cognitive changes include knowledge acquisition about the host country and students' increased awareness of international affairs. Affective changes include students' increased empathy and appreciation of the viewpoint of another person by taking their cultural values into account. Behavioral changes are reflected in whether

---

PUT IT INTO PRACTICE   13.3

Universal Standards

Read the following statements of human rights established by the United Nations and answer the questions below.

- The Universal Declaration of Human Rights
  (www.un.org/en/about-us/universal-declaration-of-human-rights)

- The Covenant of Social, Economic, and Cultural Rights
  (www.ohchr.org/en/professionalinterest/pages/cescr.aspx)

1. Could these principles constitute a universal standard against which all cultures would be judged?

2. How well do the cultures you've been reading about meet these standards?

3. How well does your culture (or cultures) meet these standards?

4. Are there rights missing from these declarations that you believe should be included?

5. Several societies with distinct cultures are not represented in the UN, such as the Kurds of Iraq, the Basques of Spain, and the Mohawks of New York and Ontario; shall we also hold these ethnic groups to these principles?

6. Are there rights in these declarations that you would exclude because they seem to be borrowed directly from the cultures of Western Europe and North America?

(Omohundro, 2008)

or not students participate effectively and interact appropriately in the host culture (Oguri & Gudykunst, 2002). The willingness to engage and be an active participant in the host culture is a predictor of success in the sojourner experience (Ruben, 1975).

Communication plays an important part in the adaptation process. Kim (1997; 2001) developed a model of adaptation and transformation that examines intercultural communication in terms of learning and growth. Kim and Ruben's (1988) Stress-Adaptation-Growth Model of the process of intercultural transformation integrates the elements of intercultural encounters, culture shock, communication, and transformation into one model. Kim's (1997; 2001) model highlights the role of the host culture, the role of communication, and the role of the pre-disposition of the sojourner to cross-cultural experience as the best predictors of a successful adjustment/acculturation. Communication competence has been a key predictor of successful adjustment (Kim, 1988). This model of transformation highlights the importance of communication and views the sojourner as an open system that is interacting on a continuous basis at all levels and in all contexts in the new culture. The sojourner affects and is affected by the new culture. In this model, culture shock is neither positive nor negative, but a necessary ingredient for intercultural transformation. Adaptation, much like culture shock, is not one-dimensional or unilateral. Similarly, Ward and Geeraert (2016) emphasize that this process of acculturation involves managing stressors in different contexts (family, work, school, sociopolitical climate). For example, sojourners in a climate that values multiculturalism will have a more positive experience than one that is strongly assimilationist. There are higher interethnic friendships among students in high-SES schools, and workers in culturally diverse organizations have more positive adjustment outcomes.

As an American teacher in a small college in Tokyo, Japan, one of the authors was pleasantly surprised by the amount of respect and deference paid to her by all of her adult students. Not only were the students models of respectful behavior in the classroom, but they also invited her to see the cultural side of Japan outside classroom hours. At the end of each semester, students thanked her for her efforts and gave her gifts that she treasured. Upon returning to the United States two years later, she was taken aback when she re-entered the US system of higher education. Her American students challenged her in class, distracted themselves with their cell phones, and were generally rude by Japanese standards. Reflecting on this experience led her to understand that the role of "teacher" in both countries was different.

Sojourners often misinterpret the meaning of an event in the new culture by viewing circumstances through their own cultural lenses. This can cripple their ability to understand the local culture and to build upon misunderstandings and incorrect information. Wendt (1984) developed *the D.I.E. Exercise*, an excellent tool to uncover confusing events in a new environment. The acronym D.I.E. stands for Description, Interpretation, and Evaluation. First the sojourner *describes* what is happening in objective terms without judging, then they identify a *possible interpretation* for the event from the perspective of the host culture, then finally the sojourner *evaluates* the various possible interpretations of the action or event. Getting at the heart of interpretation involves asking questions of those who have more experience in the country and/or the local people. The Culture Shock box on the next page provides a good illustration.

CULTURE SHOCK

The Dirty American Students

One Saturday morning in Spain, a group of American exchange students opened their 4th-floor apartment door to find an old bucket and mop propped up against it. The American students were puzzled and pulled the bucket and mop into their apartment. They began to think about possible reasons for this strange event. After discussing this among themselves, the Americans were sure that the bucket and mop were intended as an insult to the Americans. After all, they were the only foreigners living in the building. They were sure that the Spaniards wanted to insult them as being "dirty Americans." They began to look for a new place to live. One of the students described the event to a close Spanish friend by saying, "The people in our building think we are dirty Americans. They did not even have the courage to tell us to our faces that they don't like us. They left an old bucket and mop on our doorstep!" The Spanish friend began to laugh. She explained that what the American students did not know was that in an apartment building without a doorman, every resident was expected to mop the stairways. The bucket and mop belonged to all the residents of the apartment building. Propping the used bucket and mop in front of any resident's door was a nonverbal indication that it was their turn.

Had the American students in the Culture Shock box used the D.I.E. approach, they could have avoided this situation. First, they could have described what happened ("We opened the door and found an old bucket and mop propped against it.") Second, they could have asked themselves if there were more possible interpretations than just one (that they were "dirty Americans"). Third, they could have described the event and asked a Spaniard if they could tell them why this happened. Jumping to conclusions and making assumptions is very easy to do. The D.I.E. approach is a tool that all sojourners should put in their toolbox for use when cultural events are unsettling, confusing, or difficult.

The Benefits of Study Abroad

"Study abroad enables American students to obtain first-hand experience in other countries and cultures to prepare them as 21st-century professionals and leaders in all fields. The international skills they gain are crucial to their ability to succeed in global careers and work together across borders to address important world issues. It is important that we as educators work to try to ensure that all students have the opportunity to study abroad."

—Allan E. Goodman,
President and CEO, Institute of International Education

As college students, you have the opportunity right now to take advantage of international academic programs that fit your curriculum. Study abroad providers are adding both service learning and internships to their programs.

Internships for credit provide the sojourner with a meaningful full-time or part-time work experience to complement their program of study. Internships can lead to more meaningful interaction with host country nationals and the ability to add the international experience to your resume. Service-learning programs integrate academic study with volunteer service that allows direct cultural exposure to the local community. One such organization is IPSL, the International Partnership for Service-Learning & Leadership (www.ipsl.org). By participating in an IPSL Institute for Global Learning Program, students can earn academic credit for their university studies and at the same time be of service to the local community. Programs offered in Latin America allow students to take classes at a local university in the evening while volunteering in the morning. During the day, students have a choice of volunteering with local orphanages, health centers, and schools. While volunteering, students can practice their language skills and learn more about the local economy, health system, social services, and culture. Service learning allows students to be immersed in the target culture at various levels: the university, the local community, and the homestay. While the United States Peace Corps is not an example of study abroad, it is an example of an organization that welcomes those who want to live, work, and serve abroad after graduation (read about a former Peace Corps volunteer in A Closer Look 13.3).

The benefits of study abroad are well documented and have transformative potential (Borden & Monahan, 2020). Research in the field of intercultural communication and study abroad points to numerous advantages such as: learning another language, gaining new insight in your major, developing skills that will be valuable in the global workforce, and the development of a life's vocation (Kauffman, Martin, & Weaver, 1992). In particular, findings show that students for whom studying abroad is their first international experience make gains in the area of intercultural competence, intellectual development, global awareness, and enhanced cultural relativism (Granel et al.; Douglas & Jones-Rikkers, 2001; Sutton & Rubin, 2004). Documented benefits of study abroad include increased confidence, appreciation for cultural difference, open-mindedness, greater independence, greater self-confidence, greater self-awareness, and an increased desire to interact with those of another culture (Cintron, 1996; Hansel & Grove, 1986; Penington & Wildermuth, 2005; Butcher, Wiedenhoeft, & Loynachan, 2017). Some have even suggested that the most powerful influence on world relations are tourism and study abroad (Bochner, 1986).

One of the strengths of study abroad is that the personal experience is not separated from the academic experience; students are immersed in a new life in all contexts: academia, personal, and professional. Students are learning and living in a new language. Values develop and may change because being confronted with new and different ways of thinking and behaving are part of daily life. Of course, intellectual development is stirred by being able to take classroom learning out of the classroom and into the world. For example, students can experience the art of Antoni Gaudí in Spain by visiting the buildings he created, not just reading about them. An international perspective is developed where it is no longer possible to view a political or social event from only one viewpoint; it becomes second nature to look at the world and its events from various viewpoints and consider more options.

A CLOSER LOOK   **13.3**

The Similarity of Differences

The following is an account by Grant Earich of his time spent with the Peace Corps (Peace Corps Ukraine, 2006–2008; Peace Corps Response Antigua, 2011–2012).

In the over fifty years of Peace Corps history, I imagine that I am one of the only Volunteers that has served in both one of the largest and smallest Peace Corps countries. I originally served as a Peace Corps Volunteer in Ukraine (2006–2008) and recently served with Peace Corps Response in Antigua and Barbuda (2011–2012). In Ukraine, we had roughly 350 Volunteers; while in Antigua and Barbuda, there were less than 10. However, I found that the size of the Peace Corps program is only the tip of the iceberg when it comes to the differences between these two countries. There were the obvious differences between these countries—climate, culture, race, language—and there were the smaller ones. In Ukraine, it is cold, the food is devoid of spices, the language can be challenging, and the landscape is expansive. In Antigua, you sweat when you sleep, the food is spicy, the language is familiar, and the landscape is miniscule. From a tourist's point of view, the two countries could not be more different. But when you work for Peace Corps, you are not a tourist—you become a part of the country you serve. When I arrived in the Eastern Caribbean, my initial thought was, "I'm not in Ukraine anymore." But as time passed, I realized that the differences were not as vast I originally assumed. People worked, dogs barked, children played, and public transportation was unpredictable. Furthermore, I recognized the most veiled similarities were actually the problems faced by both countries—rising inflation, insolvent governments, and HIV/AIDS education. Regardless of the differences, I felt more prepared for my Peace Corps Response service in Antigua and Barbuda due to the sheer fact that I had previously been faced with many of the same concerns. I believe this is the most important fact that anyone about to begin Peace Corps Response has to undertake. Peace Corps and Peace Corps Response are similar, but not the same. Peace Corps Response is not necessarily easier than the two-year program, but rather a shorter version. Peace Corps Response Volunteers are expected to bring their professional skills and experience to their assignments. I personally feel that my previous service in Ukraine prepared me for what to expect in Antigua and Barbuda. While Volunteers are given support, Peace Corps Response Volunteers should be prepared for a rigorous, advanced-level assignment with little-to-no technical or language training. Sometimes things we think are going to be extremely different, like an Eastern Caribbean country and an Eastern European country, can be a lot more similar than we expect. And, conversely, the things that we think are going to be so similar, like Peace Corps and Peace Corps Response, can be incredibly different.

(Earich, 2014)

And, of course, one of the greatest benefits of study abroad is the opportunity to make international friendships that can last a lifetime. These forms of social support can benefit you in many different contexts both professionally and personally. Those friendships are the basis of interculturally competent communities. Nonetheless, scholars have learned that it can be difficult to establish long-term meaningful relationships in the study-abroad environment for many reasons, including linguistic and cultural barriers such as host attitudes toward foreigners, or institutional contexts that may make it difficult for such friendships to take place. In addition, because sojourn experiences are often temporary, students and expatriates may not be highly motivated to establish host country relations (Fantini, 2018; Findlay et al., 2018).

It is easier to make friends with those who are similar to us; thus, it takes work and deliberate effort to achieve many of the benefits of sojourning. Specifically, there are differences in the ease by which student sojourners are able to develop friendships with co-national or multinational students, as opposed to host nationals. In other words, it is often easier for students to befriend those who are also sojourners, instead of individuals in the host country (Hendrickson, 2018; Shiau, 2016; Meng, Li, & Zhu, 2021). This is a critical finding because one of the major benefits touted by study-abroad programs is international friendship development. What are some of the factors that could help ease this process? Shiau (2016) and Hofhuis, Hanke, and Rutten (2019) looked the role of social media and online social networks in encouraging international relations among student sojourners. Hsiau (2016) found that the adjustment period for Taiwanese students was

Study abroad provides many benefits, such as learning another language, developing global awareness, and making international friendships. (Shutterstock/Prostock-studio)

significantly shortened from six months to two months because of social media, but there were enormous barriers in sustaining intercultural friendships largely due to the language barrier. But it was not just the linguistic issue; Taiwanese students found the lack of common interests to be a major barrier. Hoshuis, Hanke, and Rutten (2019) explain that online social network sites helped sojourners foster social interaction with locals, but did not lead to a strong intent to participate in the host society. Hendrickson (2018) tried to explore mechanisms to assist in visitor-host relations and emphasized that "intercultural connectors" (p. 11) such as socially active tutors and common extracurricular activities go a long way in encouraging cross-cultural relations among sojourners and host nationals. In other words, it is not simply enough to bring people into an institution. Efforts to make sure there is active mixing of visitors and nationals go a long way in making sure the benefits of sojourning are achieved.

Opportunities for Contact and Dialogue

Opportunities for contact and dialogue exist at all stages of the sojourn experience: pre-departure, in-country, and return to the United States. Taking advantage of these resources will enable you to prepare for your experience, call on expertise and experience of other seasoned sojourners, and find like-minded travelers to share the experience with upon return to the United States. Many universities have programs that connect students who are enrolled in foreign language courses or planning to study abroad with students from those particular countries who speak the target language. University Conversation Partner Programs or programs with a similar theme are designed to encourage students to meet once a week for an hour and to practice the language of the target country. This is often a gateway to develop an international friendship with someone from another country whether you decide to travel overseas or not.

You can also take advantage of university programs such as the model developed at the Center for Citizen Peace Building (CCPB) at the University of California, Irvine. The Center "takes an integrated approach to studying the best grassroots peacebuilding methods in both domestic and international conflicts and utilizes those findings in peacebuilding projects in local neighborhoods and in international communities such as Northern Ireland and the Middle East" (CCPB, 2004). The Center builds on research, education, and action to create and promote sustainable peace through citizen peacebuilding efforts at home and abroad. The Center has been the winner of Ford Foundation grants for projects that promote open campus environments to discuss difficult topics.

Without traveling abroad you can meet international students on your campus who are eager and willing to share information about their home country while they learn about the United States. Check with the admissions office on your campus to find out how many new international students are expected for the fall and spring semesters. It is likely that these students would welcome having student connection upon arrival. Many universities, in an effort to assist new international students to feel welcome and comfortable, offer opportunities to pair students up on arrival. You may also want to check with your foreign language department to see if your university hosts visiting groups to your campus from academic institutions overseas. Visiting groups are typically on campus for 10 days participating in academic coursework and in cultural immersion experiences while accompanied by a faculty member from their home institution. There are often opportunities to be matched with individual group members to participate in co-curricular activities such as having lunch together in the cafeteria, attending campus events together, and visiting culturally significant sites in the city.

Short-term faculty-led programs of study abroad are becoming more common as a way to provide students the opportunity to experience an international academic program in 10 to 40 days (Engle & Engle, 2003). While a longer stay in country will have the greatest impact on the transformation process, short-term programs can ignite a fire to return overseas for a longer period of time. Shorter study abroad programs have also been shown to benefit personal growth and emerging intercultural communication competence of participants (Jackson, 2005). This new type of study abroad gives students who could not otherwise participate because of work or family obligations the chance to do so. Because today's students are also very concerned with social justice and the effect their visit may have on the country they visit, they are attracted to short-term faculty-led programs that include service-learning initiatives in their curriculum.

From a peacebuilding perspective, global competency is a road map to global citizenship. Global citizens are those who have developed intercultural skills not for the purpose of national dominance, be it military power or business success, but who build relationships of human solidarity (Reilly & Senders, 2009). There are innumerable benefits to participating in study abroad and international service learning. And, as this book has discussed, there are increasing opportunities to become a global citizen. In this effort we encourage you to look at programs for social justice and peacemaking between US and international groups.

Reilly and Senders (2009) raise a very important question: universities may be able to offer worlds of opportunity to their students, but can they also inspire students to live lives of consequence as global citizens? They enumerate ways in which global citizens live their lives: (1) global citizens understand themselves and their home culture; (2) global citizens have an in-depth understanding of another culture; (3) global citizens can work across cultures with facility and ease; (4) global citizens understand that culture is constantly changing; (5) global citizens seek in other cultures solutions to problems that may transform their own; and (6) global citizens feel compelled to work towards genuine understanding among peoples, work across lines of culture, class, and nationality to solve the challenges facing the whole of humanity.

The entire world benefits from the development of even one person with a whole world perspective, one who understands from intercultural contact that misunderstandings do not have to lead to negative stereotyping, prejudice, or war. Study abroad programs can actively promote a culture of peace in countries that typically have a tense and conflict-ridden relationship with the United States (Bond, Koont, & Stephenson, 2005).

> A culture of peace is an integral approach to preventing violence and violent conflicts, and an alternative to the culture of war and violence based on education for peace, the promotion of sustainable economic and social development, respect for human rights, equality between women and men, democratic participation, tolerance, the free flow of information, and disarmament. (Adams, 2005)

As Elizabeth Evans Baker noted, "peace is everybody's business" (Daniels, 1999). The sojourn experience—whether through tourism, short-term study abroad, long-term study abroad, study away, volunteerism, or service learning—are all ways of making peace *your* business.

From Sojourner to Settler

Up until this point, we have focused on the sojourner who comes to a new place as a short-term experience. However, one reality is that many sojourners transition into a different role, that of a settler or an immigrant. Woon (1983–84) and Chavez (1988) make the case that while many Chinese and Mexican sojourners come to the United States on a temporary basis, many also end up staying. One major impetus is the formation of families during the "sojourn" period. These binational families often have members who are citizens and nonresidents, and often, the family ends up deciding to live permanently in the country to be together.

While there are many pathways to acquiring citizenship or permanent residency in the United States—such as marriage, asylum, extending tourist visas, and even through undocumented entry—one of the most common ways is through extending shorter sojourns, particularly in educational and work contexts. Many sojourners who come as students desire to remain in the United States to work and eventually live permanently. In fact, a 2014 Brookings Institution report found that 45% of foreign student graduates were able to extend their visas to work in the same metropolitan area as their college or university (Israel & Batalova, 2021). Two programs give foreign workers temporary employment authorization in the US, the H-1B visa and the Optional Practical Training (OPT) visa. OPT is a visa that grants temporary employment to an individual with a student visa after they finish their education, as long as the work is related to their major area of study. The H-1B visa is one of the pathways that foreign graduates can pursue to stay in the United States once their OPT period expires. It is a temporary (nonimmigrant) visa that allows employers to petition for highly educated foreign professionals to work in "specialty occupations" that require at least a bachelor's degree or the equivalent. By the end of the 2004–2016 period, there were a total of 1,474,000 OPT approvals and 1,473,000 initial H-1B visa approvals (Ruiz & Budiman, 2018). Foreign students obtaining authorization to remain and work in the United States after graduation come from many different countries, but the majority of them are from Asia. Students from India, China, and South Korea made up 57% of all OPT participants between 2004 and 2016 (Ruiz & Budiman, 2018). These numbers give us a sense of how many students and workers come to the United States for periods longer than a short-term sojourn.

As the 2020 Census results show, the makeup of American society is more diverse than ever. (Shutterstock/Monkey Business Images)

The United States is a nation of immigrants. The first big wave of early settlers came from Europe in the 1600s, followed by a painful history that brought many African Americans into slavery, creating a White-Black dualism that rages on to this day. Over the years, immigration laws were enacted to limit specific groups of people, such as the Chinese Exclusion Act of 1882 and quotas for specific nationalities in the 1920s. Nation-based quotas were ended in 1965 with the passage of the Immigration and Nationality Act. Today, immigrants are heavily from Latin America and Asia. The changing nature of immigration over the last few decades has certainly changed the makeup of American society, with the 2020 Census results showing that the United States is more diverse than ever (Boschma et al., 2021). People of color and multiracials represented 43% of the total US population in 2020, up from 34% in 2010. Yet as much as the racial makeup of the United States has radically changed over the years, racial tension continues. Stereotypes abound regarding specific races and ethnicities (Foeman & Lawton, 2021). The perception that Whites of European origin are often the face of what it means to be an American has led minorities to continue to feel estrangement (Citrin & Sears, 2014). All of these have fueled insular attitudes about race from both nationals and immigrants alike. For example, many immigrants refuse to let their children marry outside of their ethnicity (DaCosta, 2007), and racial violence continues to target people of color. During COVID-19, this was most evident in attacks against Asians, with more than 9,000 attacks reported from March 2020 to June 2021 (Tang, 2021). Certainly, more needs to be done to reach across the aisles and move toward peace, since all these groups are living in the same country where more racial balancing is occurring with each subsequent census. As discussed in several chapters in the book, interpersonal contact is one of the strongest ways to reduce prejudice. Efforts to engage with others, through short-terms sojourns or longer-term work opportunities, play a role in helping achieve this goal.

Summary

In summary, this chapter highlights the transformative power of study abroad in particular and points to the impact of study away as a developing priority for universities and colleges in the United States. The culture shock curve describes stages of transition that occur when a person journeys to an unfamiliar location and needs new tools to understand the process. A more appropriate name for the culture shock curve would be the culture shock W. This is because students who acclimate and feel comfortable in their new environment will have a "shock" again when they return home. This is why it is so important to connect with others at home who want to share the experience and learn more. Find ways to connect with the international students who are on your home campus upon return and the students who are interested in study abroad. As a study abroad returnee, you may find that you learn just as much about your own cultural identity while you are learning about another. This is because you have the opportunity to compare and contrast the way things are done at home (e.g., raising children, celebrating holidays, marriage, and funeral customs) with the way things are done in other cultures. You will begin to realize that all cultures have their own unique traditions and that there are many different ways to accomplish the same outcome. You will begin to see that the world is not black and white, but that there are many shades of grey. One of the highlights and benefits of study abroad is the ability to improve intercultural competence and be an agent of peace. One of the most important steps toward intercultural communication competence and peacebuilding is visiting another culture, often referred to as the sojourner experience. A sojourner is someone who goes to another country to stay for a particular reason and then, after staying more than six months but less than five years, returns to his or her home country. Thus, a sojourner differs from a tourist (who doesn't stay as long) and an expatriate or immigrant (who stays longer). For students, the sojourner experience often involves participation in programs of service learning and international internships.

The sojourner experience can have a significant impact on the sojourner's cultural frame of reference or worldview, which often involves a shift from an ethnocentric to an ethnorelative point of view. Sojourners often experience some degree of culture shock, a term used to describe the feelings of sojourners as they enter a new culture and interact with others. As a process of adjustment, the culture shock curve model identifies the changes in feeling that occur with the passage of time. Research also indicates that the sojourner experience is marked by several distinct phases: the pre-departure phase, the arrival and settling-in phase, living in a new culture phase, and the returning home phase. A number of models of cultural adaptation clarify how sojourners make the adjustment and cope with the experience of living in a new culture, and how communication affects the adaptation that occurs. There are many benefits of studying abroad and many opportunities for engaging in dialogue with people of other cultures. The benefits of study abroad include a new worldview, the opportunity to grow as a global citizen, and the opportunity to share that when you return home. In the United States, the sojourn experience is often a pathway to long-term residency and citizenship, contributing to the increasing diversity of US society.

QUESTIONS

1. Compare the following types of sojourn experiences in terms of the kinds of cross-cultural experiences and intercultural communication opportunities inherent in each type of sojourning: study away, short-term study abroad, semester study abroad, international service learning, and international internships in terms of language learning.

2. Describe how you would choose and prepare for either a study away or study abroad sojourn. What skills would you need to develop prior to departure? How would you find the resources you need to learn the most about the people and country/culture you plan to live in?

3. Is it possible to experience culture shock not only when moving from one country to another, but also from one city to another, one business context to another, one college to another, and so on? Have you ever had this experience? If so, what lessons did you learn from it?

4. Look at the list of descriptions of how one lives as a global citizen. Give examples of how these descriptions would translate into action and behavior.

References

Abu-Nimer, M. (1999). *Dialogue, conflict resolution, and change: Arab-Jewish encounters in Israel*. State University of New York Press.

Abu-Nasr, D. (2005, August 28). *When flirting is forbidden, wireless chat fills in*. Los Angeles Times. www.latimes.com/archives/la-xpm-2005-aug-28-adfg-bluetooth28-story.html

Abu-Rayya, H. (2000). *Psychological and sociocultural adjustment of intermarried Jews and Arabs in Israel* [Unpublished master's thesis]. Hebrew University of Jerusalem.

ACTFL. (2012). *ACTFL Proficiency guidelines*. www.actfl.org/resources/actfl-proficiency-guidelines-2012

Adair, W., Okumura, T., & Brett, J. (2001). Negotiation behaviors when cultures collide: The US and Japan. *Journal of Applied Psychology, 86*, 371–385.

Adams, D. (2005). *Definition of culture of peace*. www.culture-of-peace.info/copoj/definition.html

Adams, R. B., Franklin, R. G., Rule, N. O., Freeman, J. B., Kveraga, K., Hadjikani, N., Yoshikawa, S., & Ambady, N. (2010a). Culture, gaze and the neural processing of fear expressions. *Social Cognitive and Affective Neuroscience, 5*, 340–348.

Adams, R. B., Rule, N. O., Franklin, R. G., Wang, E., Stevenson, M. T., Yoshikawa, S., Nomura, M., Sato, W., Kveraga, K., & Ambady, N. (2010b). Cross-cultural reading the mind in the eyes: An fMRI investigation. *Journal of Cognitive Neuroscience, 22*, 97–108.

Adler, C. (2003, November 7). *Colonel Sanders' march on China*. Time. https://content.time.com/time/subscriber/article/0,33009,543845,00.html

Agar, M. (1994). *Language shock: Understanding the culture of conversation*. William Morrow.

Agger, C., & Day, K. (2011). Accessible information and prevention strategies related to student sexual harassment: A review of students harassing students. *The High School Journal, 94*(2), 77–78.

Aizawa, Y., & Whatley. M. A. (2006). Gender, shyness, and individualism-collectivism: A cross-cultural study. *Race, Gender & Class, 13*(1/2), 7–25.

Akiba, D. (2010). Cambodian Americans and education: Understanding the intersections between cultural tradition and U.S. schooling. *The Educational Forum, 74*, 328–333.

Akimoto, T. (2008). Transferability of US education techniques to Japan: Do they cross cultural lines? *Journal of Teaching in Social Work, 28*(3/4), 396–407.

Albertsen, E. J., Connor, L. E., & Berry, J. W. (2006). Religion and interpersonal guilt: Variations across ethnicity and spirituality. *Mental Health, Religion & Culture, 9*(1), 67–84.

Allen, M., & Burrell, N. (1996). Comparing the impact of homosexual and heterosexual parents of children: Meta-analysis of existing research. *Journal of Homosexuality, 32*(2), 19–35.

Allen, K. R., & Wilcox, K. L. (2000). Gay/lesbian families over the life course. In S. J. Price, P. C. McKenry, & M. J. Murphy (Eds.), *Families across time: A life course perspective* (pp. 51–63). Roxbury.

Allport, G. W. (1954). *The nature of prejudice*. Doubleday.

Almanac of Policy Issues. (2004). *Poverty*. www.policyalmanac.org/social_welfare/poverty.shtml

Altman, L., & Taylor, D. A. (1973). *Social penetration: The development of interpersonal relationships*. Holt, Rinehart & Winston.

Amichai-Hamburger, Y., & McKenna, K. Y. A. (2006). The contact hypothesis reconsidered: Interacting via the Internet. *Journal of Computer-Mediated Communication, 11*, 825–843.

Anand, R., & Winters, M. (2008). A retrospective view of corporate diversity training from 1964 to the present. *Academy of Management Learning & Education, 7*(3), 356–372.

Anderson, B. (1983). *Imagined communities: Reflection on the origin and spread of nationalism*. Verso.

375

Anderson, L. E. (1994). A new look at an old construct: Cross-cultural adaptation. *International Journal of Intercultural Relations, 18*(3), 293–328.

Anderson, J. (2011, November 7). National study finds widespread sexual harassment of students in grades 7 to 12. *The New York Times*, p. 14.

Anderson, N., Danis, M., & Stohl, M. (2009). *Onscreen Muslims: Media, identity, terrorism, and public policy.* Paper presented to the International Communication Association, Chicago.

Andersson, M., Gillespie, M., & Mackay, H. A. (2010). Mapping digital diasporas @ BBC World Service: Users and uses of the Persian and Arabic websites. *Middle East Journal of Culture and Communication, 3*(2), 256–278.

Andreopoulos, G. (2002). Human rights education and training for professionals. *International Review of Education, 48*(3/4), 239–249.

Anicich, E. M., Jachimowicz, J. M., Osborne, M. R., & Phillips, L. T. (2021, August 11). Design physical and digital spaces to foster inclusion. *Harvard Business Review.* https://hbr.org/2021/08/design-physical-and-digital-spaces-to-foster-inclusion

Antonio, A. L. (2001). Diversity and the influence of friendship groups in college. *The Review of Higher Education, 25*(1), 63–89.

Aptheker, H. (1971). *Afro-American history: The modern era.* Carol Publishing Group.

Arasaratnam, L., & Banerjee, S. (2011). Sensation seeking and intercultural communication competence: A model test. *International Journal of Intercultural Relations, 35*(2), 226–233.

Argyle, M. (1988). *Bodily communication* (2nd ed.). Methuen.

Argyle, M., & Henderson, M. (1985). *The anatomy of relationships: And the rules and skills needed to manage them successfully.* Heinemann.

Armstrong, M. (2018). *Where tattoos are most popular.* Statista. www.statista.com/chart/13942/where-tattoos-are-most-popular

Aron, A., & McLaughlin-Volpe, T. (2001). Including others in the self. In C. Sedikides & M. Brewer (Eds.), *Individual, self, relational self, collective self* (pp. 89–108). Psychology Press.

Ashton-James, C. E., Maddux, W. W., Galinsky, A. D., & Chartrand, T. L. (2009). Who I am depends on how I feel: The role of affect in the expression of culture. *Psychological Science, 20*(3), 340–346.

Associated Press. (2004, May 26). *Gum returns to Singapore after 12 years.* USA Today. http://usatoday30.usatoday.com/news/world/iraq/2004-05-26-singapore-gum_x.htm

Associated Press. (2006, February 20). *Scientists train soldiers in nonverbal communication.* Fox News. www.foxnews.com/story/2006/02/20/ scientists-train-soldiers-in-non-verbal-communication/

-20Atkinson, D. R., Morten, G., & Sue, D. W. (1989). A minority identity development model. In D. R. Atkinson, G. Morten, & D. W. Sue (Eds.), *Counseling American minorities* (pp. 35–52). W. C. Brown.

Attar-Schwartz, S. (2009). Peer sexual harassment victimization at school: The roles of student characteristics, cultural affiliation, and school factors. *American Journal of Orthopsychiatry, 79*(3), 407–420.

Auerbach, Y. (2009). The reconciliation pyramid—A narrative-based framework for analyzing identity conflicts. *Political Psychology, 30*(2), 291–318.

Augsburger, D. (1986). *Pastoral counseling across cultures.* Westminster Press.

Aukrust, V. G., Edwards, C. P., Kumru, A., Knoche, L., & Kim, M. (2003). Young children's close relationships outside the family: Parental ethnotheories in four communities in Norway, United States, Turkey, and Korea. *International Journal of Behavioral Development, 27*(6), 481–494.

Austin, R. (2007). Reconnecting young people in Northern Ireland. In B. D. Loader (Ed.), *Young citizens in the digital age: Political engagement, young people and new media* (pp. 143–157). Routledge.

Avruch, K., & Wang, Z. (2005). Culture, apology, and international negotiation: The case of the Sino-U.S. "Spy Plane" crisis. *International Negotiation, 10,* 337–353.

Axtell, R. (1998). *Gestures: The do's and taboos of body language around the world.* Wiley.

Baderoon, G. (2002). Shooting the East/veils and masks: Uncovering Orientalism in South African media. *African & Asian Studies, 1*(4), 367–384.

Bagozzi, R. P., Verbecke, W., & Gavino, J. C., Jr. (2003). Culture moderates the self-regulation of shame and its effects on performance: The case of salespersons in the Netherlands and Philippines. *Journal of Applied Psychology, 88*(2), 219–233.

Bahns, A. J. (2019). Preference, opportunity, and choice: A multilevel analysis of diverse friendship formation. *Group Processes and Intergroup Relations, 22*(2), 233–252.

Bahr, K. S. (1994). The strengths of Apache grandmothers: Observations on commitment, culture, and caretaking. *Journal of Comparative Family Studies, 25*(2), 233–248.

Baird, V. (2010). Why do so many journalists beat the drums of war and peddle propaganda? *New Internationalist, 438*, 29–31.

Barbee, A. P., Rowatt, T. L., & Cunningham, M. R. (1998). When a friend is in need: Feelings about seeking, giving and receiving social support. In P. A. Anderson & L. K. Guerrero (Eds.), *Handbook of communication and emotion: Research, theory, application and contexts* (pp. 281–301). Academic Press.

Barber, B. K. (1994). Cultural, family, and person contexts of parent-adolescent conflict. *Journal of Marriage and the Family, 56*(2), 375–386.

Barbir, L. A., Vandevender, A. W., & Cohn, T. J. (2017). Friendship, attitudes, and behavioral intentions of cisgender heterosexuals toward transgender individuals. *Journal of Gay and Lesbian Mental Health, 21*(2), 154–170.

Bardhan, P. (1997). *The role of governance in economic development.* OECD.

Barlund, D. C. (1989). *Communicative styles of Japanese and Americans: Images and realities.* Wadsworth.

Barrios, J. (2009, June 29). *Commemorating Stonewall at the White House.* The Washington Post. www.washingtonpost.com/wp-dyn/content/article/2009/06/28/AR2009062802336.html

Bar-Tal, D. (2002). The elusive nature of peace education. In G. Salomon & B. Nevo (Eds.), *Peace education: The concept, principles, and practices around the world* (pp. 27–36). Erlbaum.

Barth, R., & Miller, J. (2000). Building effective post-adoption services: What is the empirical foundation? *Family Relations, 49*(4), 447–455.

Basso, K. (1972). To give up on words: Silence in Western Apache culture. In P. Giglioli (Ed.), *Language in social context* (pp. 67–86). Penguin.

Bauman, H. L. (2005). Designing deaf babies and the question of disability. *Journal of Deaf Studies and Deaf Education, 10*, 311–315.

Bedford, O. A. (2004). The individual experience of guilt and shame in Chinese culture. *Culture and Psychology, 10*(1), 29–52.

Bedford, O. A, & Hwang, K. (2003). Guilt and shame in Chinese culture: A cross-cultural framework from the perspective of morality v. identity. *Journal for the Theory of Social Behavior, 33*(2), 127–143.

Beersma, B., Harinck, F., & Gerts, M. (2003). Bound in honor: How honor values and insults affect the experience and management of conflicts. *International Journal of Conflict Management, 14*(2), 75–94.

Befus, C. P. (1988). A multilevel treatment approach for culture shock experienced by sojourners. *International Journal of Intercultural Relations, 12*(4), 381–400.

Begley, P. A. (2003). Sojourner adaptation. In L. A. Samovar & R. E. Porter (Eds.), *Intercultural communication: A reader* (pp. 406–412). Thomson Wadsworth.

Behar, R. (2008, June 1). *Special report: China storms Africa.* Fast Company. www.fastcompany.com/magazine/126/special-report-china-in-africa.html?page=0%2C1

Bekerman, Z., & Shhadi, N. (2003). Palestinian-Jewish bilingual education in Israel: Its influence on cultural identities and its impact on intergroup conflict. *Journal of Multilingual & Multicultural Development, 24*(6), 473–484.

Bekerman, Z., Habib, A., & Shhadi, N. (2011). Jewish-Palestinian integrated education in Israel and its potential influence on national and/or ethnic identities and intergroup relations. *Journal of Ethnic & Migration Studies, 37*(3), 389–405.

Bell, L. G. (1992). Song without words. In R. Simon, C. Barrilleaus, M. S. Wylie, & L. M. Markowitz (Eds.), *The evolving therapist* (pp. 81–86). Guilford.

Bennett, M. J. (1986). A developmental approach to training for intercultural sensitivity. *International Journal of Intercultural Relations, 10*(2), 179–196.

Ben-Porath, S. R. (2005). Multicultural education, peace, and democracy: Considerations of civic education in wartime. *Philosophy of Education Yearbook, 3*, 87–95.

Berger, P. L., & Luckmann, T. (1966). *The social construction of reality.* Doubleday.

Bezrukova, K., Perry, J. L., Spell, C. S., & Jehn, K. A. (2016). A meta-analytical integration of over 40 years of research on diversity training evaluation. *Psychological Bulletin, 142*(11), 1227–1274.

Bilewicz, M. (2009). Perspective taking and intergroup helping intentions: The moderating role of power relations. *Journal of Applied Psychology, 39*(12), 2779–2786.

Billig, M. G., & Tajfel, H. (1973). Social categorization and similarity in intergroup behavior. *European Journal of Social Psychology, 3*, 27–52.

Biracial Family Network. (2004, May 13). www.facebook.com/ pages/Biracial-Family-Network-Chicago/200576129983290

Bitel, M. (2004). *Preliminary findings from the evaluation of restorative justice in schools.* Youth Justice Board.

Black, J., & Gregersen, H. (1999). The right way to manage expats. *Harvard Business Review, 77*, 52–63.

Blair, I. V., Judd, C. M., Sadler, M. S., & Jenkins, C. (2002). The role of Afrocentric features in person perception: Judging by features and categories. *Journal of Personality and Social Psychology, 83*(1), 5–23.

Blasco, M. (2004). Stranger to us than birds in our garden? Reflections on hermeneutics, intercultural understanding and the management of difference. In M. Blasco & J. Gustafsson (Eds.), *Intercultural alternative: Critical perspectives on intercultural encounters in theory and practice* (pp. 19–39). Copenhagen Business School Press.

Blascovich, J., Mendes, W. B., Hunter, S. B., Lickel, B., & Kowai-Bell, N. (2001). Perceiver threat in social interactions with stigmatized others. *Journal of Personality and Social Psychology, 80*(2), 253–267.

Blazar, D. (2021). *Teachers of color, culturally responsive teaching, and student outcomes: Experimental evidence from the random assignment of teachers to classes.* EdWorkingPaper No. 21-501. Annenberg Institute at Brown University.

Blieszner, R., & Adams, R. G. (1992). *Adult friendships.* Sage.

Bochner, S. (1986). Coping with unfamiliar cultures: Adjustment or culture learning? *Australian Journal of Psychology, 38*(3), 347–358.

Bohm, D. (1996). *On dialogue.* Routledge.

Bond, L., Koont, S., & Stephenson, S. (2005). The power of being there: Study abroad in Cuba and the promotion of a "culture of peace." *Frontiers, 11*, 99–120.

Bonvillain, N. (2000). *Language, culture, and communication: The meaning of messages* (3rd ed.). Prentice-Hall.

Borden, J. P., & Monahan, T. F. (2020). Unique study abroad program highlights benefits to students and faculty alike. *Business Education Innovation Journal, 12*(1), 180–185.

Boschma, J., Wolfe, D., Krishnakumar, P., Hickey, C., Maharishi, M., Rigdon, R., Keefe, J., & Wright, D. (2021 August 12). *Census release shows America is more diverse and more multiracial than ever.* CNN Politics. www.cnn.com/2021/08/12/politics/us-census-2020-data/index.html

Bowen, H. (1953). *Social responsibilities of the businessman.* Harper & Row.

Bowman, N. A., & Park, J. J. (2014). Interracial contact on college campuses: Comparing and contrasting predictors of cross-racial interaction and interracial friendship. *Journal of Higher Education, 85*(5), 660–690.

Bradley, E. H. (2007). Pursuing peace: Enlisting students in the battle against bias. *Education Digest, 73*(4), 49–52.

Bradshaw, C. P., & Waasdorp, T. E. (2009). Measuring and changing a "culture of bullying." *The School Psychology Review, 38*, 356–361.

Brauer, M. & Chaurand, N. (2010). Descriptive norms, prescriptive norms, and social control: An intercultural comparison of people's reactions to uncivil behaviors. *European Journal of Social Psychology, 40*, 490–499.

Brewer, M. B., & Miller, N. (1984). Beyond the contact hypothesis: Theoretical perspectives on desegregation. In N. Miller & M. B. Brewer (Eds.), *Groups in contact: The psychology of desegregation* (pp. 281–302). Academic Press.

Brislin, R. W. (2008). *Working with cultural differences: Dealing effectively with diversity in the workplace.* Praeger.

Brislin, R. W., Cushner, K., Cherrie, C., & Yong, M. (1986). *Intercultural interactions: A practical guide.* Sage.

Brophy, I. N. (1946). The luxury of anti-Negro prejudice. *Public Opinion Quarterly, 9*, 456–466.

Brown, P. M. (1990). Biracial identity and social marginality. *Child and Adolescent Social Work, 7*, 319–337.

Brown, L. (2009). The transformative power of the international sojourn: An ethnographic study of the international student experience. *Annals of Tourism Research, 36*(3), 502–521.

Brown, H. (2022). *Understanding the digital divide.* First Book. https://firstbook.org/blog/2022/07/26/understanding-the-digital-divide

Brownlee, M. I. (2022). *The digital divide 2.0: Navigating digital equity and health equity in education.* EdSurge. www.edsurge.com/news/2022-11-10-the-digital-divide-2-0-navigating-digital-equity-and--health-equity-in-education

Buber, M. (1958). *I and thou.* Scribner Classics.

Bureau of Consular Affairs. (2013). *Statistics.* http://adoption.state.gov/about_us/statistics.php

Burgess, H., & Burgess, G. (2003). *What are intractable conflicts?* Beyond Intractability. www.beyondintractability.org/essay/meaning-intractability

Burleson, B. & Feng, B. (2005, May). *A critical review of research on cultural similarities and differences in emotional support.* Paper presented to the International Communication Association, New York City.

Burleson, B. R., & Goldsmith, D. J. (1998). How the comforting process works: Alleviating emotional distress through conversationally induced reappraisals. In P. A. Anderson & L. K. Guerrero (Eds.), *Handbook of communication and emotion: Research, theory, applications, and contexts* (pp. 245–280). Academic Press.

Burleson, B. R., & Mortenson, S. R. (2003). Explaining cultural differences in evaluations of emotional support behaviors: Exploring the mediating influences of value systems and interaction goals. *Communication Research, 30,* 113–146.

Burton, L. M., & Dilworth-Anderson, P. (1991). The intergenerational family roles of aged Black Americans. *Marriage and Family Review, 16*(3/4), 311–330.

Butcher, R., Wiedenhoeft, M. H., & Loynachan, T. E. (2017). Long-term benefit of international agricultural study abroad courses. *Natural Sciences Education, 46*(1), 1–10.

Butler, J. (1997). *Excitable speech: A politics of the performative.* Routledge.

Byon, A. S. (2005). Apologizing in Korean: Cross-cultural analysis in classroom settings. *Korean Studies, 29*(1), 137–166.

Cahn, D. D. (1985). Communication competence in the resolution of intercultural conflict. *World Communication, 14,* 85–94.

Cahn, D. D. (1987). *Letting go: A practical theory of relationship disengagement and re-engagement.* State University of New York Press.

Canary, D. J., Cupach, W. R., & Messman, S. J. (1995). *Relationship conflict.* Sage.

Canary, D. J., Spitzberg, B. H., & Semic, B. A. (1998). The experience and expression of anger. In P. A. Anderson & L. K. Guerrero (Eds.), *Handbook of communication and emotion: Research, theory, application and contexts* (pp. 189–213). Academic Press.

The Canberra Times. (2011, February 4). Internet: A tool for tyranny as well as democracy. Section A, p. 19.

Caprara, D., & Nelson, J. (2007). *Global corporations, global impact. Brookings global economy and development.* Brookings Institution Press.

Carbaugh, D. (2005). *Cultures in conversation.* Erlbaum.

Cargile, A. C. (1998). Meaning and modes of friendship: Verbal descriptions by native Japanese. *Howard Journal of Communication, 9*(4), 347–370.

Carlin, J. (2003, February 2). *Bring on the world.* The Guardian. www.theguardian.com/sport/2003/feb/02/cricketworldcup2003.cricketworldcup1

Carlin, J. (2008). *Invictus.* Penguin Books.

Carillo, S., & Salhotra, P. (2022). *The U.S. student population is more diverse, but schools are still highly segregated.* NPR. www.houstonpublicmedia.org/npr/2022/07/14/1111060299/the-u-s-student-population-is-more-diverse-but-schools-are-still-highly-segregated/

Carroll, A. B. (1991). The pyramid of corporate social responsibility: Toward the moral management of organizational stakeholders. *Business Horizons, 34,* 39–48.

Casmir, F. L. (1999). Foundations for the study of intercultural communication based on a third-culture building model. *International Journal of Intercultural Relations, 23*(1), 91–116.

Center for Citizen Peacebuilding (CCPB). (2004). *Mikhail Gorbachev.* www.peacebuilding.uci.edu/pb_gorbachev

Cencirulo, J, McDougall, T., Sorenson, C., Crosby, S., Hauser, P. (2021). Trainee experiences of racism, sexism, heterosexism, and ableism ("ISMs") at a Department of Veterans Affairs (VA) healthcare facility. *Training and Education in Professional Psychology, 15*(3), 242–249.

Chang, E. H., Milkman, K. L., Gromet, D. M., Rebele, R. W., Massey, C., Duckworth, A. L., & Grant, A. M. (2019). The mixed effects of online diversity training. *PNAS, 116*(16), 7778–7783.

Chang, Y. Y. (2021). A qualitative study of intercultural friendship through new social media. *Journal of Intercultural Communication, 21*(1), 92–105.

Channing, C. (2007). *Just lucky I guess: A memoir of sorts.* Simon & Schuster.

Chavez, L. R. (1988). Settlers and sojourners: The case of Mexicans in the United States. *Human Organization, 47*(2), 95–108.

Chen, L. (1997). Verbal adaptive strategies in U.S. American dyadic interactions with U.S. American or East-Asian partners. *Communication Monographs, 64,* 302–323.

Chen, L. (2002). Communication in intercultural relationships. In W. B. Gudykunst & B. Mody (Eds.), *Handbook of international and intercultural communication* (2nd ed., pp. 241–259). Sage.

Chen, Y. W. (2006). Intercultural friendship from the perspectives of East Asian international students. *China Media Research, 2*(3), 43–58.

Chen, M., & Bedford, O. (2022). Measuring guano quality in the workplace. *Journal of Business and Psychology, 37,* 581–599.

Chen, N. Y., & Shaffer, D. R. (1997). On physical attractiveness stereotyping in Taiwan: A revised sociocultural perspective. *Journal of Social Psychology, 137,* 117–124.

Chen, G. M. & Starosta, W. J. (1998). *Foundations of intercultural communication.* Allyn & Bacon.

Cheng, X., & Tardy, X. (2009). A cross cultural study of silence in marital conflict. *China Media Research, 5*(2), 35–40.

Chen, Y., Wu, J., & Chung, Y. (2008). Cultural impact on trust: A comparison of virtual communities in China, Hong Kong, and Taiwan. *Journal of Global Information Technology Management, 11*(1), 28–48.

Cherlin, A., & Furstenberg, F. F. (1985). Styles and strategies of grandparenting. In V. L. Bengston & J. F. Robertson (Eds.), *Grandparenthood* (pp. 97–116). Sage.

Choi, A., Chan, K. L., & Brownridge, D. A. (2010). Unraveling in-law conflict and its association with intimate partner violence in Chinese culture: Narrative accounts of Chinese battered women. *Women's Health & Urban Life, 9*(1), 72–92.

Chua, A. (2011). *Battle hymn of the tiger mother.* Penguin Press.

Chiu, L. H. (1972). A cross-cultural comparison of cognitive styles in Chinese and American children. *International Journal of Psychology, 7,* 235–242.

Chun-Seng, K., & Bond, M. H. (2008). Role of emotions and behavioural responses in mediating the impact of face loss on relationship deterioration: Are Chinese more face-sensitive than Americans? *Asian Journal of Social Psychology, 11*(2), 175–184.

Cintron, J. (1996, June). *Short-term study abroad: Integration, third culture formation and reentry.* Paper presented at the NAFSA Annual Conference, Phoenix, AZ.

Cissna, K. N., & Anderson, R. (2002). *Moments of meeting: Buber, Rogers, and the potential for public dialogue.* State University of New York Press.

Citrin, J., & Sears, D. O. (2014). *American identity and the politics of multiculturalism.* Cambridge University Press.

Clark, M. (2002). *In search of human nature.* Routledge.

Coetzer, G., & Gibbison, G. (2016). Mediating influence of time management on the relationship between adult attention deficit and the operational effectiveness of project managers. *Journal of Management Development, 35*(8), 970–984.

Cohen, D., & Gunz, A. (2002). As seen by the other . . . Perspectives on the self in the memories and emotional perceptions of easterners and westerners. *Psychological Science, 13,* 55–59.

Cohen, R. (2003). Students helping students: Peer mediation. In T. Jones & R. Compton (Eds.), *Kids working it out: Stories and strategies for making peace in our schools* (pp. 109–128). Jossey-Bass.

Cole, C. F., Arafat, C., Tidhar, C., Tafesh, W. Z., Fox, N. A., Killen, M., Ardila-Rey, A., Leavitt, L. A., Lesser, G., Richman, B. A., & Yung, F. (2003). The educational impact of *Rechov Sumsum/Shara'a Simsim*: A *Sesame Street* television series to promote respect and understanding among children living in Israel, the West Bank, and Gaza. *International Journal of Behavioral Development, 27*, 409–423.

Coleman, R. M. (2002). *Say it loud! African-American audiences, media and identity*. Routledge.

Collier, J., & Wanderley, L. (2005). Thinking for the future: Global corporate responsibility in the twenty-first century. *Futures, 37*, 169–182.

Collier, M. J. (2002). *Intercultural alliances: Critical transformation*. Sage.

Collier, M. J. (2009). Contextual negotiation of cultural identifications and relationships: Interview discourse with Palestinian, Israeli, and Palestinian/Israeli young women in a U.S. Peacebuilding program. *Journal of International and Intercultural Communication, 2*(4), 344–368.

Collier, M. J., & Thomas, M. (1988). Identity in intercultural communication: An interpretive perspective. In Y. Y. Kim & W. B. Gudykunst (Eds.), *Theories of intercultural communication* (pp. 99–123). Sage.

Collins, P. H. (2000). *Black feminist thought: Knowledge, consciousness, and the politics of empowerment* (2nd ed.). Routledge.

Conte, Z. (2001). The gift of the arts. In L. Lantieri (Ed.), *Schools with spirit: Nurturing the inner lives of children and teachers* (pp. 77–89). Beacon Press.

Cooke, M. (1997). Listen to the image speak. *Cultural Values, 1*(1), 101–117.

Corcoran, R. (2010). *Trustbuilding: An honest conversation on race, reconciliation, and responsibility*. University of Virginia Press.

Cowan, G. (2005). Interracial interactions at racially diverse university campuses. *The Journal of Social Psychology, 145*(1), 49–63.

Cramer, D. (1998). *Close relationships: The study of love and friendship*. Arnold.

Cross, S., & Gore, J. (2003). Cultural models of the self. In M. Leary & J. Tangney (Eds.), *Handbook of self and identity* (pp. 587–617). Guilford.

Cuddy, A. J. C., Rock, M. S., & Norton, M. I. (2007). Aid in the aftermath of Hurricane Katrina: Inferences of secondary emotions and intergroup helping. *Group Processes and Intergroup Relations, 10*, 107–118.

Cunha, L. E., Pereira, C. R., Camino, L., Souza de Lima, T. J., & Torres, A. R. (2016). The legitimizing role if accent on discrimination against immigrants. *European Journal of Social Psychology, 46*, 609–620. https://onlinelibrary.wiley.com/doi/abs/10.1002/ejsp.2216

Cupach, W. R., & Imahori, T. T. (1993). Identity management theory: Communication competence in intercultural episodes and relationships. In R. L. Wiseman & J. Koester (Eds.), *Intercultural communication competence* (pp. 112–132). Sage.

Cutrone, P. (2005). A case study examining backchannels between Japanese-British dyads. *Multilingua, 24*, 237–274.

Cypher, J. M. (2008). Disability and parenting: Representations of consequence. In L. B. Arnold (Ed.), *Family communication theories and research* (pp. 355–363). Allyn & Bacon.

DaCosta, K. M. (2007). *Making multiracials: State, family, and market in the redrawing of the color line*. Stanford University Press.

Dainton, M., Zelley, E., & Langan. E. (2003). Maintaining friendships throughout the lifespan. In D. J. Canary & M. Dainton (Eds.), *Maintaining relationships through communication: relational, contextual and cultural Variation* (pp. 79–103). Erlbaum.

Daniels, M. (1999). *Peace is everybody's business: Half a century of peace education with Elizabeth Evans Baker*. Juniata College.

Daniels, M. (2000). *Dancing with words: Signing for hearing children's literacy*. Bergin & Garvey.

Danko, P. W., & Stanley, P. T. (1998). *The millionaire next door: The surprising secrets of America's wealthy*. Simon & Schuster.

Darnell, R. (1985). The language of power in Cree interethnic communication. In N. Wolfson & J. Manes (Eds.), *Languages of inequality* (pp. 61–72). Mouton de Gruyter.

Darvishpour, M. (2002). Immigrant women challenge the role of men: How the changing power relationship within Iranian families in Sweden intensifies family conflicts after immigration. *Journal of Comparative Family Studies, 33,* 271–296.

Day, E. D. M., & Remigy, M. J. (1999). Mexican and French children's conceptions about family: A developmental approach. *Journal of Comparative Family Studies, 30,* 95–112.

de Mooij, M. & Hofstede, G. (2010). The Hofstede model: Applications to global branding and advertising strategy and research. *International Journal of Advertising, 29*(1), 85–110.

Deardorff, D. (2009). Synthesizing conceptualizations of intercultural competence: A summary of emerging themes. In D. Deardorff (Ed.), *The Sage handbook of intercultural competence* (pp. 264–269). Sage.

DeGenova, M. K., & Rice, F. P. (2002). *Intimate relationships, marriages and families* (5th ed.). McGraw-Hill.

Delpit, L. (2006). *Other people's children.* The New Press.

Denson, N., & Chang, M. J. (2009). Racial diversity matters: The impact of diversity-related student engagement and institutional context. *American Educational Research Journal, 46,* 322–353. doi:10.3102/0002831208323278

Denzin, N. (1984). *On understanding emotion.* Jossey Bass.

Derakhshani, T. (2010). Depression: Should we be rid of it? *The Philadelphia Inquirer,* p. E01.

Dessel, A., Rogge, M., & Garlington, S. (2006). Using intergroup dialogue to promote social justice and change. *Social Work, 51*(4), 303–315.

Dessoff, A. (2006). Who's not going abroad? *International Educators, 15*(2), 20–27.

Deutsch, M., & Collins, M. E. (1951). *Interracial housing: A psychological evaluation of a social experiment.* University of Minnesota Press.

Devine, P. G. (1989). Stereotypes and prejudice: Their automatic and controlled components. *Journal of Personality and Social Psychology, 56,* 5–18.

Diamanduros, T., & Downs, E. (2011). Creating a safe school environment: How to prevent cyberbullying at your school. *Library Media Connection, 30*(2), 36–38.

Dibiase, R., & Gunnoe, J. (2004). Gender and culture differences in touching behavior. *The Journal of Social Psychology, 144,* 49–62.

Dietrich, W. (2013). *Elicitive conflict transformation and the transrational shift in peace politics.* Palgrave MacMillan.

Di Marco, D., Hoel, H., & Lewis, D. (2021). Discrimination and exclusion on grounds of sexual and gender identity: Are LGBT people's voices heard at the workplace? *The Spanish Journal of Psychology, 24*(e18), 1–6. doi: https://doi.org/10.1017/SJP.2021.16

Diez Pinto, E. (2004). *Vision Guatemala 1998–2000: Building bridges of trust.* United Nations Development Programme. http://reospartners.com/sites/default/files/Vision%20Guatemala%20Learning% 20History.pdf

Dillon, N. (2008). A tangled web. *The American School Board Journal, 195*(12), 14–17.

Dimock, M. (2019). *Defining generations: Where millennials end and generation Z begins.* Pew Research Center. www.pewresearch.org/fact-tank/2019/01/17/where-millennials-end-and-generation-z-begins/

Dobbin, F., & Kalev, A. (2018). Why doesn't diversity training work? The challenge for industry and academia. *Anthropology Now, 10*(2), 48–55.

Dolby, N. (2004). Encountering an American self: Study abroad and national identity. *Comparative Education Review, 48*(2).

Dong, Q., Day, K., & Collaco, C. (2008, May). *Overcoming ethnocentrism through developing intercultural sensitivity and multiculturalism.* Paper presented at the annual conference of the International Communication Association, Montreal.

Dost, A., & Yagmurlu, B. (2008). Are constructiveness and destructiveness essential features of guilt and shame feelings respectively? *Journal for the Theory of Social Behaviour, 38*(2), 109–129.

Douglas, C., & Jones-Rikkers, C. G. (2001). Study abroad programs and American student worldmindedness: An empirical analysis. *Journal of Teaching in International Business, 13*(1), 55–66.

Downey, L. A., Roberts, J., & Stough, C. (2011). Workplace culture emotional intelligence and trust in the prediction of workplace outcomes. *International Journal of Business Science and Applied Management, 6*(1), 31–40.

Dover, T. L., Kaiser, C. R., & Major, B. (2020). Mixed signals: The unintended effects of diversity initiatives. *Social Issues and Policy Review, 14*(1), 152–181.

Dovidio, J. F., Gaertner, S. L., & Kawakami, K. (2003). The contact hypothesis: The past, present, and the future. *Group Processes and Intergroup Relations, 6*, 5–21.

Dovidio, J. F., Hebl, M., Richeson, J. A., & Shelton, N. (2006). Nonverbal communication, race, and intergroup interaction. In V. Manusov & M. L. Patterson (Eds.), *The Sage handbook of nonverbal communication* (pp. 481–500). Sage.

Dresser, N. (2005). *Multicultural manners*. John Wiley & Sons.

Drexel University School of Education. (2023). *The importance of diversity & multicultural awareness in education*. Drexel.edu. https://drexel.edu/soe/resources/student-teaching/advice/importance-of-cultural-diversity-in-classroom/

Druliner, J. K., & Prichard, H. (2003). "We can handle this ourselves": Learning to negotiate conflicts. In T. Jones & R. Compton (Eds.), *Kids working it out: Stories and strategies for making peace in our schools* (pp. 98–108). Jossey-Bass.

Duncan, B. L. (1976). Differential social perception and attribution of intergroup violence: Testing the lower limits of stereotyping blacks. *Journal of Personality and Social Psychology, 34*(4), 590–598.

Durlak, J. A., Weissberg, R. P., Dymnicki, A. B., Taylor, R. D., & Schellinger, K. B. (2011). The impact of enhancing students' social and emotional learning: A meta-analysis of school-based universal interventions. *Child Development, 82*, 405–432.

Dwairy, M., & Achoui, M. (2009). Adolescents-family connectedness: A first cross-cultural research on parenting and psychological adjustment of children. *Journal of Child & Family Studies, 19*, 8–15.

Earich, G. (2014). *The similarity of differences: Peace Corps*. www.peacecorps.gov/volunteer/response/volstories/earich/

Earley, P. C., & Ang, S. (2003). *Cultural intelligence: Individual interactions across cultures*. Stanford University Press.

Eberhard, D. M., Simons, G. F., & Fennig, C. D. (Eds.). (2022). *Ethnologue: Languages of the world* (25th ed.). SIL International.

Economist, The. (2022, May). *The Chinese-African relationship is important to both sides, but also unbalanced. Special report.* www.economist.com/special-report/2022/05/20/the-chinese-african-relationship-is-important-to-both-sides-but-also-unbalanced

Edwards, J. (2010). *Language diversity in the classroom*. Multilingual Matters.

Efron, D. (1941). *Gesture and environment*. King's Crown Press.

Ehrenreich, B. (2008). *Nickel and dimed: On (not) getting by in America*. Holt Paperbacks.

Ehrenreich, S. (2010). English as a business Lingua Franca in a German multinational corporation. Meeting the challenge. *Journal of Business Communication, 47*, 408–431.

Eid, M., & Diener, E. (2001). Norms for experiencing emotions in different cultures: Inter- and intranational differences. *Journal of Personality and Social Psychology, 81*(5), 869–885.

Ekman, P. (1972). Universals and cultural differences in facial expressions of emotion. In J. Cole (Ed.), *Nebraska symposium on motivation* (pp. 207–283). University of Nebraska Press.

Ekman, P., & Friesen, W. V. (1969). The repertoire or nonverbal behavior: Categories, origins, usage, and coding. *Semiotica, 1*, 49–98.

Ekman, P., & Friesen, W. V. (1976). Measuring facial movement. *Environmental Psychology and Nonverbal Behavior, 1*, 56–75.

Elfenbein, H. A., & Ambady, N. (2002). On the universality and cultural specificity of emotion recognition: A meta-analysis. *Psychological Bulletin, 128*(2), 203–235.

Elfenbein, H. A., Beaupré, M., Levesque, M., & Hess, U. (2007). Toward a dialect theory: Cultural differences in the expression and recognition of posed facial expressions. *Emotion, 7*(1), 131–146.

Elias, M. J., Zins, J. E., Weissberg, R. P., Frey, K. S., Greenberg, M. T., Haynes, N. M., Kessler, R., Schwab-Stone, M. E., & Shriver, T. P. (1997). *Promoting social and emotional learning: Guidelines for educators*. Association for Supervision and Curriculum Development.

Ellis, D. G., & Moaz, I. (2007). Online argument between Israeli Jews and Palestinians. *Human Communication Research, 33*, 291–309.

Endrass, B., Rehm, M., & Andre, E. (2011). Planning small talk behavior with cultural influences for multiagent systems. *Computer Speech and Language, 25*, 158–174.

Engle, L., & Engle, J. (2003). Study abroad levels: Toward a classification of program types. *Frontiers: The Interdisciplinary Journal of Study Abroad, 9*, 1–20.

Erikson, E. H. (1959). *Identity and the life cycle selected papers.* International Universities Press.

Etcoff, N. (1999). *Survival of the prettiest.* Doubleday.

Evans, K. R., & Vaandering, D. (2016). *The little book of restorative justice in education: Fostering responsibility, healing, and hope in schools.* Good Books.

Facio, E. (1996). *Understanding older Chicanas.* Sage.

Fang, X., Sauter, D. A., & Van Kleef, G. A. (2019). Seeing mixed emotions: The specificity of emotion perception from static and dynamic facial expressions across cultures. *Journal of Cross-Cultural Psychology, 49*, 130–148.

Fantini, A. E. (2018). *Intercultural communicative competence in educational exchange: A multinational perspective.* Routledge.

Findlay, A. M., Stam, A., King, R., & Ruiz-Gelices, E. (2018). International opportunities: Searching for the meaning of student migration. *Geographica Helvetica, 60*(3), 192–200.

Federal Bureau of Investigation. (2001). *Hate crime statistics—2001.* www.fbi.gov/about-us/cjis/ucr/hate-crime/2001/hatecrime01.pdf

Federal Bureau of Investigation. (n.d.-a). *Hate crime—Overview.* www.fbi.gov/about us/investigate/civilrights/hate_crimes/overview

Fehr, B. (2000). The life cycle of friendship. In C. Hendrick & S. Hendrick (Eds.), *Close relationships* (pp. 71–85). Sage.

Feiler, B. (2004). *Abraham: A journey to the heart of three faiths.* Harper Perennial.

Fernald, A., & Morikawa, H. (1993). Common themes and cultural variations in Japanese and American mothers' speech to infants. *Child Development, 64*, 637–656.

Fessler, D. M. T. (2004). Shame in two cultures: Implications for evolutionary approaches. *Journal of Cognition & Culture, 4*, 207–262.

Fessler, D. M. T. (2007). From appeasement to conformity: Evolutionary and cultural perspectives on shame, competition, and cooperation. In J. L. Tracy, R. W. Robins, & J. P. Tangey (Eds.), *The self-conscious emotions: Theory and research* (pp. 174–193). Guilford Press.

Field, T. (1999). Preschoolers in America are touched less and are more aggressive than preschoolers in France. *Early Childhood Development Care, 151*, 11–17.

Fisch, S. M., Truglio, R. T., & Cole, C. F. (1999). The impact of *Sesame Street* on preschool children: A review and synthesis of 30 years' research. *Media Psychology, 1*, 165–190.

Fischer, A. H., Manstead, S. R., & Rodriguez-Mosquera, P. M. (1999). The role of honour-related vs. individualistic values in conceptualizing pride, shame, and anger: Spanish and Dutch cultural prototypes. *Cognition and Emotion, 13*, 149–179.

Fischer, K. (2012, June). *Many foreign students are friendless in the U.S.* Chronicle of Higher Education. http://chronicle.com/article/Many-ForeignStudents-Find/132275/

Fischer, M. J. (2008). Does campus diversity promote friendship diversity? A look at interracial friendships in college. *Social Science Quarterly, 89*, 631–655.

Fisher, B., & Specht, D. (1999). Successful aging and creativity later in life. *Journal of Aging Studies, 13*, 457–472.

Fisher, H. (1992). *The anatomy of love.* Fawcett-Columbine.

Fisher, S. W. (1996). The family and the individual: Reciprocal influences. In N. Vanzetti & S. Duck (Eds.), *A lifetime of relationships* (pp. 311–335). Brooks/Cole Publishing.

Fitzpatrick, M. A., & Caughlin, J. P. (2002). Interpersonal communication in family relationships. In M. L. Knapp & J. A. Daly (Eds.), *Handbook of interpersonal communication* (3rd ed., pp. 726–777). Sage.

Foeman, A., & Lawton, B. (2021). *Who am I: Identity in the age of consumer DNA testing.* Solana Beach, CA: Cognella.

Foeman, A. K., & Nance, T. (1999). From miscegenation to multiculturalism: Perceptions and stages of interracial relationship development. *Journal of Black Studies, 29*(4), 540–557.

Foeman, A. K., & Nance, T. (2002). Building new cultures, reframing old images: Success strategies of interracial couples. *The Howard Journal of Communications, 13*(3), 237–249.

Foucart, A., Santamaria-Garcia, H., & Hartsuiker, R. (2019). Short exposure to a foreign accent impacts subsequent cognitive processing. *Neuropsychologia, 129*, 1–9.

Foucault, M. (1980). Truth and power. In G. Gordon (Ed.), *Power/knowledge: Selected interviews and other writings, 1972–1977* (pp. 131–143). Pantheon.

Foucault, M. (2004). Je suis un artificier. In Roger-Pol Droit (Ed.), *Michel Foucault: Entretiens* (pp. 95). Odile Jacob.

Fox, J., & Moreland, J. J. (2015). The dark side of social networking sites: An exploration of the relational and psychological stressors associated with Facebook use and affordances. *Computers in Human Behavior, 45*, 168–176.

Frankenberg, E. (2009a). The demographic context of urban schools and districts. *Equity & Excellence in Education, 42*(3), 255–271.

Frankenberg, E. (2009b). The segregation of American teachers. *Education Policy Analysis Archives, 17*(1), 1–45.

Frankovic, K. (2021, April 21). *Only one third of Americans have a valid passport.* YouGov. https://today.yougov.com/topics/travel/articles-reports/2021/04/21/only-one-third-americans-have-valid-us-passport

Fraser, N. (2007). Creating model citizens for the information age: Canadian Internet policy as civilizing discourse. *Canadian Journal of Communication, 32*(2), 201–218.

Frey, W. H. (2018, March 14). *The US will become "minority white" in 2045, census projects.* Brookings Institution. www.brookings.edu/blog/the-avenue/2018/03/14/the-us-will-become-minority-white-in-2045-census-projects/

Frey, W. H. (2021, September 9). *America's shrinking white population needs to value youthful diversity.* Brookings Institution. www.brookings.edu/blog/the-avenue/2021/09/09/americas-shrinking-white-population-needs-to-value-youthful-diversity

Friedlander, M. L. (1999). Ethnic identity development of internationally adopted children and adolescents: Implications for family therapists. *Journal of Marital and Family Therapy, 25*, 43–60.

Friedman, J. (1994). *Cultural identity and global process.* Sage.

Friend, T. (2010). *Cheerful money: Me, my family, and the last days of WASP splendor.* Back Bay Books.

Fujikane, H. (2003). Approaches to global education in the United States, the United Kingdom and Japan. *International Review of Education, 49*(1/2), 133–152.

Fuller, G. E. (2002). The future of political Islam. *Foreign Affairs, 81*(2), 48–60.

Furnham, A. (1984). Tourism and culture shock. *Annals of Tourism Research, 11*(1), 41–57.

Furnham, A., & Bochner, A. (1986). *Culture shock: Psychological reactions to unfamiliar environments.* Methuen.

Gaertner, S. L., & Dovidio, J. F. (2000). *Reducing intergroup bias: The common ingroup identity model.* Psychology Press.

Gaertner, S. L., & Dovidio, J. F. (2009). A common ingroup identity: A categorization-based approach for reducing intergroup bias. In T. Nelson (Ed.), *Handbook of prejudice, stereotyping, and discrimination* (pp. 489–505). Psychology Press.

Gaines, S. O., & Agnew, C. R. (2003). Relationship maintenance in intercultural couples: An interdependence analysis. In D. J. Canary & M. Dainton (Eds.), *Maintaining relationships through communication* (pp. 229–253). Erlbaum.

Gaines, S. O., & Liu, J. H. (2000). Multicultural/multiracial relationships. In C. Hendrick & S. Hendrick (Eds.), *Close relationships* (pp. 97–111). Sage.

Gallagher, R. J., Reagan, A. J., Danforth, C. M., & Dodds, P. S. (2018). Divergent discourse between protests and counter-protests: #BlackLivesMatter and #AllLivesMatter. *PLoS ONE, 13*(4), 1–23.

Galovan, A. M., Fackrell, T., Buswell, L., Jones, B. L., Hill, E. J., & Carroll, S. J. (2010). The work–family interface in the United States and Singapore: Conflict across cultures. *Journal of Family Psychology, 24*, 646–656.

Galtung, J. (1990). Cultural violence. *Journal of Peace Research, 27*, 291–305.

Galupo, M. P., Bauerband, L. A., Gonzalez, K. A., Hagen, D. B., Hether, S. D., & Krum, T. E. (2014). Transgender friendship experiences: Benefits and barriers of friendships across gender identity and sexual orientation. *Feminism & Psychology, 24*(2), 193–215.

Galvin, K. (2003). International and transracial adoption: A communication research agenda. *Journal of Family Communication, 3*(4), 237–253.

Galvin, K. M., Bylund, C. L., & Brommel, B. J. (2003). *Family communication: Cohesion and change* (6th ed.). Allyn & Bacon.

Ganguly, S. (2021). *Olympics-Athletics-"Hulk" Sanders smashes her limits to Tokyo silver.* Reuters. www.reuters.com/article/us-olympics-2020-ath-idCAKBN2F20Y2

Gardner, E. (2001). The role of media in conflicts. In L. Reychler & T. Paffenholz (Eds.), *Peacebuilding: A field guide.* Lynne Reiner.

Gareis, E. (1995). *Intercultural friendship: A qualitative study.* University Press of America.

Geertz, C. (1973). *Interpretation of culture.* Basic Books.

Georgas, J., Mylonas, K., Bafiti, T., Poortinga, Y. H., Christakopoulou, S., Kagitcibasi, C., . . . Kodiq, Y. (2001). Functional relationships in the nuclear and extended family: A 16-culture study. *International Journal of Psychology, 36*(5), 289–300.

Gerbner, G. (1999). The stories we tell. *Peace Review, 11*(1), 9–16.

Gerbner, G., Gross, L., Morgan, M., Signorielli, N., & Shanahan, J. (2002). Growing up with television: Cultivation processes. In J. Bryant & D. Zillmann (Eds.), *Media effects: Advances in theory and research* (2nd ed., pp. 43–67). Erlbaum.

Gershenson, S., Hansen, M., and Lindsay, C. A. (2021). *Teacher diversity and student success: Why racial representation matters in the classroom.* Harvard Education Press.

Giddens, A. (2002). *Runaway world: How globalization is reshaping our lives.* Profile.

Gilboa, E. (2010). Media and conflict resolution: A framework for analysis. *Marquette Law Review, 93*(1), 87–111.

Gillig, T. K., & Bighash, L. (2019). Genders spaces, gendered friendship networks? Exploring the organizing patterns of LGBTQ youth. *International Journal of Communication, 13,* 4895–2916.

Goetz, J. L., & Keltner, D. (2007). Shifting meanings of self-conscious emotions across cultures: A social-functional approach. In J. L. Tracy, R. W. Robins, & J. P. Tangey (Eds.), *The self-conscious emotions: Theory and research* (pp. 153–173). Guilford Press.

Goff, W. (2011). The shades of grey of cyberbullying in Australian schools. *Australian Journal of Education, 55*(2), 176–181.

Goffman, E. (1974). *Frame analysis: An essay on the organization of experience.* Harper and Row.

Goffman, E. (1986). *Stigma: Notes on the management of spoiled identity.* Touchstone.

Gomez-Banutu, M. (2011). The influence of leadership practice "inspiring a shared vision" on group norms in the organizational culture of financial institutions, in the Gambia, West Africa. *The Journal of American Academy of Business, 17*(1), 156–167.

Gonzales, R. G. (2010). On the wrong side of the tracks: Understanding the effects of school structure and social capital in the educational pursuits of undocumented immigrant students. *Peabody Journal of Education, 85,* 469–485.

Goodnough, A. (2009, July 21). *Harvard professor jailed: Officer is accused of bias.* The New York Times. www.nytimes.com/2009/07/21/us/21gates.html?_r=0

Gopnik, A., & Choi, S. (1990). Do linguistic differences lead to cognitive differences? A cross-linguistic study of semantic and cognitive development. *First Language, 10,* 199–215.

Gordon, S. (2001). New help for disabled moms. *Parenting, 15*(2), 23.

Granel, N., Leyva-Moral, J. M., Morris, J., Šáteková, L., Grosemans, J., Bernabeu-Tamayo, M. D. (2021). Student's satisfaction and intercultural competence development from a short study abroad program: A multiple cross-sectional study. *Nurse Education in Practice, 50,* 1–6.

Graves, S. B. (1999). Television and prejudice reduction: When does television as a vicarious experience make a difference? *Journal of Social Issues, 55,* 707–727.

Greenspan, S. I. (1997). *The growth of the mind and the endangered origins of intelligence.* Addison-Wesley.

Gregory, A., & Evans, K. R. (2020). *The starts and stumbles of restorative justice in education: Where do we go from here?* National Education Policy Center.
https://nepc.colorado.edu/publication/restorative-justice.

Grewal Singh, D. (2008). *Network power: The social dynamics of globalization*. Yale University Press.

Grice, H. P. (1968). Utterer's meaning, sentence meaning, and word meaning. *Foundations of Language, 4*, 225–242.

Grice, H. P. (1975). Logic and conversation. In P. Cole & J. Morgan (Eds.), *Syntax and semantics* (Vol. 3, pp. 22–40). Academic Press.

Grossman, L. (2009, June 17). *Iran's protests: Why Twitter is the medium of the movement*. Time.
www.time.com/time/world/article/0,8599,1905125,00.html

Gudykunst, W. (1998). *Bridging differences: Effective intergroup communication*. Sage.

Gudykunst, W. B., & Matsumoto, Y. (1996). Cross-cultural variability of communication in personal relationships. In W. B. Gudykunst, S. Ting-Toomey, & T. Nishida (Eds.), *Communication in personal relationships across cultures* (pp. 19–56). Sage.

Gudykunst, W. B., & Nishida, T. (1983, May). *Social penetration in Japanese and American close friendships*. Paper presented at the annual convention of the International communication Association, Dallas, TX.

Gudykunst, W. B. & Ting-Toomey, S. (1988). *Culture and interpersonal communication*. Sage.

Gudykunst, W. B., Ting-Toomey, S., Sudweeks, S., & Stewart, L. (1995). *Building bridges: Interpersonal skills for a changing world*. Houghton-Mifflin.

Gullahorn, J. T., & Gullahorn, J. E. (1963). An extension of the U-curve hypothesis. *Journal of Social Issues, 19*, 33–47.

Guobin Y., & Calhoun, C. (2008). Media, power, and protest in China: From the cultural revolution to the Internet. *Harvard Asia Pacific Review, 9*(2), 9–13.

Gupta, U., & Singh, P. (1982). An exploratory study of love and liking and type of marriages. *Indian Journal of Applied Psychology, 19*(2), 92–97.

Gurin, P., Nagda, B., & Lopez, G. (2004). The benefits of diversity in education for democratic citizenship. *Journal of Social Issues, 60*(1), 17–34.

Gurin, P., Peng, T., Lopez, G., & Nagda, B. (1999). Context, identity and intergroup relations. In D. Prentice & D. Miller (Eds.), *Cultural divides: Understanding and overcoming group conflict*. Russell Sage Foundation.

Halabi, R. (Ed.). (2000). *Israeli and Palestinian identities in dialogue: The School for Peace approach*. Rutgers University Press.

Hale, M., Kransdorf, M., & Hamer, L. (2011, July/Aug). Xenophobia in schools. *Educational Studies, 47*(4), 317–322.

Hall, E. T. (1959). *The silent language*. Anchor Books.

Hall, E. T. (1963). A system for the notation of proxemic behavior. *American Anthropologist, 65*, 1003–1026.

Hall, E. T. (1966). *The hidden dimension*. Anchor Books.

Hall, E. T. (1976). *Beyond culture*. Anchor Books.

Hall, E. T. (1983). *The dance of life: The other dimension of time*. Anchor Books.

Hall, E. T. (1990). *Understanding cultural differences: Germans, French, and Americans*. Intercultural Press.

Hall, E. T., & Whyte, W. F. (1966). Intercultural communication: A guide to men of action. In A. G. Smith (Ed.), *Communication and culture* (pp. 567–575). Holt, Rinehart & Winston.

Hallin, D. (1986). *The uncensored war: The media and Vietnam*. Oxford University Press.

Hammer, M. R. (1999). Cross-cultural training: The research connection. In S. M. Fowler & M. G. Mumford (Eds.), *Intercultural sourcebook: Cross-cultural training methods* (Vol. 2, pp. 1–18). Intercultural Press.

Hammer, M. R., & Martin, J. (1992). The effects of cross-cultural training on American managers in a Japanese-American joint venture. *Journal of Applied Communication Research, 20*(2), 161.

Hansel, B., & Grove, N. (1986). International student exchange programs—Are the educational benefits real? *NASSP Bulletin, 70*(487), 84–90.

Harder, D. W., & Zalma, A. (1990). Two promising shame and guilt scales: A construct validity comparison. *Journal of Personality Assessment, 55,* 729–745.

Hardiman, R. (1982). White identity development: A process oriented model for describing the racial consciousness of White Americans. *Dissertation Abstracts International, 43*(1), 104A.

Hardey, M. (2004). Mediated relationships. *Information, Communication and Society, 7*(2), 207–222.

Hargrave, T. D. (1994). *Families and forgiveness: Healing wounds in the intergenerational family.* Brunner/Mazel Publishers.

Harper, D. (2017, November 21). *Starbucks falls short on environmental commitments.* Sierra Club Magazine. www.sierraclub.org/sierra/starbucks-falls-short-on-environmental-commitments

Harris, I. M., & Morrison, M. (2013). *Peace education* (3rd ed.). McFarland & Co.

Harris, T. M. (2000). Interracial dating: The implications of race for initiating a romantic relationship. *The Howard Journal of Communications, 11,* 49–64.

Harris, T. M. (2004). "I know it was the blood": Defining the biracial self in a Euro-American society. In A. Gonzalez, M. Houston, & V. Chen (Eds.), *Our voices: Essays in culture, ethnicity, and communication* (4th ed., pp. 203–210). Roxbury.

Harris, V. W., Skogrand, L., & Hatch, D. (2008). Role of friendship, trust, and love in strong Latino marriages. *Marriage and Family Review, 44,* 455–488.

Harris, S. (2021). *Lawrence man sentenced to 46 months in prison for 'vile' racist harassment of Black neighbor.* WRTV. www.wrtv.com/news/local-news/crime/lawrence-man-sentenced-to-46-months-in-prison-for-vile-racist-harassment-of-black-neighbor

Hatchel, T., Espelage D. L., Huang, Y. (2018). Sexual harassment victimization, school belonging, and depressive symptoms among LGBTQ adolescents: Temporal insights. *American Journal of Orthopsychiatry, 88*(4):422–430.

Hayes, D., & Guardino, M. (2010). Whose views made the news? Media coverage and the march to war in Iraq. *Political Communication, 27,* 59–87.

Hecht, M. L., Jackson, R. L., & Pitts, M. J. (2005). Culture: Intersections of intergroup and identity theories. In J. Harwood & H. Giles (Eds.), *Intergroup communication: Multiple perspectives* (pp. 21–42). Peter Lang.

Heinz, B. (2003). Backchannel responses as strategic responses in bilingual speakers' conversations. *Journal of Pragmatics, 35,* 1113–1142.

Held, D., & McGrew, A. G. (2007). *Globalization theory: Approaches and controversies.* Polity Press.

Helms, J. E., & Carter, R. T. (1990). Development of the White racial identity inventory. In J. E. Helms (Ed.), *Black and White racial identity: Theory, research, and practice* (pp. 67–80). Praeger Press.

Henderson, J. K. (2005). Language diversity in international management teams. *International Studies of Management and Organization, 35,* 66–82.

Hendrickson, B. (2018). Intercultural connectors: Explaining the influence of extra-curricular activities and tutor programs on international student friendship network development. *International Journal of Intercultural Relations, 63,* 1–16.

Heneghan, T. (2010, June 3). *Church rejects Anglican pressure over gay rights.* Reuters. www.reuters.com/article/2010/06/03/us-anglican-gays-episcopal-idUSTRE6522ET20100603

Henry, P. J., & Hardin, C. D. (2006). The contact hypothesis revisited: Status bias in the reduction of implicit prejudice in the United States and Lebanon. *Psychological Science, 17,* 862–868.

Herring, R. D. (1995). Developing biracial ethnic identity: A review of the increasing dilemma. *Journal of Multicultural Counseling and Development, 23,* 29–38.

Herrity, V. A., & Glasman, N. S. (2010). Training administrators for culturally and linguistically diverse school populations: Opinions of expert practitioners. *Journal of School Leadership, 20*(1), 57–76.

Herszenhorn, D. M. (2010, May 28). *House votes to allow "don't ask don't tell" repeal.* The New York Times. www.nytimes.com/2010/05/28/us/politics/28tell.html

Herzig, M., & Chasin, L. (2006). *Fostering dialogue across divides: A nuts and bolts guide from the Public Conversations Project.* Watertown, MA: Public Conversations Project. www.publicconversations.org/docs/resources/Jams_website.pdf

Hewstone, M., & Brown, R. (1986). Contact is not enough: An intergroup perspective on the "contact hypothesis." In M. Hewstone & R. Brown (Eds.), *Contact and conflict in intergroup encounters* (pp. 1–44). Blackwell.

Hochschild, A. R. (1983). *The managed heart: Commercialization of human feeling.* University of California Press.

Hodson, G., Hewstone, M., & Swart, H. (2013). Advances in intergroup contact: Epilogue and future directions. In G. Hodson & M. Hewstone (Eds.), *Advances in intergroup contact.* Psychology Press.

Hoffman, C., Lau, I., & Johnson, D. R. (1986). The linguistic relativity of person cognition: An English-Chinese comparison. *Journal of Personality and Social Psychology, 51*, 1097–1105.

Hofhuis, J., Hanke, K., & Rutten, T. (2019). Social network sites and acculturation of international sojourners in the Netherlands: The mediating role of psychological alienation and online social support. *International Journal of Intercultural Relations, 69*, 120–130.

Hofstede, G. (1980). *Culture's consequences: International differences in work-related values.* Sage.

Hofstede, G. (1983). Dimensions of national cultures in fifty countries and three regions. In J. Deregowski, S. Dziurawiec, & R. Annis (Eds.), *Explorations in cross cultural psychology.* Swets & Zeitlinger.

Hofstede, G. (1986). Cultural differences in teaching and learning. *International Journal of Intercultural Relations, 10*, 301–320.

Hofstede, G. (1991). *Cultures and organizations: Software of the mind.* McGraw-Hill.

Hofstede, G. (2001). *Culture's consequences: Comparing values, behaviors, institutions, and organizations across nations* (2nd ed.). Sage.

Hofstede, G. (2009). *Geert Hofstede—Home.* www.geerthofstede.com

Hofstede, G. (2011). Dimensionalizing cultures: The Hofstede model in context. *Online Readings in Psychology and Culture, 2*(1). http://dx.doi.org/10.9707/2307-0919.1014

Hofstede, G., & Bond, M. H. (1988). Confucius and economic growth: New trends in culture's consequences. *Organizational Dynamics, 16*(4), 4–21.

Hofstede, G., Hofstede, G. J., & Minkov, M. (2010). *Cultures and organizations: Software for the mind.* McGraw-Hill.

Hogg, M. A., & Abrams, D. (1988). *Social identifications: A social psychology of intergroup relations and group processes.* Routledge.

Hogg, M. A., & Vaughan, G. M. (2002). *Social psychology* (3rd ed.).Prentice-Hall.

Hokoda, A., Lu, H.-H. A., & Angeles, M. (2006). School bullying in Taiwanese adolescents. *Journal of Emotional Abuse, 6*(4), 69–90.

Hollenbeck, S. (2008). 2,500 students, 65 languages, and a safe haven for families. *American School Board Journal, 195*(9), 42–43.

Holohan, S. (2005). The racist murder of Stephen Lawrence: Media performance and public transformation. *Sociological Review, 53*, 576–579.

Holtgraves, T. (2002). *Language as social action: Social psychology and language use.* Erlbaum.

Horowitz, J. M. (2019). *Advantages and challenges in country's growing racial and ethnic diversity.* Pew Research Center. www.pewresearch.org/social-trends/wp-content/uploads/sites/3/2019/05/Views-of-diversity_FINAL_05.08.19.pdf

Hossain, Z., & Anziano, M. C. (2008). Mothers' and fathers' involvement with school-age children's care and academic activities in Navajo Indian families. *Cultural Diversity and Ethnic Minority Psychology, 14*(2), 109–117.

Hottela, P. (2004). Culture confusion—Intercultural adaptation in tourism. *Annals of Tourism Research, 31*(2).

Huda. (2010). *Hijab in French schools.* About.com Islam. http://islam.about.com/cs/currenteve (site discontinued).

Hudson, T. D. (2020, September 3). Interpersonalizing cultural difference: A grounded theory of the process of interracial friendship development and sustainment among college students. *Journal of Diversity in Higher Education, 15*(3), 267–287. http://dx.doi.org/10.1037/dhe0000287

Huffman, A. H., Mills, M. J., Howes, S. S., & Albritton, M. D. (2021). Workplace support and affirming behaviors: Moving toward a transgender, gender diverse, and non-binary friendly workplace. *International Journal of Transgender Health, 22*(3), 225–242.

Hung, K., Li, S., & Belk, R. (2007). Global understandings: Female readers' perceptions of the new woman in Chinese advertising. *Journal of International Business Studies, 38*, 1034–1051.

Hurrell, A. C. (2005). Civility in online discussion: The case of the foreign policy dialogue. *Canadian Journal of Communication, 30*(4), 633–648.

Hurtado, S., Dey, E. L., & Trevino, J. G. (1994). *Exclusion or self-segregation? Interaction across racial/ethnic groups on college campuses.* Paper presented at the annual meeting of the American Educational Research Association, New Orleans, LA.

Hymes, D. (1972). On communicative competence. In J. B. Pride & J. Holmes (Eds.), *Sociolinguistics* (pp. 269–293). Penguin Books.

Ibrahim, M., & Forliti, A. (2021). *Militia leader gets 53 years in Minnesota mosque bombing.* Associated Press. apnews.com/article/religion-crime-minnesota-illinois-hate-crimes-3a1819d8ea489a6a9485e60a800c0824

Ierley, A., & Claassen-Wilson, D. (2003). Making things right: Restorative justice for school communities. In T. S. Jones & R. Compton (Eds.), *Kids working it out: Stories and strategies for making peace in our schools* (pp. 199–220). Jossey-Bass.

IIE Open Doors. (2020). *United States hosts over 1 million international students for the fifth consecutive year.* https://opendoorsdata.org/wp-content/uploads/2020/11/Open-Doors-2020-Press-Release.pdf

Imamura, A. E. (1990). Strangers in a strange land: Coping with marginality in international marriage. *Journal of Comparative Family Studies, 21*, 171–191.

Imamura, M., Zhang, Y. B., & Harwood, J. (2011). Japanese sojourners' attitudes toward Americans: Exploring the influences of communication accommodation, linguistic competence, and relational solidarity in intergroup contact. *Journal of Asian Pacific Communication, 21*, 115–132.

Ince, J., Rojas, F., and Davis, C. A. (2016). The social media response to Black Lives Matter: How Twitter users interact with Black Lives Matter through hashtag use. *Ethnic and Racial Studies, 40*(11), 1814–1830.

Info Norden (n.d.) *Parental benefits in Sweden.* Accessed from www.norden.org/en/info-norden/parental-benefits-sweden

Inman, A. G., Altman, A., Kaduvettoor-Davidson, A., Carr, A., & Walker J. A. (2011). Cultural intersections: A qualitative inquiry into the experience of Asian Indian-White interracial couples. *Family Process, 50*(2), 248–266.

International Telecommunication Union. (2022). *Measuring digital development: Facts and Figures 2022.* ITU Publications. www.itu.int/hub/publication/d-ind-ict_mdd-2022/

IRIN. (2006, April 6). *Iraq: Mixed marriages confront sectarian violence.* Irinnews. www.irinnews.org/report.aspx?reportid=26268

Ishii, S., & Bruneau, T. (1988). Silence and silences in cross cultural perspective: Japan and the United States. In L. Samovar & R. Porter (Eds.), *Intercultural communication* (pp. 310–315). Wadsworth.

Isik-Ercan, Z. (2010). Looking at school from the house window: Learning from Turkish-American parents' experiences with early elementary education in the United States. *Early Childhood Education Journal, 38*, 133–142.

Isosavi, J. (2020). Cultural outsiders' evaluations of (im)politeness in Finland and in France. *Journal of Politeness Research, 16*, 249–280.

Israel, E., & Batalova, J. (2021). *International students in the United States.* Migration Policy Institute. www.migrationpolicy.org/article/international-students-united-states-2020

Istanbul Insider, The. (n.d.). *Turkish customs and etiquette.* https://theistanbulinsider.com/turkish-customs-and-etiquette/

Ivie, R. L. (2009). Breaking the spell of war: Peace journalism's democratic prospect. *Javnost-The Public, 16*(4), 5–21.

Izard, C. (1977). *Human emotions.* Plenum.

Jackson, R. L. (1999). White space, White privilege: Mapping discursive inquiry into self. *Quarterly Journal of Speech, 85*, 38–54.

Jackson, R. L. (2002). Cultural contracts theory: Toward and understanding of identity negotiation. *Communication Quarterly, 50*(3/4), 359–367.

Jackson, J. (2005). Assessing intercultural learning through introspective accounts. *Frontiers: The International Journal of Study Abroad, 11*, 165–186.

Jacobs, H. (2019). *KFC is by far the most popular fast food chain in China and it's nothing like the US brand—here's what it's like.* Business Insider.
www.businessinsider.com/most-popular-fast-food-chain-in-china-kfc-photos-2018-4

Jeffrey, L. (2003). *Dialogue on foreign policy: Report on econsultation.* Electronic Commons.

Jensen, I. (2001). *The practice of intercultural communication.*
https://rucforsk.ruc.dk/ws/portalfiles/portal/57416906/jensen-practice.pdf

Ji, L., Zhang, Z., & Nisbett, R. E. (2002). *Culture, language, and categorization.* [Unpublished manuscript]. Queens University.

Jin, C. H., Talbot, R., & Wang, H. L. (2021). *What the new census data shows about race depends on how you look at it.* NPR. www.npr.org/2021/08/13/1014710483/2020-census-data-us-race-ethnicity-diversity

Johnson, A. J., Wittenberg, E., Villagran, M. M., Mazur, M., & Villagran, P. (2004). Relational progression as a dialectic: Examining turning points in communication among friends. *Communication Monographs, 70*, 230–249.

Johnson, D. W., Johnson, R. T., & Tjosvold, D. (2000). Constructive controversy: The value of intellectual opposition. In M. Deutsch & P. Coleman (Eds.), *The handbook of conflict resolution* (pp. 65–85). Jossey-Bass.

Johnson, M. (1992). *A test of wills: Jerry Lewis, Jerry's orphans, and the telethon.* Ragged Edge.
www.ragged-edge-mag.com/archive/jerry92.htm

Johnson, S. M., & O'Connor, E. (2001). *Lesbian and gay parents: The national gay and lesbian family study (APA Workshop 2).* American Psychiatric Association Press.

Jones, S. E. (1994). *The right touch: Understanding and using the language of physical contact.* Hampton Press.

Jones, T. S. (2000). Emotional communication in conflict: Essence and impact. In W. Eadie & P. Nelson (Eds.), *The language of conflict and resolution* (pp. 81–104). Sage.

Jones, T. S. (2006). Conflict resolution education: Issues, answers and directions. In J. G. Oetzel & S. Ting-Toomey (Eds.), *The Sage handbook of conflict communication: Integrating theory, research and practice* (pp. 239–266). Sage.

Jones, T. S. (2008). *Conflict resolution education in teacher education (CRETE) project, year one report* [Unpublished report]. Temple University College of Education.

Jones, T. S. (2012). Building constructive conflict communities through conflict resolution education. In J. G. Oetzel and S. Ting-Toomey (Eds.), *The Sage handbook of conflict communication: integrating theory, research and practice* (2nd ed., pp. 403–427). Sage.

Jones, T. S., & Compton, R. (Eds.). (2003). *Kids working it out: Stories and strategies for making peace in our schools.* Jossey-Bass.

Jones, T. S., & Remland, M. S. (1993). Nonverbal communication and conflict escalation: An attribution-based model. *International Journal of Conflict Management, 4*(2), 119–138.

Jones, T. S, Remland, M., & Sanford, R. (2007). *Interpersonal communication through the lifespan.* Pearson Education.

Juvonen, J., & Graham, S. (2001). *Peer harassment in school: The plight of the vulnerable and victimized.* Guilford Press.

Kacen, L. (2006). Spousal abuse among immigrants from Ethiopia in Israel. *Journal of Marriage & Family, 68*, 1276–1290.

Kacen, L., & Keidar, L. (2006). *Intimate violence among immigrants from Ethiopia: Evaluation of prevention project 1999–2003.* Center for Qualitative Methodologies, Ben-Gurion University of the Negev.

Kahn, D. (1998). Mixed marriages in Islam: An anthropological perspective on Pakistan. *Journal of the Anthropological Society of Oxford, 29*, 5–28.

Kale, D. (1994). Peace as an ethic for intercultural communication. In L. Samovar, R. Porter, & E. McDaniel (Eds.), *Intercultural communication: A reader* (pp. 422–426). Cengage Learning.

Kalev, A., Dobbin, F., & Kelly, E. (2006). Best practices or best guesses? Assessing the efficacy of corporate affirmative action and diversity policies. *American Sociological Review, 71*(4), 589–617.

Kamperidou, I. (2008). Promoting a culture of peacemaking: Peace games and peace education. *International Journal of Physical Education, 45*(4), 176–188.

Kanazawa, S. (2002). Bowling with our imaginary friends. *Evolution and Human Behavior, 23,* 161–171.

Kasanga, L., & Lwanga-Lumu, J. (2007). Cross-cultural linguistic realization of politeness: A study of apologies in English and Setswana. *Journal of Politeness Research: Language, Behavior, Culture, 3*(1), 65–92.

Katsh, E., & Rule, C. (2016). What we know and need to know about online dispute resolution. *South Carolina Law Review, 67*(2), 329–344.

Kauffman, N., Martin, J., & Weaver, H. (1992). *Students abroad, strangers at home: Education for a global society.* Intercultural Press.

Keele, R. L., & Hammond, S. (1988, September). Support systems: To give and to receive. *BYU Today,* 1–2.

Keen, K. (2013). *My brother has been shot: Witness says homicide started with "mad-dogging."* KGUN. www.jrn.com/kgun9/news/195455871.html

Keitner, G. I., Ryan, C. E., Fodor, J., Miller, I. W., Epstein, N. B., & Bishop, D. S. (1990). A cross-cultural study of family functioning. *Contemporary Family Therapy: An International Journal, 12,* 439–454.

Keltner, D., Young, R. C., & Buswell, B. (1997). Appeasement in human emotion, social practice, and personality. *Aggressive Behavior, 23,* 359–375.

Kemper, T. D. (1978). *A social interactional theory of emotions.* Wiley.

Kemper, T. D. (1993). Sociological models in the explanation of emotion. In M. Lewis & J. M. Haviland (Eds.), *Handbook of emotions* (pp. 41–52). Guilford Press.

Kenan, S. (2005). Reconsidering peace and multicultural education after 9/11: The case of educational outreach for Muslim sensitivity curriculum in New York City. *Educational Sciences: Theory & Practice, 5,* 172–180.

Khazan, O. (2021). *Americans say immigrants should learn English. But U.S. policy makes that hard.* The Atlantic. www.theatlantic.com/politics/archive/2021/06/why-cant-immigrants-learn-english/619053/

Kibria, N., & Jain, S. (2009). Cultural impacts of *Sisimpur, Sesame Street,* in rural Bangladesh: Views of family members and teachers. *Journal of Comparative Family Studies, 40*(1), 57–75.

Kim, J., & Hatfield, E. (2004). Love types and subjective well-being: A cross-cultural study. *Social Behavior & Personality: An International Journal, 32*(2), 173–182.

Kim, M. (2005). Culture-based conversational constraints theory: Individual and culture-level analyses. In W. B. Gudykunst (Ed.), *Theorizing about intercultural communication* (pp. 93–117). Sage.

Kim, M. S. (2002). *Non-Western perspectives on human communication: Implications for theory and practice.* Sage.

Kim, Y. Y. (1988). Communication and acculturation. In L. A. Samovar & R. E. Porter (Eds.), *Intercultural communication: A reader* (5th ed., pp. 344–352). Wadsworth.

Kim, Y. Y. (1997). Communication patterns of foreign immigrants in the process of acculturation. *Human Communication Research, 41,* 66–76.

Kim, Y. Y. (2001). *Becoming intercultural: An integrated theory of communication and cross-cultural adaptation.* Sage.

Kim, Y. Y. (2005). Inquiry in intercultural communication and development communication. *Journal of Communication, 55*(3), 554–577.

Kim, Y. Y. (2009). The identity factor in intercultural competence. In D. Deardorff (Ed.), *The Sage handbook of intercultural competence* (pp. 53–62). Sage.

Kim, Y. Y., & Ruben, B. (1988). Intercultural transformation: A systems theory. In Y. Y. Kim & W. Gudykunst (Eds.), *Theories in intercultural communication.* Sage.

Kitayama, S., & Markus, H. R. (Eds). (1994). *Emotion and culture: Empirical studies of mutual influence.* American Psychological Association.

Kitayama, S., Markus, H. R., Kurokawa, M., & Negishi (1993). *The interpersonal nature of emotion: Cross-cultural evidence and implications.* [Unpublished manuscript]. University of Oregon.

Kline, S., Horton, B., & Zhang, S. (2005, May). *How we think, feel and express love: A cross-cultural comparison between American and East Asian cultures.* Paper presented to the International Communication Association, New York.

Kluckhohn, F., & Strodtbeck, F. (1961). *Variations in value orientation.* Row & Peterson.

Kluger, N., Misery, L., Seite, M., & Taieb, C. (2018). Regrets after tattooing and tattoo removal in the general population of France. *Journal of the European Academy of Dermatology and Venereology, 33,* E157–E159.

Knapp, M. & Hall, J. (2008). *Nonverbal communication in human interaction.* Cengage.

Knapp, M. L., & Vangelisti, Anita L. (1996). *Interpersonal communication and human relationships.* Allyn & Bacon.

Ko, S., Lee, T., Yoon, H., Kwon, J., & Mather, M. (2010). How does context affect assessments of facial emotion? The role of culture and age. *Psychology and Aging, 26,* 48–59.

Kochanek, K. D., Anderson, R. N., and Arias, E. (2018). *Changes in life expectancy at birth, 2010–2018.* CDC. www.cdc.gov/nchs/data/hestat/life-expectancy/life-expectancy-2018.htm

Kochman, T. (1983). *Black and White styles in conflict.* University of Chicago Press.

Kohls, R. (1984). *The values Americans live by.* Meridian House.

Konan, P. N., Chatard, A., Selimbegović, L., & Mugny, G. (2010). Cultural diversity in the classroom and its effects on academic performance: A cross-national perspective. *Social Psychology, 41,* 230–237.

Kornhaber, A. (2002). *The grandparent guide.* Contemporary Books.

Kotzur, P. & Wagner, U. (2021). The dynamic relationship between contact opportunities, positive and negative intergroup contact, and prejudice: A longitudinal investigation. *Journal of Personality and Social Psychology, 120,* 418–442.

Koutsantoni, D. (2007). "I can now apologize to you twice from the bottom of my heart": Apologies in Greek reality TV. *Journal of Politeness Research: Language, Behavior, Culture, 3*(1), 93–123.

Kovecses, A. (2000). *Metaphor and emotion: Language, culture and body in human feeling.* Cambridge University Press.

Kowalczyk, J. (2011). "The immigration problem" and European education reforms: From the education of migrants' children to intercultural education. *European Education, 42*(4), 5–24.

Kramarae, C. (1981). *Women and men speaking: Frameworks for analysis.* Newbury House.

Kreider, R. M. & Lofquist, D. A. (2014). *Adopted children and stepchildren: 2010.* U.S. Census Bureau. www.census.gov/prod/2014pubs/p20-572.pdf

Kreisberg, L. (1998). *Constructive conflicts: From escalation to resolution.* Rowman & Littlefield.

Kriesberg, L. (2003). *Identity issues.* Beyond Intractability.org. www.beyondintractability.org/essay/identity_issues/

Krys, K. (2016). Be careful where you smile: Culture shapes judgments of intelligence and honesty of smiling individuals. *Journal of Nonverbal Behavior, 40,* 101–116.

Kudo, K., & Simkin, K. A. (2003). Intercultural friendship formation: The case of Japanese students at an Australian University. *Journal of Intercultural Studies, 24,* 94–114.

Kuhn, M. (1991). *No stone unturned: The life and times of Maggie Kuhn.* Ballantine Books.

Kuldas, S., Dupont, M., Foody, M. (2021). Ethnicity-based bullying: Suggestions for future research on classroom ethnic composition. In P. K. Smith and James O'Higgins Norman (Eds.), *The Wiley Blackwell handbook of bullying: A comprehensive and international review of research and intervention* (pp. 252–272). Wiley-Blackwell.

Kuppens, P., Realo, A., & Diener, E. (2008). The role of positive and negative emotions in life satisfaction judgment across nations. *Journal of Personality & Social Psychology, 95,* 66–75.

Kurylo, A. (Ed.). (2013). *Inter/cultural communication: Representation and construction of culture.* Sage.

Kwan, I., Dickson, K., Richardson, M., MacDowall, W., Burchett, H., Stansfield, C., Brunton, G., Sutcliffe, K., Thomas, J. (2020). Cyberbullying and children and young people's mental health: A systematic map of systematic reviews. *Cyberpsychology, Behavior, and Social Networking, 23*(2):72–82.

Ladegaard, H. (2007). Global culture—myth or reality? Perceptions of "national cultures" in a global corporation. *Journal of Intercultural Communication Research, 36,* 139–163.

Laird, J. (2003). Lesbian and gay families. In F. Walsh (Ed.), *Normal family processes: Growing diversity and complexity* (3rd ed., pp. 176–209). Guilford Press.

Lambert, S. (2005). Gay and lesbian families: What we know and where to go from here. *Family Journal, 13*(1), 43–52.

Lande, B. (1998). *Strangers in the world: An ethnographic study of social change in Amish society.*
www.windycreek.com/Brian/amishsocialchangeinterview.html

Lauring, J. (2011). Intercultural organizational communication: The social organizing of interaction in international encounters. *Journal of Business Communication, 48,* 231–255.

Lawton, B., Foeman, A., & Braz, M. (2013). Interracial couples' conflict styles on educational issues. *Journal of Intercultural Communication Research, 42,* 35–53.

Lawton, B., Foeman, A., & Brown, L. (2013). Upper/middle class well-educated interracial couples' children. *Howard Journal of Communications, 24*(3), 215–238.

Lazare, A. (1995, January/February). Go ahead and say you're sorry. *Psychology Today, 76,* 40–43.

Lazarus, R. S. (1991). *Emotion and adaptation.* Oxford University Press.

LeBaron, M. (2003). Cultural and worldview frames. In G. Burgess & H. Burgess (Eds.), *Beyond intractability.* Conflict Research Consortium, University of Colorado, Boulder.
www.beyondintractability.org/essay/cultural-frames

Lederach, J. P. (1996). *Preparing for peace: Conflict transformation across cultures.* Syracuse University Press.

Lederach, J. P. (2003). Conflict transformation. In G. Burgess & H. Burgess (Eds.), *Beyond intractability.* Conflict Information Consortium, University of Colorado, Boulder.
www.beyondintractability.org/essay/transformation

Lederach, J. P. (2014). *The little book of conflict transformation.* Good Books.

Lee, P. (2006). Bridging cultures: Understanding the construction of relational identity in intercultural friendship. *Journal of Intercultural Communication Research, 35,* 3–22.

Lee, P. (2008). Stages and transitions of relational identify formation in intercultural friendship: Implications for identity management theory. *Journal of Intercultural Studies, 1,* 51–69.

Lee, S. J. (1996). *Unraveling the "model minority" stereotype: Listening to Asian American youth.* Teachers College Press.

The Legacy of Hope Foundation. (n.d.). *Transcript of statement of apology.* www.legacyofhope.ca/about-residential-schools/church-government-of-canada-apologies/the-day-of-the-apology

LePoire, B. A. (2006). *Family communication: Nurturing and control in a changing world.* Sage.

Lester, E., & Roberts, P. S. (2009). How teaching world religions brought a truce to the culture wars in Modesto, California. *British Journal of Religious Education, 31*(3), 187–199.

Levine, T. R., Park, H. S., & Kim, R. (2007). Some conceptual and theoretical challenges for cross-cultural communication research in the 21st century. *Journal of Intercultural Communication Research, 36,* 205–221.

Lewin, R. (2009). Introduction: The quest for global citizenship through study abroad. In R. Lewin (Ed.), *The handbook of practice and research in study abroad: Higher education and the question for global citizenship.* Routledge.

Lewis, H. B. (1976). *Psychic war in men and women.* New York University Press.

Lewis, M. (1992). *Shame: The exposed self.* Free Press.

Lewis, M. (1993). Self-conscious emotions: Embarrassment, pride, shame, and guilt. In M. Lewis & J. M. Haviland (Eds.), *Handbook of emotions* (pp. 563–573). Guilford Press.

Lewis, M., Haviland-Jones, J. M., & Barrett L. F. (Eds.). (2008). *Handbook of emotions* (3rd ed.). Guilford Press.

Lewis, M., Takai-Kawakami, K., Kawakami, K., & Sullivan, M. W. (2010). Cultural differences in emotional responses to success and failure. *International Journal of Behavioral Development, 34,* 53–61.

Lewis, R. (2018). *When cultures collide: Leading across cultures* (4th ed.). Nicholas Brealey Publishing.

Leyens, J. P., Cortes, B., Demoulin, S., Dovidio, J. F., Fiske, S. T., Gaunt, R., . . . Vaes, J. (2003). Emotional prejudice, essentialism, and nationalism: The 2002 Tajfel Lecture. *European Journal of Social Psychology, 33,* 703–717.

Livingston, G., & Brown, A. (2017). *Intermarriage in the U.S. 50 years after* Loving v. Virginia. Pew Research Center. www.pewresearch.org/social-trends/2017/05/18/intermarriage-in-the-u-s-50-years-after-loving-v-virginia/

Li, J. (2010). "My home and my school": Examining immigrant adolescent narratives from the critical sociocultural perspective. *Race, Ethnicity & Education, 13*(1), 119–137.

Li, J., Wang, L., & Fischer, K. W. (2004). The organisation of Chinese shame concepts. *Cognition and Emotion, 18*(6), 767–797.

Lichty, L. F., Torres, J. M. C., Valenti, M. T., Valenti, M. T., & Buchanan, N. T. (2008). Sexual harassment policies in K–12 schools: Examining accessibility to students and content. *Journal of School Health, 78*, 607–614.

Liebes, T., & Kampf, Z. (2009). Performance journalism: The case of media's coverage of war and terror. *Communication Review, 12*, 239–249.

Liem, R., Lim, B. A., & Liem, J. H. (2000). Acculturation and emotion among Asian Americans. *Cultural Diversity and Ethnic Minority Psychology, 6*(1), 13–31.

Lin, Y., & Rancer, A. S. (2003). Ethnocentrism, intercultural communication apprehension, intercultural willingness to communicate, and intentions to participate in an intercultural dialogue program: Testing a proposed model. *Communication Research Reports, 20*, 62–72.

Linder, R. (2009). Voices of American teens project helps young adolescents explore cultural diversity. *Middle School Journal, 40*(4), 13–19.

Lindner, E. (2006). *Making enemies: Humiliation and international conflict.* Praeger Security International.

Liska, J. & Cronkhite, G. (1995). *An ecological perspective on human communication theory.* Harcourt Brace.

Liss, K. (2004). *Help increase the peace program manual: Empowering youth through conflict resolution and community building* (3rd ed.). American Friends Service Committee.

The Listening Project. (n.d.). *Listening Project.* www.listeningproject.info/

ListVerse.com. (2010). *The ultimate book of top ten lists: A mind-boggling collection of fun, fascinating and bizarre facts on movies, music, sports, crime, celebrities, history, trivia and more.* Ulysses Press.

Littlejohn, S. (2021). *Theories of human communication* (12th ed.). Waveland Press.

Liu, S., Wang, Y., & Nuttall, A. K. (2020). Cross-race and cross-ethnic friendships and psychological well-being trajectories among Asian American adolescents: Variations by school context. *Developmental Psychology, 56*(11), 2121–2136.

Lohrenscheit, C. (2002). International approaches to human rights education. *International Review of Education, 48*(3/4), 173–185.

Lu, Y. & Hsu, C.-F. (2008). Willingness to communicate in intercultural interactions between Chinese and Americans. *Journal of Intercultural Communication Research, 37*, 75–88

Lubrano, A. (2005). *Limbo: Blue-collar roots, white-collar dreams.* Wiley.

Lustig, M. W., & Koester, J. (2006). *Intercultural competence: Interpersonal communication across cultures.* Allyn & Bacon.

Lustig, R. (2018). *Can English remain the "world's favourite" language?* BBC News. www.bbc.com/news/world-44200901.

Lysgaard, S. (1955). Adjustment in foreign society: Norwegian Fulbright grantees visiting the United States. *International Social Science Bulletin, 7*, 45–51.

MacKinnon, C. (1999). *Toward a feminist theory of the state.* Harvard University Press.

Mahoney, J. L., Durlak, J. A., and Weissberg, R. P. (2018). An update on social and emotional learning outcome research. *Phi Delta Kappan, 100*(4), 18–23.

Maiese, M. (2003). Peacebuilding. In G. Burgess & H. Burgess (Eds.), *Beyond intractability.* Conflict Information Consortium, University of Colorado, Boulder. www.beyondintractability.org/essay/peacebuilding

Maitland, C., & Bauer, J. (2001). National level culture and global diffusion: The case of the Internet. In C. Ess (Ed.), *Culture, communication, technology: Toward an intercultural global village* (pp. 87–120). State University of New York Press.

Mandel, J. (2006). The production of a beloved community: *Sesame Street*'s answer to America's inequalities. *Journal of American Culture, 29*(1), 3–13.

Maner, J. K., Delton, A., Kenrick, D., Becker, D., Robertson, T., Hofer, B., Neuberg, S., & Butner, J. (2005). Functional projection: How fundamental social motives can bias interpersonal perception. *Journal of Personality and Social Psychology, 88*, 63–78.

Mao, Y. (2007). *Communicating worldviews in cross-cultural friendships: Communication adaptability, interaction involvement and relational communication.* National Communication Association. Paper submitted to International and Intercultural Communication Division.

Marion, M., Rousseau, J., & Gollin, K. (2009). Connecting our villages: The Afghan sister schools project at the Carolina friends school. *Peace & Change, 34,* 548–570.

Markus, H. R., & Kitayama, S. (1991). Culture and the self: Implications for cognition, emotion, and motivation. *Psychological Review, 98,* 224–253.

Markus, H. R., & Kitayama, S. (1994). The cultural construction of self and emotion: Implications for social behavior. In S. Kitayama & H. M. Markus (Eds.), *Culture, self, and emotion* (pp. 89–130). American Psychological Association.

Marlow, M. L., & Giles, H. (2010). "We won't get ahead speaking like that!" Expressing and managing language criticism in Hawaii. *Journal of Multilingual and Multicultural Development, 31,* 237–251.

Marquardt, M., & Horvath, L. (2001). *Global teams: How top multinationals span boundaries and cultures with high-speed teamwork.* Davies-Black Publishing.

Martin, J. N., & Nakayama, T. (2000). *Intercultural communication in contexts* (2nd ed.). Mayfield.

Mas'udah, D. (2017). The use of social media in intercultural friendship development. *Profetik Jurnal Komunikasi, 10*(1), 5–20.

Masuda, T. & Nisbett, R. E. (2001). Attending holistically vs. analytically: Comparing the context sensitivity of Japanese and Americans. *Journal of Personality and Social Psychology, 81,* 922–934.

Masuda, T., Ellsworth, P. C., Mesquita, B., Leu, J., Tanida, S., & Veerdonk, E. V. (2008). Placing the face in context: Cultural differences in the perception of facial emotion. *Journal of Personality and Social Psychology, 94,* 365–381.

Market Line. (2022). *KFC sends Chinese consumers into frenzy with new promotion.* Verdict Food Service. www.verdictfoodservice.com/comment/kfc-chinese-consumers/

Matsumoto, D. (1990). Cultural similarities and differences in display rules. *Motivation and Emotion, 14,* 195–214.

Matsumoto, D. (1991). Cultural influences on facial expressions of emotion. *Southern Communication Journal, 56,* 128–137.

Matsumoto, D., Leroux, J. A., & Yoo, S. H. (2005). Emotion and intercultural communication. *Kwansei Gakuin University Journal, 99,* 15–38.

Matsumoto, D., Nezlek, J. B., & Koopmann, B. (2007). Evidence for universality in phenomenological emotion response system coherence. *Emotion, 7*(1), 57–67.

Matsumoto, D., Yoo, S. H., Fontaine. J., & 56 members of the Multinational Study of Cultural Display Rules. (2009). Hypocrisy or maturity? Culture and context differentiation. *European Journal of Personality, 23*(3), 251–264.

Matsumoto, D., Yoo, S., Hirayama, S., & Petrova, G. (2005). Development and validation of a measure of display rule knowledge. *Emotion, 5,* 23–40.

Maurer, R. (2011). *American workforce's incoming generation most diverse, startlingly least educated.* Society for Human Resource Management. www.shrm.org/about/news/pages/leasteducated.aspx

Mauro, R., Sato, K., & Tucker, J. (1992). The role of appraisal in human emotions: A cross-cultural study. *Journal of Personality and Social Psychology, 62,* 301–317.

McCall, L. (2005). The complexity of intersectionality. *Signs, 3,* 1771–1800.

McCarthy, A., Lee, K., Itakura, S., & Muir, D. (2006). Cultural display rules drive eye gaze during thinking. *Journal of Cross-Cultural Psychology, 37,* 717–722.

McCarthy, A., Lee, K., Itakura, S., & Muir, D. (2008). Gaze displays when thinking depends on culture and context. *Journal of Cross-Cultural Psychology, 39,* 716–729.

McClone, M., & Breckinridge, B. (2010, September). *Why the brain doubts a foreign accent.* Scientific American. www.scientificamerican.com/ article/the-brain-doubts-accent/

McCrae, R. P., Terracciano, A., DeFruyt, F., DeBolle, M., Gelfand, M. J., Costa, P. T., & 39 Collaborators of the Adolescent Personality Profiles of Cultures Project. (2010). The validity and structure of culture-level personality scores. *Journal of Personality, 78,* 815–838.

McCullough, M. E., Pargament, K. I., & Thoreson, C. E. (2000). *Forgiveness: Theory, research and practice.* Guilford Press.

McDonough, T. B. (2005). Intercultural forgiveness: The conditions for the possibility of peace. *Philosophy of Education Yearbook, 1,* 96–98.

McFarland, L. A., & Ployhart, R. E. (2015). Social media: A contextual framework to guide research and practice. *Journal of Applied Psychology, 100,* 1653–1677.

McGoldrick, M. (2005). Irish families. In M. McGoldrick, J. Giordano, & N. Garcia-Preto (Eds.), *Ethnicity and family therapy* (3rd ed., pp. 595–615). Guilford Press.

McGoldrick, M., Giordano, N., & Garcia Preto, X. (2005). *Ethnicity and family therapy* (3rd ed.). Guilford Press.

McGovern, K. (2019). *Why did English become the global language?* Medium. https://medium.com/english-language-faq/why-did-english-become-the-global-language-9bbc14b532cd

McIntosh, P. (1990). White privilege: Unpacking the invisible knapsack. *Independent School, 49*(2), 31–36.

McKeown, J. (2009). *The first time effect: The impact of study abroad on college student intellectual development.* State University of New York Press.

McKinney, K. D. (2008). Confronting young people's perceptions of Whiteness: Privilege or liability? *Sociology Compass, 2,* 1303–1330.

McShane, L. (2010, June). *Happy birthday, Adolf Hitler! Boy with Nazi leader's name denied ShopRite cake.* New York Daily News. www.nydailynews.com/news/world/happy-birthday-adolf-hitler-boy-nazi-leader-denied-shoprite-cake-article-1.358050

McWhorter, J. (2020). *The coronavirus generation will use language differently.* Middlebury Language Schools Blog. www.middlebury.edu/language-schools/blog/coronavirus-generation-will-use-language-differently

Medora, N. P., Larson, J. H. Hortagsu, N., & Dave, P. (2002). Perceived attitudes towards romanticism: A cross-cultural study of American, Asian Indian, and Turkish young adults. *Journal of Comparative Family Studies, 33,* 155–178.

Meng, Q., Li, J., & Zhu, C. (2021). Towards an ecological understanding of Chinese international students' intercultural interactions in multicultural contexts: Friendships, inhibiting factors and effects on global competence. *Current Psychology, 40,* 1517–1530.

Menshikova, G., Saveleva, O., & Zinchenko, Y. P. (2018). The study of ethnic attitudes during interactions with avatars in virtual environments. *Psychology in Russia: State of the Art, 11,* 20–31.

Meredith, L. (2011, July 15). *Muslim woman makes history at weightlifting event.* The Seattle Times. www.seattletimes.com/sports/muslim-woman-makes-history-at-weightlifting-event/

Mesquita, B., & Albert, D. (2007). The cultural regulation of emotion. In J. J. Gross (Ed.), *Handbook of emotion regulation* (pp. 486–503). Guilford Press.

Meyer, B. (2002). Extraordinary stories: Disability, queerness and feminism. *NORA, 3,* 168–173.

Michelman, S. O., & Erekosima, T. V. (1992). Kalabari dress in Nigeria: Visual analysis and gender implications. In R. Barnes & J. B. Eicher (Eds.), *Dress and gender* (pp. 164–182). Berg.

Miguel, C. (2016). Visual intimacy on social media: From selfies to the co-construction of intimacies through shared pictures. *Social Media + Society, 2*(2). https://doi.org/10.1177/2056305116641705

Millar, F. E., & Rogers, L. E. (1987). Relational dimensions of interpersonal dynamics. In M. E. Roloff & G. R. Miller (Eds.), *Interpersonal processes: New directions in communication research* (pp. 39–62). Sage.

Millbank, J. (2003, November). From here to maternity: A review of the research on lesbian and gay families. *Australian Journal of Social Issues, 38,* 541–600.

Miller, G. W., III. (2009, September 1). *Asian students under assault seeking refuge from school violence.* Philadelphia Weekly. www.philadelphiaweekly.com/news-and-opinion/Asian-Students-Under-Assault.html?page=4&comments=1&showAll

Miller, W. I. (1997). *The anatomy of disgust.* Harvard University Press.

Mitchell, C. (2003). Beyond resolution: What does conflict transformation actually transform? *Peace Research Abstracts, 40*(2), 123–261.

Miyahara, A. (1986). Toward theorizing Japanese interpersonal communication competence from a non-western perspective. *American Communication Journal, 3*, 279–305.

Moghadam, A. H., & Assar, P. (2008). The relationship between national culture and e-adoption: A case study of Iran. *American Journal of Applied Sciences, 5*, 369–377.

Mohanty, S. K., & Arunpasad, P. (2020). Identification of drivers of employee engagement in Indian power companies. *International Journal of Productivity and Performance Management, 70*(6), 1263–1290.

Mojon, J. B. (2009, October 5). *Fifteen years after the genocide: Reconciliation, hope and development*. Millennium Villages. http://millenniumvillages.org/field-notes/fifteen-years-after-genocide-reconciliation-hope-and-development/

Mokros, H. B. (2003). Other matters: The achievement of identity through otherness. In H. B. Mokros (Ed.), *Identity matters: Communication-based explorations and explanations* (pp. 239–275). Hampton Press.

Molinsky, A. L., Krabbenhoft, M. A., Ambady, N., & Choi, Y. S. (2005). Cracking the nonverbal code: Intercultural competence and gesture recognition across cultures. *Journal of Cross-Cultural Psychology, 36*, 380–395.

Mollov, B. (2006, June). *Results of Israeli and Palestinian student interactions in CMC: An analysis of attitude changes toward conflicting parties*. Paper presented at the annual meeting of the International Communication Association, Dresden, Germany.

Montgomery, G., & Zhang, Y. B. (2018). Intergroup anxiety and willingness to accommodate: Exploring the effects of accent stereotyping and social attraction. *Journal of Language and Social Psychology, 37*, 330–349.

Monzon, J. (2007). Termination of employment in Spain. *International Labor Organization.* www.ilo.org (page discontinued).

Moodley, L., Kuyoro, M., Holt, T., Leke, A., Madgavkar, A., Krishnan, M., and Akintayo, F. (2019). *The power of parity: Advancing women's equality in Africa*. McKinsey Global Institute. www.mckinsey.com/featured-insights/gender-equality/the-power-of-parity-advancing-womens-equality-in-africa

Moody, J. (2001). Race, school integration, and friendship segregation in America. *American Journal of Sociology, 107*, 679–716.

Moore, T. (2009, December 8). *Where are Tiger's 'Cablinasian' backers?* Golf Fanhouse. http://golf.fanhouse.com/2009/12/08/where-are-tigers-cabalasian-backers/70 (site discontinued).

Mor, Y., Ron, Y. & Maoz, I. (2016). "Likes" for peace: Can Facebook promote dialogue in the Israeli-Palestinan conflict? *Media and Communication, 4*, 15–26.

Moran, K. (2006). The global expansion of children's television: A case study of the adaptation of *Sesame Street* in Spain. *Learning, Media & Technology, 31*, 287–300.

Moreau, R. (2010, December). *Do the Taliban get PTSD?* Newsweek. www.newsweek.com/do-taliban-get-ptsd-68973

Morgan, S., & Aasaratnam, L. (2003). Intercultural friendships as social excitation: Sensation seeking as a predictor of intercultural friendship seeking behavior. *Journal of Intercultural Communication Research, 32*, 175–186.

Morita, A. (1986). *Made in Japan*. Penguin.

Morris, D. (1977). *Manwatching: A field guide to human behavior*. Abrams.

Morris, D. (1994). *Bodytalk: The meaning of human gestures*. Crown.

Morris, M. W., & Peng, K. (1994). Culture and cause: American and Chinese attributions for social and physical events. *Journal of Personality and Social Psychology, 67*, 949–971.

Morris, N. (2021). Learning probability in the Kingdom of Tonga: the influence of language and culture. *Educational Studies in Mathematics 107*, 111–134.

Morrison, D. (1992). *Television and the Gulf War*. John Libbey.

Morrison, K., & Ybarra, O. (2008). The effects of realistic threat and group identification on social dominance orientation. *Journal of Experimental Social Psychology, 44*, 156–163.

Mortazavi, S., Pedhiwala, N., Shafiro, M., & Hammer, L. (2009). Work-family conflict related to culture and gender. *Community, Work & Family, 12*, 251–273.

Morten, G., & Atkinson, D. R. (1983). Minority identity development and preference for counselor race. *Journal of Negro Education, 52*, 156–161.

Mortenson, S. T. (2006). Cultural differences and similarities in seeking social support as a response to academic failure: A comparison of American and Chinese college students. *Communication Education, 55*(2), 127–146.

Mortenson, S. T., Burleson, B. R., Feng, B., & Liu, M. (2009). Cultural similarities and differences in seeking social support as a means of coping: A comparison of European Americans and Chinese and an evaluation of the mediating effects of self-construal. *Journal of International and Intercultural Communication, 2*, 208–239.

MSNBC. (2006, January 16). *Africa's first female president.* www.msnbc.msn.com/id/10865705/

0Murray, C. (2008, November). *Presenting media representation: Influence on the African American culture.* Paper presented to the National Communication Association, New York.

Nadler, L. B., Nadler, M. K., & Broome, B. J. (1985). Culture and the management of conflict situations: A paradigm for analysis. In W. B. Gudykunst, L. P. Stewart, & S. Ting-Toomey (Eds.), *Communication, cultural and organizational processes* (pp. 87–113). Sage.

Nagda, B. A. (2006). Breaking barriers, crossing borders, building bridges: Communication processes in intergroup dialogues. *The Society for the Psychological Study of Social Issues, 62*(3), 553–576.

Nagda, R., & Zuniga, X. (2003). Fostering meaningful racial engagement through intergroup dialogues. *Group Processes and Intergroup Relations, 6*(1), 111–128.

Nakayama, T., & Krizek, R. (1995). Whiteness: A strategic rhetoric. *Quarterly Journal of Speech, 81*, 291–309.

Nardi, P. (1999). *Gay men's friendships: Invincible communities.* University of Chicago Press.

Natale, S. (2016). There are no old media. *Journal of Communication, 66*(4), 585–603.

National Captioning Institute. (n.d.). *About captioning.* www.ncicap.org/viewer-resources/about-captioning/

National Communication Association. (1999). *NCA credo for ethical communication.* www.natcom.org/uploadedFiles/About-NCA/Leadership-and-Governance/Public-Policy-Platform/PDF-PolicyPlatform-NCA_Credo_for_Ethical_Communication.pdf

NationMaster. (2002). *Female doctors by country.* www.nationmaster.com/graph/lab-fem-doc-labor-female-doctors?=50

Navarro, M. (2002, June 11). *Raquel Welch is reinvented as a Latina: A familiar actress now boasts her heritage.* The New York Times. www.nytimes.com/2002/06/11/movies/raquel-welch-reinvented-latina-familiar-actress-now-boasts-her-heritage.html

Nelson, J. (2006). *Leveraging the development impact of business in the fight against global poverty.* Corporate social responsibility initiative working paper No. 22. John F. Kennedy School of Government, Harvard University.

Neuliep, J. W., & McCroskey, J. C. (1997). The development of a U.S. and generalized ethnocentrism scale. *Communication Research Reports, 14*, 385–398.

The New York Times. (2007). *Looking around the corner: The view from the front line.* The New York Times Company.

Niedenthal, P. M., Krauth-Gruber, S., & Ric, F. (2006). *Psychology of emotion: Interpersonal, experiential, and cognitive approaches.* Psychology Press.

Nieto, S. (2004). *Affirming diversity: The sociopolitical context of multicultural education* (4th ed.). Allyn & Bacon.

Nisbett, R. (2003). *The geography of thought.* Free Press.

Nishida, H. (2005). Cultural schema theory. In W. B. Gudykunst (Ed.), *Theorizing about intercultural communication* (pp. 401–418). Sage.

Nuwer, R. (2014). *Languages: Why we must save dying tongues.* BBC Future. www.bbc.com/future/article/20140606-why-we-must-save-dying-languages

Oberg, K. (1960). Culture shock: Adjustment to new cultural environments. *Practical Anthropology, 7*, 177–82.

OECD. (2021). *Household savings.* https://data.oecd.org/hha/household-savings.htm

Oetzel, J. G. (2009). *Intercultural communication: A layered approach.* Allyn & Bacon.

Oetzel, J., Ting-Toomey, S., Chew-Sanchez, M. I., Harris, R., Wilcox, R., & Stumpf, S. (2003). Face and facework in conflicts with parents and siblings: A cross-cultural comparison of Germans, Japanese, Mexicans, and U.S. Americans. *Journal of Family Communication, 3*(2), 67–94.

Oguri, M., & Gudykunst, W. B. (2002). The influence of self construals and communication styles on sojourners' psychological and sociocultural adjustment. *International Journal of Intercultural Relations, 26*, 577–593.

Olsen, L. (2023). *Teachers like us: Strategies for increasing educator diversity in public schools.* FutureEd.

Olweus, D. (1991). Bully/victim problems among school children: Basic facts and effects of a school-based intervention program. In D. J. Pepler & K. H. Rubin (Eds.), *The development and treatment of childhood aggression* (pp. 411–448). Erlbaum.

Omenugha, K. A., & Adum, A. N. (2008). Nigeria's spiral of violence: Can the media build a culture of peace? *Media Development, 55*(1), 50–54.

Omohundro, J. (2008). *Thinking like an anthropologist: A practical introduction to cultural anthropology.* McGraw-Hill.

Orbe, M. P. (2006). Co-cultural theory and the spirit of dialogue: A case study of the 2000–2002 community-based civil rights health project. In G. M. Chen & W. J. Starosta (Eds.), *Dialogue among diversities* (pp. 191–211). National Communication Association (International and Intercultural Communication Annual, XXVII).

Orbe, M. & Drummond, D. K. (2009). Negotiations of the complicitous nature of U.S. racial/ethnic categorization: Exploring rhetorical strategies. *Western Journal of Communication, 73*, 437–455.

Orelus, P. W. (2020). Other peoples' English accents matter: Challenging standard English accent hegemony. *Excellence in Education Journal, 9*, 120–148.

Orgad, S. (2009). Watching how others watch us: The Israeli media's treatment of international coverage of the Gaza War. *Communication Review, 12*, 250–261.

Organization of Economic Co-operation and Development. (2009). *OECD reveals evolving social trends in Asia-Pacific.* www.oecd.org/indonesia/oecdrevealsevolvingsocialtrendsinasia-pacific.htm

Orpinas, P., & Horne, A. M. (2003). School bullying: Changing the problem by changing the school. *School Psychology Review, 32*, 431–445.

Ortony, A., Clore, G. L., & Collins, A. (1988). *The cognitive structure of emotions.* Cambridge University Press.

Osland, H., & Bird, A. (2000). Beyond sophisticated stereotyping: Cultural sensemaking in context. *The Academy of Management Executive, 14*, 65–69.

Osman-Gani, A., & Rockstuhl, T. (2009). Cross-cultural training, expatriate self-efficacy and adjustments to overseas assignments: An empirical investigation of managers in Asia. *International Journal of Intercultural Relations, 33*, 277–290.

Osman-Gani, A., & Tan, W. (2005). Expatriate development for Asia-Pacific: A study of training contents and methods. *International Journal of Human Resources Development and Management, 5*(1), 41–56.

Ottosson, D. (2006). *Legal survey on the countries in the world having legal prohibitions on sexual activities between consenting adults in private.* ILGA.
  http://ilga.org/historic/Statehomophobia/LGBcriminallaws-Daniel_Ottoson.pdf

Ouyang, K., Huang, I. A., Wagner, J. P., Wu, J., Chen, F., Quach . . . and Tillou, A. (2021). Persistence of gender bias over four decades of surgical training. *Journal of Surgical Education*, 2–10.

Overton, H., Kim, J. K., Zhang, N., & Huang, S. (2021). Examining consumer attitudes toward CSR and CSA messages. *Public Relations Review, 47*, 1–8.

Page-Gould, E., Mendoza-Denton, R., & Tropp, L. R. (2008). With a little help from my cross- group friend: Reducing anxiety in intergroup contexts through cross-group friendship. *Journal of Personality and Social Psychology, 95*, 1080–1094. doi:10.1037/0022-3514.95.5.1080

Painter, N. I. (2010). *The history of White people.* W. W. Norton & Co.

Parham, T. (1989). Cycles of psychological Nigrescence. *The Counseling Psychologist, 17*(2), 187–226.

Parsons, T., Shils, E., & Olds, J. (1951). Categories of the orientation and organization of action. In T. Parsons & E. A. Shills (Eds.), *Toward a general theory of action* (pp. 53–110). Harvard University Press.

Pass, S. (2009). Teaching respect for diversity: The Oglala Lakota. *The Social Studies Journal, 100*(5), 212–217.

Paz, R., Neto, F., & Mullet, E. (2008). Forgiveness: A China–Western Europe comparison. *Journal of Psychology, 142*, 147–158.

Pearce, N., Cross, D., Monks, H., Waters, S., & Falconer, S. (2011). Current evidence of best practice in whole-school bullying intervention and its potential to inform cyberbullying interventions. *Australian Journal of Guidance & Counseling, 21*(1), 1–21.

Pearce, W. B., & Pearce, K. (2004). Taking a communication perspective on dialogue. In R. Anderson, L. A. Baxter, & K. N. Cissna (Eds.), *Dialogue: Theorizing difference in communication studies* (pp. 39–56). Sage.

Pearce, W. B., & Littlejohn, S. (1997). *Moral conflict: When social worlds collide.* Sage.

Pearson, J. C., Semlak, J. L., Western, K., & Herakova, L. L. (2010). Answering a call for service: An exploration of family communication schemata and ethnic identity's effect on civic engagement behaviors. *Journal of Intercultural Communication Research, 39*, 49–68.

Pedersen, P. B., Ponterotto, J. G., & Utsey, S. O. (2006). *Preventing prejudice: A guide for counselors, educators, and parents* (2nd ed.). Sage.

Penington, B. A. (2004). Communicative management of connection and autonomy in African American and European American mother-daughter relationships. *Journal of Family Communication, 4*(1), 3–35.

Penington, B., & Wildermuth, S. (2005). Three weeks there and back again: A qualitative investigation of the impact of short-term travel/study on the development of intercultural communication competency. *Journal of Intercultural Communication Research, 34*, 166–183.

Peplau, L. A., & Beals, K. P. (2004). The family lives of lesbians and gay men. In A. L. Vangelisti (Ed.), *Handbook of family communication* (pp. 233–248). Erlbaum.

Perry, B. D., Pollard, R. A., Blakely, T. L., Baker, W. L., & Vigilante, D. (1995). Childhood trauma, the neurobiology of adaptation, and "use-dependent" development of the brain: How states become traits. *Infant Mental Health Journal, 16*, 271–291.

Peterson, C. (2003). Sámi culture and media. *Scandinavian Studies, 75*(2), 293–300.

Pettigrew, T. F. (1979). The ultimate attribution error: Extending Allport's cognitive analysis of prejudice. *Personality and Social Psychology Bulletin, 5*, 461–476.

Pettigrew, T. F. (1997). Generalized intergroup contact effects on prejudice. *Personality and Social Psychology Bulletin, 23*, 173–185.

Pettigrew, T. (1998). Intergroup contact theory. *Annual Review of Psychology, 49*, 65–86.

Pettigrew, T. F., Christ, O., Wagner, U., & Stellmacher, J. (2007). Direct and indirect intergroup contact effects on prejudice: A normative interpretation. *International Journal of Intercultural Relations, 31*, 411–425.

Pettigrew, T. F., & Tropp, L. R. (2006). A meta-analytic test of intergroup contact theory. *Journal of Personality and Social Psychology, 90*, 751–783

Pettigrew, T. F., & Tropp, L. R. (2008). How does intergroup contact reduce prejudice? Meta-analytic tests of three mediators. *European Journal of Social Psychology, 38*, 922–934.

Pew Research Center. (2010). *One-in-seven new U.S. marriages is interracial or interethnic.* Pew Research Center. http://pewresearch.org/pubs/1616/american-marriage-interracial-interethnic

Pew Research Center. (2021). *Social media fact sheet.* Pew Research Center. www.pewresearch.org/internet/fact-sheet/social-media/?tabId=tab-d102dcb7-e8a1-42cd-a04e-ee442f81505a

Pfeil, H. (2015). Understanding the dynamics of Israeli-Palestinian grassroots dialogue workshops: The contribution of a Habermasian approach. *International Journal of Politics Culture and Society, 28*, 119–141.

Phinney, J. S. (1993). A three-stage model of ethnic identity development in adolescence. In M. E. Bernal & G. P. Knight (Eds.), *Ethnic identity: Formation and transmission among Hispanics and other minorities* (SUNY Series, United States Hispanic Studies, pp. 61–79). State University of New York Press.

Pilecki, A., & Hammack, P. L. (2014). "Victims" versus "righteous victims": The rhetorical construction of social categories in historical dialogue among Israeli and Palestinian youth. *Political Psychology, 35*, 813–830.

Piller, I. (2010). Cross cultural communication in intimate relationships. In D. Matsumoto (Ed.), *APA handbook of intercultural communication* (pp. 341–359). American Psychological Association.

Planalp, S. (1999). *Communicating emotion: Social, moral and cultural processes.* Cambridge University Press.

Ponterotto, J. (1988). Racial consciousness development among white counselor trainees: A stage model. *Journal of Multicultural Counseling and Development, 16,* 146–156.

Popović-Ćitić, B., Djurić, S., and Cvetković, V. (2011). The prevalence of cyberbullying among adolescents: A case study of middle schools in Serbia. *School Psychology International, 32,* 412–424.

Poston, W. S. C. (1990, November/December). The biracial identity development model: A needed addition. *Journal of Counseling and Development, 69*(2), 152–55.

Poushter, J. & Fetterolf, J. (2019, April 22). *A changing world: Global views on diversity, gender equality, family life, and the importance of religion.* Pew Research Center. https://www.pewresearch.org/global/2019/04/22/a-changing-world-global-views-on-diversity-gender-equality-family-life-and-the-importance-of-religion/

Pratto, F., & Glasford, D. E. (2008). Ethnocentrism and the value of a human life. *Journal of Personality and Social Psychology, 94,* 1411–1428.

Preston, M. (2010, January 9). *Reid apologizes for racial remarks about Obama during campaign.* CNN. www.cnn.com/2010/POLITICS/01/09/obama.reid/index.html

Prutzman, P., & Johnson, J. (1997). Bias awareness and multiple perspectives: Essential aspects of conflict resolution. *Theory into Practice, 36,* 26–31.

Putnam, R. D. (2007). E pluribus unum: Diversity and community in the twenty-first century. The 2006 Johan Skytte Prize lecture. *Scandinavian Political Studies, 30,* 137–174.

Pyeatt, M. (2002). *Deaf lesbians criticized for efforts to create deaf child.* Baptist Press. www.baptistpress.com/resource-library/news/deaf-lesbians-criticized-for-efforts-to-create-deaf-child/

Qing, L. (2010). Cyberbullying in high schools: A study of students' behaviors and beliefs about this new phenomenon. *Journal of Aggression, Maltreatment & Trauma, 19,* 372–392.

Raddatz, M. (2010). *General Petraeus: Burn a Quran day could "endanger troops."* ABC News. http://abcnews.go.com/WN/Afghanistan/burn-quran-daysparks-protests-afghanistan-petraeus-endanger/story?id=11569820#.TtDsL-sm_-Y

Raffaelli, M., & Ontai, L. L. (2001). "She's 16 years old and there's boys calling over to the house": An exploratory study of sexual socialization in Latino families. *Culture, Health & Sexuality, 3*(3), 295–311.

Ramasubramanian, S. (2010). Television viewing, racial attitudes, and policy preferences: Exploring the role of social identity and intergroup emotions in influencing support for affirmative action. *Communication Monographs, 77,* 102–120.

Rata, A., Liu, J. H., & Hanke, K. (2008). Te ara hohou rongo (The path to peace): Māori conceptualisations of inter-group forgiveness. *New Zealand Journal of Psychology, 37*(2), 18–30.

Rawlins, W. K. (1992). *Friendship matters: Communication, dialectics and life course.* Aldine De Gruyter.

Ray, R., Brown, M., Fraistat, N., & Summers, E. (2017). Ferguson and the death of Michael Brown on Twitter: #BlackLivesMatter, #TCOT, and the evolution of collective identities. *Ethnic & Racial Studies, 40*(11), 1797–1813.

Regan, P. C., Jerry, D., Marysia, N., & Johnson, D. (1999). Public displays of affection among Asian and Latino heterosexual couples. *Psychological Reports, 84,* 1201–1202.

Reicher, S., Spears, R., & Postmes, T. (1995). A social identity model of deindividuation phenomena. *European Review of Social Psychology, 6,* 161–198.

Reilly, D., & Senders, S. (2009). Becoming the change we want to see: Critical study abroad for a tumultuous world. *Frontiers: The Interdisciplinary Journal of Study Abroad, 18,* 241–267.

Remland, M. S. (2009). *Nonverbal communication in everyday life.* Pearson.

Remland, M. (2017). *Nonverbal communication in everyday life* (4th ed.). Sage.

Remland, M., Jones, T., & Brown, T. (1994, June). *Nonverbal communication and conflict escalation: The effects of attribution and predisposition.* Paper presented at the International Association of Conflict Management Convention, Eugene, OR.

Renner, N. (2019, August 8). *How social media shapes our identity.* The New Yorker. www.newyorker.com/books/under-review/how-social-media-shapes-our-identity

Retzinger, S. M. (1991). *Violent emotions: Shame and rage in marital quarrels*. Sage.

Retzinger, S. M., & Scheff, T. (2000). Emotion, alienation and narratives: Resolving intractable conflict. *Mediation Quarterly, 18*(1), 71–85.

Reuters. (2023, May 30). *Uganda enacts harsh anti-LGBTQ law including death penalty*. Reuters. www.reuters.com/world/africa/ugandas-museveni-approves-anti-gay-law-parliament-speaker-says-2023-05-29

Reyes, A. (2006). *Language, identity, and stereotype among Southeast Asian American youth*. Erlbaum.

Rezvani, A., Barrett, R., & Khosvari, P. (2018). Investigating the relationships among team emotional intelligence, trust, conflict and team performance. *Team Performance Management: An International Journal, 25*(1/2), 120–137.

Rhodes, J. (1993). The visibility of race and media history. *Critical Studies in Mass Communication, 10*(2), 184–190.

Rime, B., Corsini, S., & Herbette, G. (2002). Emotion, verbal expression, and the social sharing of emotion. In S. R. Fussell (Ed.), *The verbal communication of emotions: Interdisciplinary perspectives* (pp. 185–208). Erlbaum.

Robinson, P., Goddard, P., Parry, K., & Murray, C. (2003). Testing models of media performance in wartime: U.K. TV news and the 2003 invasion of Iraq. *Journal of Communication, 59*, 534–563.

Rodriguez-Mosquera, P. M. (1999). *Honor and emotion: The cultural shaping of pride, shame and anger*. [Doctoral dissertation, University of Amsterdam]. https://hdl.handle.net/11245/1.160049

Rodriguez-Mosquera, P. M., Manstead, A. S. R., & Fisher, A. H. (2000). The role of honor-related values in the elicitation, experience, and communication of pride, shame, and anger: Spain and the Netherlands compared. *Personality and Social Psychology Bulletin, 26*, 833–844.

Rodriguez-Mosquera, P. M., Manstead, A. S. R., & Fischer, A. H. (2002). The role of honour concerns in emotional reactions to offences. *Cognition and Emotion, 16*, 143–163.

Rogers, E. M., & Steinfatt, T. M. (1999). *Intercultural communication*. Waveland Press.

Rogers-Sirin, L. (2009). Cultural competence as an ethical requirement: Introducing a new educational model. *Journal of Diversity in Higher Education, 2*(1), 19–29.

Rohmann, A., Niedenthal, P. M., Brauer, M., Castano, E., & Leyens, J. (2009). The attribution of primary and secondary emotions to the in-group and to the out-group: The case of equal status countries. *The Journal of Social Psychology, 149*, 709–730.

Rojas, H., Shah, D. V., Jaeho, C., Schmierbach, M., Keum, H., & Gil-de-Zuñiga, H. (2005). Media dialogue: Perceiving and addressing community problems. *Mass Communication & Society, 8*(2), 93–110.

Rokeach, M. (1973). *The nature of human values*. The Free Press.

Rokeach, M. (1979). *Understanding human values: Individual and societal*. The Free Press.

Rosenthal, D. B., Elfenbein, A. H., Matthew, J., Wadsworth, L. A., & Russell, T. L. (2009). *Training soldiers to decode nonverbal cues in cross-cultural interactions*. U.S. Department of Commerce. https://apps.dtic.mil/sti/citations/ADA507720

Ruben, B. D. (1975). Intrapersonal, interpersonal, and mass communication process in individual and multi-person system. In B. D. Ruben & J. Y. Kim (Eds.), *General systems theory and human communication* (pp. 41–56). Hayden.

Rubin, R. B., Palmgreen, P., & Sypher, H. E. (Eds.). (1994). *Communication research measures: A sourcebook*. Guilford.

Ruiz, N. G., & Budiman, A. (2018). *Federal training program sees 400% increase in foreign students graduating and working in STEM fields from 2008 to 2016*. Pew Research Center. www.pewresearch.org/global/2018/05/10/number-of-foreign-college-students-staying-and-working-in-u-s-after-graduation-surges/

Rummens, J. A., & Dei, G. J. S. (2010). Including the excluded: De-marginalizing immigrant/refugee and racialized students. *Education Canada, 50*(50), 48–53.

Russell, B. N. (2009, April 6). *For mercy's sake, it's Madonna*. Los Angeles Times. www.latimes.com/archives/la-xpm-2009-apr-06-oe-russell6-story.html

Saarni, C. (1985). Indirect processes in affect socialization. In M. Lewis & C. Saarni (Eds.), *The socialization of emotions*. Plenum.

Saarni, C. (1999). *The development of emotional competence*. Guilford Press.

Safe Schools Coalition. (2007). *A living memory LGBT history timeline*. www.safeschoolscoalition.org/livingmemory-lgbthistorytimeline.pdf

Salacuse, J. (2003). *The global negotiator: Making, managing & mending deals around the world in the 21st century*. Palgrove MacMillan.

Sallinen-Kuparinen, A., McCroskey, J. C., & Richmond, V. P. (1991). Willingness to communicate, communication apprehension, introversion, and self-reported communication competence: Finish and American comparisons. *Communication Research Reports, 8*, 55–64.

Salomon, G. (2002). The nature of peace education: Not all programs are created equal. In G. Salomon & B. Nevo (Eds.), *Peace education: The concept, principles, and practices around the world* (pp. 3–36). Lawrence Erlbaum Associates.

Saletan, W. (2011). *Springtime for Twitter: Is the Internet driving the revolutions of the Arab Spring?* Slate. www.slate.com/articles/technology/future_tense/2011/07/springtime_for_twitter.htm

Samter, W., Whaley, B. B., Mortenson, S. R., & Burleson, B. R. (1997). Ethnicity and emotional support in same-sex friendship: A comparison of Asian-Americans, African-Americans, and Euro-Americans. *Personal Relationships, 4*, 413–430.

Sanchez, J., & Medkik, N. (2004). The effects of diversity awareness training on differential treatment. *Group & Organization Management, 29*, 517–536.

Sandage, S. J., Hill, P. C., & Vang. H. C. (2003). Toward a multicultural positive psychology: Indigenous forgiveness and Hmong culture. *The Counseling Psychologist, 31*, 564–592.

Sandel, T. L., Cho, G. E., Miller, P. J., & Wang, S. (2006). What it means to be a grandmother: A cross-cultural study of Taiwanese and Euro-American grandmothers' beliefs. *Journal of Family Communication, 6*, 255–278.

Santiago, C. D., Bustos, Y., Jolie, S. A., Flores Toussaint, R., Sosa, S. S., Raviv, T., & Cicchetti, C. (2021). The impact of COVID-19 on immigrant and refugee families: Qualitative perspectives from newcomer students and parents. *School Psychology, 36*(5), 348–357.

Sapir, E. (1921). *Language: An introduction to the study of speech*. Harcourt Brace.

Sarason, S. (1974). *The psychological sense of community: Prospects for a community psychology*. Jossey-Bass.

Saulny, S. (2011, January 29). *Black? White? Asian? More young Americans choose all of the above*. The New York Times. www.nytimes.com/2011/01/30/us/30mixed.html

Saunders, H. H. (2005). Sustained dialogue in Tajikistan: Transferring learning from the public to the official peace process. In R. J. Fisher (Ed.), *Paving the way: Contributions of interactive conflict resolution to peacemaking* (pp. 126–141). Lexington Books.

Scanlan, M. (2011). Inclusion: How school leaders can accent inclusion for bilingual students, families, and communities. *Multicultural Education, 18*(2), 4–9.

Scherer, K. R. (1997). The role of culture in emotion-antecedent appraisal. *Journal of Personality and Social Psychology, 73*, 902–922.

Schiappa, E., Gregg, P. B., & Hewes, D. E. (2005). The parasocial contact hypothesis. *Communication Monographs, 72*, 92–115.

Schiappa, E. S., Gregg, P. B., & Hewes, D. E. (2006). Can one TV show make a difference? *Will & Grace* and the parasocial contact hypothesis. *Journal of Homosexuality, 51*(4), 15–37.

Schmid, H., & Klimmt, C. (2010, May). *Goodbye, Harry? Audience reactions to the end of parasocial relationships: The case of "Harry Potter."* Paper presented at the International Communication Association, Singapore.

Schroeder, K. (2005). K–6 violence is global. *The Education Digest, 70*(7), 71–73.

Schultze-Krumbholz , A., Pfetsch, J. S., Lietz, K. (2022). Cyberbullying in a multicultural context— Forms, strain, and coping related to ethnicity-based cybervictimization. *Frontiers in Communication, 7*, 846794.

Schwartz, S. H. (1992). Universals in the content and structure of values: Theory and empirical tests in 20 countries. In M. Zanna (Ed.), *Advances in experimental social psychology* (Vol. 25, pp. 1–65). Academic Press.

Schwartz, S. H. (1994). Beyond individualism/collectivism: New dimensions of values. In U. Kim, H. C. Triandis, C. Kagitcibasi, S. C. Choi, & G. Yoon (Eds.), *Individualism and collectivism: Theory application and methods* (pp. 85–119). Sage.

Searle, J. R. (1969). *Speech acts: An essay in the philosophy of language.* Cambridge University Press.

Searle, W., & Ward, C. (1990). The prediction of psychological and socio-cultural adjustment during cross-cultural transitions. *International Journal of Intercultural Relations, 14*(4), 449–464.

Sears, J. T. (1997). Centering culture: Teaching for critical sexual literacy using the sexual diversity wheel. *Journal of Moral Education, 26,* 273–284.

Segrin, C., & Flora, J. (2019). *Family communication* (3rd ed.). Routledge.

Seidlhofer, B. (2009). Accommodation and the idiom principle in English as a lingua franca. *Intercultural Pragmatics, 6,* 195–215.

Seki, K., Matsumoto, D., & Imahori, T. T. (2002). The conceptualization and expression of intimacy in Japan and the United States. *Journal of Cross-Cultural Psychology, 33,* 303–319.

Selvanathan, H. P., Leidner, B., Petrović, N., Prelić, N., Ivanek, I., Krugel, J., & Bjekić, J. (2019). A quantitative field test of the effects of online intergroup dialogue in promoting justice-versus-harmony-oriented outcomes in Bosnia and Serbia. *Peace & Conflict, 25*(4), 287–299.

Seth, R. (2008). *First comes marriage: Modern relationship advice from the wisdom of arranged marriages.* Fireside.

Sethi, A. (2002, January). Talking points. *BabyTalk, 67,* 29–30.

Shaffer, D. R., Crepaz, N., & Sun, C. (2000). Physical attractiveness stereotyping in cross-cultural perspective: Similarities and differences between Americans and Taiwanese. *Journal of Cross-Cultural Psychology, 31,* 557–582.

Shani, M., & Boehnke, K. (2017). The effect of Jewish–Palestinian mixed model encounters on readiness for contact and policy support. *Peace and Conflict, 23,* 219–227.

Shapiro, J. P. (1994). *No pity: People with disabilities forging a new civil rights movement.* Three Rivers Press.

Shaw, G. (2010). Peace and social cohesion through education: Global perspectives and experiences from the GPPAC peace education working group. *Beliefs and Values, 2*(2), 111–123.

Sheehy, S. (2000). *Connecting: The enduring power of female friendship.* Harper Collins.

Shiau, H. C. (2016) Easily connected but difficult to become intimate? Intercultural friendships on social media among Taiwanese ESL students in the US. *Cogent Social Sciences, 2*(1), 1264152. doi: 10.1080/23311886.2016.1264152

Shrestha, L. B. (2006, August 16). *Life expectancy in the United States.* CRS report for Congress. https://wikileaks.org/wiki/CRS:_Life_Expectancy_in_the_United_States,_August_16,_2006

Shunnaq, M. (2009). Cross-cultural cyber-marriages: A global socio-economic strategy for young Jordanians. *Social Identities, 15*(2), 169–186.

Shweder, R. A., Haidt, J., Horton, R., & Joseph, C. (2008). The cultural psychology of the emotions: Ancient and renewed. In M. Lewis, J. M. Haviland-Jones, & L. F. Barrett (Eds.), *Handbook of emotions* (3rd ed., pp. 409–427). Guilford Press.

Sias, P. M., & Cahill, D. J. (1998). From coworkers to friends: The development of peer friendships in the workplace. *Western Journal of Communication, 62,* 273–299.

Sias, P. M., Drzeewiecka, J., Meares, M., Bent, R., Konomi, Y., Ortega, M., & White, C. (2008). Intercultural friendship development. *Communication Reports, 21,* 1–13.

Sidanius, J., Levin, S., van Laar, C., & Sears, D. O. (2008). *The diversity challenge: Social identity and intergroup relations on the college campus.* Russell Sage Foundation.

Sicorello, M., Stevanov, J., & Hecht, H. (2019). Effect of gaze on personal space: A Japanese-German cross-cultural study. *Journal of Cross-Cultural Psychology, 50,* 8–21.

Silverstein, L., & Auerbach, C. (1999). Deconstructing the essential father. *American Psychologist, 54,* 397–425.

Simon, R. J., & Altstein, H. (1996). The case for transracial adoption. *Children and Youth Services Review, 18,* 5–22.

Singh, R. (2009). Constructing "the family" across culture. *Journal of Family Therapy, 31*(4): 359–383.

Sklad, M., Diekstra, R., De Ritter, M., Ben, J., & Gravesteijn, C. (2012). Effectiveness of school-based universal social, emotional, and behavioral programs. Do they enhance students' development in the area of skill, behavior, and adjustment? *Psychology in the Schools, 49*(9), 892–909.

Smith, H. (1991). *The world's religions.* Harper Collins Books.

Smith, E. B. (2009). Approaches to multicultural education in preservice teacher education: Philosophical frameworks and models for teaching. *Multicultural Education, 16*(3), 45–50.

Smith, E. R., & Mackie, D. M. (2008). Intergroup emotions. In M. Lewis, J. M. Haviland-Jones, & L. F. Barrett (Eds.), *Handbook of emotions* (3rd ed., pp. 428–439). Guilford Press.

Smith, G. P., & Batiste, D. A. (1999). Knowledge bases for diversity in teacher education. *Multicultural Perspectives, 1*(1), 49–58.

Smith, H., Parr, R., Woods, R., Bauer, B., & Abraham, T. (2010). Five years after graduation: Undergraduate cross-group friendships and multicultural curriculum predict current attitudes and activities. *Journal of College Student Development, 51*, 385–402. doi:10.1353/csd.0.0141

Sobaci, Z. (2010). What the Turkish parliamentary web site offers to citizens in terms of e-participation: A content analysis. *Information Polity: The International Journal of Government & Democracy in the Information Age, 15*, 227–241.

Sobania, N., & Braskamp, L. (2009). Study abroad or study away: It's not merely semantics. *Peer Review, 11*(3), 23–26.

Society for Human Resource Management. (2020, Summer). *The journey to equity and inclusion.* https://www.shrm.org/hr-today/trends-and-forecasting/research-and-surveys/documents/tfaw%20the%20journey%20to%20equity%20and%20inclusion.pdf

Sokol, D., & Sisler, V. (2010). Socializing on the Internet: Case study of Internet use among university students in the United Arab Emirates. *Global Media Journal: American Edition, 9*(6), 1–34.

Soliz, J., Thorson, A., & Rittenour, C. E. (2009). Communicative correlates of satisfaction, family identity, and group salience in multiracial/ethnic families. *Journal of Marriage and Family, 71*, 819–832.

Solomon, D. (2009, February 22). *Questions for Dambisa Moyo: The anti-Bono.* The New York Times. www.nytimes.com/2009/02/22/magazine/ 22wwln-q4-t.html?_r=0

Sorokowska, A., Hilpert, P., Cantaero, K., & Sorokowska, P. (2017). Preferred interpersonal distances: A global comparison. *Journal of Cross-Cultural Psychology, 48.* doi:10.1177/0022022117698039

Sparks, S. D. (2011, February 2). Researchers look for ways to curb "mean girls" and gossip. *Education Week, 30*, 8.

Spitzberg, B. H., & Changnon, G. (2009). Conceptualizing intercultural competence. In D. Deardorff (Ed.), *The Sage handbook of intercultural competence* (pp. 2–52). Sage.

Spitzberg, B. H., & Cupach, W. R. (1984). *Interpersonal communication competence.* Sage.

Sprecher, S., Aron, A., Hatfield, E., Cortese, A., Potapova, E., & Levitskaya, A. (1994). Love: American style, Russian style, Japanese style. *Personal Relationships, 1*(4), 349–369.

Stamato, L. (2008). Peace and the culture and politics of apology. *Peace Review, 20*(3), 389–397.

Stangor, C. (2009). The study of stereotyping, prejudice, and discrimination within social psychology: A quick history of theory and research. In T. Nelson (Ed.), *Handbook of prejudice, stereotyping, and discrimination* (pp. 1–22).Psychology Press.

Starr, D., Hayes, J., and Gao, N. (2022) *The digital divide in education.* Public Policy Institute of California. www.ppic.org/publication/the-digital-divide-in-education

Statista. (2023). *Most popular social networks worldwide as of January 2023, ranked by number of monthly active users.* www.statista.com/statistics/272014/global-social-networks-ranked-by-number-of-users

Stearns, P. N. (2008). History of emotions: Issues of change and impact. In M. Lewis, J. M. Haviland-Jones, & L. F. Barrett (Eds.), *Handbook of emotions* (3rd ed., pp. 17–31). Guilford Press.

Stephan, W. G., Ybarra, O., & Morrison, K. R. (2009). Intergroup threat theory. In T. D. Nelson (Ed.), *Handbook of prejudice, stereotyping, and discrimination* (pp. 43–59). Psychology Press.

Stewart, E. C., & Bennett, M. J. (1991). *American cultural patterns: A cross-cultural perspective* (Revised edition). Intercultural Press.

Stewart, J., Zediker, K. E., & Black, L. (2004). Relationships among philosophies of dialogue. In R. Anderson, L. A. Baxter, & K. N. Cissna (Eds.), *Dialogue: Theorizing difference in communication studies* (pp. 21–38). Sage.

Stewart. E., & Bennett, M. (1991). *American cultural patterns: A cross-cultural perspective.* Intercultural Press.

Storti, C. (1997). *The art of coming home.* Intercultural Press.

Stouffer, S. (1949). *The American soldier.* Princeton University Press.

Straubhaar, J. D. (2008). Global, hybrid or multiple? Cultural identities in the age of satellite TV and the Internet. *NORDICOM Review, 29*(2), 11–29.

Strine, M. (2004). When is communication intercultural? Bakhtin, staged performance, and civic dialogue. In R. Anderson, L. A. Baxter, & K. N. Cissna (Eds.), *Dialogue: Theorizing difference in communication studies* (pp. 225–242). Sage.

Strochlic, N. (2018). *The race to save the world's disappearing languages.* National Geographic. www.nationalgeographic.com/culture/article/saving-dying-disappearing-languages-wikitongues-culture

Suen, Y. T., Chan, R. C. H., & Badgett, M. V. L. (2020). The experiences of sexual and gender minorities in employment: Evidence from a large-scale survey of lesbian, gay, bisexual, transgender and intersex people in China. *The China Quarterly, 245,* 142–164.

Suh, E., Diener, E., Oishi, S., & Triandis, H. C. (1998). The shifting basis of life satisfaction judgments across cultures: Emotions versus norms. *Journal of Personality & Social Psychology, 74,* 482–493.

Suter, E. A. (2008). Discursive negotiation of family identity: A study of U.S. families with adopted children from China. *Journal of Family Communication, 8,* 126–147.

Sutton, R. C., & Rubin, D. L. (2004). The Glossari project: Initial findings from a system-wide research initiative on study abroad learning outcomes. *Frontiers: The Interdisciplinary Journal of Study Abroad, 10,* 65–82.

Sutzl, W. (2016). Elicitive conflict transformation and new media: In search for a common ground. *Media and Communication, 4*(1), 4–14.

Sweeney, E., & Hua, Z. (2010). Accommodating toward your audience: Do native speakers of English know how to accommodate their communication strategies toward nonnative speakers of English? *Journal of Business Communication, 47,* 477–504.

Tajfel, H., Billig, M., Bundy, R. P., & Flament, C. (1971). Social categorization and intergroup behaviour. *European Journal of Social Psychology, 2,* 149–178.

Tajfel, H., & Turner, J. C. (1979). An integrative theory of intergroup conflict. In W. G. Austin & S. Worchel (Eds.), *The social psychology of intergroup relations* (pp. 33–47). Brooks-Cole.

Tajfel, H., & Turner, J. C. (1986). The social identity theory of inter-group behavior. In S. Worchel & L. W. Austin (Eds.), *Psychology of intergroup relations* (pp. 7–24). Nelson-Hall.

Tang, M., Zhiyan, W., Mingyi, Q., Gao, J., & Zhang, L. (2008). Transferred shame in the cultures of interdependent-self and independent self. *Journal of Cognition & Culture, 8*(1/2), 163–178.

Tang, T. (2021, August 12). *More than 9,000 anti-Asian incidents since pandemic began.* Associated Press. https://apnews.com/article/lifestyle-joe-biden-health-coronavirus-pandemic-race-and-ethnicity-d3a63408021a247ba764d40355ecbe2a

Tangney, J. P., & Fischer, K. (Eds.). (1995). *Self-conscious emotions: The psychology of shame, guilt, embarrassment, and pride.* Guilford Press.

Tangney, J. P., Wagner, P., Fletcher, C., & Gramzow, R. (1992). Shamed into anger? The relation of shame and guilt to anger and self-reported aggression. *Journal of Personality and Social Psychology, 62,* 669–675.

Tannen, P. D. (1990). *You just don't understand: Women and men in conversation.* William Morrow & Company.

Tatum, B. D. (2003). *"Why are all the Black kids sitting together in the cafeteria?": A psychologist explains the development of racial identity.* Basic Books.

Taylor, R., Oberle, E., Durlak, J. A., & Weissberg, R .P. (2017). Promoting positive youth development through school-based social and emotional learning interventions: A meta-analysis of follow-up effects. *Child Development, 88*(4), 1156–1171.

Teeple, D. (2011). Communication for peace in Lebanon. *Media Development, 58*(2), 33–35.

Thierry, G. (2018). *The trouble with speaking English as a second language.* World Economic Forum. www.weforum.org/agenda/2018/04/the-english-language-is-the-worlds-achilles-heel

Thomas, D., & Inkson, K. (2003). *Cultural intelligence: People skills for global business.* Berrett-Koehler.

Thomas, D., & Inkson, K. (2009). *Cultural intelligence: Living and working globally.* Berrett-Koehler.

Thomas, S., & Kearney, J. (2008). Teachers working in culturally diverse classrooms: Implications for the development of professional standards and for teacher education. *Asia-Pacific Journal of Teacher Education, 36*(2), 105–120.

Tillewein, H., Shokeen, N., Powers, P., Rijo Sánchez, A. J., Sandles-Palmer, S., and Desjarlais, K. (2023). Silencing the rainbow: Prevalence of LGBTQ+ students who do not report sexual violence. *International Journal of Environmental Research and Public Health 20*(3): 2020.

Tincani, M., Travers, J., & Boutot, A. (2009). Race, culture, and autism spectrum disorder: Understanding the role of diversity in successful educational Interventions. *Research and Practice for Persons with Severe Disabilities, 34*(3/4), 81–90.

Ting-Toomey, S. (1988). Intercultural conflicts: A face negotiation theory. In Y. Y. Kim & W. B Gudykunst (Eds.), *Theories in intercultural communication* (pp. 213–235). Sage.

Ting-Toomey, S. (1999). *Communicating across cultures.* Guilford Press.

Ting-Toomey, S. (2002). Intercultural conflict competence. In J. N. Martin, T. K. Nakayama, & L. A. Flores (Eds.), *Readings in intercultural communication.* McGraw-Hill.

Ting-Toomey, S. (2005). The matrix of face: An updated face-negotiation theory. In W. B. Gudykunst (Ed.), *Theorizing about intercultural communication* (pp. 71–92). Sage.

Title, B. B. (2003). School bullying: Prevention and intervention. In T. Jones & R. Compton (Eds.), *Kids working it out: Stories and strategies for making peace in our schools* (pp. 221–250). Jossey-Bass.

Tobin, L. (2010, April 27). *Research into online dating: Academics are finding computer dating sites a fertile ground for research into internet communication.* The Guardian. www.theguardian.com/education/2010/apr/26/online-dating-research

Tokunaga, R. S. (2008, November). But, words can never hurt me if . . .: Cultural relativity in evaluating appraisals, attributions, and consequences of hurtful messages. *Journal of Intercultural Communication Research, 37*(3), 169–188. doi:10.1080/17475750903135358

Tokunaga, R. S. (2009). High-speed Internet access to the other: The influence of cultural orientations on self-disclosures in offline and online relationships. *Journal of Intercultural Communication Research, 38*(3), 133–147. doi:10.1080/17475759.2009.505058

Tompkins. S. S. (1962). *Affect, imagery, consciousness.* Springer.

Tornoe, J. (2007). *When bad Hispanic advertising happens to good companies.* LatPro. http://learn.latpro.com/bad-hispanic-advertising/

Trading Economics. (2022). *GDP annual growth rate.* https://tradingeconomics.com/country-list/gdp-annual-growth-rate

Trent, S. C., Kea, C. D., & Oh, K. (2008). Preparing preservice educators for cultural diversity: How far have we come? *Exceptional Children, 74*(3), 328–350.

Triana, M. D. C., Gu, P., Chapa, O., Richard, O., & Colella, A. (2021). Sixty years of discrimination and diversity research in human resource management: A review with suggestions for future research directions. *Human Resource Management, 60*,145–204.

Triandis, H. C. (1994). *Culture and social behavior.* McGraw-Hill.

Triandis, H. C. (1995). *Individualism and collectivism.* Westview.

Trooboff, S., Vande Berg, M., & Rayman, J. (2008). Employer attitudes toward study abroad. *Frontiers: The Interdisciplinary Journal of Study Abroad, 15*, 17–33.

Truth and Reconciliation Commission. *Welcome to the official Truth and Reconciliation Commission website.* Department of Justice and Constitutional Development. www.justice.gov.za/trc/

Ttofi, M. M., & Farrington, D. P. (2011). Effectiveness of school-based programs to reduce bullying: A systematic and meta-analytic review. *Journal of Experimental Criminology, 7*, 27–56.

Turistiati, A. T. (2020). The use of WhatsApp group to maintain intercultural friendship. *Komunika: Jurnal Dakwah dan Komunikasi, 14*, 297–307.

Turkle, S. (2011). *Alone together*. Basic Book.

Tyler, A. (1985). *The accidental tourist*. Random House.

UNESCO. (2001, November 2). *Universal declaration on cultural diversity*. www.unesco.org/en/legal-affairs/unesco-universal-declaration-cultural-diversity

UNESCO. (2002). *UNESCO: IBE education thesaurus* (6th ed.). UNESCO International Bureau of Education.

United Nations. (2004). *Who cares wins*. UN Environment Programme—Finance Initiative. www.unepfi.org/fileadmin/events/2004/stocks/who_cares_wins_global_compact_2004.pdf

United Nations. (2010). *Intercultural dialogue crucial for world peace, Ban tells security council*. UN News. https://news.un.org/en/story/2010/05/339772

United States Department of Health & Human Services. (2007). *Adoption satisfaction*. www.aspe.hhs.gov/hsp/09/NSAP/chartbook/chartbook.cfm?id=24

United States Census Bureau. (2018). *Hispanic population to reach 111 million by 2060*. www.census.gov/library/visualizations/2018/comm/hispanic-projected-pop.html

United States Census Bureau. (2021). *Subject definitions*. www.census.gov/programs-surveys/cps/technical-documentation/subject-definitions.html#householdfamily

United States Department of Justice. (2020a). *Utah man convicted on hate crime charges after attacking three men with a metal pole*. US Attorney's Office, District of Utah. www.justice.gov/usao-ut/pr/utah-man-convicted-hate-crime-charges-after-attacking-three-men-metal-pole

United States Department of Justice. (2020b). *Federal jury convicts Illinois man for bombing the Dar Al-Farooq Islamic Center*. US Attorney's Office, District of Minnesota. www.justice.gov/usao-mn/pr/federal-jury-convicts-illinois-man-bombing-dar-al-farooq-islamic-center

United States Department of Justice. (2020c). *Two individuals charged with carjacking, murder, firearms offenses, and destruction of property*. US Attorney's Office, District of Puerto Rico. www.justice.gov/usao-pr/pr/two-individuals-charged-carjacking-murder-firearms-offenses-and-destruction-property

United States Department of Justice. (2020d). *Colorado man pleads guilty to federal hate crime and explosives charges for plotting to blow up synagogue*. Office of Public Affairs. www.justice.gov/opa/pr/colorado-man-pleads-guilty-federal-hate-crime-and-explosives-charges-plotting-blow-synagogue

United States Department of Justice. (2021a). *2020 hate crimes statistics*. www.justice.gov/crs/highlights/2020-hate-crimes-statistics

United States Department of Justice. (2021b). *Indiana man pleads guilty to hate crime for making racially-charged motivated threats toward Black neighbor and to unlawful possession of firearms. office of public affairs*. www.justice.gov/opa/pr/indiana-man-pleads-guilty-hate-crime-making-racially-charged-motivated-threats-toward-black

United States Department of Justice. (2021c). *Southern Colorado man sentenced to more than 19 years for plotting to blow up synagogue*. Office of Public Affairs. www.justice.gov/opa/pr/southern-colorado-man-sentenced-more-19-years-plotting-blow-synagogue

United States Department of State. (2021). *Annual report on intercountry adoption*. https://travel.state.gov/content/dam/NEWadoptionassets/pdfs/FY%202020%20Annual%20Report.pdf

Urban, E., & Orbe, M. (2007). The syndrome of the boiled frog: Exploring international students on us campuses as co-cultural group members. *Journal of Intercultural Communication Research, 36*, 117–138.

Utz, S. (2000). Social information processing in MUDs: The development of friendships in virtual worlds. *Journal of Online Behavior, 1*(1).

Van Meurs, N., & Spencer-Oatey, H. (2010). Multidisciplinary perspectives on intercultural conflict: The "Bermuda Triangle" of conflict, culture & communication. In D. Matsumoto (Ed.), *APA handbook of intercultural communication* (Part 1, Section 4). American Psychological Association.

Vance, C., & Ensher, E. (2002). The voice of the host country workforce: A key source for improving the effectiveness of expatriate training and performance. *International Journal of Intercultural Relations, 26*(4), 447–461.

Vande Berg, M., Connor-Linton, J., & Paige, R. M. (2009). The Georgetown Consortium Project: Interventions for student learning abroad. *Frontiers, 18*, 1–75.

Varma, R. (2021). Dissecting culture at work: Conversation with Indian immigrant scientists & engineers in the US industrial sector. *Technology in Society*, 1–8.

Varner, I., & Beamer, L. (2005). *Intercultural communication in the global workplace*. McGraw-Hill.

Varnham, S. (2005). Seeing things differently: Restorative justice and school discipline. *Education & the Law, 17*(3), 87–104.

Verbeek, P. (2009). The need to observe forgiveness. *Evolutionary Psychology, 7*, 142–145.

Vervoort, M., Scholte, R., & Overbeek, G. (2010). Bullying and victimization among adolescents: The role of ethnicity and ethnic composition of school class. *Journal of Youth & Adolescence, 39*(1), 1–11.

Vivero, V. N., & Jenkins, S. R. (1999). Existential hazards of the multicultural individual: Defining and understanding "cultural homelessness." *Cultural Diversity and Ethnic Minority Psychology, 5*, 6–26.

Vizard, S. (2018). *Nike "proud" of Colin Kaepernick ad as campaign drives "record engagement."* Marketing Week. www.marketingweek.com/nike-proud-of-colin-kaepernick-ad-campaign

Voice of America. (2009). *Analysts explain significance of evolving relationship between China and Africa*. www.voanews.com/a/a-13-analysts-explain-significance-of-evolving-relationship-between-china-and-africa-66775502/564630.html

Vogels, E. A., & Anderson, M. (2020). *Dating and relationships in the digital age*. Pew Research Center. www.pewresearch.org/internet/2020/05/08/dating-and-relationships-in-the-digital-age/

von Frank, V. (2008). School district is eloquent in the language of cultural respect. *Journal of Staff Development, 29*(1), 12–17.

WACC. (2008). Communication for peace award. *Media Development, 75*(4), 50–52.

Wahba, P. (2020). *Starbucks will let employees wear own Black Lives Matter gear after all in wake of backlash*. Fortune. https://fortune.com/2020/06/12/starbucks-black-lives-matter-employees/

Waite, S. (2021). Should I stay or should I go? Employment discrimination and workplace harassment against transgender and other minority employees in Canada's federal public service. *Journal of Homosexuality, 68*(11), 1833–1859.

Waller, R., & Conaway, R. (2011). Framing and counterframing the issue of corporate social responsibility: The communication strategies of Nikebiz.com. *Journal of Business Communication, 48*, 83–106.

Walt, V. (2010, February 23). *School lunches in France: Nursery-school gourmets*. Time. https://content.time.com/time/subscriber/article/0,33009,1969729,00.html

Walther, J. B. (2009). Computer-mediated communication and virtual groups: Applications to interethnic conflict. *Journal of Applied Communication Research, 37*, 225–238.

Wang, W., Huang, T., Huang, H., & Wang, L. (2009). Internet use, group identity, and political participation among Taiwanese Americans. *China Media Research, 5*(4), 47–62.

Ward, C., Bochner, S., & Furnham, A (2001). *The psychology of culture shock*. Routledge.

Ward, C., & Geeraert, N. (2016). Advancing acculturation theory and research: The acculturation process in its ecological context. *Current Opinion in Psychology, 8*, 98–104.

Ward, J. G., & Al Bayyari, Y. (2010). American and Arab perceptions of an Arabic turn taking cue. *Journal of Cross Cultural Psychology, 41*, 270–275.

Watkins, D. A., Hui, E. K. P., Luo, W., Regmi, M., Worthington, E. L., Hook, J. N., & David, D. E. (2011). Forgiveness and interpersonal relationships: A Nepalese investigation. *Journal of Social Psychology, 151*(2), 150–161.

Watson, O. M. (1970). *Proxemic behavior: A cross cultural study*. Mouton.

Watson, O. M., & Graves, T. D. (1966). Quantitative research in proxemic behavior. *American Anthropologist, 68*, 971–985.

Wei, L. (2012). Number matters: The multimodality of Internet use as an indicator of the digital inequalities. *Journal of Computer-Mediated Communication, 17*, 303–318.

Wells, S. (2007). *Deep ancestry: Inside the Genographic Project*. National Geographic.

Wendt, J. (1984). DIE: A way to improve communication. *Communication Education, 33*, 397–401.

Wenzhong, H., & Grove, C. (1991). *Encountering the Chinese*. Intercultural Press.

Werkmeister-Rozas, L. (2003). *The effect of intergroup dialogue on cross-racial friendships and cross-racial interaction in a learning environment*. [Unpublished doctoral dissertation]. Smith College.

White, G. M. (1994). Affecting culture: Emotion and morality in everyday life. In S. Kitayama & H. R. Marcus (Eds.), *Emotion and culture: Empirical studies of mutual influence* (pp. 219–240). American Psychological Association.

White, F. A., Harvey, L. J., & Abu-Rayya, H. M. (2015). Improving intergroup relations in the Internet age: A critical review. *Review of General Psychology, 19,* 129–139.

Whorf, B. L. (1956). The relation of habitual thought and behavior to language. In J. B. Carroll (Ed.), *Language, thought, and reality* (pp. 134–159). MIT Press.

Wierzbicka, A. (1992). Talk about emotions: Semantics, culture and cognition. *Cognition and Emotion, 6*(3/4), 285–319.

Wiglesworth, M., Lendrum, A., Oldfield, J., Scott, A., Ten Bokkel, I., Tate, K., & Emery, C. (2016). The impact of trial stage, developer involvement and international transferability on universal social and emotional learning programme outcomes: A meta-analysis. *Cambridge Journal of Education, 46,* 347–376.

Will, M. (2020). *How COVID-19 is hurting teacher diversity.* EducationWeek. www.edweek.org/teaching-learning/how-covid-19-is-hurting-teacher-diversity/2020/09

Williams, A. (2002). Should the media contribute to a culture of peace? *New York Amsterdam News, 93*(8), 8–12.

Wimmer, A., & Lewis, K. (2010). Beyond and below racial homophily: ERG models of a friendship network documents on Facebook. *American Journal of Sociology, 116*(2), 583–642.

Windspeaker. (2008). *RSSC welcome apology but expect more.* www.ammsa.com/publications/windspeaker/rssc-welcome-apology-expect-more

Wiseman, R. L., Hammer, M. R., & Nishida, H. (1989). Predictors of intercultural communication competence. *International Journal of Intercultural Relations, 13,* 349–370.

Wittenbrink, B., Gist, P. L., & Hilton, J. L. (1997). Structural properties of stereotypical knowledge and their influences on the construal of social situations. *Journal of Personality and Social Psychology, 72,* 526–543.

Wolfsfeld, G. (2004). *Media and the path to peace.* Cambridge University Press.

Wood, J. (1995). *Relational communication.* Wadsworth.

Wood, J. T. (2005). Feminist standpoint theory and muted group theory: Commonalities and divergences. *Women & Language, 28,* 61–64.

Woodbury, A. C. (1991). *Counting Eskimo words for snow: A citizen's guide.* Princeton University. www.princeton.edu/~browning/snow.html

Woodyatt, A., Bashir, N., and Mawad, D. (2022, February 1). *French lawmakers have proposed a hijab ban in competitive sports. The impact on women could be devastating.* CNN. www.cnn.com/2022/02/01/sport/france-hijab-ban-intl-spt/index.html

Woon, Y. (1983–1984). The voluntary sojourner among the overseas Chinese: Myth or reality? *Pacific Affairs, 56*(4), 673–690.

World Population Review. (2022). *Iran population 2022 (Live).* https://worldpopulationreview.com/countries/iran-population

Worrall, J. (2009). When grandparents take custody—Changing intergenerational relationships: The New Zealand experience. *Journal of Intergenerational Relationships, 7*(2/3), 259–273.

Worthington, E. L., Jr. (Ed.). (2005). *Handbook of forgiveness.* Brunner-Routledge.

Wu, M., & Stewart, L. (2005). Work-related cultural values and subordinates' expected leadership styles: A study of university employees in Taiwan and the United States. *Journal of Intercultural Communication Research, 34,* 195–212.

Wucker, M. (2000). B is for Balkans. *Civilization, 7*(1), 25–27.

Xuechunzi, B., Ramos, M. R., & Fiske, S. (2020). As diversity increases, people paradoxically perceive social groups as more similar. *Proceedings of the National Academy of Sciences, 117,* 12741–12749.

Yanru, C. (2009). Between three worlds: The Internet and Chinese students' cultural identities in the era of globalization. *China Media Research, 5*(4), 31–40.

YeahBaby (2010, June). *Illegal baby names!* www.yeahbaby.com/article.php?page=118. (Site discontinued.)

Yeakley, A. (1998). *The nature of prejudice change: Positive and negative change processes arising from intergroup contact experiences.* [Unpublished doctoral dissertation]. University of Michigan.

Yee, S. (2020). Is noun bias universal? Evidence from Chinese and Korean compared with French and English. *Studies in the Linguistic Sciences: Illinois Working Papers 43*: 32–44.

Yilmaz, H. (2011). Cyberbullying in Turkish middle schools: An exploratory study. *School Psychology International, 32,* 645–654.

Young, B. L., Madsen, J., & Young, M. A. (2010). Implementing diversity plans: Principals' perception of their ability to address diversity in their schools. *NASSP Bulletin, 94*(2), 135–157.

Yum, J. O. (1988). The impact of Confucianism on interpersonal relationships and communication patterns in East Asia. *Communication Monographs, 55,* 374–388.

Yum, Y., & Hara, K. (2005). Computer-mediated relationship development: A cross-cultural comparison. *Journal of Computer-Mediated Communication, 11*(1), 133–152.

Zarling, B. (2006, December 6). *Manpower Inc. calls on 1,000 of the world's leading corporations to join the fight to end human trafficking now!* PRNewswire. http://multivu.prnewswire.com/mnr/manpower/26317

Zeigler, K. & Camarota, S. A. (2019) *67.3 million in the United States spoke a foreign language at home in 2018.* Center for Immigration Studies. https://cis.org/Report/673-Million-United-States-Spoke-Foreign-Language-Home-2018

Zhao, Y., & Throssell, P. (2011). Speech act theory and its application to EFL teaching in China. *The International Journal of Language, Society and Culture, 32,* 88–95.

Zhou, S., Page-Gould, E., & Hewstone, M. (2019). The extended contact hypothesis: A meta-analysis on 20 years of research. *Personality and Social Psychology Review, 23.* https://journals.sagepub.com/doi/abs/10.1177/1088868318762647

Zhu, J., & Kleiner, B. (2000). The value of training in changing discriminatory behaviour at work. *Equal Opportunities International, 19*(6/7), 5–9.

Zimmerman, A. (1998, June 25). *A mother and child reunion.* Dallas Observer. www.dallasobserver.com/news/a-mother-and-child-reunion-6401785

Zurawsky, C. (2006). Foreign language instruction: Implementing the best teaching methods. *Research Points, 4*(1), 1–4.

Index